THE IRISH STOCK MARKET ANNUAL 2003

Compiled and Edited
by
John D O'Neill, B. Comm., M.B.A.

**PRIVATE
RESEARCH**

A PRIVATE RESEARCH Publication

PRIVATE RESEARCH Ltd,
Coliemore House, Coliemore Road, Dalkey, Co. Dublin
Tel: (01) 2848911. Fax: (01) 2048177.
www.privateresearch.ie

I am writing this in August 2002 - by the time that you read it, the investment world will have changed, hopefully for the better.

Those of us who have worked in investment for a long time - 35 years in my case - think we have seen it all before. The downturn of the second quarter of 2002 is not unique, but bull and bear markets never totally replicate one another. The surprising thing about this bear market is that it has been relatively severe against a relatively mild (so far) economic recession.

How does this affect the Irish Stock Exchange? Apart fro[m] a decline in overall market capitalization, the most obvio[us] effect is on new issues which have effectively dried up. W[e] cannot expect this necessary life blood to come back un[til] markets have at least stabilized for a considerable perio[d]. But stabilize markets will, when a more robust inte[r]national economy returns. New issues I am confident w[ill] return some time in 2003/2004. I hope, too, that improvi[ng] Government finances will then allow relief of stamp du[ty] where our rates are the highest in Europe and do nothi[ng] to help us develop our business.

Meantime it has been a surprisingly good year for t[he] Exchange. Turnover is well up, we are showing goo[d] progress in expanding our dealings in Irish shares, o[ur] systems are working well and our member broke[rs]

FOREWORD

What has happened, particularly in the US, has been that equity markets were rerated over the 1990s to unprecedented levels. This happens at most once in a generation and invariably has some new justification - in this case, the internet and telecoms boom. Confidence in markets capacity to rise can become over confidence. And when the markets turn, confidence can rapidly go the other way.

continue to do a good job. Our other businesses - quotin[g] investment funds, asset backed securities etc - continue t[o] grow rapidly. Their success is a measure of the reputatio[n] of the Exchange - one we jealously guard for bot[h] regulatory and administrative excellence.

David Kingsto[n]

Chairman Irish Stock Exchang[e]

The Irish Stock Exchange

28 Anglesea Street, Dublin 2. Tel: 01-6174200. Fax: 01-6776045
Pre-Trading: 6.30 - 7.50. Opening Auction 7.50 - 8.00. Continuous Trading 8.00 - 16.28.
Closing Auction: 16.28 - 16.30. Post Trading 16.30 - 17.15.
Chief Executive: T. Healy   Secretary: B. Healy

Board of Directors:

D. Kingston (Chairman), R.P. Ahern, R.Barrett, J.B. Davy
C. Gill, J.M. Maguire, P. McGowan, B. O'Connor, C. O'Kelly, H. Sheridan, M.J. Somers, V. Sheridan

Intelligence Applied

Goodbody Stockbrokers has the biggest private client list in Ireland; thousands of investors using us to build strong portfolios on their behalf. More people pick our brains. Intelligence applied.

BALLSBRIDGE PARK, DUBLIN 4 TELEPHONE (01) 667 0400 WWW.GOODBODY.IE

Goodbody
S T O C K B R O K E R S

Published by:

PRIVATE RESEARCH

Coliemore House, Coliemore Road
Dalkey, Co Dublin
Tel: 01-2848911. Fax: 01-2048177
www.privateresearch.ie
info@privateresearch.ie

Publisher:
John O'Neill

Directors:
Mark O'Neill
Sandra O'Neill

Marketing:
Franz Savino

Head of Research:
Geri Dineen

Distribution:
C. Fennelly

Printed by: Brookfield Printing Compan
Cover Designed By: Design Desk

The Author wishes to place on record
his sincere thanks to the Executives
in the various companies who so
kindly took the time and the trouble t
supply the details on each of their
respective corporate profiles.

**The comments do not reflect
in any way the opinions of
The Irish Stock Exchange
and are the sole responsiblity
of the Publisher.**

WARNING
The price of stock market investments and the income
derived from them can go down as well as up. When yo
sell such investments you may not receive the amoun
you originally invested. They may also have poor
marketability (ie prove difficult to buy and sell).
When considering investing, it is advisable to ask
whoever deals for you about marketability. And
remember that circumstances may change after our
comments are published.

LIST OF STOCKBROKERS

Not surprisingly,
our bespoke Pensions
fit like a glove.

Self-directed pensions are what today's self-directed people want. You choose where to invest or your Portfolio manager can choose for you. Davy has used the benefits of recent legislation to make the Davy Retirement Portfolio range more attractive than anything of its kind. In short, pension funding is now one of the most efficient methods of investing capital for the longer term. And because it's self-directed, it's sure to appeal to a wide range of high net worth individuals who want to remain just that - high net worth *and* individual. Call Derek Ryan on **01 614 8998** to find out about **Davy** Personal, Directors' and ARF Retirement Portfolios.

Davy. We do our homework.

Back to Basics
or
It's Time to Look at The Fundamentals

THE TOP TEN LARGEST DIVIDEND PAYERS

Rank	Company	Price € (Gross)	Dividend Yield Times Cover	Dividend	Comment
1.	Norish	0.70	7.6%	none	Net assets 50% over price
2.	IWP International	1.35	6.7%	none	Cash rich after division sale
3.	Gresham Hotels	0.69	6.5%	none	Under new control at Boardroom
4.	Viridian Group	7.80	6.3%	none	Dividend may be reduced
5.	Waterford Wedgwood	0.52	6.0%	none	Dividend not covered due to one-offs
6.	Independent News	1.44	5.4%	2.1	Strectched b/sheet; highly lgeared
7.	Heiton Group	2.60	5.1%	2.0	Dividend well covered
8.	Donegal Creameries	2.15	5.0%	3.7	Dividend solidly covered
9.	Readymix	1.30	4.7%	3.2	Solid performer
10.	Greencore	2.75	4.6%	none	Still digesting Hazlewood

In many cases there are legitimate reasons for companies providing high yields. If you are risk averse you firstly go for companies whose dividends are well covered and are, therefore, unlikely to disappoint you incomewise in the short term. It is also essential to look at the recent interim results to make sure that profits are not going to disappear altogether. In many cases the dividend has no cover because of one-off write-offs which by their very nature should not be repeated in the short-term. The higher the dividend cover the greater the scope for an increase in the dividend stream.

HIGH ASSET BACKED SHARES

Rank	Company	Price €	Net Assets Per Share €	% Over Share Price	Comment
1.	Datalex	0.28	0.82	293%	Loss-making; assets decrease each year end
2.	Gresham	0.69	1.72	249%	Will the new owners produce profits?
3.	Alphyra	0.95	2.00	211%	Loss making reduce assets
4.	Barlo	0.21	0.34	162%	Again, losses don't improve assets
5.	Iona	2.07	3.24	157%	Loss making reduce assets
6.	Aminex	0.30	0.44	147%	Recent windfall makes assets cash-flush
7.	Norish	0.70	0.99	141%	The wagons are being circled here
8.	Donegal Creameries	2.15	3.00	140%	24% return on solid assets; deserves better rating
9.	Dunloe Ewart	0.33	0.44	133%	Major shareholders at loggerheads
10.	Unidare	1.10	1.42	129%	Low 6.7% return on assets

There are reasons why shares are trading at a discount to their net asset value. Of the ten shares listed, six of them are currently loss making. With the exception of Donegal Creameries the other three are showing disappointing returns on the capital invested.

THE PRICE/EARNINGS CONUNDRUM

Rank	Company	Price €	Rolling Price/ Earnings Ratio	Comment
1.	McInerney	2.15	4.9	There are 5 construction industry related companies in this list.
2.	Donegal Creameries	2.15	5.3	Donegal, being far from the Pale, never has strong public image.
3.	Abbey	4.55	5.7	Looks inexpensive at this level.
4.	Kingspan	1.95	5.9	Falling profits not exciting.
5.	CPL	0.48	7.1	Current economic climate not great for recruitment agencies.
6.	Readymix	1.30	7.2	Looks inexpensive with good record.
7.	FBD	5.90	8.2	Recent interims not exciting.
8.	Riverdeep	2.20	9.6	Now that it has found out how to sell profitably it could be one to note.
9.	Heiton	2.60	10.0	Recent results not exciting.
8.	DCC	9.90	11.0	Litigation clouds overhang.

The earnings per share yardstick is a conundrum. What is the cheapest earnings per share yardstick?
We have looked at the shares on the basis of the 'rolling earnings per share' yardstick which takes into account the latest interim results added to the previous six months performance.

LEXUS GS300

Refined. Intelligent.
Powerful. Distinctive.
As you'd expect of Lexus.

For drivers discerning enough to appreciate the perfect balance of intelligence, power and refinement, the culmination of the unrelenting pursuit of perfection: Lexus GS300 and GS430. With pedigree and refinement evident at first glance, one can only appreciate, however, their computerised intelligence and pulse-quickening performance when you slide behind the wheel and allow the meticulously-finished interior to cocoon you in luxury and safety. Embracing Formula One technology, the GS300's drive-by-wire throttle delivers the drive of your life with unerring precision while its wheel-mounted E-shift smoothly moves the power of its 3-litre straight-six through five gears without so much as a murmur. Those seeking even more muscle may prefer the 284bhp delivered by the GS430's potent - but remarkably silent - V8. GS300 and GS430 from Lexus. Express yourself with distinction.

GS300 | GS430

The relentless pursuit of perfection.

ABBEY plc

BUSINESS: Construction of houses.
REGISTERED OFFICE: 25/28 North Wall Quay, Dublin.
HEAD OFFICE: 2 Southgate Road, Potters Bar, Hertfordshire, EN6 5DU. Tel: 00441707-651266. Fax: 00441707-645920. **Dublin Office:** 1 Setanta Place, Dublin 2. Tel: 01-6703033. Fax: 01-6703010.
SECRETARY: D Dawson.
REGISTRAR & TRANSFER OFFICE: Computershare Investor Services (Ireland) Ltd, P.O.Box 954, Heron House, Corrig Road, Sandyford Ind Estate, Dublin.
PRINCIPAL BANKERS: AIB Bank; Barclays Bank.
STOCKBROKERS: Davy Stockbrokers; ING Barings Ltd.
AUDITORS: Ernst & Young.
SOLICITORS: A & L Goodbody.
DIRECTORS: C H Gallagher (Executive Chairman - 43), D Gallagher (42), B. Hawkins (58), J Hogan, R Humber (60), D Jackson (73), R Kennedy (50), R Shortt.
SHARE CAPITAL: Authorised: 45,000,000 €0.3174 Ord. Shares.
Issued: 34,077,782 €0.3174 Ord. Shares.
EMPLOYEES: 312
SCRIP DIVIDEND: No
WEB SITE: www.abbeyplc.ie

CAPITAL HISTORY:

May 1973 22,802,000 Ordinary 25p shares issued. Of these 20,287,000 allotted as consideration for Abbey Homesteads and Gallagher Abbey Groups, 75,000 shares for P.J. Matthews and 2,440,000 for sale to public. Sept. 1987 1-for-2 'scrip' issue. Oct. 1987 3,520,000 Ord. 25p shares placed at €4.19 each. March 2000: Buys back 2,220,450 own shares for cancellation @ average €3.61 each (cost €8m). Oct 2000: Buys back 784,000 and cancels own shares @ €2.90 each

COMPANY HISTORY:

Incorporated in 1936 as the Torc Manufacturing Co. Ltd. which became public in 1952. In April 1973 Torc, in a reverse takeover, acquired the share capital of Abbey Homesteads, and the Gallagher Abbey Group. In May 1973 5.35 million shares in the enlarged group were offered for sale at 96p each and the issue was 3.7 times over-subscribed. Family feuds led to Charles Gallagher's resignation after a short period as Managing Director in 1974 although he retained 7.5% of the equity. Acrimonious A.G.M.s led eventually to the

purchase by Charles Gallagher of the late Hubert Gallagher's shares in Abbey bringing Charles Gallagher's holding to 29%. In 1983 Charles Gallagher became Chairman. In October 1985 French Kier mounted a bid for Abbey backed by 9.1 million shares (38.7%) held by other Gallagher interests. The bid valued at 96p per share failed with only 41.17% acceptances. In December 1985 the 38.7% of Abbey was placed with 40 institutions at 121p per share. Jan. 1987: Subsidiary P.J. Matthews put into liquidation. Oct. 1987: Raised £11.6m through share plac-

ing. Dec. 1987: J. Davy and D. Gallen appointed Directors. Sept. 1989: Gallagher Investment Co. sells 875,000 shares at 190p each. Jan. 1990: Provision of £5m against land values; interim dividend skipped. April 1990: R.J. Davies, Chief Executive resigns. Sept 1990: C. Gallagher now reveals reduced holding of 26.2%. Aug. 1991: C.H. Gallagher appointed Chief Executive. Sept. 1991: Articles of Association allows for purchase of own shares. Aug 1992: Disposes of Lucan site for about £1.5m. May 1993: C Gallagher Snr, dies. April 1994: J. Davy resigns as director. Buys Irish property for €4.4m. April 1997: Sold total 600 houses in year at £86,000 each. Jan 1999: Profits warning second half 98/99. July 1999: D Dalton resigns over conflict of interest. March 1999: Buys back 2.2m own shares @ around €3.61 each for cancellation (total cost €8m). May 2000: Sells Fenian St and Trinity St properties for €21.6m. Aug 2000: Has land bank in excess of 2,300 plots. 727 houses sold in y/e April 2000. Jan 2001: Has spent €4.3m buying back own shares @ €2.92 each. July 2001: Sold 444 houses in UK and 212 in Ireland in last trading year. "Trading in new year is off to a good start". July 2002: Sold 359 houses in UK in 01/02 and 212 in Ireland. "Trading in the new year is off to a good start.....In the near term, at least, prospects remain good."

Share Price Sept 2001 - Sept 2002

1. €5.30 21.05.02
2. €4.65 '02 results announced 18.07.02

FINANCIAL DIARY

Interim Results Announced:	10.01.2002
Interim Dividend Payout:	20.02.2002
Final Results Announced:	18.07.2002
Annual General Meeting:	04.10.2002
Final Dividend Payout:	09.10.2002

FIVE YEAR SHARE PRICE TREND €

1997	High 3.36 (Oct)	Low	2.39 (Jan)
1998	High 6.03 (May)	Low	2.48 (Dec)
1999	High 4.75 (May)	Low	2.65 (Jan)
2000	High 3.80 (Jan)	Low	2.50 (Jan)
2001	High 4.15 (Feb)	Low	2.80 (Oct)

INVESTMENT PERFORMANCE

Five Year Investment Performance:	€2,268
Ten Year Investment Performance:	€6,928

HALF YEARLY PERFORMANCES: € m

Six months to:	31.10.00	30.04.01	31.10.01	30.04.02
Sales	81.5	69.6	64.6	82.1
Profit before Tax	18.7	17.6	14.6	21.6
Profit % Sales	22.9	25.3	22.6	26.3

SECTORAL ANALYSIS (previous year)

Turnover: construction 86% (84%), plant hire 14% (16%). Ireland 26% (26%), UK 74% (74%)

TEN YEAR REVIEW: € m

12 months to April 30	1993	1994	1995	1996	1997	1998	1999	2000	2001	2002
Sales	49.2	60.0	64.0	57.1	78.4	115,1	116.5	142.1	151.1	146.7
Profits (Loss) before Tax	3.4	10.3	10.6	7.9	11.6	24.5	26.6	37.9	28.6	36.2
Tax	1.4	3.2	3.2	2.4	3.8	7.9	7.7	11.7	7.9	9.5
Profit (Loss) after Tax	2.0	7.1	7.4	5.5	7.8	16.6	18.8	26.2	20.7	26.7
Available to Shareholders	2.0	7.1	7.4	5.5	7.8	16.6	18.8	26,2	20.7	26.7
Ordinary Dividend	1.0	2.5	2.6	2.7	3.3	4.4	4.9	23.0	11.6	6.8
Retained Profit (Loss)	1.0	4.7	4.8	2.8	4.4	12.2	13.9	3.2	9.1	19.9
Increase (Decrease) in Reser	(4.3) g)	4.9	2.7 h)	1.9	10.1 a)	24.5 i)	19.4 j)	3.9	2.0	22.2
Shareholders' Funds	52.8	57.7	60.4	62.3	72.4	96.9	116.2	119.1	120.6	142.9
Ordinary Dividend per Share (€)	0.025	0.064	0.067	0.07	0.09	0.11	0.13	0.65	0.43	0.20
Earnings per Share (€)	0.052	0.184	0.192	0.142	0.20	0.43	0.49	0.70	0.76	0.784 f)

a) Currency gain +€5.7m. f) Based upon 34.1m shares. g) Currency loss €3.6m, property devaluation €1.8m. h) Currency loss €2.2m. i) Property revaluation +€7.6m; currency gain +€5.7m. j) Property revaluation +€4.4m

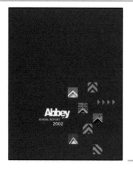

BALANCE SHEET: APRIL 30 2002. €m

Share Capital:		Fixed Assets	32.8
34,077,782 Ord. €0.3174 shares	10.9	Current Assets	160.5
Reserves	132.0	Current Liabilities	49.6
		Net Current Assets	110.9
		Medium Debt	(0.8)
Shareholders' Funds	142.9	Net Tangible Assets	142.9

Comment:
Balance sheet is as clean as a whistle with €39m in cash. This superb balance sheet has always been a favourite of ours and there is no reason to change our minds. Net assets per share stand at €4.20. The dividend is covered four times. Nearly a seven-fold increase in the 10 year investment and a profit on sales of 26%.
Some performance.

ABBEY DEVELOPMENTS LIMITED   KINGSCROFT DEVELOPMENTS LIMITED   M&J ENGINEERS LIMITED

Housebuilding   Property Development   Plant Hire

Abbey plc is listed on the Dublin and London Stock Exchanges

The company's main activities are residential housing development and plant hire in the United Kingdom and Ireland

For further information please visit our corporate Web site at www.abbeyplc.co.uk

Abbey plc

IRISH OFFICE: 1 Setanta Place, Dublin 2. Tel: (01) 670 3033. Fax: (01) 670 3010. Web: www.abbeyplc.ie
GROUP HEAD OFFICE: Abbey House, 2 Southgate Road, Potters Bar, Herts EN6 5DU. Tel: (01707) 651266. Fax: 645920. Web: www.abbeyplc.co.uk

BUSINESS: Banking and financial services.
REGISTERED OFFICE: Bankcentre, Ballsbridge, Dublin. Tel: 01-6600311. Fax: 01-6682508.
HEAD OFFICE: as regd office.
SECRETARY: W.M. Kinsella.
REGISTRARS & TRANSFER OFFICE: Computershare Investor Services (Ireland) Ltd, Heron House, Corrig Road, Sandyford Industrial Estate, Dublin.
AUDITORS: KPMG.   **SOLICITOR:** B. Sheridan.
STOCKBROKERS: Goodbody.
DIRECTORS: L Quinn (Chairman - 61), A Bourke (61), M Buckley (Ch Executive - 57), P Fallon (56), D Gleeson (54), D Godson (63), D Higgs (58), G Kennedy (44), J B McGuckian (63), C Moffett (50), J O'Leary (46), M Sullivan (63).
SHARE CAPITAL: Authorised: 1,160 million Ord €0.32 shares; 200,000,000 Non-Cum Pref. Shares of €1.27 each; 20 million Non-Cum. Pref. shares of US$25 each. **Issued:** 895,470,052 ordinary €0.32 shares; 0.25m Non-cum Preference shares of US$25 each.
STAFF: 32,397. **SCRIP DIVIDEND:** Yes

CAPITAL HISTORY:

Formed in 1966 to acquire assets of The Munster and Leinster Bank, The Royal Bank of Ireland and The Provincial Bank of Ireland. In July 1968 1-for-5 'rights' issue. July 1972 1-for-5 'rights' issue. June 1974 1-for-5 'scrip' issue. November 1977 2-for-7 'rights' issue. July 1979 1-for-2 'scrip' issue. January 1980 5.2m shares issued to employees and pensioners. May 1981 1-for-4 'rights' issue. July 1983 1-for-10 'scrip' issue. Sept 1983 18.8m shares issued as part consideration for Insurance Corporation of Ireland. Sept 1986 1-for-4 'rights' issue. October 1988 2-for-7 'rights' issue to raise £110m. May 1989 1-for-1 'scrip' issue. May 1990 1-for-6 'rights' issue. July 1997: Issued 162,947,142 Ord 25p shares (27.16m American Deposit Receipts 1-for-6) re purchase of Dauphin Deposit Corporation. April 2000: 1 ADR = 2 shares.

COMPANY HISTORY:

Allied Irish Banks formed in 1966. Dec '81 acquired 25% stake in Insurance Corporation of Ireland (cost £10.2m). Mar '83: Targets 51% stake in First Maryland Bankcorp over 5 years for $150m. Aug '83: Bought other 75% of Insurance Corporation of Ireland for £34.6m (in AIB shares). Mar '85 administrator appointed to ICI; Government takes over AIB investment in ICI for £1. AIB writes off £90.1m as a result.   May 1987: Buys 30% of Coyle Hamilton

Group for undisclosed sum. Dec. 1987: Purchased 500,000 shares in First Maryland Bank at $27.57 per share (representing 115% of net asset value). This brings AIB holding to 49.9% of FMB. December 1988: Pays $376m (£239m) for remainder of FMB. April 1990: Acquires Goodbody James Capel, stockbrokers for approx. £21m. April 1990: Bid for Baltimore Bancorp rejected.   Sept. 1990: NYSE listing. Nov. 1990: Sells 30% stake in Coyle Hamilton. Nov. 1990: Withdraws $17 per share offer for Baltimore Bancorp. Dec. 1990: Withdraws from Asset Financing in UK. Feb. 1991: Closes Allied Irish Australia Ltd. May. 1991: Pays IR£133.6m for TSB Northern Ireland. Re-enters life assurance market. June 1991: Pays IR£79.9m for York Trust & Bank in Pennsylvania.   Oct 1991: Aborts 28 million ADR issue in US due to lack of investor interest. Sept 1992: Closes Tokyo office. Dec 1992: Government levies further annual penalty of £8.8m for 20 years from '93 to fund ICI administration. Financial year changed to calendar year. October 1993: Accepts 50% of £76m in settlement of ICI action. April 1994: Buys Hill Samuel Fagan for less than £5m. Feb 1995: Buys 16.3% of Polish Bank WBK for £12.7m. April 1995: Intends buying Zirkin-Culter (Washington) for £9.2m. Dec 1995: Bought Govett Group for £99.7m. Jan 1996: Buys First Washington Bankcorp for £53.2m. April 1997: Holds 60.2% of WBK Poland (cost to date £96m). July 1997: Acquired Dauphin Deposit Corporation for £1.36 billion. Sept 1997: AIB buys 5.6m own shares at 575p each. (cost £32.8m; shares not cancelled). Oct 1998: Row over DIRT tax 'deal' with Revenue Commissioners in 1990. Feb 1999: AIB subject of takeover rumours - shares reach £14.29. June 1999: Option to acquire 24.9% of Keppel Tat Lee Bank (Singapore) by mid-2002 for £661m/Singapore$1.5bn. Aug 1999: Dropped from Eurostoxx 50 index. Sept 1999: Buys 80% Bank Zachodni, Poland for £416m (€528m). Feb 2000: Dumps brokers Warburg Dillon Read; moves to Merrill Lynch. Oct 2000: Settles with Rev Coms over "DIRT" for €114.3m. June 2001: Merges WBK (60.1%) and Bank Zachodni (83%) in Poland. AIB quits Singapore after offer from OCBC bank. Nov 2001: Deal with An Post to provide over-the-counter banking services. Feb 2002: €789m fraud at Allfirst in US; heads roll but only 1 director departs. March

Share Price Sept 2001 - Sept 2002

1. €11.35 06.02.02 Fraud revealed
2. €15.70 15.05.02 poor results at Allfirst

FINANCIAL DIARY

Interim Results Announced:	31.07.200?
Interim Dividend Payout:	27.09.200?
Final Results Announced:	20.02.200?
Annual General Meeting:	29.05.200?
Second Interim Dividend Payout:	26.04.200?

FIVE YEAR SHARE PRICE TREND

1997	High	8.82 (Dec)	Low	4.96 (Jan)
1998	High	15.27 (Feb)	Low	8.60 (Jan)
1999	High	18.14 (Feb)	Low	10.86 (Sep)
2000	High	13.10 (Nov)	Low	7.94 (Feb)
2001	High	13.80 (May)	Low	9.31 (Sept)

SECTORAL ANALYSIS (previous year)

Revenue: Ireland + other 48% (47%), USA 27% (28%), Poland 12% (12%), UK 13% (13%).
Pretax profits: Irl + other 128% (51%), USA -70% (26%), Poland 6% (7%), UK 36%(16%).

INVESTMENT PERFORMANCE

Five Year Investment Performance:	€2,917
Ten Year Investment Performance:	€6,62?

HALF YEARLY PERFORMANCES: € m

Six months to:	31.12.00	30.06.01	31.12.01	30.06.02
Profit before Tax	416	525	87	703
Pretax Profit (loss)	298	365	(192)	537

2002: External report castigates shortcoming? Class actions against Allfirst. AIBM lose €1.2bn C? pension fund. April 2002: Changes auditor. S&? downgrade AIB. 6 new directors at Allfirst. Ma? 2002: Buckley says 'no BofI merger'. Large share? holders press for sale of Allfirst. US Federal Reser? demand remedies for Allfirst weaknesses.

TEN YEAR REVIEW: € m

12 months to Dec 31	1992g)	1993	1994	1995	1996	1997	1998	1999	2000 e)	2001
Income (gross)	3,079	3,487	2,491	2,724	2978	3,952	5,029	4,987	6,539	6,967
Profit before Tax	218	249	433	473	534	736 (m)	1,049	1132	1,138	612
Tax	71	64	151	159	179	230	369	327	318	55
Profit after Tax	147	185	282	314	355	506	680	805	820	557
Minority Interest	(1)	(2)	(12)	(10)	(12)	(23)	(29)	(28)	(38)	(23)
Preference Dividends	9	14	15	14	14	18	18	16	20	50
Available for Shareholders	137	168	255	290	329	465	633	761	762	484
Ordinary Dividend	67	82	93	110	129	176	239	288	335	380
Retained Profit	70	86	164	180	200	288	394	473	427	104
Increase (Decrease) in Reserves	34 h)	174 i)	115 k)	53 q)	155	618 n)	502 a)	818 b)	641	(81)
Shareholders' Funds	1,124	1,298	1,413	1,469	1,626	2,299	2,829	3,651	4,296	5,123
Ordinary Dividend per Share (€)	0.102	0.124	0.140	0.164	0.190	0.22	0.28	0.337	0.388	0.438
Earnings per Share (€)	0.210	0.256	0.386	0.434	0.488	0.61	0.75	0.895	0.89	0.56 d)

a) Share premium +€24m, property revaluation +€141m, currency losses -€60m. b) Currency gains +€276m. d) Based upon 861.4m shares. e) Figures subsequently restated. g) 9 months to 31.12.1992. (h) Currency loss €32m. i) Currency gains €76m. k) Currency loss -€60m. m) Includes profit €76m sale of US credit card business. n) Share premium €1,025m; goodwill w/o -€849m. q) Goodwill write-off -€117m.

BALANCE SHEET: DECEMBER 31 2001 € m

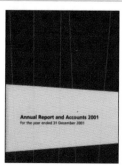

Annual Report and Accounts 2001
for the year ended 31 December 2001

Share Capital:	284	Fixed Assets	2,810
866m €0.32 Ord Shares		Associated Companies	342
		Current Assets	82,926
		Current Liabilities	78,315
Reserves	4,839	Net Current Assets	4,611
		Medium Debt	(2,320)
		Pref shares & minority	(815)
		Net Tangible Assets	4,628
		Intangibles	495
Shareholders' Funds	5,123	Net Assets	5,123

Comment:

'*Anus horribilis*' for AIB in past year. Bid rumours give support to share price. Will take a long time to overcome the criticism of weak management. Despite all the traumas of the recent past including the DIRT problem and the Allfirst fraud, the shareholders are still looking at their investment having increased by 3 times over 5 years.

AIB operates in 4 key areas - Ireland, USA, UK and Poland with a total staff of 31,895 and assets of €88.8 billion. In terms of total assets AIB is the largest banking entity in Ireland with 280 branches and outlets (9,723 staff or 31% of total employees and €23.6billion in assets or 27% of the bank's total) where it is estimated that it holds in excess of 20% of the total Irish market for euro loans and deposits.

In Northern Ireland through the First Trust brand, it operates 66 branches and outlets. In the UK AIB has 36 branches. (Total staff in NI & UK is 2,962 or 9% of total with €8.9billion in assets or 10% of total).

In the US, through the Allfirst brand, it operates through 260 branches in Maryland, adjoining states and the District of Columbia (with 5,938 staff or 19% of total and €22billion in assets or 25% of total).

Finally, in Poland it operates through the Bank Zachodni WBK (BZWBK) a 70.5% owned subsidiary with 441 branches (with 10,316 staff and €7.2billion in assets).

The services for each of the divisions are self explanatory. The Ark Life Assurance business mainly comes within the AIB Bank ROI division. In the USA division Allfirst also covers AIB New York, Cayman Islands as well as representative offices in Philadelphia, Los Angeles, Chicago, Atlanta and San Francisco. Capital Markets with the largest asset base manages the investment banking, asset management, stockbroking, corporate banking and international banking services (with the exception of Allfirst and BZWBK). On the investment side AIB Investment Managers including Govett in the UK has €15bn under management while AIB/Bank of New York and AIB/BNY Trust has €140bn in funds under administration and trusteeship.

In Poland the bank mainly operates in the western part of the country which is one of the most prosperous parts but it also has a significant presence in the major urban areas of Warsaw, Krakow and Lodz. However it is competing against some major players such as Pekao and PKO BP and its peers Bank Przemyslowo Handlowy PBK and ING Bank Slaski.

Competition in banking circles is a regularly debated 'hot potato'. In Ireland the matter has come to the fore with the suggestion by the Chief Executive of the Bank of Ireland that both the Bank of Ireland and Allied Irish Bank should get together as a form of defensive mechanism against foreign predators in the future; but there are many sides to this argument. However the recent proposed joint venture on the IT side between those two banks would appear to have been be the first step in the merging direction. But Brussels had other ideas and this adventure has duly collapsed.

In the UK the clearing banks are retrenching their branch networks and developing alternative low-cost channels of distribution. However increasing government regulation is ensuring that customer choice and industry standards remain high.

In the US the passage of financial modernization legislation in November 1999, which removed barriers to affiliation among banks, broker-dealers and insurance companies, is increasing competition in these markets. Mergers between financial institutions within Maryland and in neighbouring states have added competitive pressure.

In Poland BZWKB can only claim about 6% of the financial services market there although it is now number six in the Polish pecking order. The economy there is not in great shape these days to put it mildly. With a population of 39million people it appears AIB feel enough capital has been committed to central Europe for its size. M Buckley (CEO) has said that BZWBK is the right size to compete in the market and that if the group felt that it was not big enough,

AIB would exit the business. The value of the zloty is also important relative to this investment. From the view of competitiveness of the domestic economy, the zloty is considered too high. Pure domestic Polish companies are facing competition issue in their exports. As such, AIB is only lending to specific targeted sectors as lending to a broad spread of companies may be too risky in the current climate. Current loan growth is being achieved in lending to companies with international exposure and AIB-targeted sectors. The last annual results showed that year on year the Polish subsidiary was down 16% profitwise.

The big blot on AIB's copybook is the $789m fraud at Allfirst and in particular the fact that it had been ongoing since 1997, implying that 4 years past before anyone noticed the 'black hole' rather than the fact that it was spotted and snuffed in one year.

The risk control was lax despite banks being forewarned worldwide by the Barings/Leeson problem of some years ago. It emerged that Allfirst had not been fully integrated into the Group and the now famous Ludwig Report on the debacle made grim reading and should have evoked much more contrite reaction at top management and Board level when they digested the 67 rather basic recommendations for the operations going forward.

An outflow of deposits at Allfirst has resulted and new loan approvals slowed somewhat the two basic cornerstones of any profitable banking operation. The third cornerstone is the control of costs and AIB are paying lipservice to this element of their business. The Indians' heads that rolled were considered by some to be scapegoats and that the 'chiefs' got off lightly. Be that as it may, the bank must move forward and in the near term an acquisition abroad is probably out of the question. A fourth banana skin (firstly the acquisition of the insurance company ICI which very nearly brought the bank to its knees; secondly the DIRT debacle over what was or was not

agreed with the Revenue Commissioners and, thirdly, the forex problem at Allfirst) would hardly be tolerated by a fairly patient investment public.

In the UK AIB's operations grew by a pedestrian 8% year on year at the pretax level. Institutional investors have been alarmed by the American problem and the downturn in Poland (which was under the management of M Buckley) perhaps begging the question which has cropped up for many Irish companies trading abroad - has it the depth and spread of management to operate successfully on both continents.

We have reviewed a number of stockbrokers' reports and their estimates for the earnings in the year ending 2002 vary between €1,388m and €1,481m pretax profits with the average over the eight brokers coming out at €1,434m for the year ended December 2002. This would suggest an earnings per share of about €1.16 per share.

(We have reviewed various stockbrokers' reports including Morgan Stanley, Lehman Brother, Davy, Deutsche Bank, SG Equity Research, NCB and Goldman Sachs and in particular the AIB Form 20-F)

Division	Assets	%	Staff	%
AIB Bank ROI	€23.6 bn	27	9,723	31
AIB Bank GB&NI	€8.9 bn	10	2,962	9
USA	€22.0 bn	25	5,938	19
Poland	€7.2 bn	8	10,316	32
Capital Markets	€26.9 bn	30	2,225	7
Group/ENeb	€0.2 bn	-	731	2
	€88.8 bn	100%	31,895	100%

(formerly ITG GROUP PLC)

BUSINESS: Sale and maintenance of telephone systems and computer hardware.

REGISTERED OFFICE: 4 Heather Road, Sandyford Industrial Estate, Dublin. **HEAD OFFICE:** as regd office. Tel: 01-2076031. Fax: 01-2076039.

SECRETARY: B Hogan

REGISTRARS & TRANSFER OFFICE: Computershare Investor Services (Ireland) Ltd, Heron House, Corrig Road, Sandyford Industrial Estate, Dublin. **PRINCIPAL BANKERS:** AIB Bank. **AUDITORS:** BDO Simpson Xavier. **SOLICITORS:** P.F. O'Reilly & Co; S J Berwin & Co. **STOCKBROKERS:** Goodbody Stockbrokers; Investec Henderson Crosthwaite.

DIRECTORS: J McDonnell(Chairman - 65), J Nagle (Gr Ch Ex - 40), G Wilkinson (64), J Williamson (36), Lord Gowrie (65), N Kourmarianos (60).

SHARE CAPITAL: Authorised: 50m Ord €0.32 shares. **Issued:** 32,730,231 Ord €0.32 shares.

STAFF: 592.   **SCRIP DIVIDEND:** No

COMPANY HISTORY:

Began trading in 1989 servicing telephone systems. In 1992 acquired telephone system sales and maintenance division of Lake Electronics Ltd. Same year commenced installation of credit card swipe terminals in Bank of Ireland. 1993: Purchased assets of Allied Telephone Systems Ltd together with Harris Agency. In 1995: Bought DDT Maintenance (I) Ltd now known as INS. In 1996: Entered payphone market. May 1997: Paid €63,500 for Coin & Card Technology Ireland Ltd. Quoted in Dublin at €1.98 each. June 1998: Shares temporarily suspended. Buys Telecentral for €12.7m. Buys ICRP for €2.7m. Oct 1998: Buys 80% of The Telephone Co of Irl Ltd for €2.9m. Feb 1999: Buys Computers in Ireland Ltd for €11.2m. Buys Computercall Ltd for €4.4m. Sept 1999: Terminals deal with Ulster Bank. Dec 1999: Full listing on Dublin & London exchanges. Directors do not take up their 'rights' entitlements; 92.5% take up offer. Jan 2000: E Horgan resigns as exec dir (M.D of card services; a 'keyman'). Feb 2000 P Taggart resigns as Chairman. Buys Croft Computers for €3.87m. Invests €5.1m in Orbis Internet bringing stake to 15.3%. ITG shares reach €25.10. April 2000: Buys 20% of Cardsave (UK) for €8.35m. July 2000: Buys Targeted Transaction Managed Services (UK) for €21.6m. Sept 2000: Buys Getronics BV for €4.6m. October 2000: Buys Genidata AB for €13.6m. Oct 2000: Sells 4.9% of Orbiscom for €13.75m. Now holds 9.66% for free. Nov 2000: Buys 15% Meridian Communications for €6.3m. April 2001: Writes-off Meridian investment totalling €8.84m. Sept 2001: Rights issue raises €36.2m; directors forego their rights. Name changed from ITG. Oct 2001: Bought Transaction Services from De La Rue for €9.6m. Dec 2001: MBO of computer/telecom division for €12m; Alphyra writes off €13m. Founder director M Healy resigns. Appts Investec as joint broker.

CAPITAL HISTORY:

Incorporated February 1997. April 1997: Acquired ITG issuing 3,204,861 Ord 25p shares. Shares subdivided into Ord 25p shares. 1,12,031 Ord 25p shares issued re public flotation at 156p each. July 1998: Vendor placing and open offer (17-for-16) 5,519,138 Ord 25p shares. Issued 162,598 Ord 25p shares part consideration for Telecentral plc and 1,111 Ord 25p shares part consideration for ICRP plc. Oct 1998: Issued 115,942 Ord 25p shares part consideration for 80% of The Telephone Co of Irl Ltd. Feb 1999: Issued 1,109 Ord 25p shares part consideration for Computers in Ireland Ltd. Issued 441,000 Ord 25p shares part consideration for Computercall Ltd. Dec 1999: Placing & Open Offer (1-for-3) 1,714,285 Ord €0.32 shares @ €6.56. Full listing on Dublin and London exchanges. Sept 2001: Issues 8m Ord €0.32 shares rights-issue €5.00 each with clawback 1-for-6.

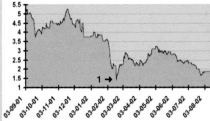

Share Price Sept 2001 - Sept 2002

1. €1.40 19.02.02 poor interim results.

FINANCIAL DIARY

Interim Results Announced:	15.08.2002
Interim Dividend Payout:	none
Final Results Announced:	28.02.2003
Annual General Meeting:	29.05.2002
Final Dividend Payout:	none

SHARE PRICE TREND

Year	High		Low	
1997	High	2.48 (Dec)	Low	2.10 (Jly)
1998	High	4.77 (Jly)	Low	2.48 (Jan)
1999	High	9.90 (Dec)	Low	4.44 (Jan)
2000	High	22.11 (Feb)	Low	6.72 (Dec)
2001	High	9.20 (Jan)	Low	3.75 (Sept)

SECTORAL ANALYSIS: (previous year)

Sales: voice and data 51% (73%), electronic 49% (27%).

HALF YEARLY PERFORMANCES €'m

Six months to	31.10.00	30.04.01	31.12.01***	30.06.02
Sales	56.5	32.0	55.4	23.8
Pretax Profits (-)	9.1*	(8.6)**	(31.5)	(3.0)
Profits % sales	16.1	-	-	-

*Includes asset sale profits of £8.2m.
Includes Meridian £7m write-off. * 8 months.

NINE YEAR REVIEW: €'000

Months to Dec 31	1994 i)	1995 i)	1996 i)	1997 i)	1998 i)	1999 i)	2000 i)	2001 i)	2001 k)
Sales	1,841	2,190	4,127	7,017	9,302	24,559	61,882	88,460	55,449
Profit before Tax	110	160	98	635	852	2,199	752	479	(31,471) m)
Tax	17	32	11	216	267	950	410	(1,843)	(163)
Profit after tax	93	128	86	419	584	1,249	342	(1,364)	(31,634)
Available for Shareholders	93	128	86	419	584	1,249	342	(1,364)	(31,634)
Ordinary Dividend	-	-	-	-	-	-	-	-	-
Retained Profit	93	128	86	419	584	1,249	342	(1,364)	(31,634)
Increase (Decrease) in Reserves	n/d	128	(147) a)	419	2,322 d)	23,874 f)	63,588	10,924	8,989 j)
Shareholders' Funds	155	284	137	556	3,286	29,164	96,260	107,657	119,686
Ordinary Dividend per Share (€)	-	-	-	-	-	-	-	-	-
Earnings per Share (€)	0.025	0.041	0.027	0.0131	0.0131	0.145	0.02 b)	-	-

a) Goodwill w/o -£184,000. b) Based upon 15.3m shares. d) Goodwill +£1.4m. f) Share premium +£17.7m. g) Share premium +£9.9m. h) Figures subsequently restated. i) Year ended April 30. j) Share premium +€39.1m. k) 8 months. m) Includes goodwill write-off -€11.9m and loss on sale of subsidiary -€13m.

BALANCE SHEET: DEC 31 2001. €'000

Comment:

This young company has found telecommunications and computers unprofitable; it is now nailing its flag to the 'transaction business through terminals' mast internationally. Only time will tell whether this has been the correct corporate strategy.

Share Capital:	10,449	Fixed Assets		28,806
32,653,125 Ord €0.32 shares		Financial Assets		23,650
		Current Assets	69,848	
Reserves	109,237	Current Liabilities	50,417	
		Net Current Assets		19,431
		Medium Debt		(6,593)
		Net Tangible Assets		65,294
		Intangibles		54,392
Shareholders' Funds	119,686	Net Assets		119,686

Since its inception in 1989 alphyra has changed from a telephone maintenance and computer sales operation to transforming itself into a pan-European electronic transaction services group, led by the mass roll-out of electronic prepaid mobile phone top-ups. Through this business alphyra simultaneously created relationships with merchants particularly supermarkets and restaurants and forged a 7-year partnership with Ulster Bank (4 years to run) taking over the merchant service operation of those terminals under maintenance contracts. As the prepaid mobile phone market exploded in the late 1990s, alphyra developed terminals and infrastructure for electronic funds transfer and the distribution of electronic PPC top-ups on behalf of mobile networks. This has become their focused core business going forward.

In 2000 they made 3 acquisitions in Sweden, Holland and the UK and in August 2001 raised €36m to expand into Germany and France. €26m of the new funds were earmarked for terminal capital expenditure with €10m for further acquisitions. alphyra has taken over De La Rue Transaction Services in the UK.

The core of the alphyra proposition is the creation of a terminal estate in merchants (i.e. shops) where millions of principally cash-economy customers can top-up their prepaid mobile phones, pay utility bills, transfer funds electronically and, in the future, receive social security payments.

Currently alphyra operates around two key service offerings, access to electronic prepaid top-ups on behalf of the mobile operators, electronic funds transfer transactions involving credit and debit cards and utility bill payments. These services go through alphyra owned and serviced terminals which are linked through a third party network and alphyra owned switching hub infrastructure which enables alphyra to process the transactions on its own servers. alphyra gets approximately 3c/4c per transaction.

To be successful in any geographical region alphyra needs to achieve critical mass in terms of access and be able to offer a portfolio of attractive services. Access is dependant on an extensive terminal roll-out and establishing the right services depends upon partnerships being achieved with the ultimate service providers be they banks, utility companies or mobile network operators. The core of alphyra's thrust is that they be strongly profitable from PPC (prepaid cellular) top-ups alone, so that each incremental service leveraged from the existing terminal estate should flow through to the bottom line.

To date they have 31,000 terminals throughout Europe and have relationships with 47,000 other merchants through its maintenance business. Each terminal costs €500 and purchase and installation comes to €1,088 per terminal. In Ireland they claim a 65% market share of total prepaid top-ups and a 40% market share of all credit and debit card transactions.

Prior to acquiring De La Rue Transaction Services alphyra paid a third of their gross margin to De La Rue for using their infrastructure in the UK. In Sweden alphyra uses its own infra structure while in Germany, France and Holland they are in the process of establishing their own switching network. Currently German and French operations are using spare capacity on the Irish servers.

As alphyra derives its revenues from two main sources - fees on transactions which are put through its terminal network and rental/maintenance revenues from its own or third party terminals - the aim is to maximise the number of transactions processed through the network so it is constantly looking for additional applications/services to add to its existing, mainly prepaid services.

alphyra has about 10,000 terminals in use in Ireland; they own and manage 7,200 for Ulster Bank. alphyra distributes 75-80% of the electronic top-ups in the Irish market where 70% of all top-ups are now delivered electronically. (If the top-ups are not done electronically alphyra competes with Easons and An Post who both major in the prepaid cards.) In the UK the mobile market has been slow to move to electronic prepaid - the top-up method used there was slow and unpopular. alphyra has 17,000 terminals in the UK providing electronic top-up and bill payment services. In March 2002 alphyra signed up Royal Bank of Scotland (Ulster Bank's parent) which is one of the largest electronic funds transfer processors in Europe. alphyra has a number of competitors in the UK such as Barclaycard (113,000 terminals), PayPoint (8,500 terminals), e-pay (7,000 terminals) and others (11,600 terminals)

In the Netherlands alphyra has 45,000 terminals (40% of the market) acquired in 2000. Interpay is the main bank owned card processor.

In Sweden terminals are owned and operated primarily by financial institutions and merchant groups. alphyra has 25-30% of the market there from 4,200 retailers with a terminal base of 12,000 machines. In Germany alphyra hopes to roll out 5000 terminals after a favourable trial but this must be seen in the context of Telecash with 141,000 terminals and Easycash with 138,000. alphyra intends to outsource the maintenance of the network to a third party. In Germany terminal applications have been mainly electronic funds transfer focused and in locations which enjoy sales of relatively high value ticket items. The terminal market there is highly fragmented with 28 service providers. The main risk to alphyra is that one or more of these networks should add electronic top-up applications to its existing network.

As in Germany, the market for prepaid is still predominantly paper-based although some electronic transactions are carried out through the ATM network. Terminal networks are predominantly used for EFT and owned by financial institutions (30%) and merchants (70%). However France is a less attractive market than Germany in terms of the proportion of prepaid mobile users. alphyra has signed a pilot deal with SFR, the second largest mobile operator in France with 34% market share and hopes to roll out 5,000 terminals. SchlumbergerSema is one of the main terminal network maintenance providers in the French market. It is also a significant supplier of terminals and software to both retailers and financial institutions. SchlumbergerSema has not added prepaid functionality to its product offering, although this is probably only a matter of time. This remains a significant risk to alphyra and, as in Germany, it is vital that alphyra signs up other operators quickly in order to persuade retailers to install its terminals and subscribe to its services. Practically no retailers would be interested in cluttering up their counter with an array of competing terminals.

What next? Southern European markets, in particular Spain, Portugal and Italy, are very attractive in terms of size and proportion of prepaid users. Italy, however, is a highly fragmented retail market with over 250,000 outlets which implies a very costly network roll out. Spain and Portugal are markets likely to be on the company's watch list.

Earnings per share for 2002 have been predicted as varying between 7.5 cents and 9.5 cents per share on profits before tax of between €4.9m and €5.6m for the 2002 calendar trading year.

(We have read some excellent stockbrokers reviews from which these details have been selected. We particularly suggest a 48-page review from Investec Securities. Others we recommend are Goodbodys, Davys and Insinger Townsley.)

On a clear day...

...you can see for miles

During your life you'll probably spend about 3.5 million minutes working hard to provide the wealth that will help you enjoy it. So it might not be a bad idea to invest a little time considering the big picture - right?

If you'd like to talk to real people with the expertise, experience and commitment to help you realise your goals, then pick up the phone and talk to us in Bloxham Stockbrokers.

We've been providing client service for over 100 years and are now Ireland's leading independent stockbroking firm.

BLOXHAM
STOCKBROKERS

International Financial Services Centre
2/3 Exchange Place Dublin 1
Tel +353 1 611 9200
Fax +353 1 829 1877

12 Marlboro Street Cork
Tel +353 21 490 6500
Fax +353 21 427 6036

46 Cecil Street Limerick
Tel +353 61 414 065
Fax +353 61 419 750

AMINEX plc

(Formerly Eglinton Exploration Plc)

BUSINESS: Oil and gas exploration.
REGISTERED OFFICE: 14 Upper Fitzwilliam Street, Dublin 2.
HEAD OFFICE: 10 Bedford Street, London WC2E 9HE. Tel: 020 7240 1600. Fax: 020 7240 0295.
SECRETARY: M Williams **REGISTRARS & TRANSFER OFFICE:** Computershare Investor Services (Ireland) Ltd, Heron House, Corrig Road, Sandyford Industrial Estate, Dublin.
PRINCIPAL BANKERS: Bank of Ireland, Barclays Bank
AUDITORS: KPMG.
SOLICITORS: O'Donnell Sweeney; Ashurst Morris Crisp; Dorosh Grishayev Malyarenko.
STOCKBROKERS: Davy Stockbrokers Ltd; Old Mutual Securities.
DIRECTORS: P Elwes (Chairman - 73), B Hall (Ch. Exec - 57), S Butterfield (56), D Hooker (60), A Prado (57), A Sarukhanov (53), F D Tughan (61), D Murcia (40).
SHARE CAPITAL: Authorised: 189,630,632 Ord €0.06 shares.
Issued: 90,207,382 Ord €0.06 shares.
STAFF: 337. **SCRIP DIVIDEND:** No

CAPITAL HISTORY:

May 1980: 1,316,000 Ord. 20p shares issued at 20p each. June 1980: 1,316,000 Ord. 20p shares issued at 20p each. August 1980: 526,400 Ord. 20p shares issued at 25p each. March 1981: 714,000 Ord. 20p shares placed on the market at 150p. June 1982: 500,000 Ord. 20p shares issued at 120p. Oct. 1983: 500,000 Ord. shares issued at 300p each. March 1984: Ord. 20; shares subdivided into Ord. 5p shares. June 1984: 1,000,000 Ord. 5p shares placed at 222p each. July 1984: 780,000 Ord. 5p shares issued in return for interest in Colombian Project. Oct. 1985: 500,000 Ord. 25p shares issued on takeover of Osceola Hydrocarbons. 700,000 shares issued in return for 500,000 shares in Ovoca Gold Exploration. 756,827 shares issued in respect of warrants. June 1987: 'rights' of 7,261,171 Ord. 5p shares at 25p each on the basis of 1-for-8 to raise £1.5m. March 1989: Ord. 5p shares consolidated to Ord. 50p shares. June 1989: 600,000 Ord. 50p shares placed at 100p each. Dec. 1989: 332,005 Ord. 50p shares issued re Albion acquisition. Dec. 1989: Placed 347,400 Ord. 50p shares at 60p each. Nov 1991: Open offer 1,722,660 'B' Ord 10p shares issued at 11p each. July 1992: 286,454 'B' 10p Ord shares issued at 11p each. July 1992: 7,627,412 Def Ord 45p shares and 7,627,412 Ord 50p shares issued in exchange for 7,627,412 Ord 50p shares. 4,236,114 Ord 5p shares and 1,772,660 Def Ord 5p shares issued in exchange for 1,722,660 'B' Ord 10p shares. Nov 1992: 477,000 Ord 5p shares placed at 5p each. 1,750,000 Ord 5p shares issued to Aberdeen Petroleum for licences in Pakistan and New Zealand. May 1993: 1,186,352 Ord 5p shares issued to East West at 5.85p stg each. 209,205 Ord 5p shares issued to East West for $17,000. 467,489 Ord 5p shares issued to East West for $46,749. 550,000 Ord 5p shares issued to Svenska Petroleum AB for interest in El Biban Tunisia and also 40,000 Ord 5p shares to BVA Consultants. May 1993: Huntwell (jersey) Ltd converts loan to 209, 205 Ord 5p shares. Bank of Ireland converts loan to 467,489 Ord 5p shares. July 1993: 11,085,817 Ord 5p shares open offer at 22.5p each. Nov 1993: 1,605,556 Ord 5p shares issued part vendor placing at 63p stg each. Jan 1994: Open offer 1-for-4 Ord shares at 83p each; issued 5,274,039 shares. March 1994: Issued 167,658 Ord 5p shares to EastWest for 79p stg each. Sept 1995: 1.06m Ord 5p shares at 60p each. Dec 195: Issued 275,000 Ord 5p shares at 60p each for 10.25% of El Biban Field. April 1996: 32,894 Ord 5p shares issued at 60p stg

for cash. June 1996: Placed 3.5m Ord 5p shares at 57p stg each. Oct 1996: Placed 6,904,358 Ord 5p shares at 57p stg with International Finance Corporation. Feb 1997: Issued 4,146,329 Ord 5p shares at 60p stg each for acquisition of Windrush Production Co. May 1997: Places 250,000 Ord 5p shares at 65p each. Aug 1997: Placing and open offer 10,382,922 Ord 5p Shares at 85p each (1-for-10). Feb 1998: 25,000 Ord 5p shares placed at 59.5p stg re acquisition of El Biban field. Dec 1998: 285,649 Ord 5p shares placed at 14.5p stg each. March 1999: 5,844,000 Ord 5p shares placed at 12p stg each. June 1999: 2,779,156 Ord 5p shares placed at 23p stg each to repay for Texas and Louisiana properties. Sept 1999: Issued warrants to subscribe for 3.5m Ord 5p shares @ 23pstg each (@ 25.5pstg 9/2000 and 28p stg 2001). Nov 1999: 6,171,600 Ord 5p shares placed at 30p stg each. Feb 2002: Repays 6.5pstg per share. Issues 13,461,538 at 26pstg each for Tanzoil (£3.5mstg)

COMPANY HISTORY:

Registered November 1979 as public company. By mid-1981 Eglinton claimed to have invested 1.4m dollars in USA and claimed value of 2.8m dollars for its American interests. Intended to acquire one-third interest in United Petrosearch Inc. in 1981 fell through. Company concentrated exploration in Columbia and eventually wrote-off £6.4m in 1986 as a result of the failure of any material progress in this area. In November 1986 took over Osceola Hydrocarbons (a company in which E. O'Connell had an interest) in a share swap of 22 Eglinton shares for every 20 Osceola shares. Osceola had net tangible assets of £623,135 including cash balances of £793,554. June 1987: 'Rights' issue raised £1.5m - 82% acceptance. Jan. 1988: Acquired 56% of Albion International Resources Inc. Acquired 25% of McKnight Exploration Company in the US. Placing of 3,500,000 shares at 13p each to raise £455,000. March 1988: Receives permission to start heap leeching for precious metals at Avoca, Co. Wicklow through Connary Minerals. June 1989: Acquires oil and gas property in Texas for $500,000 and $1 million 10% debenture maturing in 1991 with conversion rights. Nov. 1989: Acquires 45% of Albion International Resources (already owns 55%) for 1 Eglinton share for every 10 Albion resulting in issue of 332,005 new shares. April 1991: Name changed to Aminex plc. Oct 1991 open offer of new "B" 10p shares at 11p. Failed to raise £381,488 - £189,000 only subscribed. July 1992: Each 50p Ordinary share was divided into one 5p Ord share fully paid and one 45p Deferred ordinary share. The resulting 5p fully Ordinary shares were merged with the 5p "B" Ordinary shares to leave one class of 5p ordinary share. R.E.Williams resigns from the board. March 1993: Increases offer to 3 Aminex for 11 Tuskar (valued on paper at £4.7m). June 1993: Open offer (1-for-1) of 14,316,572 Aminex shares for 22.5p each. Open offer 1 for 1 @ 22.5p raised £2.28m. East West following offer holds 35%. Dec 1993: Announces Amkomi joint venture in Russia and raised £4m by way of open offer to shareholders with EastWest offering to take up 4m shares. Announces agency agreement with EastWest - EW to find further Russian deals in return for 20% of net profits in Russia. Jan 1994: Acquires 50% of Amkomi Joint Venture for £3.3m. Open offer raised £4.8m. June 1994: High Court restructuring by write-down of $21.7 million. April 1995: Agrees to lend $2.5m to Amkomi to repair oil wells. June 1996: Letter of intent from World Bank to subscribe for 7 million shares at 60p stg each (£4.2m stg) and provide additional loans of up to $30m to develop Kirtayel Field. Dec 1996: International Finance Corporation now holds 14.97%

of Aminex. Feb 1997: Bought Windrush Production Co. for $4m. 1997: Will hold 35% of Idelloil (15 oil fields in Tatarstan). Dec 19 Pays £688,000 to raise 50% stake to 55% in Amkomi Russia joint v ture. March 1998: El Biban Oilfield Tunisia (26% stake) flows at 4, barrels per day. Nov 2001: Sells Aminex Production for US$24m r Feb 2002: Returns 6.9pstg per share to shareholders (cost US$7.5 April 2002: Opportunist bid by Apple Oil & Gas (4 Apple shares for Aminex shares plus one unit of zero coupon loan notes for e. Aminex share) fails. May 2002: Buys Tanzoil (Australia) for £3.5m (all shares).

Share Price Sept 2001 - Sept 2002

1. €0.33 Results announced 22.07.02.

FINANCIAL DIARY

Interim Results Announced:	27.09.200
Interim Dividend Payout:	Not likely
Final Results Announced:	22.05.200:
Annual General Meeting:	11.07.200:
Final Dividend Payout:	Not likel

FIVE YEAR SHARE PRICE TREND

Year		High		Low	
1997	High	1.14 (Jun)	Low	0.68 (Jan
1998	High	0.95 (Apr)	Low	0.19 (Dec
1999	High	0.53(Nov)	Low	0.18 (Mar
2000	High	0.60 (June)	Low	.046 (Jan
2001	High	0.56 (Aug)	Low	0.27 (Mar

INVESTMENT PERFORMANCE

Five Year Investment Performance:	€710
Ten Year Investment Performance:	€2,756

SECTORAL ANALYSIS (previous year)

Sales: Russia 38% (12%), USA 36% (35%), Europe 26% (48%), other 0% (5%).

HALF YEARLY PERFORMANCES: $'m

6 months to:	30.06.00	31.12.00	30.06.01	31.12.01
Sales	10.0	9.0	6.5	4.8
Pretax profit/(loss)	1.8	1.5	0.6	(0.7)
Profit % sales	18.0	16.7	9.2	-

TEN YEAR REVIEW: $ '000

12 months to Dec.	1992	1993	1994	1995	1996	1997	1998	1999	2000	2001
Sales	406	399	12,745	15,157	15,636	17,409	11,844	15,894	19,000	11,305
Profit on Asset sales	-	-	-	-	-	-	-	-	-	5,709
Profit (Loss) Before Tax	(94)	(192)	2,064	(2,827)	(1,151)	(1,610)	(9,575)	1,101	3,306	5,592
Tax	-	-	-275	-250	-	-	-	25	519	319
Profit (Loss) after Tax	(94)	(192)	1,789	(3,077)	(1,151)	(1,619)	(9,575)	1,076	2,787	5,273
Minority Interest	-	-	(602)	+643	+196	+470	+907	(711)	(960)	(332)
Available for Shareholders	(94)	(192)	1,187	(2,434)	(955)	(1,140)	(8,668)	365	1,827	4,941
Ordinary Dividend	-	-	-	-	-	-	-	-	-	-
Retained Profit (Loss)	(94)	(192)	1,187	(2,434)	(955)	(1,140)	(8,668)	365	1,827	4,941
Increase (Decr) in Reserves	(94)	3,951 g)	12,557 h)	(1,509)	7,289 a)	13,274 b)	(8,622)	4,458 d)	2,192	5,011
Shareholders' Funds	824	5,849	13,930	12,505	20,699	35,181	26,589	32,035	34,227	39,251
Ordinary Dividend per Share	-	-	-	-	-	-	-	-	-	-
Earnings per Share ($)	-	-	$0.04	-	-	-	-	$0.005	$0.024	$0.065 i)

a) Share premium +$8.3m. b) Share premium $14.5m. d) Share premium +$4m. g) Share premium $4m.
h) Share capital reduced by £15.3m by High Court. i) Based upon 76.5m shares in issue.

BALANCE SHEET: 31 DECEMBER 2001. $'000

Share Capital:	5,661	Tangible Assets		11,374
76,745,844 Ord. €0.063 shares,		Investments		3,315
		Current Assets	28,047	
Reserves	33,590	Current Liabilities	3,352	
		Net Current Assets		24,695
		Medium Debt		(133)
Shareholders' Funds	39,251	Net Tangible Assets		39,251

Comment:

Not many exploration companies are so stuffed with cash.

Aminex was formed in 1980 and organised in its current form and name in 1991 with initial interests in Texas, a non-operating working interest in the El Biban field in Tunisia and exploration interests in Pakistan and offshore India.

In 1993 Zarubezhneft, the Russian state-owned foreign trade group, introduced Aminex to the Komi Republic. Aminex acquired a 50% stake in AmKomi at a cost of US$4.7million. The remaining 50% was owned by Komineft, the Komi state oil company. Aminex also launched an oilfield service and supplies business, Amossco, to support its activities in Komi. Alongside their activity in Russia Aminex's interest in Tunisia, the El Biban field, in 1998 started production at approx 4,000 barrels of oil per day.

In 2000, with oil production levels falling and considerable further investment anticipated to handle unexploited gas reserves, the El Biban interest in Tunisia was realised for $5.7m. The most recent determining development for Aminex was the 2001 agreement to sell its AmKomi stake to the Russian oil giant Lukoil for US$24m.

Circumstances in Russia have changed radically since Aminex took a 50% stake in AmKomi. Established Russian companies 're now themselves cash rich, following the lift to production levels and sharp improvements in the oil price. Foreign participation is no longer seen as essential to the oil and gas industry in Russia. The exit from the Komi Republic and a cautious approach to investing further funds toward the presently self-financing Tartarstan has led management to develop a strategy based on continued expansion of Aminex in the USA, acquisition of development opportunities in stable areas of the world and further international exploration. The company operates now in the USA, a downsized presence in Russia and entry has been gained to the emerging oil province of East Africa in Tanzania.

In February 2002 Aminex acquired Tanzoil, an Australian company with oil and gas exploration acreage in Tanzania, which was funded by the issue of 13.5m shares worth £3.5mstg at 26p per share. They have therefore acquired an exploration portfolio in a proven but highly explored hydrocarbon province along with a contracted drilling programme that will require $7.2m of funding. The immediate priority, upon which the drilling programme for two wells is focused, is the Nyuni block adjacent to the established Songo Songo discovery. Songo Songo is reported to contain over one trillion cubic feet of gas. Most importantly, the Songas project will construct a gas pipeline to Dar es Salaam and Tanzoil's production sharing agreement grants rights of access to this pipeline.

Tanzoil's Nyuni block has been independently analysed and if hydrocarbons are found to be widely present in Nyuni, this analysis identifies a number of exploration prospects with the potential to contain over 500 million barrels of oil, or more than 1.5trillion cubic feet of gas in the northern 30% of the block alone. This early opportunity is offshore but cheaply accessible from natural island drilling sites.

Tanzania has a population of 35million and is one of the poorest countries in the world. The economy is heavily dependent on agriculture which accounts for half of GDP, provides 85% of exports and employs 80% of the work force. Topography and climatic conditions limit cultivated crops to only 4% of the land area and industry is mainly limited to processing agricultural products and light consumer goods. The country has been intermittently explored over the last 50 years with most of the multinational petroleum companies being represented there at one time or another. Significant gas discoveries were made at Songo Songo and Mnzai Bay but no oil has been produced as yet although one discovery is currently under commercial development.

In the mid-90s a Songo Songo Gas to Electricity Project created Songas to utilise two onshore and three offshore natural gas wells. Produced gas from these wells will be piped to a gas plant on Songo Songo Island. Two 35million cubic feet per day processing units on the island will be built to process the natural gas from the wells. Any hydrocarbon liquids removed will be shipped to Dar es Salaam or consumed on-site as fuel. Construction of the pipeline from Songo Songo to Dar es Salaam should commence this year and the first gas may reach Dar es Salaam by the end of 2003. The turbines are already operational running on liquid fuel.

So much for the prospects in Tanzania. In the USA *Equity Growth Research* *feels that investments made in the States are expected to realise long term gains for the group and

diversify its operating portfolio but that we are unlikely to see significant returns from these American assets in this financial year.

In Russia, Aminex retains a 29.7% interest in Ideloil which operates in the state of Tatarstan and is only one of two foreign oil companies in the region. Aminex's position is not as controlling as was their position in the Komi Republic but the group provides support to the local management team. Because of local political issue the management is not willing to invest further until the outlook for the region stabilises. It remains to be seen whether local Russian interests will seek to acquire this interest as Lukoil bought the AmKomi investment.

All of this must be considered in the context of the global oil market. Oil accounts for 40% of the world's total primary energy demand and economic conditions are governed to a large degree by its availability. It has been estimated that the original recoverable oil in the earth was 2,330billion barrels (Gb). A recent study of oil and gas distribution and depletion indicates that of this amount 90% has been discovered, 50% has been produced and that at present the world consumes 4 barrels of its known reserves for every new barrel discovered. In terms of numbers this equates to a production of 22 Gb/year with only 6 Gb being discovered. So it apparent that the gap between consumption and discovery is widening as oil moves from a surplus to deficit status. Given an equal distribution of reserves, static consumption and production levels, there might be 100 years of consumption left. 65% of the world's oil reserves are located in the Middle East.

In the case of world gas, its utilisation in the past has not been optimal. Due to economic constraints, most associated gas (occurring in conjunction with oil production) was in the past flared. Increasing concerns about diminishing energy reserves and environmental hazards are applying pressure on the industry to utilise a higher percentage of this gas. As a result, legislation has been introduced to control operators and many countries are increasing their use of gas primarily for domestic consumption in order to decrease the amount of oil imported or to increase the amount of oil that can be exported.

Oil and gas prices are paramount for this industry because of their impact on the bottom line and the generation of cash flow which is the life blood of continuing exploration. We have experienced some volatility in prices in the past few years and it is a safe bet that this irregular price movement will continue into the future as the threat of war in various global territories oscillates.

*(*We have looked at a number of stockbrokers reports but would strongly recommend an excellent report from Equity Growth Research whose help has been elicited for compiling much of the above detail.)*

ANGLO IRISH BANK CORPORATION plc

BUSINESS: Banking
REGISTERED OFFICE: 18/21 St. Stephens Green, Dublin. Tel: 01-6162000. Fax: 01-6611852.
HEAD OFFICE: as regd office. **SECRETARY:** R Murphy.
REGISTRAR & TRANSFER OFFICE: Computershare Investor Services (Ireland) Ltd, Heron House, Corrig Road, Sandyford Ind Estate, Dublin.
AUDITORS: Ernst & Young. **SOLICITORS:** Matheson Ormsby Prentice. **STOCKBROKERS:** Goodbody.
DIRECTORS: P Murray (Chairman - 55), S FitzPatrick (Ch Ex - 55), M Jacob (58), P Killen (56), W McAteer (53), T O'Mahoney (44), J Rowan (45), P Wright. (62), N Sullivan (55), A Stanzel (64), F Drury.
SHARE CAPITAL: Authorised: 380 million Ord. €0.32 shares. **Issued:** 324,981,454 Ord. €0.32 shares.
STAFF: 807.　　　　**SCRIP DIVIDEND:** Yes

CAPITAL HISTORY:

In 1971 company goes public as City of Dublin Bank. Feb. '74 shares split into 25p units. June 1978 'rights' 1-for-4 at 33p. Feb. 1981 1,000,000 shares issued at 42p each. Nov. 1986 'rights' 5-for-6 at 47.5p each to raised £3.85m. July 1987 1-for-2 'rights' at 55p each raising £5m. May 1989 1-for-1 rights at 72p each raising £20.5m. Dec 1991 60,187,583 shares issued 1-1 rights issue at 46p. Jan 1994: 121,700,649 Ord 25p shares in 1-for-1 rights at 50p each. Jan 1999: Placed 13.2m 25p Ord shares at 190p each. Jan 2001: Placed 14m 0.32 Ord shares @ €3.09 each.

COMPANY HISTORY:

In 1964 City of Dublin Bank became part of Irish Financial Holdings Ltd. Jan 1971 117 Holdings (IR) Ltd. purchased City of Dublin Bank in conjunction with Slater Walker each holding 20%. 1975 bought Irish Bank of Commerce for which 1,202,096 shares issued in payment. (Irish Bank of Commerce held 30% of Credit Finance). Later in 1975 Slater Walker stake in City of Dublin Bank sold. Dec. '78 purchased Anglo Irish Bank for £100,000. In 1979 sold their stake in Credit Finance. Feb. 1981 to maintain capital adequacy ratios, issued shares raising £413.000 from insti-

tutional shareholders. Dec. 1981 sold 40% interest in Irish Bank of Commerce to Credit Commercial de France for £1m. Both CDB and CCF injected £1m in equity in IBC. Feb. 1984 Industrial Funding Trust Ltd. in UK acquired. July 1984 sold further 40% of IBC to CCF for £1.3m. June 1985 acquired Beneficial Trust of Ireland for £500,000. May 1986 acquired CH Arthur, Sales Finance and Southern Industrial Trust from Waterford Glass Plc for £6.63m. June 1986 purchased mortgage loan book from Investors in Industry (IR) Ltd. for £4.5 million. Name City of Dublin Bank changed to Anglo Irish Bank Corporation in December 1986. July 1987: 1-for-2 'rights' at 55p each raising £5m. Jan. 1988: T. Kenny resigns as Director. A.G. Murphy appointed Chairman. May 1988: Acquired Porter & Irvine, Stockbrokers. October 1988: Purchase of Irish Bank of Commerce (80%) for £6.8m. December 1988: Acquired majority of Solomons Abrahamson, Stockbrokers. Nov 1989: acquired 47% of Figurehead Finance London for £2.5m stg. July 1991: Raised £22m Long Term Floating Rate Bond. Jan 1992 : Rights Issue raises £26m. Jan 1992: 92% of rights taken up; remainder sold at 47p each. John Clegg resigns as Director. April 1992: Aborts takeover of Hill Samuel Ireland. Oct 1992: Solomons Stockbrokers close. Feb 1993: K Loughran resigns as Director. July 1993: Paid £30m stg for property loans of £30m stg bought from Chemical Bank in UK. 18m 'Clegg' shares sold at 60p each. Dec 1993: Rights issue to raise £58m; 97.5% take-up. Scrip-dividend 13% take-up. April 1994: Acquired £33m stg loan book of nursing homes from Canadian Imperial Bank in UK for £28.8m stg. Dec 1994: Bought Hill Samuel Ireland loan book for £104m (premium 5%). Jan 1995: Purchased Royal Trust Bank Austria for £13m. Dec 1995: Purchased £69m stg loan book from Allied Dunbar Assurance for IR£71.3m. March 1996: Bought Ansbacher Bank for £13m (net assets £11.6m). July 1996: High Court cancels £20m in share premium account. Jan 1998:

Share Price Sept 2001 - Sept 2002

[line graph showing share price rising from about 2 in Sept 2001 to a peak near 7 around mid-2002]

1. €6.01 07.05.02 Interims announced.

FINANCIAL DIARY
Interim Results Announced:	07.05.2002
Interim Dividend Payout:	15.07.2002
Final Results Announced:	28.11.2002
Annual General Meeting:	25.01.2002
Final Dividend Payout:	31.01.2002

FIVE YEAR SHARE PRICE TREND €
1997	High 1.74 (Dec)		Low 0.90 (Jan)
1998	High 2.69 (Jly)		Low 1.70 (Oct)
1999	High 2.88 (Oct)		Low 2.14 (Apr)
2000	High 3.17 (Dec)		Low 2.02 (Feb)
2001	High 4.66 (May)		Low 2.75 (Oct)

SECTORAL ANALYSIS
Gross Income: RoI 54% (54%), UK 40% (39%), other 6% (7%). **Profits:** RoI 53% (57%), UK 40% (35%), other 7% (8%).

INVESTMENT PERFORMANCE
Five Year Investment Performance: €6,704
Ten Year Investment Performance: € 6,866

HALF YEARLY PERFORMANCES: € m
6 months to:	30.09.00	31.03.01	30.09.01	31.03.02
Profit before Tax	72.6	90.5	104.3	115.2
Profit after Tax	59.3	71.5	75.9	86.4

Buys Credit Lyonnais Austria for £10.1m. Ja 1999: Buys Smurfit Paribas Bank for £30m (n assets £29m). May 1999: Buys UK property por folio from German bank. May 2000: Merger talk with First Active aborted. Apr 2001: Buy Marcuard Cook in Switz for €84.6m.

TEN YEAR REVIEW: € m

12 months to Sept 30	1992	1993	1994	1995	1996	1997	1998	1999	2000	2001
Income	-	138.02	139.39	183.60	243.66	305.50	403.40	540.1	809.6	1,068.7
Profit before Tax	9.32	11.75	18.44	24.29	30.60	38.47	57.27	89.1	133.6	194.8
Tax	2.62	3.01	4.9	6.44	6.86	7.75	10.28	14.7	24.7	47.4
Profit after Tax	6.70	8.74	13.45	17.85	23.74	30.73	46.98	74.4	108.9	147.4
Minority Interest	.04	(0.01)	-	-	(0.12)	-	-	-	-	-
Extraordinary Item	(0.96)	-	-	-	-	-	-	-	-	-
Pref. Dividend	-	-	-	-	-	(2.92)	(8.89)	(15.6)	(25.0)	(23.3)
Available for Shareholders	5.78	8.73	13.45	17.85	23.62	27.81	38.09	58.8	83.9	124.1
Ordinary Dividend	5.12	5.17	10.44	10.58	11.94	13.59	16.00	19.9	24.6	31.6
Retained profit	0.06	3.56	3.01	7.28	11.68	14.22	22.09	38.9	59.3	92.5
Increase (decrease) in Reserves	14.79 f)	1.10 g)	36.65 h)	(0.64) i)	0.63 j)	15.74	15.36 a)	73.5 n)	64.0	139.6 b)
Shareholders' Funds	67.83	69.34	145.14	145.63	147.54	164.30	181.06	261.1	327.2	473.6
Ordinary Dividend per Share (€)	0.043	0.043	0.043	0.043	0.047	0.053	0.062	0.072	0.087	0.104
Earnings per Share (€)	0.065	0.072	0.064	0.074	0.095	0.109	0.147	0.215	0.297	0.42 k)

a) Goodwill w/o -£8.5m; scrip dividend write back +£3.7m. f) Share premium €14.0m. g) Goodwill €3.0m written off. (h) Share premium €34.4m. i) Goodwill written off €8.9m. j) Goodwill €13.2m written off. k) Based upon 296.0m shares. n) Share premium +€27.68m. b) Share premium +€40.4m.

BALANCE SHEET: SEPTEMBER 30 2001 € m

Share Capital:		Fixed Assets	29.1
305,888,274 Ord €0.32 shares	71.7	Current Assets	15,608.9
Reserves	156.0	Current Liabilities	14,145.5
		Net Current Assets	1,463.4
		Medium debt	(476.6)
		Minority & bonds	(606.4)
		Net Tangible Assets	409.5
		Intangibles	64.1
Shareholder's funds	257.7	Net Tangible Assets	473.6

Comment:
A top class performance. Shareholders must be delighted with 6.7 fold increase in their capital over 5 years - that's one of the best performances in the financial sector.

The Seed Capital Scheme

The 2002 Finance Act extended the Seed Capital Scheme, enabling individuals establishing an operation on FINEX Europe to receive significant refunds of PAYE of up to □86,995.

Since it's founding in 1985, FINEX, the New York Board of Trade's (NYBOT) currency products division has developed a series of innovative currency futures and options contracts and carefully tailored its trading practices to accommodate the financial sectors demand for flexible risk management and investment tools. FINEX provides a global marketplace for euro-based, U.S. dollar-paired and other strategic cross-rate contracts as well as the U.S. dollar Index (USDX) futures and options.

Currency futures and options offer currency traders advantages often not found in the cash market. The exchange's open auction marketplace provides an efficient pricing mechanism, effective risk transfer and anonymity of trading. The futures market utilises margin to cover a net market position, while the currency cash market calls for the commitment of a credit line to cover every position taken. In addition, futures and options markets provide an important risk management function to participants in a number of industries. They offer price protection to hedgers and trading opportunities for investors. Their uses are broad and diverse. The NYBOT currency complex at its FINEX division features a range of futures and options contracts specifically targeted to meet the specialised needs of various segments of the global currency market.

If you have been employed in Ireland during the last 5 years and have either a proven track record or a passion for trading FX futures and options, then the FINEX Europe Seed Capital Scheme offers an exciting opportunity to put that experience into running your own business.

DEFINITIONS USED IN THE IRISH STOCK MARKET ANNUAL 2003

BEARS: Sellers expecting prices will go lower.

BLUE CHIP: A well-respected solid large company which should be a safe investment if perhaps a liitle unexciting. Sometimes disparagingly referred to as an 'elephant'.

BONDS: Government or corporate fixed interest instruments with a guaranteed regular interest (usually half-yearly) and usually a predetermined repayment date.

BOTTOM FISHING: Bargain hunting in the market when prices *look* inexpensive.

BULL: Buyers hoping prices will rise.

CAPITAL GAINS TAX: A tax levied on the profit on the sale of shares known for short, as CGT.

DIVIDEND COVER: The number of times the total cost of the dividend is covered by after tax profits (after preference dividends have been allowed for).

EARNINGS PER SHARE RATIO: The current share price divided by the last published earnings per share, where earnings per share is net profit after tax divided by the number of ordinary shares. The p/e ratio is a measure of the level of confidence investors have (rightly or wrongly) in a company. Generally the higher the figure, the higher the confidence. This is the *historic* p/e ratio. The ratio could also be based on forecast earnings and in this case it would be referred to the *future* or *prospective* p/e ratio.

IPO: Initial public offering - the issue of shares for the first time to the public

MARKET CAPITALISATION: Market capitalisation is the product of the number of ordinary shares in issue multiplied by the market share price.

MBO: Management buy out - usually when the major shareholders are not impressed with the lowly way their shares are valued by the market; they usually decide it is more peaceful to return to their 'private' rather 'public' persona.

MUTTER IN THE GUTTER: The rumours on the street!

NET ASSETS PER SHARE: We differentiate between net tangible assets per share and net assets per share. The *net tangible assets* attributable to the ordinary shareholders divided by the number of shares in issue - expressed as pence per share. The *net assets per share* exclude the intangibles which are substantial in most exploration companies.

ROLLING EARNINGS PER SHARE: Add together the earnings per share for the last two six month periods. In the case of the Annual Results there will be no change but where Interim Results have been issued subsequently, take the latest 6 months' e.p.s. and add them to the last 6 months of the last full year. It gives a more up-dated picture.

WHITE KNIGHT: A company which makes an offer to twart a bid from an unwelcome predator.

FIVE YEAR INVESTMENT PERFORMANCE: The December 31 2001 value of €1,000 invested in the company's shares at January 1 1997 with dividends accumulated. Rights issues are disregarded but obviously scrip issues are taken into account.

TEN YEAR INVESTMENT PERFORMANCE: The December 31 2001 value of €1,000 invested in the company's shares at January 1 1992 with dividends accumulated. Rights issues are disregarded but obviously scrip issues are taken into account.

INFLATION: To enable the investor assess the real return over the five and ten year investment periods, it is helpful to know that the value of €1,000 at beginning of 1997 would have to grow to **€1,182** in the five year period to December 2001 to hold its real value. Similarly €1,000 invested at the beginning of 1991 would have to grow to **€1,311** over the ten year period to December 2001 to hold its real value.

(Formerly Conroy Petroleum and Natural Resources plc + Atlantic Resources plc)

BUSINESS: Exploration company
REGISTERED OFFICE: 60 Merrion Road, Dublin. Tel: 01-6673063. Fax: 01-6673065. **HEAD OFFICE:** as regd office. **SECRETARY:** M.G. Graham **REGISTRARS & TRANSFERS OFFICE:** Capita Corporate Registrars Ltd, Unit 5, Manor Street Business Park, Dublin. **PRINCIPAL BANKERS:** Bank of Ireland, Anglo Irish Bank, ICC, Ulster Bank, National Westminster Bank, ABN Amro Bank, Bank of Scotland, Irish Intercontinental Bank, Mees Pierson, Allied Irish Bank. **AUDITORS:** Arthur Andersen.
SOLICITORS: Whitney, Moore & Keller; Matheson Ormsby Prentice.
STOCKBROKERS: Bloxham Stockbrokers; Davy Stockbrokers; Canaccord Capital (Europe) Ltd.
DIRECTORS: A O'Reilly Jnr (Chairman - 37), K Ross (CEO), J P Hayes (72), P Kidney, J S McCarthy (79), W Mulligan (60), J Tilson (71), JSD McCarthy, D Raxburgh
SHARE CAPITAL: Authorised: 2,162,488,340 Ord. £0.01 shares and 287,502,332 Deferred shares of €0.05. **Issued:** 1,581,262,825 Ord. £0.06 shares.
STAFF: 202. **SCRIP DIVIDEND:** No

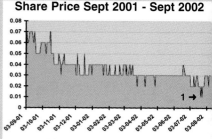

Share Price Sept 2001 - Sept 2002

1. €0.01 23.07.02 Digesting rights issue.

FINANCIAL DIARY
Interim Results announced:	28.08.2002
Interim Dividend Payout:	none
Final Results announced:	30.04.2002
Annual General Meeting:	12.07.2002
Final Dividend Payout:	none

INVESTMENT PERFORMANCE
Five Year Investment Performance:	€85
Ten Year Investment Performance:	€28

HALF YEARLY PERFORMANCES: € m
Six months to:	31.12.00	30.06.01	31.12.01	30.06.02
Sales	13.7	10.1	8.6	10.5
Loss/Profit before tax	(7.6)	(10.9)	(4.7)	(5.5)
Profit % Sales	-	-	-	-

FIVE YEAR SHARE TREND
1997	High	0.66 (Aug)	Low	0.43 (Jan)
1998	High	0.44 (Jan)	Low	0.21 (Oct)
1999	High	0.30 (Sep)	Low	0.15 (Apr)
2000	High	0.30(Jan)	Low	0.15 (Dec)
2001	High	0.18 (Jan)	Low	0.03 (Nov)

CAPITAL HISTORY:

August 1980 flotation of 1,025,034 Ord. 25p shares at £1 each. November 1982 'rights' of 11-for-8 at £1 each. May 1985 issued 1,200,000 Ord. 25p shares on acquisition of Minquest. Issued 181,772 (5%) shares to Minister for Finance. December 1985 450,000 issued for 51% Jeepflow Ltd. July 1986 100,000 Ord. 25p shares issued on acquisition of MPS Mineral Prospecting Services. August 1986 1,200,000 shares placed at 135p stg. each. December 1986 shares split into 5p units. Sept. 1987 700,000 Ord. 5p shares placed at 76p stg raising £560,000. April 1989: Rights issue on 6,696,141 Ord. 5p shares at 80p stg on the basis of 2-for-9. October 1990, 4 million Ord 5p shares placed at 100p each. Aug 1991: Issued 666,667 Ord. 5p shares part consideration Singleton Oilfield. Dec. 1991: Placed 2,045,396 Ord. 5p shares at 75p each. Jan 1992: 11,641,640 Ord. 5p shares issued re Atlantic Resources takeover at 56p each. March 1993: 728,863 issued to complete Singleton oilfield agreement. Oct 1994: Issued 840,000 Ord 5p shares to Noramco Mining at 77p each part repayment of £2.9m loan. March 1995: 218,806,203 Ord 5p shares issued in 'Rights' at €0.25 per share on 15-for 4 basis. Aug 1995: Issued 7,602,339 Ord 5p shares at €0.22 (€1.7m) to clear Ampac loan. July 2002: Creation of one Ord €0.01 share and one Deferred €0.05 share for every Ord €0.06 share held. 4-for-1 rights issue of 1,150,009,328 ord €0.01 share @ €0.025 per share

COMPANY HISTORY:

Company incorporated April 1980. Richard Conroy and Desmond Conroy were co-founders of Trans-International Oil in 1973. During 1976 Trans-International Oil Ltd. acquired exploration rights in the Irish Continental Shelf. The Conroy brothers had a 44.3% shareholding in Trans-International. In 1978 Trans-International was acquired by Aran Energy for shares. The Conroy brother's investment company Conroy Holdings (with interests in Aran and Conroy Petroleum in Texas) was acquired in July 1980 by Conroy Petroleum and Natural Resources for 237,576 Ord. 25p shares. In Aug. 1980 1,025,034 Ord. 25p shares placed at £1 each on the flotation of C.P. & N.R. Purchased 240,000 Ord. £1 shares in Berkeley Seventh Round Ltd. for £264,000 (4.58% of total BSR

equity). In 1982 commenced exploring in Galmoy acreage. Also invested further £431,250 in BSR. In December 1982 Burnett & Hallamshire Holdings took up 41.8% of C.P. & N.R. equity. August 1985 acquired Minquest Resources on the basis of 3 C.P. & N.R. shares of every 5 Minquest shares (1,200,000 C.P. & N.R. shares issued). As a result J Teeling and P Power appointed directors. Subsequent boardroom trauma led to resignation of Messrs. Teeling and Power. December 1985 acquired 51% of Jeepflow for £135,000 by the issue of 450,000 Ord. 25p shares. July 1986 acquired MPS Mineral Prospecting Services Ltd. for £140,000 by the issue of 100,000 Ord. 25p shares. In March 1986 discovery of significant zinc/lead minerals announced in Galmoy acreage in Kilkenny/Laois border. June 1986 Tara Exploration acquires Burnett & Hallamshire Holding's stake. August 1986 1.2 million Ord. 25p shares placed at 135p stg. to fund Galmoy drilling. December 1986 shares split into 5p units. Sept. 1987: Share placing raised £560,000. Nov. 1987: Joint venture agreement with American Pacific Mining Company Inc. APMC will obtain 40% interest in Galmoy. APMC responsible for raising 100% of non-recourse mining finance. APMC will pay Conroy £1m and both companies will exchange 15% of their respective equities. May 1988: Introduced to USM. Oct 1988: APMC terminates partnership with Conroy. March 1989: WGM report indicates viability of Galmoy prospect. May 1989: Rights issue raised £4.9mstg. net. Feb. 1990: Capital cost of developing Galmoy estimated at $70m. August 1990: Outukumpu controls 27% of Conroy. Canadian mining group Corona now holds in excess of 24%. Perceived battle by Outukumpu and Corona for Conroy shares pushes price to new height of 149p. Sept. 1990: Outukumpu now hold 29.83%. Sept. 1990: Outukumpu directors H. Solin and G. Mascall resign. H. Dobson rejoins Board. Oct. 1990: Share placing raises £3.96m. Feb. 1991: Peter Steen, CEO of Corona appointed Director. Aug 1991: Pays £700,000 for 20% in Singleton Oilfield (cash and shares). Nov. 1991: Corona's 21% stake transferred to Dundee Bancorp. Conroy bids 1 Conroy share for every 26 Atlantic Resources shares (values Atlantic at £7.7m). P. Steen resigns from Board. A.J. O'Reilly and Olayan purchase 2.04m Conroy new shares at 75p each. Outokumpu/Corona diluted from 53% to 43%. Major shareholders incensed at proposed takeover. Dec. 1991: Bid for Atlantic becomes unconditional with 67.5% acceptances. Jan 1992: A.J. O'Reilly resigns from Atlantic. Atlantic Resources reverses into CP & NR for £6.52m inc goodwill £2.8m. Feb. 1992: 10 Directors ousted. Elected: P. Carroll (Corona), G. Mascall (Outokumpu), G. Dempsey, J. Donnelly, E. Laatio, Lord Shaughnessy, P. Wallace, P. Steen. March 1992: O'Reilly purchases Dundee (Bancorp) 16.3% shareholding for £7.8m. B. Gilmore, T. O'Reilly Jnr, J. Meagher, J. McCarthy appointed Other Directors appointed R. Conroy, D. Conroy, M. Jones, W. Mulligan, P. Hayes and J. Jones. May 1992: R. Conroy sells 492,662 shares at 40p; D. Conroy sells 1 million at 40p. Purchaser Columbia Investments (O'Reilly) now holds 24.45%; R. Conroy holds 1.2m; D. Conroy 0.94m. Name changed to ARCON International Resources Plc. Nov 1992: Columbia Investments (AJF O'Reilly) purchases 1.3m shares on market at 43p each - now holds 23%

plus 6.99% with concert parties. May 1994: Galmoy licenc obtained: annual rent for 21 years £100,000 p.a. plus 3% of re enues. July 1994: Galmoy zinc concentrates presold to 5 smelte (120,000 tonnes p.a.). Oct 1994: Major executive row. R. Conro replaced by B. Gilmore . Dec 1994: R. Conroy, D Conroy, J Jone and Miss M Jones resign as Directors. May 1995: Turnkey Galmo project given to the Cementation Co (Ir) Ltd for £37.8m. April 199 Rights issue raised £41.3m. Outokumpu declines to take up i rights. A. O'Reilly ends up with 45% of equity. Sept 1995: Que Capital Corp holds 4% after buying 7.6m shares at 17.1p eac May 1996: Outokumpu sells 24.5% at 27p each. March 1997: Fir ore produced at Galmoy. Goodman & Co (Canada) acquire 5.56% Arcon's equity. Aug 1997: Each Arcon share to get or share in Providence Resources. Feb 1995: Invests $4.5m in con vertible debenture in Princess Resources (Convertible Oct 1998 Oct 1999: AJ O'Reilly mops up more shares - now holds 44.1% Feb 2000: Capital Group now holds 5.49% (up from 4.9%). Ju 2002: Complete refinancing. Rights issue raises €28.8m, bar debt reduced by US$62m, banks issued with equity in lieu (€3.6m debt.

TEN YEAR REVIEW: € m

12 Months to 31 Dec	1992a)	1993a)	1994a)	1995a)	1996a)	1997 b)g)	1998	1999	2000	2001
Turnover	1,096	1,945	1,855	1,802	2,073	16,753	15,997	26,946	27,185	18,726
Profit (Loss) before Tax	(1,541)	(4,115)	(361)	(603)	272 j)	(4,566)	(10,428)	(1,651)	(10,478)	(15,637)
Tax	-	-	+471	-	-	-	-	-	-	-
Profit (Loss) after Tax	(1,541)	(4,115)	110	(603)	272	(4,566)	(10,428)	(1,651)	(10,478)	(15,637)
Extraordinary Item	-	-	-	-	-	-	-	-	-	-
Available for Shareholders	(1,541)	(4,115)	110	(603)	272	(4,566)	(10,428)	(1,651)	(10,478)	(15,637)
Ordinary Dividend	-	-	-	-	-	-	-	-	-	-
Retained Profit (Loss)	(1,541)	(4,115)	110	(603)	272	(4,566)	(10,428)	(1,651)	(10,478)	(15,637)
Increase (Decrease) in Res	(3,780) f)	(3,606)	-	37,674 h)	(625)	(29,478)	(12,094) j)	1,006 k)	(9,659)	(14,967)
Shareholders' Funds	16,310	12,758	13,323	65,426	64,933	36,768	24,674	25,679	16,020	51
Ordinary Dividend per Share (€)	-	-	-	-	-	-	-	-	-	-
Earnings per Share (€)	-	-	0.002	-	0.001 i)	-	-	-	-	-

a) Year ended Aug 31. b) 16 months. d) Share premium €4.6m. f) Goodwill w/o €3.6m.
h) Share premium +€40.3m. i) Based on 285.1m shares. j) Currency loss -€1.7m. k) Currency gain +€2.7m.

BALANCE SHEET: DECEMBER 31 2001. € m

Share Capital:		Fixed Assets		13.2
287,502,332 Ord. 5p shares	17.3	Current Assets	1.9	
		Current Liabilities	18.1	
		Net Current Liabilities		(16.3)
Reserves	(17.2)	Medium Debt		(26.5)
		Net Tangible Liabilities		(29.6)
		Intangibles		29.5
Shareholders' Funds	0.1	Net Assets		0.1

Comment:

There seems to be

no bottom

to this pit.

Auditors Note: *There is a 'Going Concern' note attaching to these accounts.*

ARDAGH plc

(Formerly Irish Glass)

BUSINESS: Glass container manufacture.
REGISTERED OFFICE: South Bank Road, Ringsend, Dublin. Tel: 01-6052400. Fax: 01-6683416.
HEAD OFFICE: as regd office.
SECRETARY: B. J. Butterly
REGISTRARS & TRANSFER OFFICE: Capita Corporate Registrars plc, Unit 5 Manor Street Business Park, Dublin.
PRINCIPAL BANKERS: Bank of Ireland, Allied Irish Banks, National Westminster Bank, Anglo Irish Bank, BNP Paribas, Royal Bank of Scotland.
AUDITORS: PricewaterhouseCoopers.
SOLICITORS: McCann Fitzgerald.
STOCKBROKERS: Davy Stockbrokers.
DIRECTORS: P Coulson (Chairman - 51), E Kilty (Ch Exec 55), F J Davies (72), M Downes (71), B Dowling (56), R French (58), B Somers (54), J Riordan (45).
SHARE CAPITAL: Authorised: 50,000,000 Ord. shares of €0.30 each. **Issued:** 37,110,085 Ord. €0.30 shares (incl 2,484,395 treasury shares).
STAFF: 1,458.   **SCRIP DIVIDEND:** Yes.

CAPITAL HISTORY:

March 1969 'rights; of 500,000 Ord. 25p shares @ 75p each on the basis of 5-for-19. June 1969 600,000 Ord. 25p shares 'scrip' issue on the basis of 2-for-3. November 1973 'scrip' issue of 1-for-2. Dec 1977 'scrip' issue of 1-for-3. Dec 1987 'scrip' issue 1-for-1. Nov 1990: 1-for-1 'scrip' issue. March 1999: Open offer 8,471,997 Ord. 5p shares (10-for-33) at €1.52 each. Rockware's holding of 7,336,423 shares deemed and cancelled. June 2000: Bought back 2,484,472 own shares @ €1.61 each.

COMPANY HISTORY:

Founded in 1925 to take over restructured Irish Glass Bottle Co. and Ringsend Bottle Co. In 1932 Joseph McGrath and Richard Duggan along with a Belgian company acquired the operation which in turn became involved with Waterford Glass in 1952. In 1967 Waterford Glass was hived off. In 1976 the UK glass producers Rockware Group took over 20.4% of the equity of Irish Glass formerly held by the Belgian interest. In 1978 Irish Glass disposed of its 2.3% shareholding in Waterford Glass for €1.85m. June 1987: Irish Plastic Packaging (60%) ceased manufacturing. 1988: Company entered into conditional agreement to invest in 40% of Consolidated Plastics Ltd. June 1989: Interest in Consolidated Plastics Ltd. reduced to 17.5%. Aug 1989: Acquired remaining 25% of Irish Plastic Packaging Ltd. Feb 1990: Name changed to Ardagh plc. September 1991: £475,000 loan stock repaid to stockholders. June 1992, E. Kilty appointed Group M.D.. Mercury Asset Management Ltd indirectly acquires 29.9% of Ardagh. 1997: Yeoman International buys 2.7m shares at €1.74 each. Sept 1997: Quinn's new £60m bottling plant in North to compete with Ardagh. Nov 1997: Amazement at Ardagh's proposed £25m investment in bottling plant. March 1998: Major board changes - P. Murray goes with I. Morrison and K. O'Donovan later. Announced that Flavius (91% owned by Mercury Asset Management) had taken 29.09% of equity. March 1999: Pays €359m for Rockware (reverse takeover). July 1999: Quoted in London. Ardagh claims 79% of 149,000 tonne market in all Ireland; Rockware claims 34% of UK glass packaging production. Oct 1999: Ringsend to make 100 redundant. April 2000: Will repurchase €4m worth of 2,484,472 own shares by tender at €1.61 each. S'holders offered back 4.6m shares! July 2000: Yeoman now holds 19%. April 2001: Acquires 50.9% Consumers International, Canada for $31.7m. Fails to gain outright control. Sept 2001: Decides to sell its bonds in Consumers International - likely profit $36m. Dec 2001: Shares delist in London. July 2002: Closes Ringsend plant. Lease worth €20m. May build warehouse on site.

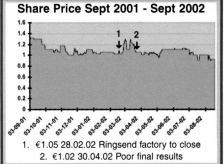

Share Price Sept 2001 - Sept 2002

1. €1.05 28.02.02 Ringsend factory to close
2. €1.02 30.04.02 Poor final results

FIVE YEAR SHARE PRICE TREND

Year	High		Low	
1997	High	1.78 (Apr)	Low	1.46 (Oct)
1998	High	2.73 (Mar)	Low	1.39 (Dec)
1999	High	2.60 (Mar)	Low	1.35 (Dec)
2000	High	2.10 (Aug)	Low	1.20 (Apr)
2001	High	1.50 (June)	Low	1.00 (Nov)

INVESTMENT PERFORMANCE

Five Year Investment Performance:	€838
Ten Year Investment Performance:	€ 854

HALF YEARLY PERFORMANCES: €'m

Six Months to	30.06.00	31.12.00	30.06.01	31.12.01
Sales	151.4	168.4	139.6	164.7
Profits (-) before tax	3.8	5.1	6.59	(4.18)
Profits % Sales	2.5	3.0	4.7	-

TEN YEAR REVIEW: €'000

12 months to Dec 31	1992 d)	1993 d)	1994 d)	1995 d)	1996 d)	1997 d)	1998 d)	1999 b)	2000	2001
Sales	41,203	38,545	40,992	43,061	45,486	46,537	51,160	273,635	319,760	304,278
Profit (Loss) before Tax	5,347	2,124	5,670	6,577	7,382	8,249	9,179	20,515	8,924	2,410 f)
Tax	565	283	498	730	970	1,192	1,232	5,520	4,000	+29
Profit (Loss) after Tax	4,782	1,841	5,172	5,847	6,412	7,057	7,947	14,995	4,924	2,439
Minority Interest	-	-	-	-	-	-	-	-	-	119
Available for Shareholders	4,782	1,8,41	5,172	5,847	6,412	7,057	7,947	14,995	4,924	2,558
Ordinary Dividend	1,335	1,406	1,642	1,814	2,016	2,261	2,615	1,063	2,522	1,255
Retained Profits	3,447	436	3,530	4,033	4,396	4,796	5,332	13,932	2,402	1,303
Increase (Decrease) in Reserves	3,525	538	3,578	4,148	4,509	4,873	5,518	12,822	(1,926)	3,021
Shareholders Funds	38,750	39,330	42,923	47,107	51,657	56,553	62,308	74,952	73,026	76,197
Ordinary Dividend per Share (€)	0.039	0.042	0.048	0.053	0.059	0.066	0.074	0.033	0.074	0.037
Earnings per Share (€)	0.056	0.055	0.0152	0.171	0.188	0.206	0.22	0.41	0.14	0.075 a)

a) Based upon 34.1m shares. b) 78 weeks to 31.12.99, d) Year ended June 30. f) Includes Ringsend write-off -€7.6m; property sale +€6.6m.

BALANCE SHEET: DECEMBER 31 2001 €'000

Comment:
Is Ardagh trying to prove, in merger terms, that one plus one is not greater than two. Intangibles now account for 98% of Ardagh's net assets and borrowing is now going through the roof.

Share Capital				
36,931,563 Ord. €0.30 shares	11,079	Fixed Assets		248,583
(inc 2,484,395 treasury shares)		Current Assets	189,039	
Reserves	65,118	Current Liabilities	127,799	
		Net Current Assets		61,240
		Medium Debt		(304,346)
		Minority		(3,837)
		Net Tangible Assets		1,640
		Intangibles		74,557
Shareholders' Funds	76,197	Net Assets		76,197

ARNOTTS plc

BUSINESS: Department store operators.
REGISTERED OFFICE: 12 Henry Street, Dublin.
Tel: 01-8050469. Fax: 01-8721403.
HEAD OFFICE: as regd office.
SECRETARY: P Donnelly.
REGISTRARS & TRANSFER OFFICE: Capita Corporate Registrars plc, P.O.Box 7117, Dublin
PRINCIPAL BANKERS: Allied Irish Banks; HSBC Bank; National Irish Bank; Investment Bank of Ireland.
AUDITORS: PricewaterhouseCoopers.
SOLICITORS: William Fry.
STOCKBROKERS: Davy Stockbrokers.
DIRECTORS: M O'Connor (Chairman - 73), B. Davy (60), V Dudgeon (68), J Duignan (Mgr Dir - 60), W Kelly (56), H Kilroy (67), R Nesbitt (51), C Tolar (62).
SHARE CAPITAL: Authorised: 25,000,000 Ord. €1.27 shares; £90,000 6% (now 4.50% + tax credit) cumulative preference €1.27 stock units. **Issued:** 18,508,534 Ord. €1.27 shares (inc 604,467 treasury share); 90,000 cumulative preference €1.27 stock units.
STAFF: 999.   **SCRIP DIVIDEND:** No.

CAPITAL HISTORY:

April 1970 1-for-2 'scrip' issue. 1977: 1-for-2 'scrip' issue. May 1980 1-for-1 'scrip' issue. May 1990 1-for-1 'scrip' issue.

COMPANY HISTORY:

Founded in 1843 under the name Cannock White. Sir John Arnott took over the running of the business in the 1860's and Arnotts was incorporated in 1872. Destroyed by fire in 1894. In the 1930's engaged in manufacturing and the retail side was expanded in the '60s with the addition of two new outlets - Boyers in North Earl Street, Dublin and Arnotts in Grafton Street. In 1974 entered cash in transit security business with Allied Couriers but revamped in 1987 with joint venture with Brink's-Mat. In 1980 Arnotts acquired remaining 40% of Ballet International from Courtaulds for estimated €0.57m. In 1983 shirt making discontinued. March 1987: Rebuffed takeover approach from Glen Abbey plc. May 1987: R.S. Nesbitt appointed President. Nov. 1987: Ballet International (net assets €2.9m) sold to John Crowther Ltd. for €3.7m cash. Jan 1990: Closed wholesale. Oct 1992: Completed refurbishment of main store. March 1993: M Nesbitt moves from Mng Dir and appointed Director of Development. Sept 1993: Morgan Stanley Asset Mgt builds up 11.12% stake. Jan 1995: £2.8m robbery at Brinks Allied (50% owned). March 1995: Brinks 50% stake for sale. June 1995: M. R. Nesbitt resigns. Morgan Stanley reduces stake to 7%. April 1999 JB Davy buys 50,000 shares at €6.75 each. June 2000: Buys 326,000 own shares @ €6.70 each; Davy/Nesbitt/O'Connor buy 105,000 shares; Setanta off-loads 431,000 shares. BIAM buys 1.5m shares (8.2%) @ €6.70 each. Oct 2001: Buys 138,566 own shares @ €6.30 each. Nov 2001: Buys 140,000 own shares @ €6.30 each (total treasury shares now 604,467 or 3.3%).

Share Price Sept 2001 - Sept 2002

1. €8.15 27.03.02 results announced.

FINANCIAL DIARY

Interim Results Announced:	28.08.2002
Interim Dividend Payout:	18.10.2002
Final Results Announced:	27.03.2002
Annual General Meeting:	30.05.2002
Final Dividend Payout:	01.07.2002

FIVE YEAR SHARE PRICE TREND €

1997	High 6.47 (Dec)	Low 4.50 (Jan)
1998	High 8.38 (July)	Low 6.47 (Dec)
1999	High 7.85 (July)	Low 6.01 (Dec)
2000	High 7.30 (July)	Low 5.79 (Apr)
2001	High 7.40 (June)	Low 6.20 (Oct)

INVESTMENT PERFORMANCE

Five Year Investment Performance:	€1,699
Ten Year Investment Performance:	€3,591

HALF YEARLY PERFORMANCES: € m

6 months to:	31.01.01	31.07.01	31.01.02	31.07.02
Sales	70.9	62.1	78.5	66.03
Profit before Tax	10.5	5.6	7.1	6.7
Profit % Sales	14.8	9.0	9.0	10.1

TEN YEAR REVIEW : €'000

12 months to January	1993	1994	1995	1996	1997	1998	1999	2000	2001	2002
Sales(excluding concession sales)	54,721	55,616	59,629	64,336	66,170	75,049	93,175	107,688	124,375	140,583
Profit before Tax	2,844	3,943	5,725	6,888	8,638	9,801	11,834	14,227	15,646	17,882
Tax	1,279	1,676	2,527	2,294	2,054	- a)	2,112	3,483	3,446	3,043
Profit after Tax	1,566	2,266	3,198	4,594	6,584	9,801	9,722	10,744	12,200	14,839
Preference Dividend	5	5	5	5	5	6	6	6	6	6
Available to Shareholders	1,561	2,261	3,193	4,589	6,579	9,795	9,716	10,738	12,194	14,833
Ordinary Dividend	1,658	1,306	1,882	2,108	2,466	2,933	3,592	4,273	4,935	5,715
Retained Profit	(98)	603	1,312	2,481	4,113	6,862	6,124	6,465	7,259	9,118
Increase (Decrease) in Reserves	(98)	612	1,326	2,579	4,523	37,629 f)	6,878	40,190 g)	39,141 b)	7,385 h)
Shareholders' Funds	57,638	58,261	59,599	62,259	66,988	104,671	111,957	152,274	191,610	199,014
Ordinary Dividend per Share (€)	0.095	0.095	0.108	0.121	0.14	0.165	0.20	0.235	0.273	0.32
Earnings per Share (€)	0.09	0.13	0.18	0.26	0.37	0.55	0.54	0.59	0.68	0.826 e)

a) No Tax due to capital allowances. b) Property revaluation +€33.6m. e) Based upon 18.1m shares. f) Revaluation surplus +€26.9m. g) Revaluation surplus +€33.4m. h) Purchase of own shares -€1.8m.

BALANCE SHEET: JANUARY 31 2002. €'m

Share Capital:			Fixed Assets	225,385
18,373,000 €1.27 Ord. shares	23,334		Current Assets	38,354
			Current Liabilities	47,727
Reserves	175,680		Net Current Liabilities	(9,373)
			Medium Debt	(16,884)
			Pref Shares	(114)
Shareholders' Funds	199,014		Net Tangible Assets	199,014

AVIVA plc

(formerly CGNU plc; previously CGUplc and Norwich Union plc)

BUSINESS: Insurance

REGISTERED OFFICE: St Helen's, 1 Undershaft, London.

HEAD OFFICE: as above. Tel: 0044 020 72832000.

SECRETARY: R Whitaker.

REGISTRARS & TRANSFER OFFICE: Lloyds TSB Registrars, The Causeway, Worthing, West Sussex.

PRINCIPAL BANKERS: HSBC plc; Natwest Group.

AUDITORS: Ernst & Young.

SOLICITORS: A&L Goodbody; Clifford Chance LLP.

STOCKBROKERS: Hoare Govett; Davy Stockbrokers.

DIRECTORS: P Gyllenhammar (Chairman - 67), G Paul (63), R Harvey (Gr Ch Exec - 52), P Scott (49), M Biggs (50), P Twyman (58), G de la Dehesa (61), V Dik (64), M Partridge (67), P Snowball (52), D Stevens (64), E Vallance (57), A Villeneuve (58), T Wyand (59).

SHARE CAPITAL: Authorised: 3 billion Ord 25p shares.

Issued: 2,255,693,925 Ord 25p shares.

STAFF: 68,107

SCRIP DIVIDEND: Dividend reinvestment plan.

CAPITAL HISTORY:

Feb 1997: 499,998 ord shares issued to Fileco (No. 4) Ltd for cash. May 1997: Issues 1.3 billion ord shares re flotation. Aug 1997: First dealings 290p stg. June 2000: CGNUplc issues 48 new CGNU Ord 25p stg shares for every 100 Norwich Union shares valuing Norwich Union at £7.4billion stg. Issued 1,312,541,748 Ord 25p shares to Norwich Union shareholders.

COMPANY HISTORY:

Norwich Union traces its history from 1797 and is one of the UK's largest insurance groups with funds under management of £40 billion stg at end 1996 and worldwide gross premium of just over £5 billion in 1996. They have over 7 million customers and their premium income split down as between life and pensions 48%, general insurance 23%, healthcare 3% and the balance of 26% is international. In 1995 NU was third largest in UK in life insurance based on assets under management, second largest in motor insurance and third largest in medica insurance. 96% of NU's life and pensions business comes through independent financial advisers. In 1994 deficiencies were detected in NU's direct sales force which were withdrawn and retrained. Aug 1997: Quoted on Dublin Stock Exchange following flotation in London in June at 290p stg. 231 million free shares issued to members and 630 million new shares issued to raise £1.75 billion stg for NU. Oct 1997: Invites purchasers for Irish building society. Nov 1998: Acquired London & Edinburgh Assurance.

CGNU plc: On Feb 21 2000 the boards of CGU and Norwich Union announced agreed terms of a merger, henceforth to be known as CGNU plc. Becomes UK's largest insurer with premium income and retail investment sales of £26billion stg, second largest life and pensions operator in UK with leading positions in France, the Netherlands, Ireland and Poland. CGU emerged from the 1998 merger of Commercial Union and General Accident. June 2000: Norwich Union valued at £7.4billion stg holding 930m CGNU shares (41.5%) with CGU shareholders holding 1,313million CGNU shares (58.5%). Jan 2001: Boardroom exits. Feb 2001: Sells New Zealand arm for £125mstg. May 2001: Sells Belgian business for £72m stg. June 2001: Sells US general insurance division for £1.3billion stg. April 2002: Name changed to Aviva. 40% dividend cut in 2002 to 23p per share with growth of 5% p.a; shares lose 10%.

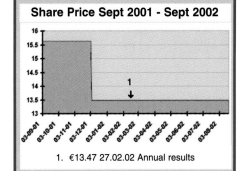

Share Price Sept 2001 - Sept 2002

1. €13.47 27.02.02 Annual results

FINANCIAL DIARY

Interim Results Announced:	01.08.2002
Interim Dividend Payout:	15.11.2002
Final Results Announced	27.02.2002
Annual General Meeting:	23.04.2002
Final Dividend Payout:	17.05.2002

HALF YEARLY PERFORMANCES: £m stg

Six months to	31.12.00	30.06.01	31.12.01	30.06.02
Gross Premium	16,693	13,842	14,973	14,495
Profit before Tax	(1,144)	106	408	(384)

SECTORAL ANALYSIS: (previous year)

Profits: UK 53% (51%), other Europe 37% (30%). elsewhere 10% (19%).

SHARE PRICE TREND

2000: High 1395p (Nov)   Low 1280p (Nov)

2001: High 1771p (Jan)   Low 1347p (Dec)

EIGHT YEAR REVIEW: £ m stg

12 months to 31 December	1994	1995	1996	1997	1998 g)	1999	2000	2001
Premium Income	4,655	4,519	5,012	5,723	5,649	26,677	28,720	28,815
Profit Before Tax	224	803	528	722	777	1,468	(1,406)	514
Tax	128	230	154	216	222	382	255	424
Profit After Tax	96	573	374	506	555	1,086	(1,661)	90
Minority	-	-	(3)	(11)	(10)	(66)	(52)	(57)
Preference dividends	-	-	-	-	-	-	(17)	(17)
Available to Shareholders	96	573	371	495	545	1,003	(1,730)	16
Ordinary Dividend	-	-	-	152	251	773	855	857
Retained Profit	96	573	371	343	294	230	(2,585)	(841)
Increase (Decrease) in Reserves	n/a	n/a	n/a	2,337 a)	614	n/a	(2,043) h)	(1,562) j)
Shareholders funds	n/a	n/a	n/a	5,098	5,713	15,673	13,433	11,672
Ordinary Dividend per Share (stg)	-	-	-	7.75p	12.8p	34.3p	38.0p	38.0p
Earnings per Share (stg)	7.5p	44.6p	28.9p	25.2p	27.8p	44.8p b)	-	0.7p b)

a) Currency loss - £51m; share premium +£1,795m. b) Based upon 2,250m shares in issue. f) Norwich Union payout only.
g) Subsequently adjusted. h) Foreign currency gain +£303m. j) Revaluation reserves -£821m stg.

BALANCE SHEET: DECEMBER 31 2001. £ m stg

Comment:

Prior to the merger of CGU and Norwich Union pretax profits of both companies totalled £1,468m stg - one has to wonder was this a step too far! And 2002 will hardly go down as the insurance industry's best year after the stock market turmoil.

Share Capital:		
2,254,928,378 Ord 25p shares		564
Reserves		11,108
Shareholders' Funds		11,672

Fixed Assets		307
Investments		136,009
Current Assets	22,073	
Current Liabilities	13,074	
Net Current Assets		8,999
Medium Debt		(132,776)
Minority & pref		(2,008)
Net Tangible Assets		10,531
Intangibles		1,141
Net Assets		11,672

BUSINESS: Financial services.
PRINCIPAL OFFICE: Lr Baggot Street, Dublin.
Tel: 01-6615933. Fax: 01-6615671.
SECRETARY: T.H. Forsyth.
REGISTRARS: Computershare Investor Services (Ireland) Ltd, Heron House, Corrig Road, Sandyford Ind Estate, Dublin. **AUDITORS:** PricewaterhouseCoopers.
SOLICITORS: F Murphy.
STOCKBROKERS: Cazenove & Co; J. & E. Davy.
DIRECTORS: L Crowley (Chairman - 66), M Soden (Group Ch Exec - 56), M Keane (62), R Bailie (59), A Barry (68), R Burrows (57), D Geaney (52), B Goggin (51), R. MacSharry (65), C Marland (57), T Moran (50), D O'Brien (45), M Redmond (52), J O'Donovan.
SHARE CAPITAL: Authorised: Ordinary Stock 1.5billion units of €0.64; Non-cumulative Pref. Stock: - 8m units of US $25 Pref. Stock; 100m units of stg £1 Pref. Stock; 100 units of €1.27 Pref. Stock. ADRs: One ADR equals 4 Stock Units. **Issued:** 1,008,550,285 units (excl 42,557,815 treasury units) of €0.64 Ord Stock. 1.9 million non-cum £1 stg Pref Stock 3.0m non-cum €1.27 Pref Stock.
STAFF: 18,438.   **SCRIP DIVIDEND:** No

CAPITAL HISTORY:

March 1969 1-for-2 'scrip' issue. May 1973 1-for-5 'scrip issue. June 1975 1-for-2 'scrip' issue. June 1976 1-for-5 'rights' at 250p plus 1-for-14 Conv. Loan Stock. July 1977 1-for-3 'scrip' issue. July 1983 1-for-2 'scrip' issue. May 1984 1-for-5 'rights' issue at 350p to raise £45m. May 1986 1-for-1 'scrip' issue. June 1987 2-for-9 'rights' issue at 150p to raise £53.3m. April 1988 1-for-4 'rights' at 150p to raise £73.5m. June 1989 scrip issue of 1-for-3. June 1991 scrip issue of 1 for 5. Aug 1993: Rights Issue 67,097,092 units (1-for-6) at €1.90 each. Oct 1997: Placed 23.5m stock units of £1 each at €10.75 each. July 1999: £1 Stock Units sub-divided into 50p Stock Units.

COMPANY HISTORY:

Established in 1783 by Royal Charter. In 1958 acquired Hibernian Bank Limited. April 1966: Took over National Bank of Ireland. March 1972: The three banks (Bank of Ireland, Hibernian, and National) were integrated into Bank of Ireland. April 1977 Bank of Ireland, P.J. Carroll and Fieldcrest Mills Inc. announced £43m. joint venture to manufacture towels in Kilkenny. Bank of Ireland held 25% at cost of £4.2m. May 1978 acquired British Credit Trust for £11m. Placed 3.4m shares at 345p to finance acquisition. November 1984 acquired 20% stake in Development Capital Corp. for £3.4m. 1986 acquired 99% of the Investment shares in the ICS Building Society. Feb. 1987: Acquired Bank America Finance Ltd. UK house mortgage subsidiary of Bank of America with net assets of £7m stg. for £25m stg. Sept. 1987: Established a new independent life company, Lifetime. Nov. 1987: Bad debt provision of £23.3m for rescheduled sovereign debt. Dec1988: Announced purchase of First NH Banks Inc. of New Hampshire USA at a cost of $370m, funded by 'rights' issue of 1-for-4 at 150p per share (£74 million), and a $75m Preferred Stock issue in the US and internal resources. July: Raises $150m in subordinated capital repayable in 1998. November: Purchases 49% of stockbroker J. & E. Davy from Gandon Group. December 1988: N.H. Banks Inc. purchase completed. March 1989: Sells stake in Hibernian Group. March 1990: Stung for £16m in 'unlawful' UK Local Authorities interest 'swap' transactions. Sept. 1990: F. Buhl resigned as Director. Nov. 1990: M. Hely Hutchinson resigns as Chief Executive and Director. Jan 1991: Closes BCT in UK with expected closure cost of £10.6m. Jan 1991: Moodys downgrade Bank of Ireland longterm rating. Feb 1991: Announces pretax loss of £60.0m for year at US subsidiary. July 1991: Tony Ryan sells 16.7m shares at 162p and resigns as Director. Oct 1991: Purchased certain assets and liabilities of BankEast, Amoskeag, Meridian N.A. and Nashua Trust Co. for £14.5m. Increased its share in J & E Davy from 49% to 89.8% for £12.2m. Feb 1992: 5 million Non-cum £1stg Pref Stock issued at £10.01p stg each and £6.5m non-cum £1 Pref Stock Series A issued at Ir £10.09p each raising in total £119.4m. March 1992: Losses at First NH Banks reach $123.4m for 1991. B of I close Tokyo office. April 1992: Bill Marshall announces his resignation as Chairman and CEO of First NH Banks. Sept 1992: D.O'Brien appointed CEO First NH Bank. Feb 1993: BES company (Shannon Companies) formed in UK to take over repossessed B of I properties for re-letting. AIB Investment Services sold 5m shares over seven months. March 1993: Raises £41m through sale of Preference Stock. July 1993: Sale of New York retail operation agreed. 300 B of I staff to retire by October 1994. Aug 1993: Rights Issue rais £100m (94.8% take up). Dec 1993: 36% shar holders opt for scrip-dividend. Offloa 2,732,738 DCC shares at £10 each. July 199 Securitisation of mortgages in UK raises £500 stg. Aug 1994: Sells British Credit Trust f £25.8m stg. Buys Great Bay Bankshares in U for £34.6m. Jan 1995: 44% of shareholders o for scrip dividend. April 1995: Buys 2 Cre Lyonnais branches in London. July 1995: On share-one-vote adopted. April 199 Amalgamates Bank of Ireland First Holding I with Citizens Financial Group; ends up wi 23.5% of merged group and will write-c £48.1m. Sept 1996: ADRs quoted on NYSE. M 1997: Closes New York office. July 199 Acquires Bristol & West Bld. Socy for £600 (goodwill £295m). Dec 1997: Purchased Ne Ireland Assurance for £274m (goodwill £93n May 1998: Acquires Amex card franchise f Ireland. Sept 1998: Sells its 23.5% of Citizer Bank for £545m. May 1999: £11.4bn merger wi Alliance & Leicester (UK) proposed (BofI share hit €20.3). June 1999: Merger aborted with ce tain acrimony. Sept 1999: Buys back 52m share @ €8.45/€8.15 each. Dec 1999: Ends ICC tak over discussions. May 2000: Cost cuttir announced; up to 40 branches to close and 7C staff to go (€64.8m cost savings). June 200 DIRT liability settled for €38.7m. July 200 Acquires Chase Vere (UK financial advisor) f €162.3m. Nov 2000: Buys *Moneyextra* (U online) for €43m. June 2001: Australian take-ov rumour quashed. May 2002: Buys 61% Iridia Asset Management (US) for €196m. July 200 Buys Willis National (UK) for €66.4m. Feb 200 M Soden floats suggestion of merger with tro bled AIB. June 2002: To merge BofI's IT dept wi AIB. Aug 2002: IT merger aborted.

Share Price Sept 2001 - Sept 2002

1. €13.50 16.05.02 Results announced.

TEN YEAR REVIEW: € m

12 Months to March 31	1993	1994	1995	1996	1997	1998	1999	2000	2001 c)	2002
Income	2,347	2,131	1,985	2,215	2,070	3,266	3,977	4,014	5,317	5,363
Pretax Profits	158	356	409	401	502	673	1,054 d)	920	960	1,088
Tax (inc levy)	65	124	124	129	163	197	253	196	196	165
After Tax Profits	93	232	285	272	339	476	801	724	764	920
Minority Interests	(0.5)	(1)	(0.4)	(0.4)	(0.6)	(7)	(7)	(9)	(10)	(10
Preference Dividend	23	27	19	19	19	20	23	25	26	17
Available for shareholders	70	204	266	253	320	449	771	690	728	893
Ordinary Dividends	50	63	76	93	110	150	192	233	290	333
Retained Profit	20	141	190	160	210	299	579	457	438	560
Increase/(Decrease) in Reserves	37 i)	210 j)	161 k)	241 b)	228	179 a)	841 m)	416	518 f)	382 g
Stockholders' Funds	846	1,143	1,310	1,557	1,772	1,986	2,833	3,257	3,777	4,193
Ordinary Dividend per Share (€)	0.063	0.067	0.079	0.093	0.113	0.145	0.185	0.235	0.290	0.330
Earnings per Share (€)	0.088	0.210	0.281	0.264	0.330	0.451	0.745	0.681	0.730	0.890 e

a) Stock premium +€257m; goodwill w/o -€526m; unrealised profits +€41m; exchange gains +€146m. b) Goodwill write-back €81m.
c) Subsequently restated. d) Includes €218m profit on sale of Citizens Financial Group. e) Based on 1,005.6m stock units.
f) Property revaluation +€85m, currency loss -€48m. g) Preference stock buyback -€247m. i) Pref stock premium +€45m; currency loss -€23m.
j) Share premium +€44m, unrealised profits +€17m, currency uplift +€20m, k) Currency losses -€15m; goodwill w/o -€20m.
m) Share premium +€50m, goodwill written back on disposal of Citizens Bank +€230m, currency losses -€23m.

Stockbrokers wanted.
No experience necessary.

FINANCIAL DIARY:

Interim Results Announced:	15.11.2001
Interim Dividend Payout:	08.01.2002
Final Results Announced:	16.05.2002
Annual General Meeting:	10.07.2002
Final Dividend Payout:	19.07.2002

FIVE YEAR SHARE PRICE TREND

Year		High		Low	
1997	High	6.95 (Dec)	Low	3.43 (Jan)
1998	High	10.03 (July)	Low	6.18 (Oct)
1999	High	10.50 (Jan)	Low	7.42 (Oct)
2000	High	10.55 (Dec)	Low	5.68 (Mar)
2001	High	12.00 (July)	Low	7.85 (Sept)

HALF YEARLY PERFORMANCES: €m

6 months to	30.09.00	31.03.01	30.09.01	31.03.02
Profits before Tax	629	369	556	529
Profits after Tax	458	306	476	444

INVESTMENT PERFORMANCE:

Five Year Investment Performance:	€ 3,400
Ten Year Investment Performance:	€11,443

SECTORAL ANALYSIS (previous year)

Gross Income: Ireland 52% (52%), Britain 46% (43%), other 2% (3%). **Profits:** Ireland 75% (77%), Britain 23% (20%), other 2% (3%).

BALANCE SHEET: MARCH 31 2002. € m

Capital Stock:		Fixed Assets	1,234
1,007.6m €0.64 stock	672	Other Assets	2,337
(excl 42,557,815 Treasury Stock)		Current Assets	77,828
		Current Liabilities	74,773
Reserves	3,521	Net Current Assets	3,055
		Loans, Pref Stock, Minority	(2,704)
		Net Tangible Assets	3,922
		Intangibles	271
Shareholders' Funds	4,193	Net Assets	4,193

Comment:
The profits graph has been moderately upwards of late. Under new management. Unrecognised derivatives losses (net) for year ended March 2002 of €297m not accounted for in P&L A/c - represents 27% of disclosed profits - Chairman Crowley tells stockholders 'this is standard accounting policy'!

The Bank of Ireland Group was restructured recently into six main divisions - retail banking Republic of Ireland, Bank of Ireland Life, wholesale financial services, UK financial services, asset and wealth management and, finally, Group and Central. The breakdown staff wise is:

Retail Republic of Ireland	7,702
BOI Life	1,097
Wholesale Financial Services	1,663
UK Financial Services	5,369
Asset and Wealth Management	662
Group and Central	1,945
Total	18,438

The pretax profit and assets are:

Division	Pretax Profit €m	%	Assets € m	%
Retail Republic of Ireland	321	27	23,427	21
Bank of Ireland Life	122	10	6,028	5
Wholesale Financial Services	355	30	43,538	39
UK Financial Services	318	27	33,338	29
Asset & Wealth Management	126	11	930	1
Group and Central	(64)	(5)	5,767	5
	1,178	100	113,028	100

Retail banking in the Republic operated from 265 branches. This division also includes ICS Building Society, direct telephone banking, credit card operations and Banking 365 a direct selling operation offering loan facilities. The group claims a market share in the Republic of over 20% of resources and loans outstanding. They claim that a new product, Life Loan, which enables older customers to borrow up to the assessed value from their principal residence without repayment during their lifetime, has been particularly successful. The telephone channel, Banking 365 Telephone has 300,000 active users and handles 8 million calls annually. Its sister operation, Banking 365 Online has in excess of 200,000 customers handling 4 million transactions annually. In the Bank of Ireland Life division which embraces Lifetime and New Ireland Assurance, the group now claims a 19% share of the life and pension market.

The wholesale financial services incorporates corporate banking, treasury and international banking, Davy stockbrokers, private banking, First Rate Enterprises and IBI Corporate Finance. The First Rate Enterprises recently announced a 50:50 venture with the Post Office in the UK where they will offer foreign currency and other travel products to 17,500 post offices across the UK.

In the UK the UK Financial Services (UKFS) has now been delineated by customer segments rather than by traditional brand considerations. Bristol & West is the group's player in the mortgage business in the UK while

the financial advisors of Wills National, Moneyextra (a business to consumer online advisory service on mortgages, pensions, life assurance and credit cards) attracting some 500,000 visitors or 'hits' each month and Chase de Vere are important in both the mortgage and life assurance areas. Competition is aggressive in the UK which is serviced by over 500 licensed banks, 80 building societies and nationwide Girobank operated by the Post Office.

Assets & Wealth Management accounts for only 11% of the group's profits and this division has been relatively unexciting if solid over the past few years. Assets under management are now at the €57 billion mark.

The Group & Central section reflects the impact of the Preferred Securities raised in 2001 and the buyback of preference shares at the end of that year.

The analysis of loans by the group (€57 billion) is interesting:

Sector	% Irl	% UK	€ bn
Agriculture	1.8	0.1	1.1
Energy	1.2	0.2	0.8
Manufacturing	6.7	1.0	4.4
Construction & Property	3.3	3.7	4.0
Distribution	2.0	0.4	1.4
Transport	1.5	0.1	0.9
Financial	3.5	0.3	2.1
Business + other services	6.5	1.9	4.8
Commercial mortgages		3.5	2.0
Personal mortgages	13.2	40.2	30.5
Personal other lending	7.1	1.8	5.0
	46.8	53.2	57.0

Not many would have realised that the largest chunk (38%+) of the group's lending is devoted to the personal mortgage market in the UK and just goes to show the importance of the

Bradford & Bingley operation there. In the Form 20-F which the BofI files with the Securities Exchange in the US it is obvious how sweet this mortgage lending in the UK is for the bank. In the last year's accounts only €2.9 million was provided for bad debts in UK residential mortgages compared with €63.4m for bad debts in Irish personal 'other lending'. Percentage wise, UK residential mortgage bad debts are running at 0.0126% compared with Irish personal loan bad debts of 1.57% - no doubt the Irish credit cards account for a fair whack of the latter and the interest rates charged reflect this.

Profit before tax in the past two years has risen by 18% (last year) and 8% (the year before). Let us look at where the major changes in this trend have occurred.

Division	2002	2001
Retail RoI	+11%	+27%
B of I Life	-7%	+22%
Wholesale	+25%	+30%
UKFS	-2%	+13%
Asset Management	-5%	+11%

Despite the competitive nature of the local domestic market the recent growth rates are commendable as indeed has been the super performance of the wholesale services. However the other three divisions of life assurance, UKFS and asset management hardly set the world on fire. In each of these no doubt there have been extenuating circumstances such as the global equity markets. But these are the main factors for potential investors to get their teeth into because if it is not the wielding of the cost cutting axe then the only hope for growth is from the individual divisions or by acquisitions.

A new factor going forward is the recently announced purchase for €196m/220m of 61% in Iridian, a US asset management firm with €12.1 billion under management with 33 staff. As no profit details have been disclosed, this is an unknown quantity.

The recent announcement that the intended merger with the AIB IT division has been aborted because there has been too much sniffing around by Brussels looks as if the merger 'kite' flown by Mike Soden has for the moment taken quite a dive.

(We have looked at a number of stockbrokers' reports including Deutsche Bank and Morgan Stanley, Schroder Salomon Smith Barney, Goodbody, NCB and Dresdner Kleinwort Wasserstein as well as the Bank of Ireland's own 20-F Form from which much of this detail has been extracted.)

BARLO plc

BUSINESS: Radiators, plastics and agri products.
REGISTERED OFFICE: Alexandra House, Sweepstakes, Ballsbridge, Dublin. Tel: 01-2310700. Fax: 01-2310700
HEAD OFFICE: as regd office   **SECRETARY:** J Bourke
REGISTRARS & TRANSFERS OFFICE: Computershare Investor Services (Ireland) Ltd, Heron House, Corrig Road, Sandyford, Dublin.
PRINCIPAL BANKERS: Allied Irish Banks, Bank of Ireland, IIB Bank, KBC Bank, Fortis Bank, Royal Bank of Scotland.   **AUDITORS:** KPMG.
SOLICITORS: William Fry; Dibb Lupton Alsop; Gaedertz Rechtsanwaelte; Stibbe Simont Monahan Duhot.
STOCKBROKERS: Davy Stockbrokers.
DIRECTORS: N Carroll (Chairman - 62), A Mullins (Mgr. Dir. - 56), A Barlow (70), B Beausang, J Bourke (57), A De Smet, J. Farrell (71), R Skelley.
SHARE CAPITAL: Authorised: 250million Ord €0.125 shares . **Issued:** 175,050,288 Ord €0.125 shares.
STAFF: 1,627.   **SCRIP DIVIDEND:** No.

CAPITAL HISTORY:

Incorporated March 1973 February 1988: private placing to raise £2.63m through issue of 270,000 Ord. 25p shares at 975p each. Scrip issue on basis of 4-for-1. Ord. shares divided into 10p units Sept 1988. Placing of 4,750,000 Ord. shares of 10p each at 85p per share.   Oct. 1990: Rights issue of 21,171,875 Ord. 10p shares at 20p each. Issue of 1,875,000 Ord. 10p shares to Syden (a Mullins) company) at 20p each. Option granted to A. Mullins to purchase 1.5m Ord. 10p shares at 40p each by mid 1994. Further option to A. Mullins to purchase 1.5m Ord. 10p shares by 31.7.1997 at 85p each. July 1991 2,846,090 Ord. 10p shares placed at 32.5p each. April 1992: 8,500,539 Ord 10p shares issued at 51p each for investment portfolio. July 1992: 42,846,147 Ord 10p shares issued on acquisition of IRG Plc. July 1992: Placing and open offer of 19,607,843 Ord 10p shares at 51p each. July 1993: Placing and open offer (2-for-7) of 35,006,273 Ord 10p shares at 58p each. March 1994: 7.5m 10p Ord shares issued by way of placing at 88p each to purchase Kingspan Veha and Warmstyle.

COMPANY HISTORY:

Started manufacturing radiators in Clonmel in 1965, at first for the Irish market and later for the U.K. In 1972 established a U.K. subsidiary (Barlo Products). 1973 Allied Combined Trust acquired a 25% shareholding in reformed group. 1981 disposed of farm machinery division. 1985 acquired Coppas, a British based control equipment manufacturer for stg£104,000. 1987 acquired Halsted, a supplier of gas boilers for stg£575,000. Feb1988: raised £2.63m by way of a private placing. Sept 1988: Raises £4m in placing full listing on Stock Exchange. Oct 1989: M.J. Hickey, Financial Director resigns, C. Glass appointed Director. Jan 1990: D. McKenna resigns as Managing Director, Aidan Barlow becomes Group Managing Director. April 1990: S. McHale resigns as Director. Sept. 1990: T. Mullins appointed Managing Director. Rights issue and new shares raise £4.75m. Eight month strike at Clonmel ends. Oct 1990: 22% of rights issue left with underwriters. C. Glass appointed Finance Director. Sold Halstead Boilers for IR£276,000. July 1991: J. Bourke replaces C. Glass as Finance Director. Purchases Merriot in Thurles. 2.8m shares placed at 32.5p each to raise £0.9m. Changed Auditors. April 1992: purchased investment portfolio valued at £4.3m for 8,500,539 Ord 10p (51p each) Portfolio included 8.87% of IRG plc and 5.37% of Bridgend plc. Purchased 6% of IRG plc in the market for £1.2m. May 1992: Bids £21.7m for IRG plc. Dec 1992: High Court reduces Share Premium Account by £29.8m. July 1993: Pays £14.5m for Veha NV and raises £19m by way of placing. Feb 1994: Buys Kingspan Veha for £4m. Share placing raises £6.5m. March 1994: High Court reduces Share Premium by £16m. May 1994: J. Beloff, M. Delahunty, J. Kennedy and S. Barlow resign as directors. June 1994: Syden Investments (Mullins) exercised warrant for 1.5m shares at 40p each and immediately sold them at 81p. Also redeemed pref shares for 1.8m 10p Ord shares at 20p each. Sept 1994: Must write-off £600,000 Curragh Carpets bad debt. Feb 1996: D. Desmond's IIU Ltd buy 3.9% equity. March 1996: Downsizing to cost Barlo £5.9m in 1996/97. May 1996: Sells Earls Wire for £1.4m. Nov 1997: Buys Resart and Critesa for £6.4m. Buys Celair (France/plastics) for £3.6m. July 1999: Sells Stanley Smith for £5.3m. Dec 1999: Buys ICI Acrylics Gmb for £7.2m. Nov 2000: Buys PSC in Slovakia f £10.7m/€13.6m. Jan 2001: Buys Athlone Extrusior for €55.8m. May 2001: Closes plant at Gee Belgium. Dec 2001: Sells strapping business f €5.2m. Issues profits warning. June 2002: Sells pro erty in Athlone for €4m.

Share Price Sept 2001 - Sept 2002

1. €0.24 05.10.01 - Large share sales
2. €0.26 07.12.01 Profits warning

FINANCIAL DIARY:

Interim Results Announced:	07.12.2001
Interim Dividend Payout:	none
Final Results Announced:	22.05.2002
Annual General Meeting:	26.07.2002
Final Dividend Payout:	none

FIVE YEAR SHARE PRICE TREND €

1997	High	0.77 (Dec)	Low	0.53 (Apr)
1998	High	1.27 (May)	Low	0.70 (Oct)
1999	High	0.93 (Nov)	Low	0.63 (Apr)
2000	High	1.05 (Aug)	Low	0.72 (May)
2001	High	1.19 (Feb)	Low	0.21 (Dec)

SECTORAL ANALYSIS (previous year)
Turnover: Radiators 32% (36%), Plastics 68% (64%). Ireland 12% (12%), UK 32%(27%), other 56% (61%)

INVESTMENT PERFORMANCE

Five Year Investment Performance:	€ 634
Ten Year Performance	€ 813

HALF YEARLY PERFORMANCE: * m

Six Months To	30.09.00	31.03.01	30.09.01	31.03.02
Sales	123.3	151.2	143.5	152.4
Pretax (-) profit	9.44	11.9	(6.7)	(2.5)
Profit % Sales	7.7	7.9	-	-

TEN YEAR REVIEW: € m

12 Months to 31 March	1993	1994	1995	1996	1997	1998	1999	2000	2001 g)	2002
Sales	63.109	123.559	146.751	145.812	142.720	175.794	223.292	232.053	274.559	295.899
Profit (loss) before Tax	4.952	9.884	7.037	(3.149)	8.704	10.774	17.963	23.606	21.347	(9.172)
Tax	0.099	0.041	0.102	0.162	0.514	0.381	1.778	1.903	1.750	1.400
Profit/(Loss) after Tax	4.853	9.843	6.935	(3.311)	8.190	10.393	16.185	21.703	19.597	(10.572)
Minority Interest	(0.097)	(0.178)	(0.100)	(0.075)	(0.127)	(0.149)	(0.187)	(0.234)	(0.311)	(0.234)
Available for Shareholders	4.756	9.665	6.835	(3.386)	8.063	10.244	15.998	21.469	19.286	(10.806)
Ordinary Dividend	0.778	2.057	2.138	2.140	2.465	2.697	3.238	4.244	4.760	
Retained Profit	3.978	7.608	4.697	(5.526)	5.598	7.547	12.760	17.225	14.526	(10.806)
Increase (-) in Reserves	11.981 c)	15.120 d)	4.457	(6.615)	5.481	13.431 e)	12.494	20.616 f)	14.459	(7.631) h)
Shareholders' Funds	35.824	56.342	61.227	54.630	60.136	73.645	86.251	106.522	121.176	115.274
Ordinary Dividend per Share (€)	0.006	0.013	0.013	0.013	0.015	0.0137	0.019	0.025	0.0275	-
Earnings per Share (€)	0.046	0.063	0.041	-	0.048	0.061	0.094	0.13	0.114 a)	-

(a) Based upon 169.9m shares. (c) Share premium €30.1m; goodwill w/o €21.3m. d) Share premium €27.6m, goodwill w/o €20.3m. e) Currency gain +€5.7m. f) Currency gain +€3.3m. g) Figures subsequently restated. h) Share premium +€2.5m

---

BALANCE SHEET: MARCH 31 2002 € m

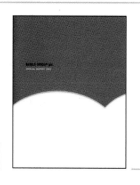

Share Capital: 175,050,288		Fixed Assets		173.464
Ord. €0.125 shares	21.881	Current Assets	123.055	
		Current Liabilities	121.035	
Reserves	92.080	Net Current Assets		2.020
		Medium Term Debt		(114.921)
		Minorities & grants		(1.313)
		Net Tangible Assets		59.250
		Intangibles		54.711
Shareholders' Funds	113.961	Net Assets		113.961

Comment:

No dividend - no joy.

With inflation running at an average of 3% over the decade we take a close look at the companies whose dividends have looked after shareholders over time.

important of these is that you must keep a close eye on the companies that have announced or are about to announce cuts in their dividend payout. Such an aberration however temporary can dull the shine on any good track record.

We have therefore looked for a steady dividend growth of 10% per annum over the five or ten year life spans to keep investors ahead of inflation. We would prefer this steady growth rather than dividend increases in fits and spurts. A steady growth of 10% per annum would translate into a dividend stream €100 in year one growing to €146 in year five and amounting to €235 in year ten. These are vitally important where investors are planning for the longterm and particularly for their retirement.

Of those on the Honour's List in the 2002 Annual the most notable drop off is **Ulster Television** which has been finding it tough to continue its 10% increase in annual dividend. The weakness in the advertising market has taken its toll. This is quite a shame as it had built up a formidable reputation over the decade having paid out a total of 112.5p in ten years including two bonus payments; maybe it would have better to conserve these wind-falls for the rainier days.

The Dividend Classic

10 Years

DCC
FBD Holdings
Irish Continental Group

9 Years

Allied Irish Banks
Grafton Group
Kerry Group
Kingspan

8 Years

Arnotts
Bank of Ireland
IAWS
Jurys Doyle Group

7 Years

Irish Life & Permanent
Readymix

6 Years

Abbey
Anglo Irish Bank
United Drug

5 Years

IFG Group

4 Years

Galen Holdings
McInerney Holdings

...fe havens for investors are the order of the day ...en markets hit rock-bottom and while cash and ...'s would normally be attractive the returns in ...ese are not very attractive these days either.

...th the short-term outlook for equities both ...certain and volatile we turn once again to good ...I fashioned dividends which at least should give ... income stream while investors long for the elu-...e capital appreciation at the end of the rainbow.

...e contribution of dividends to stock market ...urns has been overlooked in recent years as ...estors chased growth stocks. They were urged to ...get dividend income as yields dropped to 1% and ...s and were exhorted that they were hardly worth ...thering about. Growth was the new income and a ...x efficient one if you were not already making full ...e of your capital gains tax allowance.

...t times are a changing! Once again we are happy ... applaud the companies who well reward ...estors for risking their capital. And this year is no ...ception.

...s we highlight elsewhere in this publication €1,000 ...uld have to grow to €1,182 over the five year ...riod ended December last if you were to take ...re of the erosionary affect of inflation. So also ...,000 back in 1991 would have to grow to €1,311 ... make sure you didn't get any poorer as a result ... rising prices in the intervening years. This bench-...ark is the same whether it is capital appreciation ... dividend income you are concerned with.

...ere are some pitfalls that investors need to keep ... mind when dealing with dividend income. Most

In the era of dot.com fever the basic fundamentals fell out the window. Instead of talking about dividend income and price earnings ratios, the get-rich-quick brigade could only talk about b2b, b2c and cash-burn and all the other mumbo jumbo that doesn't put bread on the table. So now, with a little bit of hindsight let's get back to basics.

Out of the 74 companies on the Irish stock market only 42 paid any dividend in the past twelve months. Of the 32 who didn't pay any dividend two highflyers had no intention of paying out any return to the investor anyway. They were Elan and Ryanair both of whom have voracious appetites for funds and feel they would be better off reinvesting their cashflows rather than rewarding their shareholders who were quite satisfied with their capital appreciation instead of dividend income. But that was until Elan developed an accounting colic which decimated any chance of capital appreciation and proved that where there is no dividend fall-back the price free-fall can be really detrimental to your wealth.

The rule used to be - why bother about an interim or final dividend when you can slice off a few shares to pay for the little luxuries of life. But sentiments have changed. There is a realisation that with growth stocks you get a double hit when times are bad. The price goes down and there is no reward in the dividends for holding them. Equity income also has the potential to grow over the years and with our benchmark demand to increase the dividend each year by 10%, if you buy well before retirement and reinvest the dividends to boost returns, then when the twilight years come such a policy should stand you in good stead in your leisure days.

That leaves us with three winners at the top of the ladder: **FBD, DCC and Irish Continental Group**. Their payouts over the decade have really been fabulous. In 1991 **FBD** paid €0.0457 per share; in 2001 the insurance group paid €0.195 per share - a whopping compound growth rate of 17% per annum. At the turn of the last decade **Irish Continental Group** paid out €0.028 annually by way of dividend; this had grown over the next ten years to €0.195 which converts to an annual compound rate of 22%. But the best of the lot has been **DCC** which only this year can claim ten years of at least 10% per annum in dividend growth. In **DCC's** case they not only achieved the base requirement easily but ended up paying out just over 28% compound per annum. That is quite spectacular. Well done to Jim Flavin and his team.

BULA RESOURCES (HOLDINGS) plc

BUSINESS: Oil and gas exploration.
REGISTERED OFFICE: 7 Priory Hall, Stillorgan, Co Dublin.
HEAD OFFICE: as regd office. Tel: 01-6775222. Fax: 01-6775106.
SECRETARY: C Casey **REGISTRARS & TRANSFER OFFICE:** Computershare Investor Services (Ireland) Ltd, Heron House, Corrig Road, Sandyford Industrial Estate, Dublin.
PRINCIPAL BANKERS: AIB. **AUDITORS:** Arthur Andersen.
SOLICITORS: Matheson Ormsby Prentice.
STOCKBROKERS: Corporate Synergy plc.
DIRECTORS: T Kelly, O Yazigi.
SHARE CAPITAL: Authorised: 3,283,769,182 Ord 1.0p shares.
Issued: 2,236,375,553 Ord €0.012 shares.
EMPLOYEES: 2. **SCRIP DIVIDEND:** No

CAPITAL HISTORY:

May 1981 Bula Resources plc. acquired Bula Oil Ltd and Shenandoah Ireland Inc. in return for 59,739,838 Ord. 25p shares. Public flotation in May 1981 by AIIB - 24m Ord. 25p shares at 50p each. May 1981 4,407,362 Ord. 25p shares were issued to the Minister for Energy. June 1981 issued 5,191,838 Ord. 25p shares in consideration of the acquisition of 1,018,000 shares in Gaelic Oil Ltd. May 1984 issued 4,428,622 Ord. 25p shares in consideration for 57% of the issued share capital of Gaelic Oil Ltd. Jan. 1986 placing of 82,857,143 "B" Ord. 2.5p shares at 3.5p each. January 1986 4,360,902 "B" Ord. 2.5p shares were issued to the Minister for Finance. Bula Resources (H) plc: March 1986 issued 1 Ord. share of £1 each to each of four nominees and 30,000 Ord. shares of £1 each to J. Stanley. March 1986: Ord. £1 shares sub-divided into a total of 2,000m Ord. 2.5p shares. July 1986 issued 184,985,705 Ord. 2.5p shares at 5p each to the shareholders of Bula Resources plc. in consideration of the acquisition of its entire issued share capital. July 1986 issued 3.6m Ord. 2.5p shares at par to TCC Nominees Ltd. in consideration of the acquisition of 650,000 Ord. shares of 5p stg. each in New Court Resources plc. July 1986 issued 180,000 Ord. 2.5p shares to the Minister for Energy. Jan 1987 issued 22.5m Ord. 2.5p shares at par to the shareholders of Mossrigg Ltd. in consideration of the acquisition of its entire issued share capital. June 1987 issued 20m Ord. 2.5p shares at 4.4p each in a placing, raising approximately IR£840,000 net of expenses. June 1987 issued a total of 20m Ord. 2.5p shares at 5p each to the shareholders of Middle Sea Resources S.A. in consideration of the acquisition of its entire issued share capital. 29th July 1987 issued 22,753,000 Ord. shares at 5.5p each in a placing, raising £1.2m. Oct. 1987 issued 50m Ord. shares at 8.9p each (8p stg) in a placing, raising £4.3m. Oct 1987 Rights issued 27,522,894 Ord. shares at 7.8p each (7p stg). March 1988 issued 12m Ord. shares as part of the consideration for the acquisition of Highland UK Holdings Ltd. April 1988 issued 28,144,562 Ord. shares in consideration for the acquisition of 1,764,996 shares in Norminol A/S. May 1989 issued 22.25m Ord. 2.5p shares for 4.6% interest in the Non Buchan area of licence P241 from Charterhall plc. Sept. 1990: Issued 65,652,735 Ord. 2.5p shares at 4.2p for acquisition of oil and gas interests in Texas and raised £1.5m. Aug 1991: Rights issue 1-for-1 480,789,136 Ord. 2.5p shares at 2.5p, only 58,634,943 shares taken up. Jan 1993: All Ord 2.5p shares subdivided into one Ord 1p shares and one Deferred Share of 1.5p. Rights Issue (2-for-1 and open offer) of 1,078,848,158 Ord 1p shares at 1p each. Only 125,159,115 shares issued. June 1993: 17,764,862 Ord 1p shares issued in connection with the acquisition of a similar number of Tuskar shares (Bula hold 16.3% of Tuskar). July/Aug 1993: 5,804,519 Ord 1p shares issued in connection with the acquisition of a similar number of Tuskar shares. Jan 1994: 68.2m Ord 1p shares placed at 3.5p each. Nov 1994: 287.7m Ord 1p shares issued at 2.5p each. 604.7m Def. 1.5p shares issued by capitalising part of share premium account. 1,144,153,879 1.5p Def shares extinguished. Jan 1995: 18.4m Ord 1p shares issued re Aki-Otyr. June 1995: 71.9m Ord 1p shares issued re 51% option over Aki-Otyr. Sept 1995: Bought 25% Mir Oil Developments for 101,562,587 Ord 1p shares. Oct 1995: Placed 134.3m Ord 1p shares at 2.8p each. July 1996: Places 147.7m Ord 1p shares at 2.75p stg. Feb 1998: Placed 90m Ord 1p shares at 1.125p stg per share. May 1998: Placed 35.5m Ord 1p shares at 1.127p stg per share. March 1999: Placed 111.9m Ord 1p shares at 1p each. May 1999: Placed 63.1m Ord 1p shares at 1p each. EGM resolved to cancel, subject to High Court approval, 73.7m shares regd in name of Chamonix Nominees Ltd. Oct 1999: Placed 100m Ord 1p shares at par. Jan 2000: Placed 55.4m Ord 1p shares at 3pstg/Ir5p per share. March 2000: Placed 36m Ord 1p shares at 5pstg each. 2001: Placed 71.6m Ord €0.012 at €0.012 to €0.018. Options exercised over 45,175,160 Ord €0.012 @ €0.012 each (mainly A Reynolds).

COMPANY HISTORY:

Incorporated January 1981. May 1981 acquired Bula Oil Ltd. and Shenandoah Ireland Inc. in return for 59,739,838 Ord. 25p shares. Public flotation in May 1981. June 1981 acquired 21% of Gaelic Oil in return for 5,191,838 Bula Ord. 25p shares. Through further purchases rights issue Bula ended up with 29.9% of Gaelic Oil by Dec. 1981. Further loans made to Gaelic Oil. December 1983 converted these loans to equity and increased holding to 37.6%. May 1984: Successfully offered 4.4m Bula shares for remainder of Gaelic. May 1985: sold Bula Exploration to Saxon Oil plc. and wrote-off £2.2m. December 1985 founder directors M.J. Wymes, T.C. Roche, R.F. Wood and T.J. Roche resigned. July 1986 Bula Resources (Holdings) plc acquired the whole of the issued share capital of Bula Resources plc in return for 184,985,705 Ord. shares. Jan. 1987: Acquired Mossrigg in all share deal - 22.5m Bula shares. June 1987: Acquired Middle Sea Resources including cash resources of US$1.2m in return for 20 million Bula shares. June 1987: Acquired Floyd Oil America Inc. and Floyd Oil Ltd. and raised IR£1,213,872 by issuing 22.75 million Bula shares. Sept. 1987: Acquired a 12% net revenue interest in a gas producing field offshore Louisiana. Sept. 1987: Acquired 14% interest in Norminol A/S at a cost of IR£761,000. Oct. 1987: Gaelic Resources acquired Gaelic Oil from Bula in return for 21% of equity of Gaelic Resources. Subsequently holding increased to 26%. March 1988: Purchased Highland UK Holdings for 12 million Bula shares plus £734,000 cash. April 1988: Increased its stake in the enlarged Norminol group to 20% by the issue of 28.1 million Bula shares. Nov. 1988: Buys 32.13% stake in Galveston Block 464, Gulf of Mexico for $1.6m and acquired a 0.5% royalty of S. Timbalier block offshore Louisiana, the latter to revert to an 8.75% working interest. April 1989: Disposed of their holding in Gaelic Resources for £1.3m. Nov 1991: Full Stock Market listing. Jan 1993: Agreed to sell Shandeal UK (Holdings) Plc to Tuskar Resources Plc for a consideration of $450,000 and 30 million Tuskar shares. Acquired a further 17,764,862 Tuskar shares during the period June/Aug 1993. May 1994: Shares suspended pending Russian deal. Aug 1995: AGM told of problems with Russian investment a paying £3.6m and issued 90m Bula shares. 4 Russian Directors not attend heated A.G.M. Sept 1995: Bought 25% Mir Developments for £2.5m with option on remainder for 304.7m B shares. April 1997: J. Stanley resigns suddenly as Chairman a Mgr Dir. Dec 1997: Capital and reserves reduced by £17.2m. Ju 1997: Writes off £8m Aki-Otyr Venture. Hunt to find real owners Mir Oil and their 74m shares in Bula. Aug 1997: Angry A.G.M. c Russian fiasco. Oct 1997: Trade Minister orders investigation i Bula shares. July 1998: Trade report castigated Bula Board. A 1998: Obtains injunction against Stanley prohibiting disposal of B assets. March 1999: Major Board changes. Aug 1999: Disclosed t Chairman Reynolds gets 'kick-back' if certain Iraq exploration s ceeds, and also holds options over 87.1m shares at 1p each. J 2000: German IAB now holds 7.2%. Aug 2000: T Peart sudde departs as Mng Dir; J Hogan apptd Ch Ex. Nov 2000: Litigation w Stanley ends. Jan 2001: Ir Stock Exchange forces clarification Libya activities. J Hogan departs after 6 months. June 2001 T K apptd Ch Ex. Dec 2001: Ghaddafi International Foundation to b 50m shares @ €0.018 each (€0.9m). Bula denies that this is investment arm of the Libyan Govt. Placed 25m shares with Liby O&M Management @ €0.018 each. Sept 2001: 2 directors resi Jan 2002: Davy stockbrokers resign. Feb 2002: B Johnston opt over 70m shares. April 2002: Shares suspended. June 2002: T K (M.D) resigns. July 2002: Stock Exchange censures A Reynol option exercise in Aug 2001 during 'closed period'. Sept 2002 Reynolds resigns at acrimonious meeting.

Share Price Sept 2001 - Sept 2002

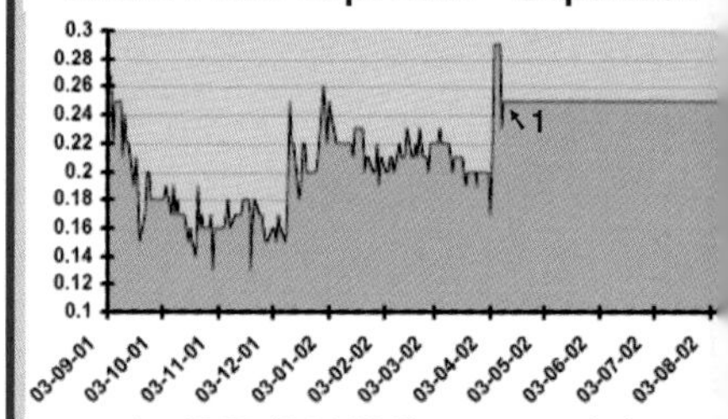

1. €0.25 10.04.02 Share suspended.

Bula share prices are in units of ten shares.

FIVE YEAR SHARE PRICE TREND €

1997	High	0.4p (Jan)	Low	0.13p (July
1998	High	0.13 (Jan)	Low	0.13 (Dec
1999	High	0.70 (Dec)	Low	0.10 (Jan
2000	High	10.8 (June)	Low	0.60 (Jan
2001	High	0.038 (Jan)	Low	0.013 (Oct

INVESTMENT PERFORMANCE

Five Year Investment Performance	€1,040
Ten Year Investment Performance	€1,040

FINANCIAL DIARY

Interim Results Announced:	27.09.2001
Interim Dividend Payout:	not likely
Annual Results Announced:	24.06.2002
Annual General Meeting:	09.09.2002
Final Dividend Payout:	not likely

TEN YEAR REVIEW : €'000

12 months to 31 Dec.	1992	1993	1994	1995	1996	1997 a)	1998	1999 a)	2000	2001
Turnover	1,580	1,635	650	383	1,021	588	336	630	399	420
Profit (Loss) before Tax	(2,569)	(2,477)	(4,373)	(4,955)	(13,546)	(16,006) e)	(1,493)	(848)	(1,401)	(981)
Tax	(2)	(4)	(8)	(5)	(6)	(4)	(1)	(1)	-	-
Profit (Loss) after Tax	(2,571)	(2,481)	(4,381)	(4,960)	(13,552)	(16,010)	(1,494)	(849)	(1,401)	(981)
Available for Shareholders	(2,571)	(2,481)	(4,381)	(4,960)	(13,552)	(16,010)	(1,494)	(849)	(1,401)	(981)
Ordinary Dividend	-	-	-	-	-	-	-	-	-	-
Retained Profit (Loss)	(2,571)	(2,481)	(4,381)	(4,960)	(13,552)	(16,010)	(1,494)	(849)	(1,401)	(981)
Increase (Decrease) in Reserves	(2,320)	(244) b)	(9,707)	1,465 c)	(2,433) d)	(15,646)	966	1,441	(1,412)	(610)
Shareholders' Funds	9,501	14,123	20,448	27,487	18,199	2,553	1,817	6,636	6,444	6977
Ordinary Dividend per Share	-	-	-	-	-	-	-	-	-	-
Earnings per Share	-	-	-	-	-	-	-	-	-	-

(a) Figures subsequently restated. b) Currency gain €1.4m. c) Share premium €6.5m net. d) Reduction in reserves - €21.7m; share premium +€2.7m. e) Write-off investment Salymskoye Oilfield -€15.6m.

BALANCE SHEET: DECEMBER 31 2001 €'000

		Fixed Assets		29
Share Capital:	26,860	Current Assets	2,476	
2,238,375,553,119 Ord €0.012 shares		Current Liabilities	1,554	
Reserves	(19,883	Net Current Assets		922
		Medium debt		(113)
		Net Tangible Assets		838
		Intangibles		6,139
Shareholders' Funds	6,977	Net Assets		6,977

Auditors' Note: *Going Concern '......we have considered the adequacy of the disclosures...concerning the recoverability of the carrying value of the Group's Oil and Gas Interests held outside the cost pools of €6.1m....'*

Comment:

There is more excitement in the boardroom than in the prospecting area.

No apparent reason for investing in this exploration company.

CPL RESOURCES plc

(Quoted on DCM)

JSINESS: Employment agency.
EGISTERED OFFICE: 83 Merrion Square, Dublin **HEAD FFICE:** as regd office. Tel: 01-6146000. Fax: 01-6146011
ECRETARY: William Fry Ltd **REGISTRARS & TRANSFER FFICE:** Computershare Investor Services (Ireland) Ltd, Heron ouse, Corrig Road, Sandyford Industrial Estate, Dublin
RINCIPAL BANKERS: AIB Bank **AUDITORS:** Arthur ndersen **SOLICITORS:** William Fry; Lawrence Graham.
OCKBROKERS: Davy Stockbrokers
RECTORS: J Hennessy (Chairman - 45), A Heraty (Carroll) r Mgr Dir - 42), P Carroll (38), P Garvey (56), P Malone (58). Roche (31), J Tierney.
HARE CAPITAL: Authorised: 50million Ord €0.10 shares **sued:** 36,196,825 Ord €0.10 shares
AFF: 272 **SCRIP DIVIDEND:** no

CAPITAL HISTORY:

rporated June 1998 as Forkhill Trading Ltd. Dec 8 name changed to CPL Recruitment International April 1999 name changed to CPL Resources plc. e 1998 2 £1 Ord shares issued. Dec 1998 acquired nputer Placement for 13,278,720 Ord 10p shares CPL Solutions for 13,278,720 Ord 10p shares. June 1999 the 26,557,460 Ord 10p shares were replaced by 33,196,825 Ord 8p shares and redesignated Ord €0.10 shares of which 6million Ord €0.10 shares were placed at €0.77 each (50pstg).

COMPANY HISTORY:

The business of Computer Placement was set up in Oct 1989 by A Heraty and K O'Malley. Then owned 67% by Professional Placement Group owned by K O'Malley and 33% by A Heraty.. In 1992 A Heraty acquired Computer Placement. 1994 company restructured allowing recruiters specialise in software developers, localisation, network and technical support. In 1996 set up CPL Solutions responding to demand for flexible staffing for software development, networking and support, database design and software testing. Late 1996 CPL Engineering formed, April 1998 CPL Sales started, June 1998 CPL Financial commenced and Nov 1998 CPL Telecom began. In 1997 Limerick office started Jan 1999 Galway office opened. Fees are 15% to 20% of first year basic salary. In 1999 CPL had over 500 clients. Operates in fragmented industry with approx 300 employment agencies in Ireland. June 1999 public flotation - 16.6% of equity placed raising £1.5m for company and same amount for directors. Placed @ $0.77, closed at $0.80 on first day. April 2000: Buys Careers Register for $3.77m. Feb 2002: Agrees to buy temporary contract busines from Marlborough Group/Ann O'Brien.

FINANCIAL DIARY

Interim Results Announced:	28.01.2002
Interim Dividend Payout:	08.04.2002
Final Results Announced:	20.09.2001
Annual General Meeting:	15.11.2001
Final Dividend Payout:	20.11.2001

HALF YEARLY PERFORMANCE: € m

Six months to	30.06.00	31.12.00	30.06.01	31.12.01
Sales	14.5	17.2	17.8	12.1
Pretax Profit	2.6	2.7	2.4	0.67
Profit % Sales	17.9	15.7	13.5	5.5

SHARE PRICE TREND

1999	High 0.90 (Dec)	Low 0.65 (Nov)
2000	High 1.70 (Apr)	Low 0.80 (Jan)
2001	High 0.95 (Feb)	Low 0.30 (Dec)

SIX YEAR REVIEW: $ m

months to June 30	1996	1997	1998	1999	2000	2001
es	3.475	6.107	11.901	20.760	26.004	35.003
fits Before Tax	0.086	0.292	1.254	3.153	4.609	5.148
	0.047	0.099	0.420	0.968	1.211	1.182
fits After Tax	0.039	0.193	0.734	2.185	3.357	3.966
ilable to Shareholders	0.039	0.193	0.734	2.185	3.357	3.966
inary Dividend	0.013	-	-	-	0.364	0.452
ained Profits	0.027	0.193	0.734	2.185	2.993	3.514
rease (Decrease) in Reserves	n/a	0.193	0.734	4.504 a)	2.993	3.514
reholders' Funds	0.136	0.329	1.063	5.348	8.217	11.731
inary Dividend Per Share €	-	-	-	-	0.011	0.0125
nings Per Share €	0.011	0.058	0.022	0.066	0.093	0.11 b)

Share premium +€1.8m. b) Based upon 36.2m shares

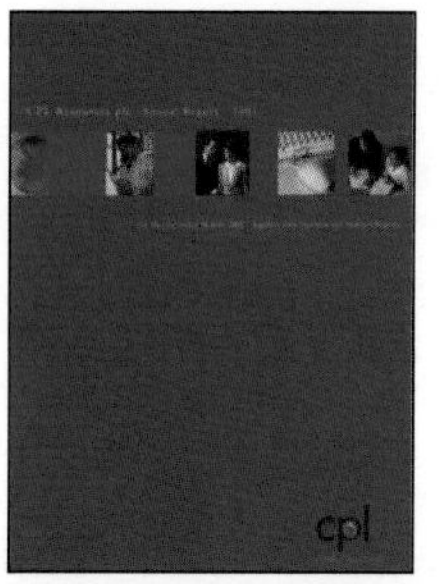

BALANCE SHEET: JUNE 30 2001.€ m

Tangible Assets		1.3
Current Assets	13.8	
Current Liabilities	5.7	
Net Current Assets		8.1
Medium debt		(1.3)
Net Tangible Assets		8.1
Intangibles		3.6
Net Assets		11.7
Share Capital:		
36,196,825 Ord €0.10 shares		3.6
Reserves		8.1
Shareholders' Funds		11.7

Comment: Too tightly held (80%) to interest market and now at less than flotation price.

CELTIC RESOURCES HOLDINGS plc

(Exploration Securities Market)

SINESS: Exploration company. **REGISTERED OFFICE:** 14 Upper zwilliam St, Dublin. Tel 01-6611245. Fax: 01-6611056. **HEAD OFFICE:** as d office. London Office: 59/65 Upper Ground, London SE1 9PQ **SECRETARY:** ingley. **REGISTRARS & TRANSFER OFFICE:** Computershare Investor rvices (Ireland) Ltd, Heron House, Corrig Road, Sandyford Industrial Estate, blin. **PRINCIPAL BANKERS:** Ulster Bank, Bank of Scotland, Allied Irish Bank. **DITORS:** Deloitte & Touche. **SOLICITORS:** O'Donnell Sweeney; Kerman & Co; rosh Grishayev Malyarenko. **STOCKBROKERS:** Davy Stockbrokers. **RECTORS:** P Hannen (Chairman - 49), K Foo (53), M. Nesbitt (62) Vorthington (47), M Palmer (59), N McDermott (52). **ARE CAPITAL: Authorised:** 250m Ord €0.025 shares, 5m 5% Red Conv Pref .26 shares, 2m A Pref £1 shares **Issued:** 231,840,623 Ord €0.025 shares, m 5.% Red Pref €1.26 shares. **STAFF**: 156. **SCRIP DIVIDEND:** No.

CAPITAL HISTORY:

porated Nov 1994. Issued 980,000 Ord 2p shares at 25p each and 000 £1 Pref shares to Fishers in return for licences (value £1.1m). d 2.8m Ord 2p shares at 25p each and 1.65m £1 Pref shares to on for their companies and loans (value £2.35m). Sept 1995: ed 5,114,900 Ord 2p shares at 25p each. Issued 0.8m Ord 2p es to Kanamura in lieu of fees owing of £200,000. Redeemed 98 founders £1 shares for £30,000. Nov 1996: Issued 1m shares at each for cancellation of an agreement. Jan 1997: Issued 2m Ord 2p es at 27p over to Goldking Ltd, plus 2m warrants at 30p each till h 1999. March 1997: Issued 0.96m Ord 2p shares at 30p each. In on the holders of 2,040,000 share warrants exercised their entints at 30p per share. July 1997: Issued 0.6m warrants exercisable e year at 35p each. Dec 1997: Issued 2m shares at 10p each. July : Rights issue (4-for-3) up to 29,859,867 Ord 2p shares at 6p each. Sept 1998: Allotted 3.95m Ord 2p shares to Dragon Oil at 6p each. July 1998: Issued 1,616,238 Ord 2p shares at 6p each and 3.95m Ord 2p shares at 6p each as part of rights issue. Sept 1998: Issued 146,291 Ord 2p shares at 6p each to creditors in lieu of cash. Nov 1998: Issued 0.25m Ord 2p shares at 6p each to creditors in lieu of cash. Aug 1999: Issued 16m Ord 2p shares at 2p each (to Redhaven). Nov 1999: Issued 4,785,819 Ord 2p shares to creditors. Issued 11,724,506 Ord 2p shares on conversion of A Pref £1 shares. March 2000: Placed 6,087,775 Ord 2p shares at 11.25pstg each. Issued 1,664,000 Ord 2p shares for licences in North Sea Gas. Issued 0.22m Ord 2p shares to Tyry Ltd terminating consultancy. June 2000: Issued 20,381,500 Ord 2p shares for Millennium Oil and Dabney plus warrants for 3m Ord 2p shares. Sept 2000: Placed 3,441,900 Ord 2p shares @ 0.094pstg each. Oct 2000: Placed 18,297,594 Ord 2p shares @ 0.94pstg each with warrants attached. May 2001: Issued 1.2m Ord 2p shares (value US$250,000) for Kazakhstan interests of Goldbelt Resources. Placed 10,854,700 Ord 2p shares @ €0.117 each (warrants for 5,427,350 Ord 2p shares attached @ €0.1625 each). July 2001: Placed 12,157,478 Ord 2p shares @ 8pstg each (warrants for 12,157,478 Ord 2p shares @ 8pstg/10pstg each). July/Oct 2001: Placed 4,729,763 Ord shares @ 8pstg each. Oct/Dec 2001: Placed 14,507,941 Ord shares @ 12.5pstg each. May 2002: Placed 28.6m Ord shares @ 13.5pstg each.

COMPANY HISTORY:

Formed Nov 1994 as Celtic Explorations Ltd subsequently changed to Celtic Resources Holdings Plc in May 1995. The company was formed to acquire mineral interests of Fishers (formerly Celtic Gold) and the entire equity and certain loans of the Dragon companies all wholly owned subsidiaries of Dragon Oil Plc (formerly Oliver Resources Plc). Aug 1995: Raised £1m in placing. After the placing Fishers owns 10.4% of ordinary shares and Dragon Oil owns 46.9%. June 1996: Yorkton Securities Inc to subscribe for 3.5m Ord 2p shares at 27p each. Sept 1998: Turmoil in Russia causes problems. Sept 1998: Creditors approached to postpone payments. May 1999: Dragon Oil agreed to convert US$2.36m into £1 pref shares and further to convert to ord shares at a price of at least 15p each. Other creditors settled for 40p in the £ (being cash 10p and shares 30p) which will involve the issue of 4.5m Ord 2p shares. Aug 1999: Redhaven holds 28% of Celtic. Aug 2000: Acquires Millennium Oil & Gas and Dabney Holdings with oil and gold interests in Kazakhstan. June 2001: Bought Danae's interest in FIC Alel JSC for $1.8m. June 2002: Standard Bank provides $12m loan. July 2002: Preparing to move to AIM Listing in London.

FINANCIAL DIARY

Interim Results Announced:	31.10.2001
Interim Dividend Payout:	Not likely
Final Results Announced:	21.06.2002
Annual General Meeting:	26.07.2002
Final Dividend Payout:	Not likely

INVESTMENT PERFORMANCE:

Five Year Investment Performance: €330

SHARE PRICE TREND

1997	High 0.55 (Jan)	Low 0.38 (Apr)
1998	High 0.13 (May)	Low 0.025 (Nov)
1999	High 0.90 (Dec)	Low 0.025 (Jan)
2000	High 0.28 (Mar)	Low 0.10 (Jan)
2001	High 0.22 (Sep)	Low 0.08 (Apr)

SEVEN YEAR REVIEW:

	£'000	£'000	£'000	£'000	£'000	$'000	$'000
nths to 31 Dec.	1995	1996	1997	1998	1999	2000	2001
e	19	222	0	0	0	0	0
Profits (loss)	2	(354)	(1,362)	(5,970)	(462)	(1,034)	334
	1	-	-	-	-	-	596
ax Profit	1	(354)	(1,362)	(5,970)	(462)	(1,034)	(262)
y Interest	-	-	+25	+755	(18)	+73	+26
ole for Shareholders	1	(354)	(1,338)	(5,215)	(480)	(961)	(236)
nd	-	-	-	-	-	-	-
ed Earnings	1	(354)	(1,338)	(5,215)	(480)	(961)	(236)
se in Reserves	1,786	1,182 a)	442 b)	(2,830) d)	1,216 e)		4,771 f)
holders' Funds	4,479	5,661	3,717	1,494	2,871	7,341	16,373
ry Dividend per Share	-	-	-	-	-	-	-
gs per share	-	-	-	-	-	-	-

hare premium +£1.4m. b) Share premium +£1.4m; goodwill +£0.3m. d) Share premium +£0.2m; currency loss -£0.3m. e) Share premium £1.6m. f) Share premium +$5m.

Auditors Note-' Fundamental uncertainty: *"In forming our opinion, we have considered the adequacy of the disclosure made in the financial statements concerning the valuation of intangible fixed assets and financial assets. The realisation of the intangible fixed assets of $20,148,000 and financial assets of $899,000 included in the consolidated balance sheet and of financial assets of $13,810,000 and amounts owed by subsidiaries of $9,022,000 in the company balance sheet is dependent on the successful development of mineral and hydrocarbon reserves........"*

Comment: The Auditor's note speaks volumes. Major fundraising in progress whereupon they will up sticks and transfer to the AIM market in London. Not a happy experience for Irish investors. Their stated objectives are: *"To create shareholder wealth .... pay a dividend by June 2004."* We shall await with bated breath.

BALANCE SHEET: DECEMBER 31 2001. $'000

Fixed Assets		1,954
Financial Assets		899
Current Assets	3,262	
Current Liabilities	6,285	
Net Current Liabilities		(3,023)
Pref Shares		(3,184)
Minority		(3,605)
Net Tangible Liabilities		(6,959)
Intangibles		20,148
Net Assets		13,189
Share Capital: 159,587,355		
Ord €0.025 shares		3,910
Reserves		9,279
Shareholders' Funds		13,189

CONDUIT plc

BUSINESS: Provider of telephone directory information.
REGISTERED OFFICE: Conduit House, East Point Business Park, Dublin
HEAD OFFICE: as above. Tel 01-8190000. Fax: 01- 8190088
SECRETARY: C Coyle
REGISTRARS & TRANSFER OFFICE: Capita Corporate Registrars plc, Unit 5, Manor Street Business Park, Manor St, Dublin.
PRINCIPAL BANKERS: Allied Irish Banks
AUDITORS: Deloitte & Touche
SOLICITORS: LK Shields; Linklaters
STOCKBROKERS: Davy Stockbrokers; Merrion Stockbrokers Ltd
DIRECTORS: E Kerr (Chairman - 52), L Young (Mng Dir - 39), D Creighton, R Nealon (35), G Purcell, L Shields (53), P McDonagh (51), M Tunney (50).
SHARE CAPITAL: Authorised: 423.2m Ord €0.03 shares
Issued: 17,361,069 Ord €0.03 shares
EMPLOYEES: 1,408
SCRIP DIVIDEND: No

CAPITAL HISTORY:

Incorporated April 2000 to hold Conduit Enterprises Ireland, Conduit Software and Fournir. May 2000: Issued 4,923 £1 Ord shares in Conduit Enterprises Ireland at £406.26 each. Conduit redeemed and acncelled 595 redeemable £1 Ord shares. Converted 35,000 redeemable convertible 3% cum pref shares into 20,000 Ord £1 shares in Conduit Enterprise Ireland. 8,922 Red Ord £1 shares converted into 8,922 Ord £1 shares. Issued Conduit 291,131 Ord £1 shares in exchange for entire capital of Conduit Enterprise Ireland. 118 issued 54 Ord £1stg shares to Conduit Enterprises Ireland at par. 118 issued 45 Ord £1stg shares to Sonera Media BV at par. June 2000: Conduit plc issued 42.32 Ord €0.03 shares for every Ord €1.2696 shares held; this resulted in 423,200,000 €Ord 0.03 shares in issue. June 2000: Floated on Neuer Markt in Germany by issuing 3,500,000 Ord €0.03 shares at €15.97 per share. April 2001: Lists on Dublin market @ €9.40 per share.

COMPANY HISTORY:

Established in 1996 to provide outsourced teleservices, telesales, teleresearch, customer care and direct assistance ('DA') services. Sept 1996 contract to provide DA services to Esat Digifone (renewed in June 2000 for another 2 years). June 1998: contract with One in Austria. Dec 1998: contract with COLT in UK. May 1999: Launched 11850 in Ireland. Launched DA service in Switzerland. Dec 2000: Launches 118811 in Austria. Various agreements were struck between Conduit and BT in UK, Tele Danmark in Denmark, France Telecom in France, Belgacom in Belgium, and Deutsche Telekom in Germany. Future growth in Europe and America will reflect the speed of deregulation. June 2000: Raises €50m (net) from flotation on Neuer Markt. April 2001: Dublin share listing. Oct 2001/April 2002: 3 directors resign. Nov 2001: Shares fall 29% on interim results. Feb 2002: Sonera sells 10% stake of Conduit for €3.8m (@ €2.20 per share). Conduit buys Sonera's 45% stake in 118 Ltd for €4m. June 2002: Reports 82.6m calls in 2001 up from 45.2m and has 11% of the UK directory market. June 2002: L Shields increases stake to 3.95%.

Share Price Sept 2001 - Sept 2002

1. €5.80 15.11.02 Results announced
2. €2.10 06.06.02 Results announced

FINANCIAL DIARY

Interim Results Announced:	15.11.2001
Interim Dividend Payout:	none
Final Results Announced:	06.06.2002
Annual General Meeting:	05.09.2002
Final Dividend Payout:	none

HALF YEARLY PERFORMANCE: € m

Six months to	30.09.00	31.03.01	30.09.01	31.03.0:
Sales	12.6	17.8	23.9	28.4
Pretax profits/(-)	(1.56)	(4.70)	(6.37)	(1.59
Profits % sales	-	-	-	

SECTORAL ANALYSIS (previous year)

Sales: directory assistance 99% (97%), other 1% (3%). Ireland 59% (80%), UK 27% (3%), rest of Europe 13% (16%), other 1% (1%).

SHARE PRICE TREND: €

2001:	High 9.40 (Apr)	Low 2.92 (Dec)

FIVE YEAR REVIEW: €'000

12 months to March 31	1998	1999	2000	2001	2002
Sales	1,334	2,885	10,996	30,408	52,342
Profits (Loss) Before Tax	77	(797)	(2,276)	(6,352)	(7,955)
Tax	10	+3	20	171	11
Profits After Tax	67	(794)	(2,296)	(6,524)	(7,965)
Minority Interests	-	-	-	-	-
Available to Shareholders	67	(794)	(2,296)	(6,524)	(7,965)
Ordinary Dividend	-	-	-	-	-
Retained Profits (Losses)	67	(794)	(2,296)	(6,524)	(7,965)
Increase (Decrease) in Reserves	n/a	(808)	(2,296)	46,564 a)	(7,233)
Shareholders' Funds	437	90	1,466	48,160	40,927
Ordinary Dividend Per Share €	-	-	-	-	-
Earnings Per Share €	-	-	-	-	-

Accounting standards are American. a) Share premium +€52m

BALANCE SHEET: MARCH 31 2002. €'000

Share Capital:	521	Fixed Assets		19,149
17,361,069 Ord €0.03 shares		Current Assets	36,620	
		Curent Liabilities	13,033	
Reserves	40,406	Net Current Assets		23,587
		Medium debt		(4,466)
		Net Tangible Assets		38,270
		Intangibles		2,657
Shareholders' Funds	40,927	Net Assets		40,927

Comment:
Critical mass appears to be very important in achieving profitability. It is disappointing to see a 72% jump in revenues producing a 25° increase in losses. However, the second half figures to March 2002 show the company could be within striking distance of being profitable.

REGISTRARS

Bank of Ireland, Registration & Securities Dept
P.O. Box 4044 Hume House,
Ballsbridge, Dublin 4
Tel: 01-6605666

BDO Simpson Xavier,
20 Merchants Quay, Dublin 8.
Tel: 01-6170100

Capita Corporate Registrars Plc,
Unit 5 Manor Street Business
Park, Manor Street, Dublin 7.
Tel: 01-8102429

Computershare Investor Services (Ireland) Limited,
Heron House, Corrig Road,
Sandyford Industrial Estate,
Dublin 18. Tel: 01-2163100

Computershare Investor Services plc,
Registrar's Dept PO Box 435
Owen House, 8 Bankhead
Crossway North,
Edinburgh EH11 4BR.
Tel: 0044-8707020010

Computershare Investor Services plc,
The Pavilions, Bridgewater Road,
Bedminster Down,
Bristol BS99 7NH.
Tel: 0044-8707020000

Lloyds Bank Registrars,
The Causeway, Worthing,
West Sussex BN99 6DA
Tel: 0044-1903 502541

CRH plc

Liam O'Mahony

CAPITAL HISTORY:

May 1974 'scrip' 1-for-2. March 1976 15.3 million shares issued in 'rights' 1-for-4 at 55p. May 1978 'scrip' 51.7 million shares issued in 2-for-3. April 1979 34.3 million shares issued in 'rights' at 88p in 1-for-4. March 1981 7.75 million shares placed. March 1984 'rights' at 62p on the basis of 1-for-4 raising £27m.. March 1985 15.6 million shares placed at 74p bringing in £11.5m. January 1987 17 million shares placed at 170p each. November 1987 18.8 million shares placed at 200p each. Sept 1993: Rights issue (1-for-5) of 58,379,839 Ord 25p shares at 260p each. July 1995: Issues 2,791,659 Ord 25p shares at 415p each for Staker Paving. Sept 1996: Placed 17.94m Ord 25p shares at 575p each. Sept 1998: Issued 482,531 Ord 25p shares re purchase of Raboni. Sept 2000: Placed 19,570,000 Ord €0.32 shares @ €18.00 each. March 2001: 1-for-4 rights issue (103,622,311 Ord €0.32 shares) at €10.50 each.

COMPANY HISTORY:

Cement Roadstone Holdings Ltd. was formed in 1970 by the merger of Cement Ltd (est. in 1935) and Roadstone Ltd (est. in 1948). In Nov. '70 25.5m Ord. share and 0.87m 7% cum. pref. shares issue re acquisition of Cement Ltd. November '73 acquired Breton Ltd. and Van Neerbos Beheer. 1977: joint venture with Hepworth Ceramics of seawater magnesia plant in Drogheda (Premier Periclase). 1978 purchased J. & W. Henderson in Scotland, Amcor in USA, DeSchelde in Holland. 1979 acquired T.B.F. Thompson in Nth Ireland, El Paso Precast in USA and also Carder Concrete Products. In 1981 paid $12 m for Concrete Conduit Inc. 1983 Bought Robert Abraham in UK. Jan '85 purchased Callanan Industries for $40m cash. May '86 acquired Blyth & Taylor and Area Lighting Systems in USA. Aug '86 acquired Wimpey Merchants in UK for £23.5m stg. Sept '86 CRH issues American Depository Receipts

(ADR) in USA. Purchased for $6m California Concrete Pipe Corp. and Hurst Concrete Products Inc. Nov '86 paid £7.8m for Heras Holding in Holland. Dec '86 acquired Boorhem Fields Inc. (50%) and Faulkner Concrete Pipe Co. Inc. (50%) for $11.5m in USA. Spent £122.9m in 1987 on various acquisitions. Jan '87: Bought NC Products Corporation and Adams Products Co of North Carolina at a total cost, including debt acquired, of $39m. The outstanding stg£6.0m redeem. pref. shares in Cement-Roadstone Merchants Ltd. were acquired from George Wimpey Plc. April '87: 10% of Radex-Heraklith A.G., an Austrian refractories manufacturer acquired for Austrian Schillings 84.8m in cash. July '87: Assets of Miller Material Co. Kansas City bought for $4m cash. Oct 87: Big River Industries Inc. Louisiana acquired for $22m. Nov '87: Acquired the Spanish Catalan Concrete Group for IR£62.2m. Mar '88: Acquires Irish Clay Industries for £4m, Wath Concrete and Von Campen BV (plumbing components) in Holland for a combined £4.9m. Pike Holdings (CRH 50%) acquires Pike Industries for $77m with option on other 50%. May '88: Acquires Pioneer Building Supplies in UK for Stg£10m. June '88: Acquires Severn Artstone for stg£2.7m. Feb. '89: Acquires Facade Beek BV and Flevobeton BV in the Netherlands for £4.3m. May '89: Acquired 50% Arizona Block, Deer Valley Block and Superlite Builders Supply in U.S. - CRH investment $10m. June '89: Purchased Anchor Building Products in U.K. for £16.1m. July '89: Listed on NASDAQ. Oct '89: Acquired A Muys & Co. and Kleiwarenfabriek Joosten BV in Holland for £11.7m. Dec '89: Purchased Kleiwarenfabriek Buggenum in Netherlands. Jan '90: Bought Coalite Building Supplies in UK for £50m in U.K. Feb '90: Purchased Betco, Goria and Eastern Prestressed for $22.4m. Mar '90: Raised £121m through issue of IR£75m 6.5% Convertible Capital Bond 2005 and US$72m (IR£46m) 5.75% Convertible Capital Bond 2005. Apr '90: Joint venture purchase of HPG Industries in U.S. for $100m (£62.5m). Dec '90: Invested £108m in acquisitions, etc. in 1990. Jan '91: Acquired Stradalit in Germany for IR£9.5m. Nov 1992: Buys remaining 50% of Pike Holdings and sells its 50% of Carder. Total net cost IR£27m. Sept 1993: Purchases Pennsy Supply and Clemente-Latham Concrete Corp for IR£30m. Rights issue for £147m. May 1994: Acquires 90% of Marlux in Belgium. Aug 1994:

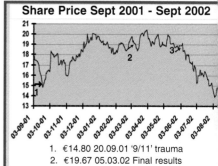

Share Price Sept 2001 - Sept 2002

1. €14.80 20.09.01 '9/11' trauma
2. €19.67 05.03.02 Final results
3. €16.50 10.07.02 Expansion announced

Buys 4 US companies (Keating, Lebanon Rock, Ba Sullivan Lafarge) for £44.3m. Sept 1994: Buys Roton in US for £14.6m. 40% of CRH shareholding now fe eign owned. Nov 1994: Buys Tempglass (US) £135m. Pays $5.7m for 20% of Cateras Cerro Neg (Argentina) and invests further $27.3m in loans. Fin £2.8m for part of EU cartel. Dec 1994: Pays £7.7m Schusters Block and Bosse Concrete. Jan 1995: Bu Dy-Core Systems (Dutch) for £15.7m. July 1995: Pa £15.3m for Staker Paving in Utah. March 1996: Bu J.B. Parson for $87m. Gartmore sells 22.2m CF shares at 500p/530p having bought them at 230p. Ap 1996: £7m deal gives CRH 50% of Materiaux in Par May 1996: Pays £12m for 2 Dutch Builders Merchan July 1996: Pays Goodwill of £18.8m for Allied Buildi Products in USA. Sept 1996: Pays £213m for Tilcon, BTR building materials subsidiary in America. Vario sales will reduce cost to £157m. June 1997: Spe £34m in early '97 on buying Weegels Beton BV a other companies: disposed of £43m in assets. Ju 1997: Buys Allied Building Products (USA) for £76 Sept 1997: Pays £63m for CPM Development Cor Spends £44m on various US acquisitions. Oct 199 Buys New York Trap Rock for £27.4m. Sept/Dec 199 Paid £35m for various US acquisitions. May 1998: Pa £43m for Segale Inc. Sept 1998: Buys 2 French comp nies, Raboni and Prefaest, for £14.3m. Oct 1998: Pa £23m for 47% of Holding Cement Polski (now hol 96%). Dec 1998: Successfully bids £326.4m for Ibsto plc (UK). April 1999: Sells Keyline (UK) for £220m. Ju 1999: Pays £117m for Millington and Dell (US). Pay £327m for Finnsementti and Rudus (Finland). Pa £10.8m stg for Hepworth's bricks. Aug 1999: Boug Thompson-McCully (US) for £325m. Jan 2000: €114.5 in Europe & US. Feb 2000: Buys Shelley in Ohio f US$362m (£283m). April 2000: Loses bid for Polis Trzuskawica. July 2000: Total invested €339m in Europ & US in H1 2000. Nov 2000: Buys Jura Group f €268m. Sells 50% Huntstown Power to Viridian. Ja 2001: Acquisition spend €354m in H2 2000 - total sper 2001 €1.5m. March 2001: 94.7% take-up of rights issu Capita Registrars error necessitates buy-in of 8.2 shares to correct their mistake. April 2001: Eyeing 25 stake in Nesher Israel. June 2001: Fails in bid for 25 Suez Cement. May 2001: Pays €154m for Mount Hop Rock (USA), 25% Mashav Group Israel $48m, Halle Materials and Des Moinee Asphalt $75m. March 2002 Buys US Aggregates for $140m. Negotiates $1bn glol al bond finance. June 2002: Bids €178m for Egyptia cement co.

TEN YEAR REVIEW: € m

12 months to Dec. 31	1992	1993	1994	1995	1996 c)	1997	1998	1999	2000	2001
Sales	1,414.5	1,811.9	2,048.1	2,425.2	3082.9	4,079.6	5,034.3	6,599.4	8,701.8	10,206.8
Profit before Tax	73.1	97.1	147.4	203.8	245.6	321.5	408.9	634.9	696.7	802.9
Tax	13.3	17.6	27.6	41.8	55.0	75.7	99.9	177.7	193.7	217.0
Profit after Tax	59.8	79.5	119.9	161.9	190.7	245.8	309.0	457.2	503.0	585.9
Minority Interest	(0.6)	(0.6)	(1.9)	(1.7)	(1.8)	(2.2)	(3.3)	(3.1)	(4.6)	(3.8)
Preference Dividend	(0.1)	(0.1)	(0.1)	(0.1)	(0.1)	(0.1)	(0.1)	(0.1)	(0.1)	(0.1)
Available for Shareholders	59.2	78.7	118.0	160.2	188.8	243.5	305.6	454.0	498.3	582.0
Ordinary Dividend	24.9	30.9	36.2	41.5	48.6	57.1	66.6	78.5	93.4	120.0
Retained Profit	34.3	47.9	81.8	118.7	140.2	186.4	239.0	375.5	404.9	462.0
Increase (Decrease) in Reserves (4.2) j)		243.5 k)	22.5 l)	109.7 n)	180.4 a)	251.3 b)	243.1 d)	642.6 e)	865.6 g)	1,623.9 h)
Shareholders' Funds	471.7	733.9	756.5	868.2	1,055.9	1,308.4	1,553.8	2,200.5	3,073.9	4,734.2
Ordinary Dividend per Share (€)	0.086	0.092	0.103	0.116	0.130	0.149	0.171	0.200	0.228	0.23
Earnings per share (€)	0.204	0.251	0.335	0.452	0.516	0.637	0.791	1.164	1.249	1.153 f)

a) Share premium +€138.4m; currency loss -€45.7m; goodwill w/o -€5.2m. (b) Currency gains +€98.5m; goodwill w/o -€56.9m; share premium +€21.8m.
c) Figures subsequently restated (average exchange rates instead of year end rates 1996 +€10.3m; 1997 -€12.6m). d) Currency loss -€21.7m, share premium +€25.9m e) Share premium +€34.0m; currency gains +€179.3m; goodwill write-back +€57.5m. f) Based upon 504.7m shares. g) Share premium +€377.2; currency gain +€90.9m. h) Share premium +€1,071.6m; currency gain +€84m. j) Goodwill w/o -€15.1m, currency loss -€25.4m.
k) Share premium +€169.5m, currency gain +€29.8m. l) Currency loss -€15.7m, goodwill w/o -€45.7m. n) Share premium +€23.4m; goodwill w/o -€31.7m.

Continued on page 36

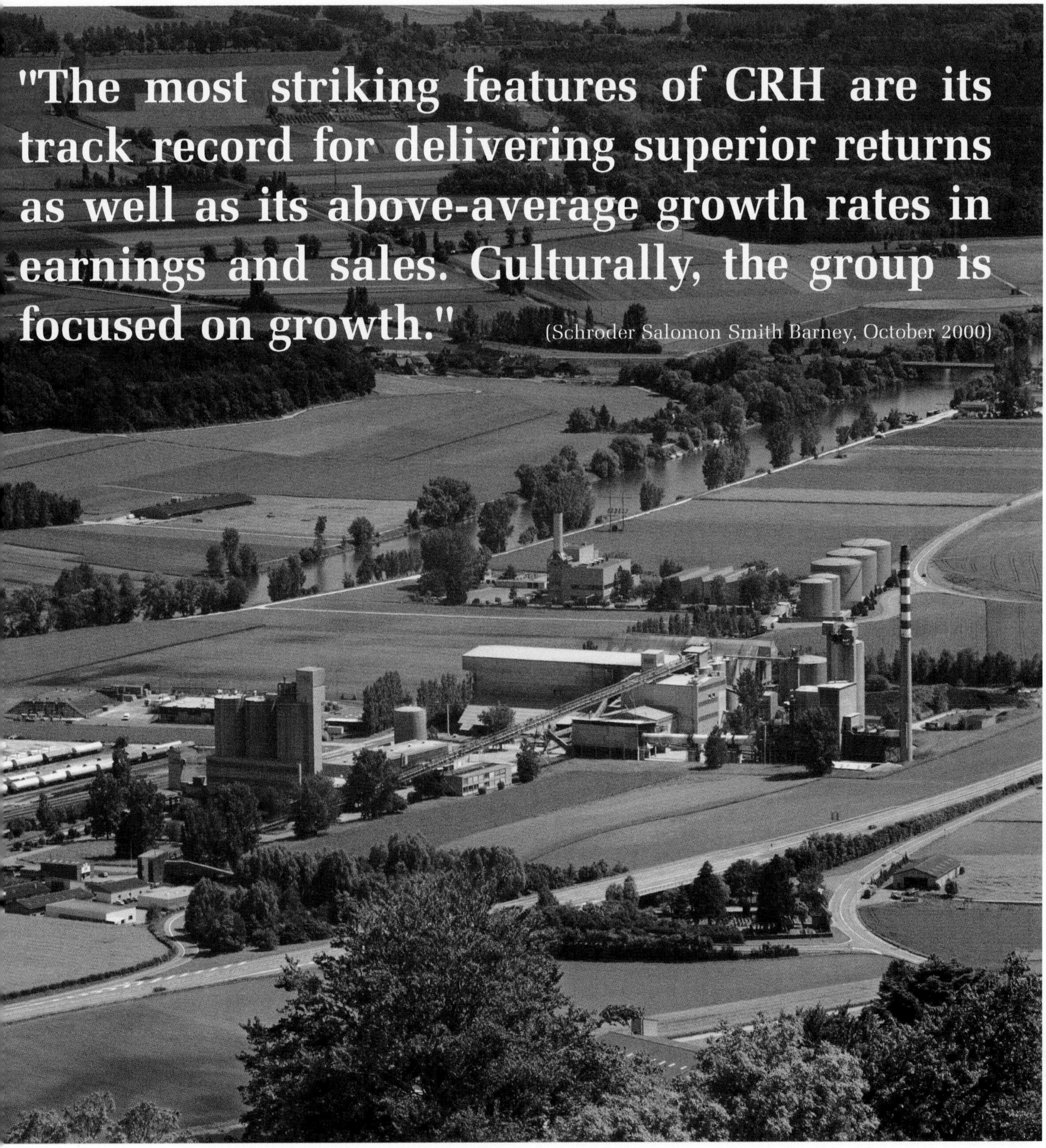

"The most striking features of CRH are its track record for delivering superior returns as well as its above-average growth rates in earnings and sales. Culturally, the group is focused on growth." (Schroder Salomon Smith Barney, October 2000)

A shareholder who invested the equivalent of €100 in 1970 and reinvested gross dividends would now hold shares worth €37,989 based on the share price as of 31st December, 2001. This represents a 21.1% compound annual return.

Visit our website for the latest news and updates:-
www.crh.com

Total shareholder return 1970-2001

€37,989

Compound annual return of 21.1%

40,000

30,000

20,000

10,000

€100

1970 — 2001

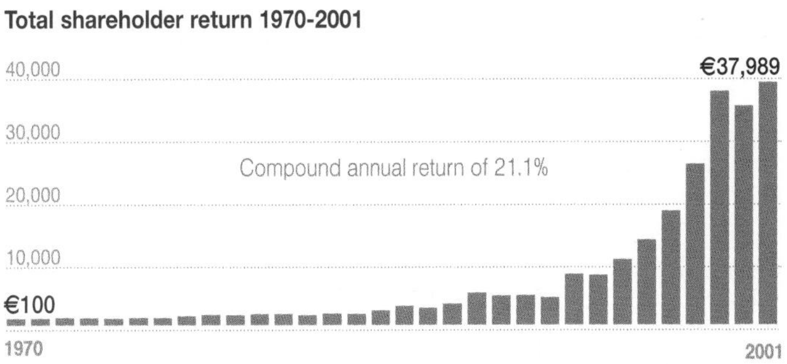

CRH

The International Building Materials Group

CRH plc

Continued from page 34...

FINANCIAL DIARY

Interim Results Announced:	03.09.2002
Interim Dividend Payout:	08.11.2002
Final Results Announced:	05.03.2002
Annual General Meeting:	08.05.2002
Final Dividend Payout:	13.05.2002

FIVE YEAR SHARE PRICE TREND €

Year		High		Low	
1997	High	10.86 (Dec)	Low	7.73 (Jan)
1998	High	15.68 (Dec)	Low	9.71 (Aug)
1999	High	21.65 (Sept)	Low	13.65 (Jan)
2000	High	21.88 (Jan)	Low	16.13 (Nov)
2001	High	21.51 (June)	Low	18.79 (Sept)

HALF YEARLY PERFORMANCE: £'m

Six months to	31.12.00	30.06.01	31.12.01	30.06.0
Sales	5,145.1	4,418.1	5,788.7	4,665.
Profit before Tax	516.5	185.9	617.0	195.
Profit % Sales	10.0	4.2	10.7	4.

INVESTMENT PERFORMANCE

Five Year Investment Performance:	€ 2,705
Ten Year Investment Performance:	€ 7,637

SECTORAL REVIEW: (previous year)

Sales: RoI 8% (9%), UK 8% (13%), Europe 22% (24%), US 62% (54%), building materials 49% (78%), merchanting 51% (22%).

Profits: RoI 16% (17%), UK 6% (9%), Europe 18% (16%), US 60%(58%), building materials 56% (91%), merchanting 44% (9%).

BALANCE SHEET: DECEMBER 31 2001. € m

Share Capital:		Fixed Assets	5,150.5
521.408m Ord. €0.32 shares		Financial Assets	315.8
& 521.408m		Current Assets	4,158.4
€0.02 Income shares	177.3	Current Liabilities	2,158.8
		Net Current Assets	1,999.6
		Long Term Debt etc	(3,733.2)
Reserves	4,556.9	Minority & Grants	(150.8)
		Pref Shares	(1.2)
		Net Tangible Assets	3,580.7
		Intangibles	1.153.5
Shareholders Funds	4,734.2	Net Assets	4,734.2

Comment:

Every equity market downturn presents a buying opportunity and this is equally true about this well managed global group.

DATALEX plc

BUSINESS: e-Business infrastructure and solutions provider for the travel industry.
REGISTERED OFFICE: Howth House, Harbour Road, Howth, Co Dublin.
HEAD OFFICE: as above. Tel 01-8391787. Fax: 01-8391781.
SECRETARY: L Booth
REGISTRARS & TRANSFER OFFICE: Computershare Investor Services (Ireland) Ltd, Heron House, Corrig Road, Sandyford Industrial Estate, Dublin.
PRINCIPAL BANKERS: AIB, Anglo Irish Bank, Bank of Scotland.
AUDITORS: Arthur Andersen
SOLICITORS: McCann FitzGerald; Lennon Heather & Co.
STOCKBROKERS: Goodbody Stockbrokers
DIRECTORS: M Quinn (Chairman), N Wilson (53), P Blackney (56), B Kilcoyne (69), P Lennon (47), N Beck (CEO), P Taggart.
SHARE CAPITAL: Authorised: 100million Ord $0.10 shares, 3m A convert redeem $0.10 shares, 1.5m B convert redeem $0.10 shares, 30,000 def £1 shares. **Issued:** 65,555,859 Ord $0.10 shares, 1,371,247 A convert red $0.10 shares, 1,170,456 B convert red $0.10 shares. One ADR = 2 Ord $0.10 shares.
EMPLOYEES: 416   **SCRIP DIVIDEND:** No

CAPITAL HISTORY:

March 2000: Placed 5,195,382 Ord $0.10 shares @ $2.81 each being less than fair value of $5.67 each (difference being $3.6m charged to P&L). Issued 3,852,555 Ord $0.10 to Atraxis AG @ $0.8m (fair value difference of $11m capitalized and being amortized over 3 years. Issued 90,400 Ord $0.10 shares for 30% of Hyperion. Sold 6,064,209 Ord $0.10 for $17m ($2.80 per share) to Monad Ltd (N Wilson company) at $7.4m less than fair value which was written off P&L. Issued warrant for 356,718 Ord $0.10 shares to DUNC LLC (US airline consortium) at exercise price of $5.67 per share. April 2000: Issued 2,140,305 Ord $0.10 shares (value $6.3m) re acquisition of Teamwork. May 2000: Issued 4,226,469 Ord $0.10 shares (value $23.9m or $5.65 per share) re purchase of Sight and Sound. August 2000: Issued 36,000 Ord $0.10 shares (value $0.2m or $5.55 per share) re purchase 25% of Datalex Australasia. Sept 2000: Sold 1.5m Ord $0.10 shares for $10m ($6.66 per share). Issued 88,020 Ord $0.10 shares re earn-out for ATS. Oct 2000: Sold 12,360,061 Ord $0.10 shares for $71.1m ($5.75 each) as part of IPO on NASDAQ and flotation on Irish Stock Market @ $6.84 per share. Nov 2000: Issued 900,000 Ord $0.10 shares valued $4.7m ($5.22 each) for 50% of Yatra Corp. Feb 2001: Issued 150,000 Ord $0.10 shares (value $780,000) to vendors of ATS.

COMPANY HISTORY:

1985: Founded by N Wilson and S Metzler to provide data communications products to the airline industry. A model was developed to connect mainframe reservation systems to a web server to enable internet access to user groups.such as travel suppliers to distributors. Principal customers include Aer Lingus, American Airlines, British Airways, Delta and KLM and distributors *ebookers*, *expedia* and *orbitz*. July 2000: High Court settlement re dispute over shares to Elginmount (issued 468,661 shares in Datalex (I) Ltd for $3,125,969 ($6.67 per share). Oct 2000: Cancelled warrants issued to Buy.com. Size of offering and flotation price reduced to $6.84 compared with target price of $8.31 per share. May 2001: D Desmond (IIU) and ICC buy 100,000 and 874,050 shares respectively from N Wilson @ €1.85 each. August 2001: 108 staff layoffs, cutbacks in spending, closure of 2 offices abroad and goodwill write-off in Q3 of $35m. Sept 2001: Chairman J Tierney resigns. March 2002: Bought remaining 50% of Yatra Corp. April 2002: Delisted from NASDAQ. April 2002: Chairman N Wilson and 3 directors resign. May 2002: L Booth resigns as Finance Director.

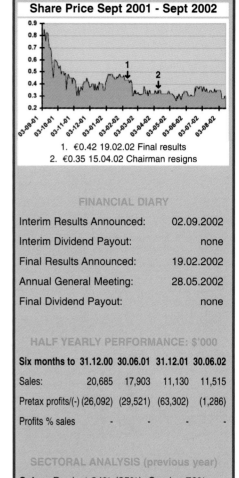

Share Price Sept 2001 - Sept 2002

1. €0.42 19.02.02 Final results
2. €0.35 15.04.02 Chairman resigns

FINANCIAL DIARY

Interim Results Announced:	02.09.2002
Interim Dividend Payout:	none
Final Results Announced:	19.02.2002
Annual General Meeting:	28.05.2002
Final Dividend Payout:	none

HALF YEARLY PERFORMANCE: $'000

Six months to	31.12.00	30.06.01	31.12.01	30.06.02
Sales:	20,685	17,903	11,130	11,515
Pretax profits/(-)	(26,092)	(29,521)	(63,302)	(1,286)
Profits % sales	-	-	-	-

SECTORAL ANALYSIS (previous year)

Sales: Product 24% (35%), Service 76% (65%).

SHARE PRICE TREND: €

2001	High	6.30 (Jan)	Low 0.30 (Nov)

FIVE YEAR REVIEW: $'000

12 months to December 31	1997 e)	1998 e)	1999 e)	2000 e)	2001 f)
Sales	6,590	9,181	13,073	33,322	29,033
Profits (Loss) Before Tax	949	693	(7,512)	(66,068)	(92,823) d)
Tax	+32	+116	+80	+300	+64
Profits (Loss) After Tax	917	577	(7,432)	(65,768)	(92,759)
Minority Interests	-	-	-	-	572
Available to Shareholders	917	577	(7,432)	(65,768)	(92,187)
Ordinary Dividend	-	-	-	-	-
Retained Profits (Loss)	917	577	(7,432)	(65,768)	(92,187)
Increase (Decrease) in Reserves	n/a	4,524 b)	18,986 c)	126,141 a)	(89,685)
Shareholders' Funds	1,747	8,045	27,557	159,155	65,188
Ordinary Dividend Per Share	-	-	-	-	-
Earnings Per Share ($)	0.07	0.04			

a) Share premium +$196.1m. b) Share premium +$5.7m. c) Share premium +$26.7m. d) Includes 'impairment charge' of $44.8m. e) Accounts are compiled under American standards. f) Accounts compiled according to Irish standards.

Comment:

Last year the company postulated: "Working towards achieving the objective of a return to profitability in early 2002". We said: wait for the progress towards this before taking a plunge. In the meantime there has been a rearrangement of the seats at the boardroom table and we are still waiting to see if and when the red ink turns into black.

BALANCE SHEET: DECEMBER 31 2001. $'000

Share Capital:	6,817	Fixed Assets	5,468
65,555,859 Ord $0.10 shares,		Financial Assets	911
1,371,247 A convert red $0.10 shares,		Current Assets	66,248
1,170,456 B convert red $0.10 shares.		Current Liabilities	15,028
		Net Current Assets	51,220
Reserves	58,371	Medium debt	(1,568)
		Minorities	(2,530)
		Net Tangible Assets	53,501
		Intangibles	11,687

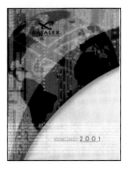

DCC plc

CAPITAL HISTORY:

Incorporated April 1976 as Development Capital Corporation Ltd. May 1991 name changed to DCC plc. May 1991 13,374,465 £1 Ord shares and 107,201 Ord £1 shares 1p paid were in issue. Between Sept 1991 and Feb 1993 various options were exercised. June 1993 150,000 £1 Ord shares issued re Employee Partly Paid Share Scheme with 1p paid thereon (variable premium to maximum of £9.50 per share). Jan 1994 further 180,500 Ord £1 shares issued re Employee Partly Paid Share Scheme 1p paid (variable premium to max £10 per share). March 1994: Ord £1 shares split into 5 Ord 20p shares. Exec options on Ord 20p shares issued. April 1994 issued 349,990 Ord 20p shares issued at 240p per share to 60 staff of subsidiaries. Issued 603,703 Ord 20p shares to shareholders in Fannins (bringing DCC's stake to 83.7%). May 1994: 3m Ord 20p shares placed at €3.17 in connection with flotation.

COMPANY HISTORY:

Founded in 1976 as a venture capital business. In 1985 it acquired Share & Loan Trust portfolio from Bank of Ireland and the 3i portfolio on its exit from Ireland. Institutional investors put up more than £60m in equity up to 1989. One of its flagship investments has been its association with Fyffes plc. In 1990 DCC changed direction from venture capitalist to conglomerate. It spent £77m in 3 years to March 1994 in acquiring controlling stakes in Wardell Roberts, Flogas, Printech, Fannins and Sharptext together with its interest in Emo Oil/Greenway. In 1979 acquired 27% of Wardell Roberts which was increased to 80% in 1993. In 1981 acquired 9% of FII Ltd (now Fyffes) which was subsequently increased to 11%. Played an active role in Fyffes' warehousing of Irish Distillers shares ahead of Pernod Ricard takeover resulting in substantial capital gain for Fyffes. In 1989 acquired 25% of Allied Foods in financing an MBO. May 1992 bought additional 27.4% Sharptext Group bringing stake to 72.7% subsequently increased to 76.8%. In preparation for public flotation acquired in Feb 1993 45.1% of Printech International bringing DCC's holding to 91.6% subsequently reduced to 75.02%. Feb 1993 acquired Wardell Roberts (previous stake 29.8%). In December 1993 Bank of Ireland sold its 20% stake in DCC for £2 per share. April 1993 got 75% control of Emo Oil. Aug 1993 increased stake in Flogas to 60.3% (Flogas was valued at £39m, Emo £4.3m, Printech £20.5m. Wardell £14.8m, Sharptext £7.7m). May 1994: Public flotation disappoints; no premium. July 1994: Buys 3.5m shares in Heiton Holdings for £1.5m (now holds 16%). Dec 1994: Increases Heiton stake to 20% by buying 1.65m shares at 65p each. March 1995: Paid up to £4.6m stg for Gem Distribution. April 1995: Spent £835,000 on increasing its stakes in Fannin (to 88.7%) Broderick (to 68.1%0 and Allied Foods (to 30.4%). Sept 1995: D. Gavagan resigns. Jan 1996: Sold 29.4% holding in Greenway for £4m (Profit £39,000). May 1996: Offloads 25% Heitons with profit of £5.1m. May 1996: Purchased remaining 20.1 of Ochil for £2.1m, paid £1.5m for 11.3m of Fannin. Sept 1996: Bought 20% of Oare Plc for £3.8m and bought 50% of Millais Investments (Allied Foods). November 1996: Pays £0.6m for Mitchells Wine Merchants. May 1997: Pays £4m for 45% of ITP. June 1997: Paid £3.38m for 7.5% of Sharptext and Runsole. July 1998 : Acquires remaining 7.6% of Sharptext for £6.35m. Oct 1998: Pays £14.9m for BM Brownes. Dec 1998: Pays £13.5m for Burmah Ireland. Dec 1998: Pays £6m for 50% Kylemore bakery and shops. Jan 2000: Pays £7.3m for 55% Distrilogie with possible £22.7m earn-out to 3/2003 for remaining 45%. Feb 2000: Dumps Fyffes entire equity holding 31.2m shares(10.5%) @ €3.41 per share yielding £83.7m. Denies DCC had any forewarning of Fyffes profits warning. March 2000: Sells 90% of ITP for €19.8m. July 2000: Buy-back 2,563,045 Ord €0.25 shares @ €9.50 each. Sept 2001: Buy-back 2,275,000 own shares @ €9.25. Buys BP Scottish distribution for €15m. Dec 2001: Pays €16m f Altagas (UK). Feb 2002: Pays €8.3m for 75% TechnoPharr Feb 2002: 2 US, 3 Irish Institutions and Fyffes sue DCC re Fe 2000 sale of Fyffes shares.

TEN YEAR REVIEW: € m

12 Months to March 31	1993	1994	1995	1996	1997 g)	1998	1999	2000	2001	2002
Turnover	100.24	302.69	355.74	441.72	527.22	639.59	791.71	1,220.24	1,870.14	2,048.89
Profit before Tax	18.88	28.16	32.11	36.64	44.79	46.35	57.66	139.17 m)	82.41	90.91
Tax	3.63	5.56	5.48	6.53	8.44	7.46	8.88	18.70	13.10	13.68
Profit after Tax	15.26	22.60	26.63	30.12	36.35	38.89	48.78	120.47	69.31	77.23
Minority	(0.84)	(5.78)	(6.33)	(6.61)	(2.68)	(1.42)	(0.80)	(0.63)	(1.23)	(0.94)
Available for Shareholders	14.42	16.82	20.30	23.51	33.67	37.47	47.98	119.84	68.08	76.29
Ordinary Dividend	1.98	4.37	5.69	6.65	8.35	10.27	12.99	15.37	18.14	20.47
Retained Profit	12.44	12.45	14.61	16.86	25.32	27.20	34.99	104.47	49.94	55.82
Increase (Decrease) in Reserves	(6.99) a)	(10.01) b)	13.24	(10.17) d)	17.87 e)	31.00 f)	40.32 h)	134.20 k)	25.36 n)	37.71 p)
Shareholders' Funds	113.80	104.04	118.32	108.55	128.25	154.08	195.22	329.12	354.69	391.43
Ordinary Dividend per Share (€)	0.029	0.063	0.078	0.088	0.102	0.122	0.147	0.176	0.210	0.245
Earnings per Share (€)	0.213	0.249	0.282	0.318	0.420	0.45	0.55	0.69	0.790	0.903 j)

a) Goodwill w/o €17.1m. b) Goodwill w/o €23.4m. d) Goodwill write-off -€35.0m; associated companies reserves +€2.9m. e) Share premium + €18.7m; goodwill write-of - €17.8m; equity reserve written off - €7.6m. f) Share premium +€9m; goodwill w/o -€5.8m. g) Figures subsequently re-stated. h) Share premium +€8.8m. j) Based upo 84.5m shares. k) Goodwill write-back +€20.7m. m) Includes one-off profits of €71.4m on asset sales. n) Share buy-back -€24.6m. p) Share buyback -€21.3m

BALANCE SHEET: MARCH 31 2002. € m

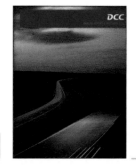

Share Capital:				
88,224,000 Ord. €0.25 shares	22.03	Tangible Assets		159.16
(inc 2.275m Treasury shares)		Financial Assets		38.98
Reserves	369.40	Current Assets	751.80	
		Current Liabilities	517.14	
		Net Current Assets		234.66
		Medium Debt		(154.56)
		Minority and grants		(5.13)
		Net Tangible Assets		273.11
		Intangible Assets		118.32
Shareholders' Funds	391.43	Net Assets		391.43

Comment:
Not too many Irish plcs have increased their pretax profits by 6 times over the decade and the dividend has exploded 9.8 times. An excellent performance with shrewd management who may be preoccupied with the Fyffes litigation over the short-term.

Pension schemes - so much to consider.

Trustees, regulators, beneficiaries.

Overwhelmed, anxious?

Let us guide you.

pensions and actuarial
assurance
financial advisory services
legal
tax

www.kpmg.ie

Running a pension scheme effectively can be a daunting task. So many elements involved, so many people to please. At KPMG our pensions and benefits professionals can provide you with a "pension strategy review" to benchmark those benefits and the effectiveness and value for money of the benefits you provide. So to cultivate the right scheme contact KPMG Pensions and Actuarial on 01 410 2815.

understanding Irish business @ *KPMG*

DCC is the original Irish conglomerate having been founded in 1976 by the current CEO, Jim Flavin and started its corporate life as a venture capital company. The early 1990s saw DCC refocus out of the venture capital arena where it had varying successes and into its present strategy of building a limited core of defensive companies with growth potential. As the 'conglomerate' description developed a tarnished image DCC has been inclined to have its shares moved from under the 'diversified industrial' to 'distributors' title which means little to investors generally. However shortly they will side step again into the 'services support' sector. Flavin probably thinks that each stepping stone has helped his share price to move steadily upwards but we feel pigeon holes have little merit when it comes to market support.

DCC can be divided into four different sectors: IT distribution, energy, healthcare, and other activities which embrace food, supply chain solutions and 49% of Manor Park.

DCC			
IT Distribution	Energy	Healthcare	Others
Hardware	Oil	Mobility	Food
Software	LPG	Hospital Supplies	Supply Chain Solutions
Storage	Environmental Services	Nutraceuticals	49% Manor Park

The best way to get a grip on the DCC group is to show the revenue and profitability for each division remembering the total sales are just over €2billion

DCC				
Division	Annual Sales €m	%	Pretax Profit €m	%
IT	815	40%	31	30%
Energy	717	35%	35	34%
Healthcare	192	9%	21	20%
Food	184	9%	11	11%
Other	141	7%	5	5%
Total	2,049	100%	103	100%

From a casual investor's viewpoint the fact that 40% of DCC's revenue is generated by its investment in the IT sector is hardly the stuff that makes punters queue up outside stockbrokers offices panting to get their hands on blocks of equity. This comment is made primarily because the division trades under the heading of SerCom Distribution which to those not directly involved with the industry means absolutely nothing to them. To throw some light on the division 55% of its turnover comes from selling computer hardware in the UK, the balance is shared between storage in continental Europe, hardware and software sale in Ireland and, finally, software sales in the UK. DCC markets hardware and software to resellers and traders but not end users. The

mixed product offering means that software (22%) is the largest single product category while PCs (including laptops) only represent about 18%; printers and peripherals account for another 20%. SerCom distributes to 8,000 resellers, dealers, computer superstores, general retailers and mail order catalogues of which 4,500-5,000 are regular monthly customers with none of them accounting for over the worrying 5% level of sales. MicroP is the largest company in the SerCom Distribution division accounting for about 55% of sales. Operating from Basingstoke, Romsey and Accrington, MicroP is one of the largest UK distributors of hardware. Much of the product is despatched from the Accrington base within 24 hours. The broad customer base spreads the risk. Key suppliers include Tecktronixs, Epson, Phillips, Fujitsu-Siemens and Sony. In Ireland this division operates under the Sharptext banner whose sales are 50% in PCs. This subsidiary's growth has probably peaked in the short-term. The PC market is considered a cut-throat commodity market. DCC has secured the exclusive distribution contract for Microsoft's X-Box for the UK and Ireland's indirect market being 25% of the total market.

In the energy sector 22% of the revenue is in Scotland (BP's oil products), 7% in the UK, 35% in Northern Ireland, with balance of 36% in Ireland. DCC tends not to be involved in the supply of large bulk contracts with major oil or gas producers. In LPG the product is either delivered to customers, storage tanks or delivered in cylinders. In oil, which is the faster growing side, the customer base is wide-ranging covering domestic heating and cooking requirements, automotive and agricultural, commercial and industrial usage. As this is a mature industry, it begs the question what value can DCC leverage from it? Distribution is not perceived as a key activity by the oil/gas majors but exploration and retail are of greater importance. Oil distribution is very fragmented and this should provide the opportunity for acquisitions and small bolt-ons and from them DCC can gain economies of scale. While oil prices are volatile DCC's profit comes from a mark-up on the tonnage handled. There are some lag impacts from rising or falling prices but generally price movements do not affect

returns much in oil. Not so in LPG as the LPG price is more consistent and usually only changes twice a year. The energy industry major attraction is that it is very cash generative.

Healthcare has grown in importance in the DCC camp in recent years growing from a level of 9% to 20% of group profits. Fannin is the leading distributor of hospital supplies in Ireland and estimates are that it is twice the size of Baxter and Johnson & Johnson. Fannin sells such items as operating theatre lights, hospital beds, minimally invasive surgery equipment orthopaedic implants and syringes from such suppliers as Bard, Huntleigh, Stratec and Tyco. Hospital supplies would account for 40% of the revenue in this division while 35% comes from mobility and rehab with nutraceuticals accounting for the remainder. There does not, however, appear to be much scope for growth into the UK where the market size there is fully serviced by OEMs.

However DCC is the leading integrated UK supplier of mobility and rehab equipment such as bath aids, toilet aids, homecare beds and powered mobility products where it is the exclusive European distributor for the Shoprider range of products which will be helped further by the acquisition of Casacare in Germany. The ageing population means that the demand for generalised mobility products is growing fast. Healthcare offers the highest margins. However it should be remembered that Jim Flavin to his credit has a hang up about return on capital as a key measure; so while returns on capital employed for healthcare are 45% (excluding goodwill) working capital requirements are more demanding than in other areas of the group.

In the area of nutraceuticals DCC markets distributes and manufactures its branded and private label vitamins and supplements for the UK and Europe. This segment looks like growing as the ageing population seeks more kicks from supplement popping.

DCC's food operations are Irish based and major on snackfoods (KP which is currently Walkers are growing - second only to Tayto) health foods (market leader with Kelkin) coffee (second in ground coffee through its own brand Robert Roberts), soft drinks and wine (through the acquisition of Woodford Bourne and Mitchells).While a toe in the food industry does provide DCC with some defensive quality the particular segments are highly competitive (which segments are not!) Their products are really up against some aggressive 'big boys' and the onward surge by Walkers crisps with its mega advertising budget shows how hot the temperature can get in the kitchen. Robert Roberts has some 4,500 customers in the retail grocery, retail confectionery, off-licence and catering sectors. They have a long-term contract with KP with which it has a manufacturing joint venture. DCC has a 50% interest in Allied Foods (distributor of frozen and chilled foods) and a 50% stake in Kylemore Group which (not unlike IAWS's Cuisine de France) manufactures frozen part baked bread.

(We have examined a number of stockbrokers' reports including an exceptional review by Dresdner Kleinwort Wasserstein from which much of this short overview has been drawn. Another excellent report has been produced by Davys.)

DONEGAL CREAMERIES plc

BUSINESS: Agri-trading.

REGISTERED OFFICE: Ballyraine, Letterkenny, Co Donegal

HEAD OFFICE: As above. Tel: 074-21766 Fax: 074-24823

SECRETARY: D Kelly

REGISTRARS & TRANSFER OFFICE: Computershare Investor Services (Ireland) Ltd, Heron House, Carrig Road, Sandyford Industrial Estate, Dublin

PRINCIPAL BANKERS: Ulster Bank.

AUDITORS: PricewaterhouseCoopers.

SOLICITORS: Arthur Cox; V.P. McMullin & Son; Matheson Ormsby Prentice.

STOCKBROKERS: NCB Group Ltd

DIRECTORS: L Tinney (Chairman - 64), _ Keon (Mgr Dir - 64), I Bates, F Browne, B Byrne, _ Callaghan, J Carlin, F Devenney (57), S Gallagher, _ Gregg (54), I Grier (58), D Kelly (46), P Kelly (58), _ Kerr, G McClay, M. McNulty (57), J Moody, E Moore, _ Rankin, M Robinson, R Russell, F Scott, D Sweeney, _ Tindal (66), G Vance (52), N Witherow.

SHARE CAPITAL: Authorised: 50m Ord €0.13p shares. **Issued:** 10,034,590 Ord €0.13p shares.

STAFF: 335

SCRIP DIVIDEND: No

dairy products and agri-trading. In the 70's and 80's operated a cheese plant with Japanese partners in Letterkenny until losses forced its closure. Concentrated then on milk evaporation which ceased in 1991. Milk is now collected and sold to processors in Nth Ireland. 1990: acquired 75% of Maybrook, a processor and distributor of packaged milk in Derry for £0.74m and Jan 1992 bought remainder for £0.25m. 1995 closed Maybrook's plant in Derry and operated from Killygordon. July 1995 bought 74% of Smyth Group in animal feeds for £1.16m; has option to buy 26% by mid-2000. As a result now owns 30% McCorkell in shipping and storage. 1995 bought 1million 9.9% cum pref shares in Waterford Foods. Oct 1996 bought An Grianan's 3,000 acres (with 413,000 gallon milk quota) at Lifford for £3.9m from receivers. May 1997 bought 23% Ennis Foods for £100,000 producing a milk based breakfast product. Sept 1997 bought Irish Potato Marketing Ltd (principally in seed potatoes) for £8. Dec 1997: Public flotation at €2.10 each netting the company €2.8m. First day's trading ends at €2.86. Dec 1997: Holds 107,828 Treasury shares bought in 1996 and 1997 at €1.17 each. Feb 1999: Acquired 76% (with option on remainder) of Wm McKinney & Sons (sweet mfg) for €1.02m. June 1999: Joint venture (Donegal 40%, NCF 26%, Carbury management 34%) acquires Carbury Mushrooms group for €12.15m + earnout 0f €2.41m. Donegal to subscribe €4.44m for loanstock. May 2000: Animal feed fire; insurance €3.3m in excess of book value. Nov 2000: Buys W Patterson Ltd for €6.5m. March 2001: Closes part Carburry Mushrooms cost €2m. May 2002: Wm Lord (Leeds) placed in liquidation (owns 40%)

CAPITAL HISTORY:

Incorporated Dec 1989 with issued capital of 40,022 £1 Ord shares. 1995: issued 7,366 Ord _ shares. 1996: issued 2,343 Ord £1 shares for _,709. July 1996 848,985 Ord £1 shares were sub-divided into 10 Ord 10p shares. 1997 re-issued 100,492 Treasury shares at 92p each in lieu of dividend. Nov 1997: Placing and Open Offer (2-for-11) 1,523,750 Ord 10p shares at 2.10 each.

COMPANY HISTORY:

Donegal Co-operative Creameries Ltd was founded in 1970 by the merger of Finn Valley Co-op, Taughboyne Co-op and Letterkenny Co-op. 1973 acquired Drumholm Co-op. 4 co-ops traded in milk assembly, sale of milk, manufacture of

Share Price Sept 2001 - Sept 2002

1. €2.00 19.09.01 Interim results
2. €2.20 29.05.02 Final results

HALF YEARLY PERFORMANCE: €'000

Six months to	30.06.00	31.12.00	30.06.01	31.12.01
Sales	49.4	48.3	70.7	43.9
Profit before Tax	2.9	3.3	3.2	1.9
Profit % Sales	5.9	6.8	4.5	4.3

SHARE PRICE TREND

1998	High	3.30 (Jan)	Low	2.29 (Dec)
1999	High	2.35 (Jan)	Low	1.50 (July)
2000	High	2.25 (Mar)	Low	1.63 (Nov)
2001	High	2.40 (Dec)	Low	1.70 (Apr)

FINANCIAL DIARY

Interim Results Announced:	19.09.2001
Interim Dividend Payout:	22.12.2001
Final Results Announced:	17.04.2002
Annual General Meeting:	04.07.2002
Final Dividend Payout:	02.09.2002

SECTORAL ANALYSIS (previous year)

Sales: Dairy 42% (44%), farm inputs 38% (34%), other 20% (22%), RoI 68% (54%), UK 24% (39%), other 8% (7%).

EIGHT YEAR REVIEW: €'000

12 months to December 31	1994	1995	1996	1997	1998	1999	2000	2001
Sales	47,008	54,803	58,192	64,283	73,763	90,172	97,653	114,572
Profit Before Tax	2,227	2,556	2,746	3,179	3,955 d)	4,391	6,215 f)	5,074
Tax	724	502	492	494	660	630	1,274	972
Profit After Tax	1.503	2,054	2,254	2,685	3,295	3,761	4,942	4,102
Minority Interests	+14	+6	-	-	-	(66)	(74)	(96)
Available to Shareholders	1,517	2,060	2,254	2,685	3,295	3,695	4,868	4,006
Ordinary Dividend	320	430	432	521	681	879	1,010	1,074
Retained Profits	1,197	1,630	1,822	2,164	2,614	2,816	3,858	2,932
Increase (Decrease) in Reserves	n/a	1,832	1,742	4,862 b)	2,646	2,703	3,675	2,879
Shareholders' Funds	11,486	13,327	15,073	20,128	22,777	25,480	29,154	32,063
Ordinary Dividend Per Share €	0.038	0.05	0.051	0.057	0.069	0.889	0.10	0.108
Earnings Per Share €	0.182	0.245	0.265	0.320	0.333	0.037	0.49	0.404 a)

a) Based upon 9.9m shares. b) Share premium +€2.5m. d) Includes w/o -€0.43m Ennis Foods and +€0.46m profit on sale of IAWS shares. f) Includes asset sales and closure cost +€3.2m.

BALANCE SHEET : DECEMBER 31 2001.€'000

Comment:

Revenue increasing, dividend payout increasing (which is four times covered), and net assets per share €3.20 but the share price is only marginally up on the flotation price in 1997.

Share Capital:		
10,034,990 Ord €0.13p shares	1,304	
Reserves	30,759	
Shareholders' Funds	32,063	

Fixed Assets		21,553
Financial Assets		10,102
Current Assets	43,124	
Current Liabilities	34,990	
Net Current Assets		8,134
Medium Debt		(8,453)
Minority		(1,368)
Net Tangible Assets		29,968
Intangibles		2,095
Net Assets		32,063

(Formerly OLIVER RESOURCES Plc)

BUSINESS: Oil mineral and gas exploration in Turkmenistan.
REGISTERED OFFICE: 7 Fitzwilliam Square, Dublin. **HEAD OFFICE:** Dublin: 60 Lr Baggot Street, Dublin 2. Tel: 01-6766693. Fax: 01-6618025. Middle East: c/o Dragon Holdings Ltd, P.O. Box 34666, Dubai, UAE.
SECRETARY: G. Thomson.
REGISTRARS & TRANSFER OFFICE: Computershare Investor Services (Ireland) Ltd, Heron House, Corrig Road, Sandyford Ind Estate, Dublin. **PRINCIPAL BANKERS:** AIB; Bank of Ireland.
AUDITORS: Arthur Andersen.
SOLICITORS: Ashurst, Morris, Crisp; Mason Hayes & Curran.
STOCKBROKERS: J & E Davy.
DIRECTORS: H. Sultan (Chairman & Ch Exec), J Key (49), M Al Sayegh (53), B Kinney (60), C Dixon (59), N McCue (51), E Almulla.
SHARE CAPITAL: Authorised: 510 million Ord. €0.317 shares.
Issued: 362,153,112 Ord 25p shares. Warrants outstanding 11,694,259 (exercise by Oct 2011 at 24.75/62.5p stg).
STAFF: 660.   **SCRIP DIVIDEND:** No

CAPITAL HISTORY:

Went public in 1978. Placed 500,000 Ord. 5p shares at 64p in June 1981. Aug. 1984 acquired Candecca Ireland in return for 800,000 Ord. 5p shares. Aug. 1984 Celtex Exploration Services receive 50,000 Ord. 5p shares. Sept. 1984 2,000,000 Ord. 5p shares placed at 138p. March 1985 'rights' issue of 2-for-2 at 40p stg. (49p IR) and placing of 1,650,000 Ord. 5p shares at 40p stg. (49p IR). June 1986 8.5 million Ord. 5p shares placed at 8p stg. April 1987 2.4 million Ord. 5p shares placed at 11p stg. In May 1987 interest free loan of £361,000 stg. given to Oliver Resources by Enterprise Oil plc in return for a right to convert loan into 1,940,000 Ord. 5p shares, which option was taken up in Aug. 1987. In June 1987 acquired 64% of a producing gas field in Texas, USA for 1,675,050 Ord. 5p shares in Oliver Resources. Dec. 1987 placement of 3.6m new Ord. 5p shares at 20p stg. Dec. 1987 exchange of 1,651,413 Oliver shares at 27p for 1,651,413 in Burmin. March 1988 acquired working interest in 24 producing oil and gas wells in Texas in exchange for 8,000,000 new Ord 5p shares at 39p each. March 1988 purchased 1,910,090 Ord. 20p shares of North West Exploration in exchange for 3.6m new Ord. 5p shares at 27.2p each plus the transfer of 1,831,413 in Burmin. April 1989 placed 6m Ord. 5p shares at 42p each. May 1989 issued 1,707,065 Ord. 5p shares at 52p each and 652,273 Ord. 5p shares at 51.75p. And in July 1989 147,700 Ord. 5p shares at 52.87p in exchange for 2,257,652 shares in North West Exploration plc (29.46%). June 1990 rights issue 1-for-1 at 15p per share (including 2 warrants for every 11 shares exerciseable by 30.04.91 at 20p per share) involving 48,078,376 Ord. 5p shares. Nov. 1990: 300,000, Ord. 5p shares issued at 15p each. Aug. 1991: 2,928,000 Ord. 5p shares issued at 7p each. June 1992: Placing and open offer (1-for-1.05) of 134,653,034 Ord. shares at 2.19p each. 4,170,350 Ord. 1p shares to creditors in lieu of £83,407. Oct 1992: Issued 14,118,000 Ord. 1p shares

part payment re Jennings purchase. Dec 1992: 1m Ord 1p shares issued at 2.25p each. Jan 1993: issued 28.5m Ord 1p shares for 114,000 Kirkland shares. May 1993: 932,977,500 Ord 1p shares issued on takeover of Kirkland. 178million Ord 1p shares 'open offer' placement at 2.25p each. Oct 1993: 118,172,332 Ord 1p shares placed at 2.25p each. Oct 1994: Placed 221,919,853 units (unit = 2 Ord 1p shares plus one warrant to subscribe for a share at 2p up to 1.11.1999) with Sinoil. Rights issue (1-for-26) 56,919,853 units at 4p each. Dec 1994: Issued 4,402,500 Ord 1p shares in return for 17,610 shares in Kirkland. Oct 1995: Placed 96m Ord 1p shares at 2p stg each. Nov 1995: Placed 90 million Ord 1p shares at 2p stg each. June 1996: Placed 2.5 billion Ord 1p shares with SOL for 1.5p stg each. Open offer 843,931,208 (2-for-5) at 1.5p stg each to raise max. £12.7m stg. Issues 100 million APC warrants (for 5years) at 1.5p each. June 1997: Rights issue 129,968,297 Ord 25p shares at 50p stg each (3-for-5). Aug 1997: EGM reduces shares in issue by 25-to-1. Dec 2001: 14,567,030 Ord €0.317 shares placed @ 29.5p stg

COMPANY HISTORY:

Originally launched in 1971 as Oliver Prospecting & Mining. went public in 1978. Took over Candecca Ireland in 1984 in all share deal. Vendors, Plascom, obtained a 10% interest in Oliver. In March 1985 acquired Wington Enterprises. May 1985 name changed to Oliver Resources. August '87: Enterprise Oil exercise option. Dec '87: Share exchange with Burmin. March '88: Acquired interest in Texas Wells for issue of shares. March '88: Acquired interest in North West Exploration for equity plus transfer of holdings in Burmin. Dec '88: Bid for North West Exploration fails. Oliver offered 7 new Ord. Oliver shares for every two shares in North West. June '91: Offered Enterprise Oil a 20% option on Argentine exploration in return for funding. Oct '92: Acquired 25% of J.D. Jennings Ranch for $0.5m plus 14.1m shares. Dec '92: Intends offering 250 Oliver shares for each Kirkland AS shares. Oliver shares suspended. Jan '93: Acquired 114,000 (3%) Kirkland shares in return for 28.5m Oliver shares - values Kirkland at £20m. May '93: Name changed to Dragon Oil plc. May 1993: Bought Kirkland AS for $33.6m. June '93: Share quotation reinstated. Oct 1993: GT Management holds 8.1% of equity. Oct 1994: Sinoil (Chinese consortium) invest £11.2m with options on 165m shares at 2p till end 1999. and take 4 seats on board. O. Waldron relinquishes chair and 3 directors resign. Sept 1995: Announces £35m contract with others to build and operate 50 megawatt diesel power plant in Philipines. Oct 1995: Will pay up to £21.7m for 30% in 2 gas fields in Turkmenistan. May 1996: Reverse takeover by Larmag Energy Assets Ltd (LEA). New listing documents issued. A. Panigord pays £37.5m for 47% stake in Dragon. Nov 1997: Converts loan to LEA Ltd into shares ($15m)

Share Price Sept 2001 - Sept 2002

1. €0.29 15.02.02 Boardroom changes

FINANCIAL DIARY

Interim Results Announced:	15.09.2001
Interim Dividend Payout:	unlikely
Final Results Announced:	30.04.2002
Annual General Meeting:	05.07.2002
Final Dividend Payout:	unlikely

FIVE YEAR PRICE TREND €

1997	High	1.37 (Sept)	Low	0.04 (July)
1998	High	1.04 (Feb)	Low	0.25 (Sept)
1999	High	0.34 (Jan)	Low	0.25 (Sept)
2000	High	0.34 (Nov)	Low	0.23 (Apr)
2001	High	0.65 (July)	Low	0.28 (Jan)

HALF YEARLY PERFORMANCE $US (previous year)

6 months to	30.06.00	31.12.00	30.06.01	31.12.01
Sales:	22.8	10.4	11.3	10.9
Pretax Profit(-):	1.8	-	(1.3)	(4.1)
Profit % Sales:	7.9	-	-	-

bringing holding to 75%. Pays $28m for remaining 25%. M 1998: Chairman announces he wishes to sell 46% of Drago and Bell wants to sell its 18.8%. Nobody prepared to pay 5 per share. Nov 1998: Malaysian interests sell 160m Ord share to Emirates National Oil Co (ENOC). Dec 1998: ENOC ma offer of 15p stg for remaining shares. Jan 1999 ENOC achieve 69.4% (241m shares) of equity. 6 Board resignations. Major ba ance sheet clean-up. Major operation now in Turkmenistan Central Asia with head office in Dubai. Nov 1999: New agre ment with Turkmenistan government; total concentration now this Cheleken contract. Withdraws from Thailand, Philippine and coal mine gas licences in UK. Jan 2001: Drilling starts Caspian Sea. Jan 2002: Sold interest (9.1%) in Celt Resources for US$2.6m. Feb 2002: 3 Directors leave. Marc 2002: Producing 9,500 bopd of oil.

TEN YEAR REVIEW

12 months to December 31	£'000 1992 k)	£'000 1993 k)	$'000 1994 q)	$'000 1995	$'000 1996	$'000 1997	$'000 1998	$'000 1999	$'000 2000	$'000 2001
Revenue	12	3,351	6,359	4,303	10,439	17,560	10,525	40,598	33,187	22,248
Profit/(Loss) before Tax	(184)	631	1,200	(1,514)	(414)	501	(64,057)	2	1,873	(5,433)
Tax	-	125	710	+167	-	+80	+100	+302	+79	-
Profit/(Loss) after tax	(184)	506	490	(1,347)	(414)	421	(63,957)	304	1,952	(5,433)
Minority	-	-	(295)	-	+953	+1,126	+4,720	(3,049)	(350)	-
Available for Shareholders	(184)	506	195	(1,347)	539	1,547	(59,237)	(2,745)	1,602	(5,433)
Ordinary Dividend	-	-	-	-	-	-	-	-	-	-
Retained Profit/(loss)	(184)	506	195	(1,347)	539	1,547	(59,237)	(2,745)	1,602	(5,433)
Increase (Decrease) in Reserves	4,716 d)	22,513 j)	5,787 m)	1,605 n)	17,458 e)	56,077 a)	(59,239)	(2,745)	1,602	(3,630)
Shareholders' Funds	5,266	49,903	62,445	66,985	135,710	242,139	182,914	180,170	181,772	182,107
Ordinary Dividend per Share	-	-	-	-	-	-	-	-	-	-
Earnings per share	-	-	-	-	0.28c	0.52c	-	-	0.46cents b)	-

a) Share premium +$54.5m. b) Based upon 347.6m shares. d) Share premium €19.7m written off. e) Share premium +$16.9m.
j) Share premium $22m. k) Year end Oct. m) Share premium $5.6m net. n) Share premium +$2.9m. q) 14 months.

BALANCE SHEET: DECEMBER 31 2001. $ m

Share Capital:		Tangible Assets	0.3	
362,153,112 Ord. €0.317 shares	138.3	Current Assets	21.7	
Reserves	43.8	Current Liabilities	58.5	
		Net Current Assets		(36.8)
		Medium debt		(20.6)
		Net Tangible Assets		(57.1)
		Intangibles		239.2
Shareholders' Funds	182.1	Net Assets		182.1

Comment:

Investors would want to have similar agenda and deep pockets as major Middle Eastern (66.7%) shareholder.

DUNLOE EWART plc

(Formerly Dunloe House plc)

BUSINESS: Property investor and developer.
REGISTERED OFFICE: 9 Fitzwilliam Square, Dublin 2. **HEAD OFFICE:** as regd office. Tel: 01-6614344. Fax: 01-6614322. **SECRETARY:** A.M. Smyth. **REGISTRARS & TRANSFER OFFICE:** BDO Simpson Xavier, 20 Merchants Quay, Dublin 8 **PRINCIPAL BANKERS:** Bank of Ireland, IIB Bank, Morgan Stanley Dean Witter, Northern Bank, Ulster Bank Markets. **AUDITORS:** KPMG. **SOLICITORS:** Mason Hayes & Curran, N. Smyth & Partners; Slaughter & May. **STOCKBROKERS:** Davy Stockbrokers.
DIRECTORS: N Smyth (Chairman - 52), H Ennis (73), D Fell (60), S Carrington (60), T Kenny (41), N Murray (53), B O'Connor, A Smyth (51).
SHARE CAPITAL: Authorised: 500 million Ord 50.10 shares.
Issued: 387,915,285 Ord 50.10 shares.
STAFF: 48.   **SCRIP DIVIDEND:** No.

CAPITAL HISTORY:

Incorporated September 1934 as Ideal Weatherproofs. Went public in 1960. March 1983: Foir Teo and others converted loans into equity and as a result 1,320,160 shares issued. In 1984 1 million shares issued for cash as par. 140,000 issued for remaining 50% of Metromead, 240,000 issued for conversion of loans, 60,000 issued to discharge rental arrears. In August 1985 1 million shares issued at par for cash. September 1986: 11,778,000 issued to pay for a number of properties. Also 300,000 issued at par for cash. March 1989: Placing of 833,000 Ord. shares at 45p per share to raise £375,000. Dec 1995: Issued 6,497,650 Ord 5p shares at 10p each buy Nabola. issued 1,064,180 Ord 5p shares at 10p each discharge loans to N. Smyth. Issued 8 million Ord 5p shares acquire Kalbourne Upr Merrion Street development. Rights issue 2-for-1 35,540,320 Ord 5p shares at 10p each. Capital reorganisation: Ord 25p shares dividend into Ord 5p shares and the deferred 20p share (of no value). October 1996: Issued 4.4 million Shares to Mainstream Ltd for units at Airways Industrial Estate. September 1997: Placing and open offer (9-for-5) 36,569,158 Ord 5p Shares at 18p each. March 1998: 6,655,485 Ord 5p shares issued to Ewart shareholders who opted for shares (19-for-5) at 81p stg each.

COMPANY HISTORY:

Company (as Ideal Menswear) suffered losses due to recession in clothing industry. Name changed to Ideal Menswear in July 1975. July 1980: Name changed to Dunloe House Ltd. In December 1982 formalities to restructure capital could not be drawn up in time for A.G.M. Plans to reverse a £3 million property portfolio were frowned upon by Stock Exchange. Foir Teo and Western International Trust Co. Ltd., an Isle of Man company associated with M.S. Birrane, increased its stake to 48% of equity on conversion of loans. Further options at that time to convert other loans to 60.6% of equity. Both Birrane and J. Kutchera were co-opted to Dunloe Board in 1981. Metromead, acquired in 1985, owns 7 acres in Newbridge, Co. Kildare. August 1985: Dunloe ceased manufacture of clothing. In September 1986 11,779,000 shares issued for purchase of properties as follows: 12 & 14 Northwick Terrace London NW8 (flats) costing £325,000 stg-1,560,000 shares; Green Tiles, Denham, Nr. Uxbridge, UK (flats), costing £185,000 stg-888,000 shares; Northwick and Green Tiles were sold in 1988. 19/21 Aston Quay, Dublin costing £279,000-1,116,000 shares; 15 Adelaide Street, Dun Laoghaire, Co. Dublin (occupied by Irish Tam Ltd.) costing £181,000-24,000 shares; The Galleria, 6/7 St. Stephen's Green, Dublin 2 (commercial lettings) costing £1.87m-749,000 shares. All have since been sold. Jan. 1988: Dealing suspended. March 1988: Trading resumes, shareholders approve acquisition worth £13m. June 1988: Dealing suspended temporarily pending re-issue of documents on proposed acquisitions. June: John Biranne (M.D.) dies. August 1988: Announces that it will not proceed with intended package of acquisitions. March 1989: Clayform Properties acquired 5,247,153 (29.99%) from Western International Trust. D. Jones, B. Burleston, R. Ware appointed Directors. Placing of 833,000 at 45p raises £375,000. April 1990: Clayform acquired remaining shares from Western International Trust bringing holding to 60.2% and makes outright offer at 45p per share. Bid not accepted. May 1990: J. Birrane and J. Kutchera resign as Directors. Sept 1990: Sells Galleria Centre, Dublin for £5m. Oct 1990: Partner in £20m development at Arran Quay, Dublin. April 1991: Clayform Properties which now owns 77.5% of Dunloe reports loss of £39.1m stg. June 1991: B. Burleston resigns as Chairman of Clayform and Dunloe. R. Ware appointed Chairman. March 1993: Ben Dunne, supermarket chief, pays £900,000 for Clayform's equity in Dunloe at 6.75p per share. April 1993: B Dunne offers 6.75p per share for Dunloe which subsequently fails. Share transfers result in B Dunne holding 49%, N Smyth 15%, M Dunne 5.6%, M Cosgrove 5.6%. July 1993: Director E McMahon dies. R. Ware resigns as director. July 1995: Fitzwilliam Trust Holdings Ltd (Noel & Mrs Smyth) offers 5p each for each share (valuing Dunloe at £900,000). Fitzwilliam now holds 54% and N. Smyth holds 15%. Dec 1995: Buys Nabola (Maynooth Shopping Centre) from N. Smyth for £650,000 in shares. Buys Upr Merrion St Development for £1.5m. Rights issue raises £3.35m (83.6% take-up). N. Smyth diluted to 42%, McDermott & O'Donnell hold 10.4%, NatWest Smaller Companies hold 3.9%. April 1996: High Court approves share reduction of £4.2m. July 1996: Auditors BDO Simpson Xavier change to KPMG. May 1997: Buys shopping centre in Clondalkin, Dublin for £9m. June 1997: Shares suspended at 35p each pending outcome of talks with Monarch Properties. September 1997: Acquires Cradder Group (involving Monarch Group, Aviette Group and Cherrywood) for £21.2m. Rights issue to raise £25m net. Dec 1997: Announced purchase of Sir John Rogerson's Quay Dublin site from N. Smyth for £7.5m. March 1998: Acquired Ewart Plc for £31m. P. Monahan offloads 11.5m shares for £3m (26p per share). June 1998: Name changed to Dunloe Ewart. April 1999: British Land pays £33.5m for 50% Dunloe's development at Cherrywood, Loughlinstown.

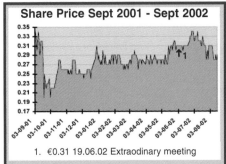
HALF YEARLY PERFORMANCE: € m

Six months to:	30.06.00	31.12.00	30.06.01	31.12.01
Revenue	22.3	48.7	36.8	21.6
Pretax Profit (loss)	3.1	5.9	(12.2)	(1.2)
Profit % Income	13.9	12.1	-	-

INVESTMENT PERFORMANCE

Five Year Investment Performance:	€1,033
Ten Year Investment Performance:	€1,632

FIVE YEAR PRICE TREND

1997	High	0.50 (Feb)	Low	0.24 (Nov)
1998	High	0.47 (Apr)	Low	0.27 (Jan)
1999	High	0.43 (Jan)	Low	0.30 (Apr)
2000	High	0.50 (Oct)	Low	0.34 (June)
2001	High	0.45 (Feb)	Low	0.20 (Sept)

FINANCIAL DIARY

Interim Results Announced:	18.09.2001
Interim Dividend Payout:	None
Final Results Announced:	30.04.2002
Annual General Meeting:	19.06.2002
Final Dividend Payout:	None

SECTORAL ANALYSIS (previous year)

Revenue: Rentals etc 29% (37%); property sales 71% (63%). RoI 77% (43%), UK 23% (58%).

British Land buys 5% of Dunloe Ewart equity @ 32p per share. July 1999: £400mstg development venture in Belfast with MEPC and John Laing. Oct 1999: Buys 4 properties from Dawnay Group for £23m. July 2000: Decides to go private; offers $0.51 (cash & 3yr loan note) provided 50% acceptance.(values DE at €199m; NAV €67.3). Oct 2000: Offer to privatise withdrawn. L Carroll buys more shares @ €0.50 each; now has 20%. May 2001: Offer to repurchase 34m (8.8%) Ord €0.10 @ €0.55 per share. P Byrne charged with insider trading - subsequently cleared. Property developer L Carroll (Zoe)(27.2%) blocks repurchase scheme at e.g.m. Dec 2001: P Byrne resigns. June 2002: Disposes of Nth Ireland properties for £90.75mstg (€146m). Aug 2002: Buys 50% Cherrywood Properties for €64m. L. Carroll increases stake to 27.45%. Sept 2002: 5m shares bought.

TEN YEAR REVIEW: € m

months to December 31	1992	1993	1994	1995	1996	1997	1998	1999	2000	2001
Sales	0.999	1.197	0.415	0.646	5.035	21.271	58.479	89.023	70.954	58.430
Profit (Loss) before Tax	(4.318)	(0.532)	(0.189)	(0.047)	0.263	1.934	9.614	25.713	9.001	(13.421)
Tax	0.006	-	0.011	-	0.126	0.467	2.531	6.448	2.075	1.958
Profit (Loss) after Tax	(4.312)	(0.532)	(0.201)	(0.047)	0.137	1.467	7.084	19.266	6.926	(15.379)
Available to Shareholders	(4.312)	(0.532)	(0.201)	(0.047)	0.137	1.467	7.084	19.266	6.926	(15.379)
Ordinary Dividend	-	-	-	-	-	-	-	-	-	-
Retained (Loss) Profit	(4.312)	(0.532)	(0.201)	(0.047)	0.137	1.467	7.084	19.266	6.926	(15.379)
Increase (Decr) in Reserves	(4.830)	(0.531)	(0.201)	(0.047)	10.941 f)	44.758 g)	33.666 a)	33.613 h)	21.007 b)	(6.624) e)
Shareholders' Funds	1.535	1.003	0.803	0.758	11.226	72.013	107.943	156.969	177.976	171.394
Ordinary Dividend per Share (€)	-	-	-	-	-	-	-	-	-	-
Earnings per Share (€)	-	-	-	-	0.002	0.009	0.02	0.050	0.018 d)	-

a) Share premium +€9.0m; property revaluation +€17.6m. b) Property revaluation +€13m. d) Based upon 387.5m shares. e) Property revaluation +€6.7m. f) Share premium +€4.8m; property revaluation +€1.4m; elimination of def. 20p Shares +€4.6m. g) Share premium +€43.3m; goodwill w/o -€0.4m. h) Property revaluation +€15.7m.

Comment:

Sale and exit of Northern Ireland properties should straighten out the balance sheet and make it attractive to a bidder with net assets of €0.42 per share. But looking back over the 5 and 10 year performances when property values went sky-high, the investor must be sorely disappointed.

BALANCE SHEET: DECEMBER 31 2001.   € m

Share Capital:				
		Tangible Assets		91.1
		Financial Assets		59.0
387,915,285 Ord. €0.10 shares	38.8	Current Assets	242.9	
		Current Liabilities	153.4	
Reserves	132.6	Net Current Assets		89.4
		Medium Debt		(68.1)
Shareholders' Funds	171.4	Net Tangible Assets		171.4

ELAN CORPORATION plc

BUSINESS: Pharmaceutical manufacturer
REGISTERED OFFICE: Monksland, Athlone, Co Westmeath.
HEAD OFFICE: Lincoln House, Lincoln Place, Dublin.
Tel: 01- 7094000; Fax: 01- 6624949. **SECRETARY:** M. Pearson
REGISTRAR & TRANSFER OFFICE: Computershare Investor
Services (Ireland) Ltd, Heron House, Corrig Road, Sandyford
Industrial Estate, Dublin. Depositary for ADS: Bank of New York,
101 Barclay Street, 22 West, New York, NY 10286, USA
PRINCIPAL BANKERS: Barclays Bank plc; Bank of Ireland
AUDITORS: KPMG   **SOLICITORS:** A & L Goodbody;
McCann Fitzgerald; Cahill Gordon & Reindel.
STOCKBROKERS: Davy Stockbrokers
DIRECTORS: G Armen (Chairman - 50), B Boushel (72),
L Crowley (66), A Gillespie (52), A Gray (57), J Groom (64),
K McGowan (59), K McIntyre (67), K. McLaughlin (58),
D Selkoe (59), R. Thornburgh (70), D Tully (71).
SHARE CAPITAL: Authorised: 600m €0.05 shares, 1,000
Exec €1.25 shares, 25,000 'B' Exec €0.05 shares. **Issued:**
350,106,441 Ord €0.05 shares, 1,000 Exec €0.0125 shares,
21,375 'B' Exec €0.05 shares.
STAFF: 4,528.   **SCRIP DIVIDEND:** No.

CAPITAL HISTORY:

Nov 1990 rights issue at £5.63 each for 3,926,273 Units (1 Callable Ordinary Share in Drug Research Corp plc 'DRC' plus 1 Warrant to buy 1.5 Ord shares of Elan). June 1991: 2,141,997 Ord shares at $20.11 each. Issued 1,806,021 Ord shares at $10 each in exchange for subordinated notes. Feb 1992: issued 75,845 Ord shares at $29.667 each re purchase of Vega Biomedical Corp. Issued 97,500 Ord shares at $32 each. June 1992: 115,470 Ord shares issued at $32.83 each for 70% of Elan Pharma S.A. Issued 22,290 Ord shares for $32.83 each raising $732,000 in cash. July 1992 Issued 23,592 Ord shares for $30.60 per share raising $722,000 in cash. Nov 1992 Units separated into 2 underlying securities with the warrants exercisable at $15.38 per share from 14.11.1992 to 14.11.1995. During 1993 33,314 Ord shares issued to former shareholders of DDS. April 1993: 43,604 Ord 4p shares issued at $30.625 & shareholders of DDS. July 1993: 2,485,358 Ord 4p shares issued at $33.175. 28,726 Ord 4p shares issued at $31.00. Aug 1993: 3,922,766 Units of one share in ATS plus one Elan warrant for $73.5m . Warrants exercisable at $39.26 each. Jan 1996: 1.6 million ADS offered at $54.50 each. June 1996: 9.8 million Ord 4p shares issued on take-over of Athena. Aug 1996: 2-for-1 scrip issue. Jan 1998: Elan and Neuralab placed 1,250,000 units of one share in Neuralab plus one warrant to purchase Elan ADS at $65.01 per ADS. May 1999: Scrip issue 1-for-1. May 2000: Issued 15.6m Ord $0.05 shares re purchase of The Liposome Co for $732m. Nov 2000: Issued 30.6m Ord $0.05 shares re purchase of Dura Pharmaceuticals for $1.59billion.

COMPANY HISTORY:

Elan was founded in 1969 by D Panoz and its first product was launched in 1972. 1980: Elan agent appointed in US resulting in contract in 1981 with AH Robins Co and Marion Merrell Dow. Formed Elan Pharmaceutical Research Corp in US. In 1982 shares in EPRC offered on NASDAQ raising US$4.8m to construct facility in Georgia. In 1984 did a 1-for-1 share swap with publicly quoted EPRC and itself floated publicly on NASDAQ raising US$9.2m to expand Athlone. In 1986 raised US$34.2m in share placing. Invested US$3.8m in O'Brien Pharmaceuticals Inc and acquired Hi Chem Diagnostics Inc in California for US$5.1m. In 1989 raised US$20m through subordinated notes in EPRC to fund purchase of Knight Medical Inc. This debt was redeemed in 1991 by payment of US$8.3m with subsequent payment of US$1.5m earn-out. Elan bought remaining shares in O'Brien for 226,329 Elan shares. 1990: purchased Drug Delivery Systems Inc for US$4.5m plus earn-out of which US$4.1m has been paid. Nov 1990: rights issue of Units raised US$38.5m. In 1991 rights issue at US$33 per share raised US$47.1m. Oct 1992 Elan International Finance Ltd (EIF), a subsidiary, issued at substantial discount US$431.25m Liquid Yield Option Notes (LYONs) due 2012. Gross proceeds: US$138.78m (£77.6m) at $321.81 per $1,000 nominal at maturity with no interest giving 5.75% p.a. yield to maturity. Jan 1993: Panoz trust, Fountainhead (Bermuda), offers 1,376,206 Elan shares at approx £20 each (reducing holding from 18% to 14%). July 1993: Panoz predicts pre-tax profits to rise by 50% p.a. over next 4 years. Plans rights issue for £55m for investment in Advanced Therapeutic Systems (ATS) - 1 ATS at $20 for every 8 shares in Elan and will receive a 5year warrant to acquire 1 Elan share. Nov 1993 Obtains official quote on Dublin Stock Exchange. April 1994: pays £2.1m for 4.5% of loss-making Dura Pharmaceuticals. May 1994: D. Panoz has sold 679,500 Ord 4p shares. July 1994: Paid £0.7m for 51% of Elan Pharma (Taiwan) Ltd. Oct 1994: Invested £6.9m in Nale Laboratories Ltd for 26.6% of equity. Jan 1995: Shares listed on NYSX. Profits dependent on Cardizem CD and Verelan in mature markets. Feb 1995: Bought minority partner in Elan Medical Technologies for £2.2m. May 1995: N. Panoz and J. McCabe resign as Directors. July 1995: Received warning re plant approval from FDA. Sept 1995: Paid £5m licence fee to mfg patch drugs for Ethical Holdings. Dec 1996: D. Panoz sells 1.5 million shares grossing approx £52m. May 1996: Year end change to Dec. June 1996: $537m (£406m) takeover of Athena. Nov 1996: Axogen, an Elan related company raises $83 (£50m) on NYSE. Jan 1997: Sold Nutritional Medical for $4.3m incurring a book loss of $18m. Dec 1997: Announced purchase of Sano Corp for £425m in shares. April 1998: Buys Carrnick Laboratories for $150m. April 1999: *Fortune* criticises Elan for putting some development costs 'off balance sheet'. Application to FDA re ziconotide; shares reach $59 from a year high of $88. Jan 2000: Buys Neuralab for $76.3m. May 2000: Acquires Liposome for $732m. June 2000: Ziconotide approved. July 2000: Makes provision of $344m re change in accounting methods concerning amortising 'up-front' fees. Sept 2000: Buys Dura for $1.6billion in shares. Dec 2000: Buys Quadrant Healthcare for $86m. Jan 2001: Elan ranked in *Forbes* Global 400 Best Companies. Top products in 2000: Zanaflex $91m sales, Skelaxin $82m, Diagnostics $70m, Abelcet $64m, Permax $53m, Maxipime $51m, 6 others total $171m. Sept 2001 Buys portfolio of products from Roxane. Buys Delsys Pharma for $50m. Jan 2002: *Wall Street Journal* queries Elan's accounts. Feb 2002: Profits warning. March 2002: 30 class actions against Elan. Abandons Alzheimer's drug. Moodys downgrade Elan's debt to junk status. July 2002: D Geaney & T Lynch resign. Aug 2002: To raise cash $1.5bn from asset sales; 1,000 staff to go.

Share Price Sept 2001 - Sept 2002

1. €47.50 10.01.02 Wall Street Journal queries
2. €15.90 21.03.02 Moody's downgrade
3. €2.35 09.07.02 Geaney & Lynch resign

FINANCIAL DIARY:

Interim Results Announced	30.07.2002
Interim Dividend Payout	None
Final Results Announced	04.02.2002
Annual General Meeting	19.08.2002
Final Dividend Payout	None

FIVE YEAR SHARE PRICE TREND

1997	High	48.53 (Oct)	Low	24.76 (Apr)
1998	High	69.45 (July)	Low	44.86 (Jan)
1999	High	80.00 (Mar)	Low	22.35 (Nov)
2000	High	66.75 (Oct)	Low	26.35 (Jan)
2001	High	73.80 (June)	Low	44.60 (Dec)

INVESTMENT PERFORMANCE:

Five Year Investment Performance: €4,152

HALF YEARLY PERFORMANCES: $ m

Six month to	31.12.00	30.06.01	31.12.01	30.06.02
Revenue	595.3	890.6	850.1	899.8
Pre-tax profit/(-)	171.7	218.7	(1,088.5)	(750.0)
Profit % Sales	28.8	34.6	-	-

SECTORAL ANALYSIS: (previous year)

Revenue: Ireland 39% (44%), Europe 5% (5%), US 53% (46%). Drug delivery 19% (38%), biopharmaceuticals 81% (62%).

TEN YEAR REVIEW:

12 months to December 31	£'000 1993 f)	£'000 1994 f)	£'000 1995 f)	£'000 1996 f)	US $'000 1996	US $'000 1997	US $'000 1998	US$'000 1999 9 Months	US$'m 2000	US$'m 2001
Revenues	89,771	107,023	118,899	141,686	235,559	389,156	676,734	1,007,795	1,302.0	1,740.7
Profits before Tax	22,288	(51,101)	40,487	56,987	(352)	180,555	150,328	343,136	351.1	(869.8)
Tax	1,141	797	433	340	774	1,186	3,874	7,288	9.0	17.4
Profit after Tax	21,147	(51,898)	40,054	56,647	(1,126)	179,369	146,454	335.848	342.1	(887.2)
Minority	+234	+1,577	+1,628	(203)	+338	+260	(38)	(31)	-	-
Available for Shareholders	21,381	(50,321)	41,682	56,444	(788)	179,629	146,416	335,817	342.1	(887.2)
Dividend	-	-	-	-	-	-	-	-	-	-
Retained Profit (Loss)	21,381	(50,321)	41,682	56,444	(788)	179,629	146,416	335,817	342.1	(887.2)
Increase (Decr) in Reserves	31,413 b)	11,456	31,895 d)	129,682 e)	(32,261) g)	305,866 h)	1,560,093 i)	355,543 k)	2,625.5	(262.2)
Shareholders' Funds	137,879	149,442	184,430	314,385	464,075	770,444	2,332,102	2,687,668	5,315.5	5,054.5
Net Ordinary Dividend per Share	-	-	-	-	-	-	-	-	-	-
Earnings per Share	11p		19.5p	26.2p		$0.91	$0.62	$1.26	$1.19 j)	-

b) Share premium £4.9m; currency gain £5.0m. d) Currency loss £9.8m. e) Share premium +£68.6m f) Year ended March 31 g) Goodwill w/o - $584.2m; share premium +$550.8m. h) Share premium +$147m; currency loss -$20m. i) Share premium +$1.39billion j) Based upon 267.1m shares. k) Share premium +$39.6m

BALANCE SHEET: DECEMBER 31 2001. US$ m

Share Capital:		Tangible Assets	401.1
349,836,938 Ord €0.05shares,		Financial Assets	1,957.1
1,000 Exec €0.0125 shares,	19.9	Current Assets 2,552.2	
21,375 'B' Exec €0.05 shares		Current Liabilities 1,331.7	
		Net Current Assets	1,223.5
Reserves	5,034.6	Medium Debt	(3,048.2)
		Minority	(5.2)
		Net Tangible Assets	528.3
		Intangibles	4,526.2
Shareholders' Funds	5,054.5	Net Assets	5,054.5

Comment:

2002 will be a year Elan will prefer to forget. Top marks to American finacial journalists for rumbling the Elan accounts. No great plaudits for Elan board.

To say it has not been a happy year for Elan is probably an understatement. Right from the off in

The second important consideration for investors is the competition for each of the products. Generic forms of Ceclor Myambutol were approved and in 2001 significantly reducing the and profitability of these products. ult Elan had to write-off a total of in intangibles in 2001 but in the year a further write-down for l, which stands in the balance sheet , is expected. So it can be seen that g the intellectual property value over ted life of a drug can be sometimes e expectations of Elan.

June 2002 an Elan competitor FDA approval to market a generic for Zanaflex 4mg dose form. The ere is that 75% of prescriptions for are for the 4mg dose. In 2002 or Zanaflex were $161.7m. Zanaflex ed approximately 9% of Elan's total s a result Elan expects a significant the sales and profitability of this e carrying value of Zanaflex, fortu-nly $12.1 million.

e area of intangibles, intellectual and impairment of values is well in Elan's Form 20-F. In August 1998 red Neurex for $810miilion. At that

efficacy

e of drugs in humans

ups of patients to determine xpanded evidence of safety

cted in patients to l proof of efficacy and safety

ex was developing a ziconotide price paid for Neurex was primarily o acquired intellectual property. In was forced to write down this intel-perty by a whopping $500million ays in the product launch schedule d revenue projections for Prialt due tion in the projected target patient for that drug whose reduced sales are now estimated to be in excess ion.

ample of this unhappy state of en in the purchase of Sano in 1998 nillion. Sano was developing l drugs. The purchase price was located to intellectual property but the value was decimated by n to reflect reduced revenue The bottom line for all of these s is that the bottom-line has had to f a massive $1,010 million in 2001. As if these weren't bad enough the FDA told

,000 out of a total of 4,500 people (chart B).

the pharmaceutical industry to cease producing drugs containing PPA. This little product euthanasia cost Elan $36million for product returns and inventory write-offs.

Much of the recent controversy has highlighted the business ventures carried out by Elan. They had approximately 55 active business ventures in May 2002. The pipeline of products in development by these business ventures includes approximately 30 products in clinical development including 4 in Phase 111 stages. The business ventures focus primarily on neurology, pain, oncology and the utilisation of drug delivery techniques. Elan received and recorded initial revenue from the business ventures $173million in 2001, $321million in 2000 and $226million in 1999. Elan's initial investments in the businesses were $229 million in 2001, $436million in 2000 and $329million in 1999. In 2000 the SEC instructed Elan to begin deferring and amortising non-refundable up-front licence fees received from these 'business ventures' over the performance period of 2 to 3 years. The SEC enquiries are ongoing and until they are complete final adjustments are conjecture.

Elan's gearing is not a pretty sight. In the short-term the company owes over $700 million and a further $250m in 2002/3 while a further $2,318million needs to be coughed-up over the near term. The newly elected chairman, Garo Armen, (about whom many analysts said 'who?' when they learned of his appointment), has vowed to raise $1billion through asset sales over the next nine months. "We have to shore up our balance sheet so there is absolutely no concern whatsoever about liquidity. We also want to streamline and simplify our balance sheet so that you don't have to go through 55 footnotes in order to interpret what our cash level is, what our cash earnings are and what our future looks like."

Meanwhile Elan will have to fight off a batch of class actions in the US from the likes of Fox Asset Management who lost $12million when the shares slumped in value. And on top of this there is the question of downsizing the operation with up to 1,000 jobs on the line. Whether all the bad news is out of the way yet and whether running the company 'by committee' is a recipe for future growth is a moot point. Each quarterly report and each product development announcement will be picked over assiduously.

(Most of the details here have been culled from Elan's Annual Report and Form 20-F which we recommend as compulsory reading for any astute investor)

Chart B Sales Force	Primary Care	Hospital	Neurology	Specialty/ Dermatology	Clinical Sales Consultants
Number in US	520	200	165	70	50
Products	Skelaxin Sonata	Abelcet Azactam	Frova Roxicodone	Aclovate Cutivate	Myobloc
	Zanaflex	Maxipime	Slexaxin Zanaflex Zonegran	Temovate	

ENNEX INTERNATIONAL plc

(Exploration Securities Market)

BUSINESS: Natural resource exploration company.
REGISTERED OFFICE: 11 Mespil Road, Dublin.
Tel: 01-6677310. Fax: 01-6677311.
HEAD OFFICE: as regd office.
SECRETARY: C Casey. **REGISTRARS & TRANSFER**
OFFICE: Computershare Investor Services (Ireland) Ltd, Heron House, Corrig Road, Sandyford Industrial Estate, Dublin.
PRINCIPAL BANKERS: AIB Bank.
AUDITORS: Ernst & Young
SOLICITORS: Whitney, Moore & Keller
STOCKBROKERS: J&E Davy.
DIRECTORS: B. Cusack (Chairman - 53), C. Schaffalitzky (Mgr Dir - 49), J. McCarthy (42), M. McCarthy (75), C Casy, J Craven, G Wrafter.
SHARE CAPITAL: Authorised: 450m Ord. €0.0125 shares.
Issued: 282,004,322 Ord. €0.0125 shares.
STAFF: 20.   **SCRIP DIVIDEND:** No.

CAPITAL HISTORY:

Incorporated May 1984. May 1984 issued 30,000 Ord. 10p shares of 10p each for 100p each. June 1984 issued 27,837,493 share at 100p for acquisition of Summit Exploration. June 1984 public flotation of 24,000,000 Ord. 10p shares at 50p each. June 1987 'rights' issue and placing of 25m shares raising £14m stg. at 62p on the basis of 46.62 shares per 100 (neither Northgate nor Westfield took up their entitlements). Feb. 1988: 4,310,345 Ord. 10p shares issued on acquisition of 50.4% of Oil Search Corporation. April 1997: 10 million Ord 10p shares issued on purchase of Oranmore Resources Ltd. Also 6 million warrants issued to subscribe for shares at 10p each till 21/4/98. Dec 1997: Issued 22.5m Ord 10p shares on purchase of Zinc Corporation of Kazakhstan and 15 million warrants at 30p per share. Feb 1998: 10 million Ord 10p shares issued at 27.5p each on exercise of warrants. Shares offloaded at 34.65p each. April 1998: 6 million Ord 10p shares issued at 10p each. Dec 1998: Issue of 30m Ord 1p shares and Warrants to subscribe for 15m Ord 1p shares @ 30p each re purchase of Zinc Corp. April 1999: Rights issue (2-for-7) 37,874,496 Ord 1p shares @ 5p each. June 2000: Placed 7,580,785 Ord 1p shares @ €0.063 with warrant to subscribe for 1 share for every 2 shares by 30.06.2001 at €0.076 per share. Feb 2001: Placed 14,231,470 Ord 10p shares @ €0.057 each. Sept 2001: Shares changed to €0.0125 and deferred shares of €0.114 each. 78m Ord €0.0125 shares issued re Ariam and Gostem @ €0.038 each. Placed 11,756,834 Ord shares @ €0.034 each.

COMPANY HISTORY:

Ennex originally set up to acquire the principal European mineral interests of Northgate and Westfield and the oil and gas interests of Westfield. During 1985 Ennex reported excellent drilling results on the Sperrin Mountains gold prospect. Also participated in an open pit gold mine in Nevada. In 1986 announced 300,000 ounce gold reserve in the Sperrin Mountains. Developments 1987-94: August 1987: Announced 150,000 ounce Gold reserve in Scotland. Acquired 20% interests in two gold mine properties in Australia. January 1988: Acquired controlling interest in Oil Search Corp. by issue of 4,310,345 shares at 40p each. April 1988: Base metal discovery in Rathdowney. Nov. 1988: Announces that it has increased reserves at the Cononish property in Scotland and re-organisation of U.K. oil interests. September 1989: Exploration staff reduced by 5 to 18. October 1989: Sold 20% in 2 Australian mines to Whim Creek for $8m and as a result Ennex lost $5m. December 1989: Oil and Gas interests sold for $2.5million. January 1990: Northgate announces it has acquired Westfield's holding and now holds 33% of Ennex. April 1990: Share premium account reduced from IR£47.6m to IR£27.3m by offsetting deficit in P & L of IR£20.3m. 21% interest in Little Bald Mountain Mine Nevada sold for $250,000. October 1990: High Court informed that Ennex has lost £20m on unsuccessful exploration. March 1991: Scottish gold mine has at most 5 year life. Would need 7 year life for commercial viability. Exploration continuing. May 1992: J. Teeling plus associate company (Norwest Holdings) acquire Northgates 25m shares (29.8%) for £1.3m or 5.2p each share. "Gold prices of under $350 per oz make new gold mines uneconomic in most developed countries" - P. Hughes. April 1993: Hughes acquires 20m shares from Teeling and other. May 1993: Breakeven gold price at Cononish now less than $400 per oz. Jan 1995: Sold Scottish (Cononish) Mine for US$4.25m plus 0.5m shares in Caledonia Mining Corporation (total value US$7.925m). Aug 1995: Pat Hughes interests reduce holdings from 23.8% to 4.76%. March 1997: Buys Oranmore

Resources for £1m in shares. April 1997: Intention acquire option mine in Kazaksan by 31.12.199 May issue 30 million shares and warrants to buy million shares at 30p each. Norwest Holdings ha sold 16 million Ennex shares at about 22p eac June 1997: Pat Hughes sells 2.5m Shares at 20p s each. Dec 1997: Buys 95% of Zinc Corporation Kazakhstan for 22.5m shares (at 36p each wor £8m) plus £1.65m cash. Shares not to be so before Jan 1999. First ingot to be produced b 2,001. Aug 2000: Endeavour Capital buy 15% Ennex. Feb 2001: Raised £640,000 from sha placing. Sept 2001: Buys 25% in Marathon Royal and 5% in oil deposits in Faroes-Shetland.

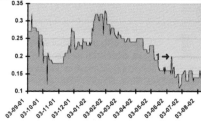
Share Price Sept 2001 - Sept 2002

1. €0.20 12.06.02 Final results

FINANCIAL DIARY

Interim Results Announced:	28.09.2001
Interim Dividend Payout:	Not likely
Final Results Announced:	12.06.2002
Annual General Meeting:	17.08.2002
Final Dividend Payout:	Not likely

FIVE YEAR SHARE PRICE TREND €

1997	High	0.036 (Apr)	Low	0.011 (Mar)
1998	High	0.046 (May)	Low	0.01 (Nov)
1999	High	0.01 (Mar)	Low	0.0025 (Nov)
2000	High	0.01 (Aug)	Low	0.008 (May)
2001	High	0.066 (Jan)	Low	0.012 (Oct)

INVESTMENT PERFORMANCE

Five Year Investment Performance:	€242
Ten Year Investment Performance:	€383

TEN YEAR REVIEW: $'000

12 months to Dec. 31	1992	1993	1994	1995	1996	1997	1998	1999	2000	2001
Revenue	-	-	-	-	-	-	-	-	-	119
Profit (Loss) before tax	(2,787)	(336)	(91)	(198)	(5,167)	(1,314)	(690)	(3,921)	(4,238)	(23,094)
Tax	+3	+1	+2	1	-	-	-	-	-	21
Profit (Loss) after tax	(2,784)	(335)	(89)	(199)	(5,167)	(1,314)	(690)	(3,921)	(4,238)	(23.115)
Minority Interests	-	-	-	-	-	-	-	-	-	-
Available for Shareholders	(2,784)	(335)	(89)	(199)	(5,167)	(1,314)	(690)	(3,921)	(4,238)	(23.115)
Ordinary Dividend	-	-	-	-	-	-	-	-	-	-
Retained Profit/(Loss)	(2,784)	(335)	(89)	(199)	(5,167)	(1,314)	(690)	(3.921)	(4,238)	(23.115)
Increase (Decrease) in Reserves	(2,784)	(335)	(89)	(199)	(5,167)	6,087 a)	1,763 b)	(2,164) d)	(3,880)	(20,588)
Shareholders Funds'	17,864	17,529	17,440	17,241	12,074	22,969	26,960	25,293	21,505	2,070
Ordinary Dividend per Share	-	-	-	-	-	-	-	-	-	-
Earnings Per Share	-	-	-	-	-	-	-	-	-	-

a) Share premium +$7.4m. b) Share premium +$2.5m. d) Share premium +$1.8m.

BALANCE SHEET: DECEMBER 31 2001 US $'000

Share Capital: 282,004,322 Ord. €0.0125 shares	19,268	Fixed Assets	31
		Current Assets	557
		Current Liabilities	694
Reserves	(17,198)	Net Current Liabilities	(137)
		Medium debt	(601)
		Net Tangible Assets	(707)
		Intangibles	2,777
Shareholders' Funds	2,070	Net Assets	2,070

Comment:

This is a pure gamble.

FBD HOLDINGS plc

BUSINESS: Insurance broking and underwriting.

REGISTERED OFFICE: FBD House, Bluebell, Dublin. Tel: 01-4554292 Fax: 01-4554303

HEAD OFFICE: as regd office.

SECRETARY: D. Flynn.

REGISTRARS & TRANSFER OFFICE: Computershare Investor Services (Ireland) Ltd, Corrig Road, Sandyford Industrial Estate, Dublin.

PRINCIPAL BANKERS: AIB Bank.

AUDITORS: Deloitte & Touche.

SOLICITORS: P. O'Riade & Co

STOCKBROKERS: Bloxham Stockbrokers.

DIRECTORS: M Berkery (Chairman - 54), P O'Callaghan (Ch. Executive - 63), J Donnelly (54) J Duggan, W Duron (67), P Fitzsimons (55), P. Lynch (57), M Morley (63), O'Keeffe (80), J Rea (65), H Ryan (73), A Wouters (63), Dillon.

SHARE CAPITAL: Authorised: 51,326,000 Ord. €0.60 shares, 1,340,000 14% Non-cum. pref. €0.60 shares, 2,750,000 8% non-cum. pref. €0.60 shares. **Issued:** 41,816,683 Ord. €0.60 shares, 1,340,000 14% non-cum. pref. €0.60 shares, 3,532,292 8% non-cum. pref. €0.60 shares.

STAFF: 995. **SCRIP DIVIDEND:** No

CAPITAL HISTORY:

Incorporated October 1988. 300,000 Ord. 10p shares issued. Oct. 88 acquired FBD Insurance 68,859,126 Ord. 10p shares plus 500,000 % non-cum. pref. £1 shares. Dec 1988 issued million Ord. 10p shares at par in private placing. Issued 170,000 14% non-cum. pref. £1 shares and 1.7m 8% non-cum. pref. 10p shares Assurances du Boerenbond Belge for 40,000 cash. Issued 8,480,000 Ord. 10p shares and 7.5m 8% non-cum. pref. 10p shares 90% of F.B.D. Ltd. Issued 4.25m Ord. 10p shares and 6.25m 8% non-cum. pref. 10p shares 90% of Strongbow Underwriting Agencies d. Issued 500,000 Ord. 10p shares for purchase of International Loss Control Services Ltd.

Issued 100,000 Ord. 10p shares for purchase of International Risk Management Services Ltd. June 1989: 14% Non-Cum Pref £1 shares subdivided into 10p shares. Issued 1,438,350 Ord. 10p shares and 2,211,460 8% non-cum. pref. 10p shares for 50% of FBD Life & Pensions. Issued 15m Ord. 10p shares to Farmers Business Developments and 10m Ord. 10p shares to Assurances du Boerenbond Belge for £2.5m cash. Aug 1989: All Ord. 10p shares converted to Ord. 50p shares and all pref. 10p shares converted to pref. 50p share. Sept 1989: 3,973,187 Ord. 50p shares issued under terms of rights issue at €1.02, raising £3.2m. Sept. 1989: 4.5m Ord. 50p shares placed at €1.22 each.

COMPANY HISTORY:

F.B.D. Insurance commenced trading in 1970 with approximately 3,000 farmer shareholders (75% of equity) and Assurances du Boerenbond Belge (25% of equity). In 1974 Life and Pensions Division established and also engaged in non-agricultural and commercial business. 1988 reformed itself into a holding company. Sept. 1989 quoted on stockmarket. Feb 1992: Acquires additional 52% Ranches Reunidos S.A. (bringing total to 100%) on which £25m spent to date with £7m to go. Previous partner takes over 380 acres out of 1,000 acres instead. Oct 1992: FBD rumoured to be interested in ACC Bank in partnership with Credit Agricole. Feb 1994: Merger talks with Hibernian Group aborted. April 2001: Bought 206,000 own shares @ €4.32 each. June 2002: Buys 200,000 own shares @ €5.25 each.

Share Price Sept 2001 - Sept 2002

1. €4.95 04.03.02 Final results
2. €5.25 26.06.02 Buys own shares

FINANCIAL DIARY

Interim Results Announced:	28.08.2002
Interim Dividend Payout:	04.10.2002
Final Results Announced:	04.03.2002
Annual General Meeting:	23.04.2002
Final Dividend Payout:	26.04.2002

SHARE PRICE TREND €

Year	High		Low	
1997	High	4.51 (Dec)	Low	2.73 (Jan)
1998	High	7.11 May)	Low	4.57 (Jan)
1999	High	5.33 (Jan)	Low	4.49 (Mar)
2000	High	5.20 (Jan)	Low	4.25 (June)
2001	High	5.20 (Dec)	Low	4.00 (Sept)

INVESTMENT PERFORMANCE:

Five Year Investment Performance:	€2,182
Ten Year Investment Performance:	€4,991

HALF YEARLY PERFORMANCE: € m

Six months to:	31.12.00	30.06.01	31.12.01	30.06.02
Turnover	138.1	151.0	154.8	172.3
Profit before Tax	33.0	8.4	20.3	14.1
Profit % Sales	23.9	5.6	13.1	8.2

SECTORAL ANALYSIS (previous year)

Sales: Insurance 80% (78%); financial services 4% (4%); leisure property 16% (18%); Ireland 89% (87%); Europe 11% (13%)

TEN YEAR REVIEW: € m

months to Dec 31	1992	1993	1994	1995	1996	1997	1998 a)	1999	2000	2001
Premium Income	118.40	139.83	152.19	173.43	184.61	199.28	211.92	230.0	269.5	305.8
Profit before Tax	14.57	16.91	16.92	17.72	18.63	18.09	21.20	(7.2)	40.4	28.7
Tax	5.38	5.61	4.84	3.85	3.94	1.96	2.52	+7.7	5.3	2.8
Profit after Tax	9.19	11.30	12.08	13.87	14.69	16.13	18.68	0.5	35.1	25.9
Minority Interests	0.01	+0.04	(0.19)	+0.02	0.02	+0.06	(0.04)	(0.2)	(0.5)	(0.3)
Preference Dividends	0.25	0.22	0.22	0.22	0.22	0.30	0.3	0.3	0.3	0.3
Available for Shareholders	8.93	11.12	11.67	13.67	14.45	15.89	18.34	0.0	34.3	25.3
Ordinary Dividend	2.30	2.65	3.00	3.47	3.96	4.57	5.45	6.2	7.2	8.1
Retained Profit	6.63	8.47	8.67	10.20	10.49	11.32	12.89	(6.2)	27.1	17.2
Increase (Decrease) in Reserves	0.69 e)	13.99 f)	0.67 g)	14.22 h)	12.71 i)	18.62 j)	33.06 m)	(4.4)	27.7	38.6 n)
Shareholders' Funds	47.27	61.34	62.05	76.28	89.04	107.93	141.26	136.9	164.8	202.0
Net Ordinary Dividend per Share (€)	0.057	0.066	0.074	0.086	0.098	0.111	0.132	0.15	0.173	0.195
Earnings per Share (€)	0.222	0.276	0.288	0.338	0.357	0.390	0.446	0.08	0.824	0.60 k)

a) Subsequently restated. e) Exchange loss €3.9m; goodwill w/o €0.6m. f) Asset revaluation + €6.7m; currency loss - €1.3m. g) Investment portfolio devaluation -€7.7m. h) Revaluation of reserves +€4.2m net. i) Revaluation surplus net +€2.8m. j) Revaluation surplus +€12.3m minus def. tax -€3.2m. k) Based upon 41.8m shares. m) Revaluation surplus net +€22m. n) Property revaluation +€20.5m.

Comment:

This is unexciting and seems to have nothing better to do but to buy back its shares in the marketplace. With net asset value per share of €4.83 and the dividend covered three times, the shares look fairly valued.

BALANCE SHEET: DECEMBER 31 2001. €'m

Share Capital:	25.1	Fixed Assets		17.2
41,816,683 Ord. €0.60 shares		Investments		765.9
Reserves	176.9	Current Assets	94.9	
		Net Current Liabilities	59.8	
		Net Current Assets		35.1
		Medium debt		(608.3)
		Minority & Pref shares		(7.9)
Shareholders' Funds	202.0	Net Tangible Assets		202.0

47

Knowledge is Power

Private Research Ltd, Ireland's premier company information and corporate research firm, provides services to companies in Ireland, Europe and Internationally. We pride ourselves on offering the customer an accurate, efficient service while keeping value for money in mind, enabling you to be fully informed and to make the correct decisions.

Call us for all your company information, analysis and company formation requirements.

● COMPANY INFORMATION

Private Research provides public and private company information and analysis to clients on five continents. We specialise in Irish and UK company information within one hour. Call us to enquire on any company, director, company name or business name. Get the latest information released from the Companies Office in Dublin, Belfast and London

Contact: Geri

● PRIVATE RESEARCH SOUTHERN IRELAND

Private Research supplies Ireland with it's only monthly dedicated analysis of private Irish companies as they file their results in the Companies Registration Office, detailing their results, directors, advisors and revealing incisive information gleaned from their filed results. This analysis is used by companies to judge creditworthiness, view competitor assessment throughout Irish business and contains up to date, accurate and incisive company information - a must for all people in Irish business today.

Contact: Sandra

● IRISH INDUSTRY REPORTS

From industries as diverse as Advertising to Steel, Private Research produces specific reports on the companies involved in Irish industry in an easy to read format.

These reports are an excellent way of benchmarking your company's performance against competitors in your own industry as well as providing information for potential acquisitions and industry credit worthiness information.

Contact: Franz

● MARKETING DATABASES

The most up-to-date contact information on the premier Irish Companies (North and South) is held within Private Research's database on 380,000 Irish companies. Generate sales leads, up to date company executive names, specific industry targeting as well as the ability to mail and fax merge.

Contact: Brian

● COMPANY FORMATION

We provide the most efficient, company formation facility in Ireland, the UK and elsewhere in the world with professionalism and discretion assured. Contact us with the company name you require and we will inform you of its availability. Should you wish to form the company, it will be live within 5 working days at the cost of €252 plus VAT.

Contact: Mark

We do not compromise on quality.... Why should you.

PRIVATE RESEARCH

● Private Research Southern Ireland ● PARAGON ● Company Formations ●
● Private Research Motor Edition ● Industry Reports ● Individual Company Searches ●
● The Irish Stock Market Annual ● ASPECT Premier 2,500 Irish Companies ●

Private Research Ltd. Coliemore House, Coliemore Road, Dalkey, Co Dublin. Tel: 01-2848911. Fax: 01-2048177
Web site: www.privateresearch.ie   E-Mail: info@privateresearch.ie

FIRST ACTIVE plc

BUSINESS: Residential mortgages and retail savings.
REGISTERED OFFICE: Skehan House, Booterstown, Co Dublin **HEAD OFFICE:** First Active House, Central Park, Leopardstown, Dublin. Tel: 01-2075000.
Fax: 01-2074900. **SECRETARY:** R K Bergin
REGISTRAR & TRANSFER OFFICE: Computershare Investor Services (Ireland) Ltd, Heron House, Corrig Road, Sandyford Industrial Estate, Dublin.
PRINCIPAL BANKERS: Bank of Ireland, Lloyds Bank
AUDITORS: PricewaterhouseCoopers
SOLICITORS: Arthur Cox; Simmons & Simmons
STOCKBROKERS: Davy Stockbrokers; Hoare Govett Ltd
DIRECTORS: J Callaghan (Chairman - 60), T Gaffney (43), J Kelly (62), C McCarthy (Ch Ex - 40), K Milliken (52), H Murdoch (64), M Torpey (43), E Whelan (62), B Wilson (57).
SHARE CAPITAL: Authorised: 200million Ord €0.32 shares. **Issued:** 143,228,349 Ord €0.32 shares.
STAFF: 696 **SCRIP DIVIDEND:** No

CAPITAL HISTORY:

Founded in 1861. Sept 1998 converted to First Active plc. Issued 8 Ord 25p shares at par and a further 119,992 Ord 2p shares at par to First Active Nominees on behalf of Qualifying Members Free Shares on Conversion. Issued 3,430,500 Ord 25p shares free to Qualifying Members shares on flotation. 46,222,222 Ord 25p shares issued on flotation @ 225p each for 1.6m 1-for-10 loyalty bonus issue in Sept 1999 to those who have not sold their free shares. Public flotation Oct 1998 by 'tender' between 265p and 380p. However due to stock market collapse price struck at 225p. Jan 1999: Issued 306,700 Ord 25p shares for entitlements under conversion scheme. Sept 1999: Issued 425,400 'loyalty' Ord 25p shares free (23-for-50 shares). Oct 2000: Issued 3,645,000 'loyalty' and free shares (22 shares).

COMPANY HISTORY:

Formerly known as First National Building Society, its origins go back to 1861 when it was formed as the Workingman's Benefit Building Society and was incorporated in 1875. In 1960 it became First National Building Society and since then has expanded organically and by the acquisition of five small building societies including the Grafton Savings and Building Society in 1974 and the Irish Life Building Society in 1993. It has 75 branches in RofI and in 1993 opened in Northern Ireland followed by the purchase of Cheltenham & Gloucester in 1997 with assets of £68m stg. Entered UK market in 1994 when it bought Mortgage Trust (assets £550m stg) and in 1996 bought Mortgage Corporation (assets £1.2billion stg mainly off balance sheet). From 1977 to 1987 assets grew from £107m to £764m and since then assets have grown fivefold to £3.66billion with another £1.2billion non-recourse off balance sheet. In 1998 FNBS (assets £2,646m) is second to Irish Permanent (assets £5,471m), equals EBS (assets £2,642m) and is larger than ICS (assets £1,538m) and Irish Nationwide (assets £1,391m). Oct 1998: Public flotation - first day price reached 290p. Dec 1998: 93k shareholders (95%) hold less than 501 shares. Moves 'tied insurance agency' from Irish Life to Friends First. June 1999: Third mortgage securitisation raises £197m. Aug 1999: Bank of Scotland enters mortgage market. Branch managers criticise executive. Dec 1999: 175 redundant and 25 of 76 branches to close (£10m savings). Jan 2000: J Smyth forced to resign (payoff £540,000 + pension bonus of £249,000). Feb 2000: 85 'agents' to be cancelled. March 2000: Head office to move to Leopardstown. May 2000: Merger talks with Anglo Irish Bank aborted. E Dunphy and S Ross's orchestrated endeavour to oust board-members fails. As 6 shareholders hold 15m shares (11%) democracy (166,050 shareholders) had little say on the day. June 2000: T Shanahan resigns (payoff £400k). Aug 2000: Sells 60% of First Active Financial (UK). Oct 2000: Buys-back own shares and 'placed' in the market; discontinued in March 2001. Nov 2001: Sells Booterstown head office for €20.3m. Sept 2001: €27m free shares unclaimed. Take-over protection to end in Oct 2003. Dec 2001: Buys back 0.4m own shares @ €2.50 each. July 2002: Announces it will buy-back more own shares.

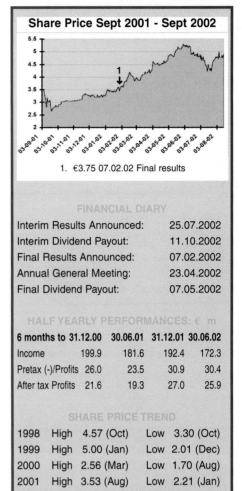

Share Price Sept 2001 - Sept 2002

1. €3.75 07.02.02 Final results

FINANCIAL DIARY

Interim Results Announced:	25.07.2002
Interim Dividend Payout:	11.10.2002
Final Results Announced:	07.02.2002
Annual General Meeting:	23.04.2002
Final Dividend Payout:	07.05.2002

HALF YEARLY PERFORMANCES: € m

6 months to	31.12.00	30.06.01	31.12.01	30.06.02
Income	199.9	181.6	192.4	172.3
Pretax (-)/Profits	26.0	23.5	30.9	30.4
After tax Profits	21.6	19.3	27.0	25.9

SHARE PRICE TREND

1998	High	4.57 (Oct)	Low	3.30 (Oct)
1999	High	5.00 (Jan)	Low	2.01 (Dec)
2000	High	2.56 (Mar)	Low	1.70 (Aug)
2001	High	3.53 (Aug)	Low	2.21 (Jan)

SEVEN YEAR REVIEW: € m

12 months to Dec 31	1995	1996	1997	1998	1999	2000	2001
Income	232.0	265.5	350.4	400.1	355.5	393.1	374.0
Profit (Loss) before Tax	30.6	35.8	40.2	46.5	23.2	41.2	54.4
Tax	7.8	8.9	9.8	11.2	4.6	7.6	8.1
Profit (Loss) after Tax	22.8	26.9	30.4	35.3	18.6	33.6	46.3
Available for Shareholders	22.8	26.9	30.4	35.3	18.6	33.6	46.3
Ordinary Dividend	-	-	-	3.2	14.3	16.5	19.2
Retained Profit	22.8	26.9	30.4	32.1	4.3	17.1	27.1
Increase (Decrease) in Reserves	n/a	n/a	n/a	96.7	(5.5) f)	23.5 g)	26.7
Shareholders' Funds	246.3	226.4	151.4	289.9	286.3	310.9	338.2
Net Ordinary Dividend per share (€)	-	-	-	0.024	0.105	0.118	0.135
Earnings per share (€)	0.213	0.251	0.284	0.362	0.135	0.238	0.33a)

a) Based upon 141.8m shares. b) Share premium +€93.3m, flotation costs -€27.5m. d) After €25.4m restructuring charge.
f) Currency loss -€7.1m. g) Goodwill write-back +€8.4m.

Comment:

The revenue stream is hardly impressive with every chance that the outcome for the current year will not be a record. Their own share buying should support the share price in the short term but the ending of the take-over protection in October 2003 may be too tempting for some.

BALANCE SHEET: DECEMBER 31 2001. € m

Share Capital:		Fixed Assets	56.7
141,800,000 Ord €0.32 shares	45.4	Current Assets	6,080.8
Reserves	292.8	Current Liabilities	5,438.0
		Net Current Assets	642.8
		Medium debt	(361.3)
Shareholders' Funds	338.2	Net Tangible Assets	338.2

FYFFES plc

BUSINESS: Importer and wholesaler of fruit and vegetables
REGISTERED OFFICE: 1 Beresford Street, Dublin.
HEAD OFFICE: as regd office. Tel: 01-8730733. Fax: 01-8730546.
SECRETARY: P. Halpenny.
REGISTRAR & TRANSFER OFFICE: Computershare Investor Services (Ireland) Ltd, Heron House, Corrig Road, Sandyford Ind Estate, Dublin.
PRINCIPAL BANKERS: Allied Irish Banks; Barclays Bank; ABN AMRO.
AUDITORS: KPMG. **SOLICITORS:** Arthur Cox & Co.; S.J. Berwin & Co; Niles Barton & Wilmer. **STOCKBROKERS:** J. & E. Davy, HSBC Securities.
DIRECTORS: N McCann (Chairman - 79), D Bergin (75), J Gernon, C McCann (51), D McCann (Ch Ex - 45), G Scanlan (69), J Tolan, P Cluver.
SHARE CAPITAL: Authorised: 438,000,000 Ordinary $0.6 shares; 58,000,000 IR8.25p (net) Convertible Cumulative Pref. Shares of $1.27 each; 6,5000,000 Unclassified Shares of stg £1 each. **Issued:** 354,326,336 Ord $0.06 shares (including 9,021,610 delisted treasury shares).
STAFF: 2,436. **SCRIP DIVIDEND:** No

CAPITAL HISTORY:

Incorporated January 1980. 15,000,000 Ord. 5p shares issued in December 1980 when Ord. 25p shares split into 5p units. Feb: 1981: Floated on market. In 1983 1,575,332 shares were issued against acquisitions. In 1984 issued 35,617 Ord. 5p shares against acquisitions. March 1985 200,129 Ord. 5p shares issued against acquisition of F.E. Benner Ltd. Sept. 1985 738,518 Ord. 5p shares issued to United Brands (valued at £2.10p each) on acquisition of Fyffes Group, placing of 6,000,000 Ord. 5p share at £2.10p each and issue to United Brands of 6,500,000 7.5% Convertible Cum. Pref. shares of £1 stg. each. March 1987 'scrip' issue of 4-for-1. Dec. 1987 13.5 million Ord. 5p shares issued as part consideration for 14.7% of IDG Plc. July 1988, 329,707 Ord. 5p shares issued on acquisition of H. Marshall Ltd. Dec 1988, 4.378m Ord. 5p shares issued on purchase of J. Dolan Ltd. May 1989, £6.5m Cum. Pref. £1 shares converted to 13,793,396 Ord. 5p shares by United Brands (18.5% of total equity). Nov 1989: 'scrip' of 1-for-2 involving 91,350,461 new Ord. 5p shares. June 1991: Rights issues 56,792,500 IR8.25p (net) convert. cum. Pref. shares (1-for-5) at 110p each. April 1993: 6m 5% Conv Cum Red Pref £1stg shares redeemed. Feb 1996: Issued 3,050,000 Ord 5p shares for purchase of Peviani. Dec 2000: 5.27m ord €0.06 shares issued re conversion of pref shares. Nov 2001: Issues 50,732,000 Ord €0.06 shares on conversion pref shares.

COMPANY HISTORY:

FII was built up in the late 1960s and 1970s by Neil McCann by acquiring a number of private fruit importers and wholesalers. In January 1981 DCC and other institutional investors purchased 25% of FII and in February 1981 dealings began on the Stock Exchange. In 1982 FII increased its shareholding in Torney Bros. Belfast to 45% and Uniplumo to 85%. During 1983 acquired F.E. Benner Ltd. for 1.6m shares. In 1984 took over remaining equity in Torney Bros. and increased its holding in Amalgamated Bottlers to 51.82%. They also acquired an interest in the 2,000 ton 'Arklow Bridge' for tax reasons. May 1985: Purchased Kinsealy Farms Ltd. for £1.5m. They also paid £1.3m (cash and shares) for D.P. McHale (F.I.) Ltd. and £430,000 for

Gillespie. In May 1986 purchased Fyffes Group a UK subsidiary of United Brands USA, for £29.4m and also announced a placing of 6 million shares at 210p each. Sept. 1987: Shares admitted to Full Listing. Oct. 1987: Purchased 3,335,000 shares in Irish Distillers fir £8.1m. Nov. 1987: Acquired 9,244,249 shares in Irish Distillers for £21.4m. March 1988: Bought fruit importer Marshall & Co. for undisclosed sum. June 1988: Pays £5.25m for fruit and veg importer Jack Dolan. Oct 1988: High Court rules that FII sell Irish Distillers stake to Pernod Ricard. Dec 1988: Buys UK based fruit & veg wholesaler Rowe & Co. and GM Gerrards for £14.8m stg. (1.72m ord. shares, £6m worth of 5% convertible preference stock and £2m in unsecured loan stock). Sept 1989: United Brands 18.5% stake placed with institutions. Nov. 1989: Name changes to Fyffes plc. February 1990: Acquired Glass Glover in Scotland for £6.2m. May 1990: Paid £7.5m for Padwa Group. September 1990: Paid £11.1m for J. Lindsay in Scotland. October 1990: Gerrards, Fruit Retail chain, sold. January 1991: Purchased second refrigerated ship for £19m. June 1991: John Callaghan announced as Group Chief Executive. June 1991: Rights issues raises £60.2m. July 1992: Intention to buy 50% of Swedish Saba Trading for £47.5m with option on remaining 50%. Sept 1992: Saba deal aborted. Dec 1992: Balkan Investments (McCann company) sold 10.7m shares at 64p each - DCC took up 7.7m shares. Sold 3m Conv. Pref. shares at 103p each. P McNamee sold 300,000 shares having sold 440,000 at 96p each in June. March 1993: 3 management staff leave and consider competing in fruit market. April 1993: Approach from Dole Foods push up share price to 130p. Dole prepared to pay 115p only (£420m). No deal. May 1993: Joint venture with Coplaca in Canaries. July 1993: Acquires 50% Brdr Lembcke A/s (Denmark). Aug 1993: J Callaghan resigns after less than 2 years. July 1993: Buys 50% Velleman & Tas for £15.9m. Aug 1994: Acquires 70% J.A. Kahl & Co in Germany for £7m. Takes 33% of Sofiprim (France). Oct 1994: Acquired 50% Tropic International. Bought 40% Jamaica Banana Holdings. April 1995: Sells Vangen Services in UK for £16.5m stg. Oct 1995: N. McCann retires as Ch Exec. Jan 1996: Bought Geest Bananas for £150.6m stg with Windward Island Banana DC. Feb 1996: Bought 50% of Peviani in Italy for £3.1m. R. Benner sells 650,000 shares at 105p each. April 1996: C. Comerford (Ex - Greencore) emerges as head of Geest Bananas. Sept 1996: Abandons US market. Feb 1998: Balkan Investments (McCanns) spend £3.2m increasing its stake to 9.6% at prices between 100p and 132p per share. Aug 1998: Sues Geest for £50m stg. Sept 1998: Buys 5.075m own shares at 127p each (£6.5m). Buys further 2.055m shares at 180p each (total now 7.13m). March 1999: Sells 18.5% United Beverages for profit of £2.2m. June 1999: Allegro merges with Gillespies (Fyffes). Sept 1999: Since March 99 Fyffes have bought in 2.6m shares at a cost of £4.17m (prices from &2.20/173p down to &1.75/138p). Nov 1999: Invests £28.4m (shares and cash) + £16.4m (performance related) in European alliance with South African exporter Capespan. Granted option to Capespan to subscribe for 14.568m Fyffes shares @ £1.21stg (Ir149p/$1.89) before Nov 2000.

Share Price Sept 2001 - Sept 2002

1. €1.28 27.02.02 Final results

INVESTMENT PERFORMANCE
Five Years Investment Performance: €1,069
Ten Year Investment Performance: €1,351

SECTORAL ANALYSIS (previous year)
Sales: Ireland/UK 47% (48%), Continent 53% (52%).

FINANCIAL DIARY

Interim Results Announced	02.09.2002
Interim Dividend Payout	04.10.2002
Second Interim Payout	09.01.2002
Final Results Announced	27.02.2002
Annual General Meeting	28.05.2002
Final Dividend Payout	31.05.2002

FIVE YEAR SHARE PRICE TREND €

1997	High	1.50 (Jan)	Low	1.14 (Jly)
1998	High	2.67 (May)	Low	1.40 (Jan)
1999	High	2.40 (Jan)	Low	1.60 (Nov)
2000	High	3.97 (Feb)	Low	0.69 (Nov)
2001	High	1.47 (Sept)	Low	0.80 (Mar)

HALF YEARLY PERFORMANCES: € m

Six months to	31.12.00*	30.06.01	31.12.01	30.06.02
Sales	1,054.4	863.3	739.5	757.0
Profits (-)Before Tax	(12.9)	30.4	27.2	32.6
Profits % Sales	-	3.5	3.7	43

*8 months

Feb 2000: DCC sells 17.9m Fyffes shares @ 252p ($3.20) netting £45.1m. Then sells remainder of its 10.2% stake @ $3.90 each (307p) netting £83m. Marathon Asset Management now holds 5.3% March 2000: Calls off litigation against Geest and Morgan Grenfell pays all costs. Profits warning. Dec 2000: McCanns buy shares €1.00/€0.85 each. May 2001: Winds down worldoffruit.com at £12m cost. Jan 2001: Sues DCC over sale of Fyffes shares in Feb 2000 Aug 2002: Buys 70% Hortim (Czech) for €10.25m.

TEN YEAR REVIEW: € m

12 months to December 31	1992 c)	1993 c)	1994 c)	1995 c)	1996 c)	1997 c)	1998 c)	1999 c)	2000 b)	2001
Sales	665.7	776.3	1,110.5	1,422.4	1,468.6 a)	1,673.8	1,708.8	1688.5	1,859.3	1,602.8
Profit (Loss) before Tax	36.2	40.4	45.8	53.3	61.5	68.6	78.9	83.9	7.5	57.6 q
Tax	7.9	11.1	11.1	11.9	14.6	16.2	18.1	18.1	8.1	14.0
Profit (Loss) after Tax	28.3	29.3	34.7	41.4	46.9	52.4	60.8	65.8	(0.6)	43.6
Minority Interest	(1.2)	(1.4)	(3.6)	(7.1)	(11.7)	(7.6)	(7.2)	(5.8)	(6.9)	(6.7)
Preference Dividend	(6.2)	(6.1)	(5.9)	(5.9)	(5.9)	(5.9)	(5.9)	(5.9)	(6.3)	(4.4)
Available for Shareholders	20.9	21.8	25.1	28.4	29.3	38.9	47.7	54.0	(13.8)	32.5
Ordinary Dividend	4.4	4.9	5.4	6.0	6.7	8.6	10.5	12.4	12.6	14.3
Retained Profit (Loss)	16.5	16.8	19.7	22.4	22.6	30.3	37.2	41.6	(26.4)	18.2
Increase (Decrease) in Reserves	0.9 g)	20.6 h)	(10.3) i)	11.0 j)	16.4 k)	25.4	6.7	54.2	(22.6)	87.7 p
Shareholders' Funds	144.3	165.0	154.7	165.8	182.4	153.0	159.7	213.1	190.8	260.4
Ordinary Dividend per share (€)	0.016	0.018	0.019	0.021	0.023	0.029	0.036	0.043	0.043	0.047
Earnings per Share (€)	0.075	0.077	0.089	0.100	0.103	0.13	0.16	0.18	-	0.109 e

a) Figures subsequently restated. b)14 months. c) Year ended Oct 31. e) Based upon 298.2m shares. g) Currency loss -€14m; goodwill w/o -€2.3m. h) Goodwill w/o -€11.3m, currency uplift +€10.9m. i) Goodwill w/o -€25.5m; currency loss -€5m. j) Goodwill write-off -€5.5m net; currency loss -€6.2m. k) Goodwill write-off -€14.2m; currency profit +€3.4m.
m) Share premium +€6.9m; currency gain +€15.2m; goodwill w/o -€55.2m. n) Goodwill write-off -€23.6m; currency loss -€3.7m, purchase of own shares -€8.3m. p) Currency gain +€7.4m; disposal of assets -€2.6m net. q) Includes asset sales and losses of -€2.6m net and reduction in pref interest €4.5m due to conversion of debt to equity.

BALANCE SHEET: DECEMBER 31 2001. € m

Share Capital:		
354,326,000 Ord €0.06 shares		21.3
(inc 9,021,610 delisted treasury shares)		
Reserves		260.3
Shareholders' Funds		281.6

Tangible Assets		139.3
Financial Assets		57.3
Current Assets	587.3	
Current Liabilities	372.7	
Net Current Assets		214.6
Medium debt		(96.7)
Minority & grants		(41.8)
Pref shares		(0.6)
Net Tangible Assets		272.1
Intangible Assets		9.5
Net Assets		281.6

Comment:

A really disappointing

investment over the

5 and 10

year term.

Back in April 1993 rumours were rife that Fyffes were going to fall into the clutches of Dole, one of the majors in fruit sales internationally. The price then was at 1.46 per share at a multiple of 18.9 times the then earnings per share. Just imagine if Dole were to come around again and make such a generous offer to the disillusioned shareholders of this favourite monkey food distributor - they would break Dole's arm off at the elbow rushing to grab hold of such largesse.

If you were unfortunate enough to invest 1,000 in Fyffes a decade ago and reinvested the dividends the nest egg would now be a disappointing €1,069. If you did the same exercise five years ago the end result would be just as disappointing with an accumulated amount of €1,351.

So what has happened this fruit company controlled by the octogenarian Neil McCann and his offspring? One of the inherent difficulties is the fact that it is so closely allied to the most unexciting high energy product - the banana.

Global production of bananas amounts to some 65 million tonnes. Most of this is consumed domestically as the fruit is a staple product in several regions. Only 20% of the output is traded internationally. The bulk of this trade is from Latin America (which accounts for 80% of world exports) to North America and Europe (65% split roughly equally between these two regions). The EU banana regime limits the import of bananas from outside EU territories and certain ACP regions essentially former colonies of EU countries) to 3.3 million tonnes annually. Licences are distributed for the importation of these bananas in accordance with a company's historic share in handling banana imports into the EU. In total (including EU and ACP output), EU sales amount to 4.1 million tonnes per annum. The current regime is due to be replaced by a tariff only system after January 2006 although it is not certain that the system will necessarily be replaced at that time.

The main producing countries are: India 11m tonnes, Brazil 7m tonnes, Ecuador 7m tonnes, Indonesia 5m tonnes, Philippines 4m tonnes, China 4m tonnes and Columbia 4m tonnes. The key exporters are Latin America and the Caribbean at least 10 m tonnes while the Philippines exports 1.2m tonnes. The main consumers are North America for 3.8m tonnes, EU countries 3.3m tonnes and Japan 1.0 m tonnes.

The business of distributing this fruit to the market is concentrated in a handful of operators. Five companies - Chiquita, Dole Foods, Fresh Del Monte, Fyffes and Noboa - account for three- quarters of all bananas traded globally. Furthermore the nature of this fruit, which requires sophisticated temperature controlled logistics, means that there is an unusually high degree of vertical integration compared with other segments of the fruit industry. Many of the leading exporters own plantations to grow bananas, own the ships to

transport them as well as the ripening and distribution centres to bring the fruit through its final stages on its way to the market. The industry is, as a consequence, capital intensive, much more so than other fruit distribution operations, in which most of these companies are also involved.

Despite the high level of consolidation within the industry, the past decade has seen banana prices and processor profit margins at very low levels. To a large extent the EU regime protected profitability within that market, though the plummeting prices in the second half of 1998 and the strong dollar in 2000 showed that even this protected zone was not immune to global trends. The essential problem has been one of perennial oversupply. Investment in new capacity especially by some of the leading trading companies like Chiquita on the back of rising global demand in the 1990s proved optimistic and lower prices were the consequence in order to balance the market. In particular Chiquita did not anticipate that the EU would impose quota restrictions after the arrival of the Single European Market. EU imports fell by 10% as a result of the regime (by circa 300,000 tonnes or 3% of global trade). The high investment in new plantations means that the cost of exit is high and the global trade is quite inflexible in matching production with demand.

In its excellent review of Fyffes, Goodbody Stockbrokers spotlighted Chiquita and its problems. The severity of the downturn in the industry from a processor standpoint was most evident from Chiquita's slide into bankruptcy proceedings, out of which it has just emerged. There were other factors contributing to Chiquita's demise such as the huge investment in reefer ships, but the main problem was that it over-extended its commitment to the global banana market at the wrong time and misread the regulatory environment in the EU. Following its restructuring, Chiquita's debt has been halved with debt holders exchanging debt for new equity. The new agreement with the US on the banana regime sees the company getting an extra 100,000 tonnes of quota in the EU market. This will reduce its requirement to buy licences from other players in the EU, while providing a new environment of stability until at least 2006.

Goodbodys are convinced that at this stage the options for the industry are to improve margins by taking out capacity and/or to squeeze unit production costs even further.

After a decade of pruning costs the clearest way to make any significant headway is for further merger and acquisition activity. This would open new possibilities for greater

Share of the EU Banana Market	
Fyffes	6%
Del Monte	16%
Chiquita	26%
Dole Foods	25%
Others	27%
	100%

efficiencies right through the cost chain from banana supplies to logistics and ripening. According to the brokers, to make a structural difference to the industry any merger activity will need to include a combination of the big five players - the four quoted enterprises of Fyffes, Chiquita, Dole and Del Monte plus the Ecuador privately owned Noboa which has a 12% share of the global market.

Critical factors will include the financial capacity of each of the five, regulatory hurdles and 'goodness of fit'. The borrowing capacity among the three quoted players, excluding Chiquita, is according to Goodbody's analysis, surprisingly similar. Fyffes, despite its relatively small size in terms of enterprise value has as great a gearing potential as Dole Foods due to its current balance sheet strength. Fyffes has not far short of €400 million cash in the bank with minimal bank borrowings.

It is Goodbodys considered opinion that Dole has the strongest financial firepower when its capacity to raise new equity is also taken into account. A one for three rights issue for them would raise in the region of $600 million whilst such an exercise would only increase Del Monte's war chest by $320 million and would only add €150 million to Fyffes' coffers. All would be severely stretched to make an all-out bid for Chiquita's entire operations, with Chiquita's enterprise value currently standing at $1.28 billion. Goodbody's estimates of the 2002 sales for the various companies are: Fyffes €1.7 billion, Dole Foods $4.2 billion, Chiquita $2.2 billion and Fresh Del Monte (which is different from Del Monte canned) $2 billion.

Finally, there are two risks with the Fyffes scenario. Banana prices in Europe could soften relative to last year or the dollar could strengthen further. So far this year prices have been broadly similar to last year. But then Chiquita will be adding an additional 100,000 tonnes to the current EU market. There has been disruptive illegal importation and dumping of 50,000 tonnes by some French companies last year which has now ceased. The second risk with Fyffes is that a major acquisition might go sour within the context of a stretched balance sheet. And will the regime of nepotism in the McCann sons be able to digest successfully an enlarged organisation? Many imponderables indeed including the outcome of the legal fisticuffs with their old ally DCC. It could be exciting times ahead.

(Much of this pen picture of Fyffes has been distilled from an excellent concise stockbroker's review from Goodbody)

BUSINESS: Pharmaceutical manufacturers
REGISTERED OFFICE: Seagoe Industrial Estate, Craigavon, Co Armagh **HEAD OFFICE:** as regd office. Tel: 0044 2838334974 Fax: 0044 2838350206.
SECRETARY: A Bruno **REGISTRARS & TRANSFER OFFICE:** Computershare Investor Services plc, P.O. Box 82, The Pavillions, Bridgewater Road, Bristol, UK.
PRINCIPAL BANKERS: Bank of Ireland
AUDITORS: PricewaterhouseCoopers.
SOLICITORS: Ashurst Morris Crisp.
STOCKBROKERS: Merrill Lynch International, Credit Suisse First Boston, ABN AMRO Equities Ltd, Goodbody Stockbrokers.
DIRECTORS: J King (Chairman - 53), R Boissonneault (CEO - 53), M Carter (64), G Elliott (50), H Ennis (72), D Gibbons (64).
SHARE CAPITAL: Authorised: 250m 10p ord. shares.
Issued: 185,458,725 10p ord. shares.
STAFF: 1,692 **SCRIP DIVIDEND:** No

CAPITAL HISTORY:

Incorporated Aug 1991 as Moyne Shelf Co. Ltd. Nov 1991: Name changed to Galen Holdings Ltd which became Galen Holdings Plc in June 1997. July 1997: Authorised capital increased from 10 million Ord 10p shares to 170 million Ord 10p shares. Alloted 119,933,322 Ord 10p shares on the basis of 74-to-1. Placed 30,266,662 Ord 10p shares at 150p stg per share on flotation (21,266,666 were new shares and 8,999,996 were existing shares). Sept 2000: Issued 31,698,554 Ord 10p shares re takeover of Warner Chilcott. ADRs listed on NASDAQ (1ADR=4 Ord 10p shares). Nov 1999: Placed 6m Ord 10p shares at 605p each. July 2001: Open offer 39.7m (26,490,011 new shares + 13.2m shares from Directors) Ord 10p shares @ 755pstg each.

COMPANY HISTORY:

Incorporated August 1968 by Allen McClay to market Prescription Pharmaceuticals the manufacturing of which was sub contracted. In 1977 manufactured their own products. 1988: acquired IVEX. 1989: manufactured controlled release intravaginal rings and established clinical trial services division. 1992: acquired Connors Chemists. Aug 1996: demerged Connors Chemists, which was acquired by 3 Galen directors (McClay, King & Elliott). 1997: established clinical trial services facility in Pennsylvania to service US market. Galen now sells over 40 products in the UK and Ireland including Paramol, Kapake and Tramake and Laxatives such as Capsuval. The Ivex division manufactures 66 products for intravenous and sterile solutions. In May 1997: Charitable Trust in Queens University, Belfast received 6 million shares as a bequest and subsequently sold through the placing, 1 million shares leaving it with 4.1% of Galen. July 1997: Shares placed at 150p, first day's dealings ended at 179p. September 1997: first quoted in Dublin at 282p each. June 1998: Shares suspended at 415stg pending outcome of merger talks with Ferring Pharmaceuticals. Oct 1998: Merger talks aborted - shares relisted at 300stg. Nov 1998: Directors J King (1.35m) and G Elliott (0.75m) sell 2.1m shares at £4stg each. June 1999: Paid £19.8m stg cash for Bartholomew Rhodes. July 2000: Buys 2 US companies (Applied Clinical Concepts & DCRI Pharmacy) £10.2mstg. Sept 2000: Buys Warner Chilcott for £201.7mstg in shares with options on futher 875,000 shares (valuing WC at £275.7mstg). Eventually WC shareholders will hold 25% of Galen. Dec 2000: Directors off-load 3.5m (£30mstg/€49.3m worth) shares. June 2001: Buys Estrace Tablets from Bristol Myers for €67.2m. July 2001: Directors sell more shares 13.2m shares (£100mstg/€162.4m). Jan 2002: Sells Chemical Synthesis Services to A McClay for £25mstg. A McClay resigns as Director. March 2002: Pays €46m for US rights of antibiotic Duricel and Moisturel skin cream. May 2002: Sells Clinical Trials Services business to A McClay for £130mstg. A McClay to sell 12m (6.5% of equity) shares for £65mstg. Aug 2002: Sells ICTI for €16.5m.

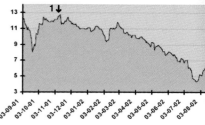

Share Price Sept 2001 - Sept 2002

1. €12.75 13.11.01 Final results

FINANCIAL DIARY

Interim Results Announced	08.05.2002
Interim Dividend Payout	23.08.2002
Annual Results Announced	13.11.2001
Annual General Meeting	19.02.2002
Final Dividend Payout	28.02.2002

SECTORAL ANALYSIS (previous year)

Sales: UK 19% (49%), Nth America 70% (36%), other 11% (15%). **Profits:** UK 21% (78%), Nth America 63% (22%), other 16% (0%)

HALF YEARLY PERFORMANCES: £'m stg

Six months to	30.09.00	31.03.01	30.09.01	31.03.02
Sales	43.6	44.4	138.3	107.5
Profits before Tax	7.9	6.4	10.5	20.5
Profit % Sales	18.1	14.4	7.6	19.1

SHARE PRICE TREND €

1997	High	5.03 (Dec)	Low	3.58 (Sept)
1998	High	8.18 (Mar)	Low	4.90 (Oct)
1999	High	10.46 (Nov)	Low	6.08 (Jan)
2000	High	16.30 (Nov)	Low	8.00 (Jan)
2001	High	15.50 (Feb)	Low	8.04 (Sept)

EIGHT YEAR REVIEW: £'000 stg

12 months to 30 September	1994	1995	1996	1997	1998	1999	2000	2001
Sales	45,483	57,218	74,865	39,252	48,867	67,010	86,020	182,683
Profit before Tax	2,046	5.168	8,510	11,364	11,970 d)	18,405	19,073	16,946
Tax	446	1,377	2,303	2,948	3,580	4,396	4,699	3,594
Profit after Tax	1,600	3,791	6,207	8,416	8,390	14,009	14,574	13,352
Minority Interests	-	-	-	-	(12)	(19)	(89)	(122)
Available to shareholders	1,600	3,791	6,207	8,416	8,378	13,990	14,285	13,230
Ordinary Dividend	-	-	5,822	445	1,601	1,915	3,036	4,413
Retained Profit	1,600	3,791	685	7,971	6,777	12,075	11,249	8,817
Increase (Decrease) in Reserves	n/d	3,791	685	25,978 e)	6,681	11,907	338,654 f)	183,538 g)
Shareholders funds	7,086	10,877	11,562	49,534	56,215	68,122	410,546	607,118
Ordinary Dividend per share (pstg)	-	-	4376p a)	0.367p	1.32p	1.65p	2.07p	2.49p
Earnings per share (pstg)	1.6p	3.9p	6.2p	8.03p	6.91p	12.03p	11.76p	8.2p b)

a) Based upon 143,000 shares in issue. b) Based upon 161.4m shares. d) Wrote-off £2.7m re aborted merger talks. e) Bonus issue -£9.9m, net share premium +£27.9m. f) Merger reserve +£290.7m; share premium +£35.8m. g) Share premium +£185.2m.

BALANCE SHEET: SEPTEMBER 30 2001. £'000 stg

Share Capital:
189,311,298 Ord 10p shares 18,931

Reserves: 588,187

Shareholders' Funds: 607,118

Tangible Assets	89,180
Current Assets	274,526
Current Liabilities	62,324
Net Current Assets	212,202
Medium Debt	(204,764)
Minority Interests	(242)
Net Tangible Lilibities	(96,376)
Intangibles	510,742
Net Assets	607,118

Comment: At the time of going to press there is a 3.8% tranche of shares owned by Elan which will come on the market sooner or later. Galen seems to have had no problems in the past either raising funds or disposing of significant stakes such as that held by Allen McClay. The Elan overhang will hardly be a major event. Galen paid a lot for Warner Chilcott but the Galen shares may well prove inexpensive if their growth record continues in its focused womens' healthcare niche

Founded in 1968, Galen started life as a sales and marketing operation focused on branded pharmaceutical products in the UK and Ireland. In 1977 they began to develop and manufacture their own products from a facility at Craigavon. In 1988 they added the manufacture of sterile solutions with the acquisition of IVEX and the following year began manufacturing the intravaginal ring (IVR) drug delivery vehicle and later developed the IVR drug delivery technology. In 1989 the UK product portfolio was broadened with the acquisition of the Bartholomew Rhodes group for $32.7million. They extended their branded pharmaceutical products business into the US and in September 2000 bought Warner Chilcott, a marketer of branded prescription pharmaceutical products focused primarily on women's healthcare for $325.5million. In June 2001 Galen acquired Estrace tablets from Bristol-Myers Squibb, a branded oestrogen replacement therapy for $95million.

In 1989 Galen began providing a range of highly specialised services to research oriented pharmaceutical companies to enable them to more efficiently manage clinical trials. In 1997 global demand meant expansion of the clinical trial services into the US.

Galen's pharmaceutical products business including their research and development activities, focuses on women's healthcare therapeutic area and other product areas such as dermatology and urology. Their product portfolio includes the Estrace cream and tablets, Ovcon oral contraceptives acquired in February 2000 and Doryx for the treatment of acne.

Out of a total staff of 1,800, Galen has a salesforce of 225 people now in the US and claim to have one of the largest women's healthcare sales forces calling on physician specialists including obstetrician/gynaecologists, dermatologists and urologists in the States. In Ireland and the UK their is a salesforce of 125 reps selling to GPs, community pharmacists and hospital consultants. Most of the products for the UK and Irish markets are manufactured at Craigavon and Larne. Other products for the Irish and UK markets and all the products for the American market are manufactured under contract with third parties.

In 2001 Galen's turnover was split 70% in pharmaceutical products and 30% in pharmaceutical services. These pharmaceutical services involved Chemical Synthesis Services (CSS) including SynGel and QuChem which provided an integrated service from basic R&D and small-scale chemical synthesis to kilogram scale chemical synthesis. Back in January this division representing under 3% of total sales was sold to Allen McClay for £25m stg. In May Galen sold off its CTS business which provides clinical packaging services to pharmaceutical companies that choose to outsource their manufacturing, packaging and distribution of both active drugs and placebos to targeted clinical trial patients. Galen got £130m stg for this operation, again from McClay. In August Interactive Clinical Technologies (ICIT) was also sold to McClay for £16m. These disposals amounted to 25% of Galen's turnover.

As a result of all of these sell-offs Galen is now focusing on growing its core specialty pharmaceutical products business. It believes that the Warner Chilcott acquisition opened up the US pharmaceuticals market. They have spent £100m stg on various products including Estrace tablets. To expand in this US market Galen bought an antibiotic Duricef and a skin moisturizer Moisturel which helped to grow their specialties of women's healthcare, dermatology and urology. Both of these products were bought from Bristol-Myers Squibb for $40m and had sales of $17million with gross margins of 85% in 2001. In May, Chairman John King stated: "In women's healthcare Galen has products in the two most important therapeutic categories: contraception and hormone replacement therapy (HRT), the US market for which is approximately $4.5 billion in sales and controlled by the obstetrician and gynaecologist. Our oral contraceptive continues to demonstrate strong growth." In the HRT market Estrace tablets are the second most widely prescribed oestrogen replacement therapy brand in the US.

In a review on the company by Credit Suisse First Boston the breakdown of Galen's pharmaceutical division looked like:

Product	% of Sales	Therapeutic Application
Ovcon	21%	Oral Contraceptive
Estrace (cream)	14%	Vaginal Atrophy
Estrace (tablets)	13%	Estrogen Replacement
Doryx	13%	Acne Treatment
Kapake	6%	Analgesics
Sterile fluids	7%	
Regurin	2%	Urinary incontinence
IVR	1%	
Other	23%	

The US market for Galen's products is moving ahead strongly but meanwhile their European pharma business is in a transformation phase as it moves from selling a myriad of products across several therapeutic categories to a more focused approach to women's health. For instance, selling in Ireland and the UK is gradually shifting time and resources away from promoting the more GP-type drugs to the newer, speciality pharma-type products such as Regurin (for stress incontinence) and the intravaginal ring (IVR) to specialists such as urologists, obstetricians and gynaecologists.

One of Galen's latest products this year is Menoring, an anti-bacterial IVR treatment which after being on the market in the UK for a year has finally got the green light from the American FDA where the market for the product is $150m. This is an intravaginal ring oestrogen replacement

therapy whose strengths are that the ring offers three months of treatment without the hassle of taking pills or stick on patches. This is obviously more convenient for the user and from the doctor's perspective makes it more likely the user is complying with her treatment. The second plus is the ability of the ring to deliver local treatment as well as systemic therapy thus eliminating the use of creams with pills or patches.

Credit Suisse First Boston goes on to illustrate the immediate future for Galen. CSFB believes Galen's main challenge in trying to maintain sales of the standard Estrace tablets is to persuade doctors to prescribe the product while preventing generic substitution. While Estrace is a well-known brand that is commonly prescribed by US physicians, only a fraction of the prescriptions lead to the dispensing of the branded Estrace product. This is because the dispensing pharmacist will often substitute prescribed Estrace tablets for a generic substitute, which is usually cheaper. Galen's challenge is to persuade doctors not only to continue prescribing Estrace but also to prevent pharmacists substituting the product with a generic drug. Doctors can easily do this by adding DAW (dispense as written) to the prescription. It is felt that given the size of the salesforce Galen is likely to have sufficient success in its task to grow the brand.

The pharmaceutical industry is highly competitive. Galen's branded products compete with brands marketed by other pharmaceutical companies including companies with resources substantially greater than the Irish operator. The principal competitors in the women's health therapeutic category are in the US and include the women's healthcare divisions of Johnson & Johnson, American Home Products, Pfizer, Schering, A.G. and Akzo-Nobel. The principal competitors for their other products are Medicis, Pharmacia and Sanofi.

On top of this competition there is the problem of government agencies and medical insurers challenging the pricing of pharmaceutical products and limiting the number of products on their formulary lists to reduce costs. Added to these negatives is the fact that Galen's branded products are up against generic equivalents because there is no proprietary protection for most of the branded pharmaceutical products they sell. Their Estrace tablets, NataFort and NataChew are in direct competition with generics. To copperfasten the quality of their products Estrace cream and Ovcon contraceptives are manufactured by Bristol-Myers Squibb under long term agreements up to 2009 and Estrace tablets are also made by Bristol Myers up to mid July 2006. These account for a substantial proportion of Galens sales in the US. To keep ahead of the competition Galen increased their expenditure on R&D in the first half of 2002 by 79% to £6.4m stg. On top of this they retired £46m stg of bonds with a high yield of 12.6% acquired at the time of the Warner Chilcott takeover.

Overtures to acquire Elan's 4% stake in Galen have been spurned for the moment but as Elan's dash for cash progresses the pressure to turn these readily realisables shares into cash will no doubt become acute; at least, they will hardly overhang the market as Galen or its friends will only be too pleased to pick them up.

(We have relied on a Credit Suisse First Boston stockbroker's report for some of the details in this review along with Galen's own 20-F Report file with the SEC)

GARTMORE IRISH GROWTH FUND plc

BUSINESS: Investment company
REGISTERED OFFICE: 23 Cathedral Yard, Exeter, UK
HEAD OFFICE: Gartmore Investment Ltd, 8 Fenchurch Place, London. Tel: 0044 2077822000
SECRETARY: Sinclair Henderson Ltd
REGISTRARS & TRANSFER OFFICE: Computershare Investor Services plc, P.O. Box 82, The Pavilions, Bridgewater Road, Bristol.
PRINCIPAL BANKERS: Ulster Bank Markets Ltd
AUDITORS: Ernst & Young
SOLICITORS: -
STOCKBROKERS: HSBC Securities
DIRECTORS: H Sheridan (Chairman), R Baillie (59), G Caldwell, R Milliken.
SHARE CAPITAL: Authorised: 40m Ord 25p shares. **Issued:** 23,113,944 Ord 25p shares.
EMPLOYEES: none
SCRIP DIVIDEND: Dividend Reinvestment Scheme.

CAPITAL HISTORY:

Placed (as Natwest Irish Smaller Companies Invest Trust) 5million Units of 5 Ord 25p shares and 1 Warrant at 500p each. Warrant exercisable between July 97 and 2001 for 0ne share @ 100p each. Company can borrow up to 25% of net asset value. Management fee is 1% of funds. Fund has an end date of 2002 but may be extended by e.g.m. every 3 years thereafter.

COMPANY HISTORY:

Launched June 1995 as Natwest Irish Smaller Companies Investment Trust plc to invest (North & South) in companies outside the 10 largest quoted plcs in RoI. March 1996: 3 largest holdings DCC (5.7%), Green Prop (5.4%), ICG (5.1%). Jan 1997: Name changed to Gartmore Irish Smaller Companies Investment Trust plc. March 1997: 3 largest holdings Kingspan (5.7%), Grafton (4.7%), Green Prop (4.7%). March 1998: 3 largest holdings Kingspan (6.2%),

Harry Sheridan

Gartmore

ICG (4.5%), Green Prop (4.5%). March 1999: 3 largest holdings Anglo Irish (7.0%), Green Prop (6.2%), Esat Telecom (5.9%). March 2000: Name changed from Gartmore Irish Growth Fund plc. 3 largest holdings Horizon (12.0%), DCC (6.8%), Iona (6.7%). March 2001: 3 largest holdings DCC (7.7%), Anglo Irish (6.7%), Kingspan (5.9%). June 2001: 3 largest holdings

First Active (6.7%), Glanbia (6.6%), Anglo Irish Bank (5.5%). June 2002: Three largest holdings First Active (6.7%), Glanbia (6.6%), Anglo Irish Bank (5.5%).

Share Price Sept 2001 - Sept 2002

FINANCIAL DIARY

Interim Results Announced:	none
Interim Dividend Payout:	none
Final Results Announced:	05.06.2002
Annual General Meeting:	28.08.2002
Final Dividend Payout:	27.09.2002

SHARE PRICE TREND:

2000	High	3.64p (Oct)	Low	3.44 (Mar)
2001	High	4.04 (May)	Low	3.50 (Jan)

SEVEN YEAR REVIEW: £'000 stg

12 months to March 31	1996	1997	1998	1999	2000	2001	2002
Investment dealing/(loss)	4,068	7,723	18,943	(8,043)	19,164	(3,294)	(1,771)
Dividend income	677	1,129	1,250	1,515	850	1,205	1,326
Profits/(Loss) Before Tax	4,384	8,422	19,896	(8,113)	18,133	(4,160)	(1,596)
Tax	92	166	99	169	+5	2	-
Profits After Tax	4,292	8,256	19,797	(8,282)	18,138	(4,162)	(1,596)
Minority Interests	-	-	-	-		-	
Available to Shareholders	4,292	8,256	19,797	(8,282)	18,138	(4,162)	(1,596)
Ordinary Dividend	145	65	-	-	-	-	35
Retained Profits	4,147	8,191	19,797	(8,282)	18,138	(4,162)	(1,631)
Increase (Decrease) in Reserves	19,601 a)	8,191	19,797	(8,282)	18,138	(4,139)	(463)
Shareholders' Funds	24,982	33,173	52,970	44,688	62,826	58,695	58,621
Ordinary Dividend per share	0.675p	0.2p	-	-	-	-	0.15p
Earnings per share (p stg)	26.16p	38.13p	91.97p	-	84.3p	-	-
Net Asset Value per share (p stg)	116.05	154.1p	246.07p	207.6p	291.86p	272.28p	253.62p

a) Share premium + £14.5m

BALANCE SHEET: MARCH 2002 £'000stg

Share Capital:		Investments	54,908
23,113,944 Ord 25pstg shares	5,778	Current Assets	3,989
		Current Liabilities	276
Reserves	52,843	Net Current Assets	3,713
Shareholders' Funds	58,621	Net Tangible Assets	58,621

Comment:
Its seven year life-span is up this year but it will be kept alive tri-annually by way of a resolution at the agm. The current year's performance will be very dependent on the proces of the secondary equities on the Irish market. Net asset value at August 2002 was 245p stg or €3.81 per share.

Gartmore Irish Growth Fund PLC

Chairman's Statement

Harry Sheridan
Chairman

The Company recorded a fall of 2.7% in diluted Net Asset Value (NAV) in the year to 31 March 2002. This reflected a deteriorating global and domestic economic background for much of the year under review.

Over the same period, the Davy Mid Cap Index rose by 0.5% and the ISEQ Index fell by 7.8%, both in sterling terms. The Hoare Govett Smaller Companies Index (excluding investment companies) fell by 5.6%, whilst the FTSE All-Share Index fell by 5.7%.

The Company seeks to provide Shareholders with long-term capital growth and will distribute income when revenue permits. The revenue return per share was 0.97p, substantially better than the previous year's return of 0.59p. This increase means that the Company will be required to make a dividend payment in order to maintain its investment trust status. Accordingly, your Directors have proposed a dividend of 0.15p per ordinary 25p share to be paid on 27 September 2002 to the members on the register on 6 September 2002.

The increased revenue return per share offsets in part a negative capital return of 8.04p per share, resulting in a negative total return per share of 7.07p. Whilst this is disappointing, it should be seen in the context of the long-term returns achieved by the Company since it was floated in 1995. The increase in diluted NAV since that date represents a compound rate of growth of 15.1% per annum. I thank the Managers for their efforts in achieving this excellent return.

At 31 March 2002 the share price discount against the NAV was 11.9%. This level of discount is disappointing, but it represents an improvement over the average of the past several years and compared with a discount of 14.3% at 31 March 2001. On 31 July 2001 the Company's remaining Warrantholders exercised their right to subscribe in cash for ordinary shares in the Company at a price of 100p per share since this was the last opportunity to do so. All 1,556,542 outstanding warrants in issue were converted as at that date, increasing the total number of ordinary shares in issue to 23,113,944.

Prospects for the Company over the coming year are felt to be very favourable. Ireland's annualised rate of economic growth continues to outpace that in other eurozone economies, albeit at a slightly more moderate rate than before. The Irish economy continues to enjoy the benefit of the low level of interest rates in the eurozone, the country's low rate of corporation tax and the inward investment that these factors attract. As the global economy has recovered from last year's downturn, investors have gained confidence and this is being reflected in a rise in the Irish stockmarket. The recent announcement by Intel of its plans to invest a further $2.2bn in its Irish operations reinforces this trend. The consensus forecast for growth in Ireland in 2002 is 3.7% and 5% in 2003. In contrast, the consensus forecast for growth in Europe is 1.3% for 2002 and 2.7% for 2003. In this environment, the Directors look forward to favourable returns in the coming years.

Under the Company's Articles of Association, the Directors shall be proposing at the Annual General Meeting to be held in August 2002 that the Company should continue as an investment trust for a further three years. Since it commenced operations on 8 June 1995, the Company's investment performance has been excellent, with an increase of 160.6% in diluted NAV by comparison with a rise of 94.6% for the Davy Mid Cap Index and a return of 103.3% for the ISEQ Index. The Company has produced returns amongst the highest of any conventional trust managed by Gartmore in the period. Your Board is confident that the investment approach adopted by the Managers should continue to produce good returns over the next three years and recommends that Shareholders vote in favour of continuation, as the Directors intend to do in respect of their own holdings which, in aggregate, amount to 63,000 ordinary shares.

The Irish economy continues to enjoy the benefit of the low level of interest rates in the eurozone, the country's low rate of corporation tax and the inward investment that these factors attract.

Gartmore

Harry Sheridan
Chairman
5 June 2002

GLANBIA plc

CAPITAL HISTORY:

Incorporated March 1988. Authorised share capital on incorporation was £1m divided into 9,250,000 'A' Ord. shares of 10p each and 750,000 'B' Ord. shares of 10p each. April 1988 'A' Ord. shares divided into 18.5m 'A' Ord. shares of 5p each, authorised capital increased to £4.875m by the creation of 77.5m 'A' Ord. shares of 5p each and consolidated all 'B' Ord. shares of 10p each into 375,000 'B' Ord. shares of 20p each. 149,998 'B' Ord. shares allotted to Avonmore Co-op for cash at a premium of 1p per share. May 1988 re-registered as a plc. Authorised share capital increased to £24.8m by the creation of an additional 99.625m 'B' shares of 20p each. The company issued 31,748,315 'B' shares credited as fully paid to Avonmore Co-op in exchange for the entire issued share capital of certain subsidiaries and associates of Avonmore Co-op and allotted 68,101,685 'B' shares to Avonmore Co-op for cash at par fully paid. July 1988 28,145m 'A' Ord. 5p shares allotted at 45p per share to farmer members, suppliers of Avonmore Co-op. August 1988 placing of 11m 'A' Ord. 5p shares at 75p per share to raise £8.25m. September 1988 admission of 'A' Ord. shares to Stock Exchange. Aug. '89: 511,364 'A' Ord. shares issued re purchase of Glenmills Dairy. Nov 1991 Rights Issue 34,914,091 A Ord shares at 91p each. Nov 1996: Redesignated 100 'B' Ord 20p shares as 100m 5p Ord shares and eliminated 'A' from the other Ord 5p shares. June 1997: Offers 29 Avonmore Ord 5p Shares for every 50 Waterford Foods Ord Shares (values Waterford Foods at £378.1m). Jan 1998: Issues 116,581,669 Ord 5p shares on acquisition of Waterford Foods.

COMPANY HISTORY:

Avonmore Creameries Federation formed in 1967. Avonmore Co-op formed in mid '70s from the amalgamation of a number of these creameries. It controls over 91% of Roscrea Bacon in March 88 : purchased Edmund Burke & Sons, for £1.6m. August 88: acquired a 42% shareholding in T.H. Goodwin for IR£3.52m with option to acquire balance. May 89 : purchased Irish Country Bacon for £3.3m cash. June 89 :purchased Glenmills Dairy for £900,000 stg cash and shares. June 89 : purchased Roys Dairy Inc. in Wisconsin for IR£6.7m cash. September 89: acquired Golden Dairy Co. £2.7m stg. March 90 bought assets of Falbo Cheese, Illinois for $2.7m. May 90: Admission of "A" Ord. shares to London Stock Exchange. June 90: completed the acquisition of T.H. Goodwin & Sons Ltd. July 90: acquired fixed assets, stocks and goodwill of the Ashmount Foods Ltd, for £5.5m stg. business at Bradford and equity of Handsworth Dairies Ltd., Birmingham at a total cost IR £11.0m. August 90: acquired Ward's Cheese Inc., Richfield, Idaho for IR£6.4m plus earnouts. This brings total spent on acquisitions over 88/89 to £48.8m. May 91: discussions with Waterford Foods which may lead to merger. September 91: merger talks with Waterford Foods aborted. Nov 91: Rights Issue raises £31m. 60% of issue left with underwriters. Jan 92: buys certain Whitecroft Dairy assets in UK for £4.5m stg. April 92: pays £5.5m for 4 UMP meat plants. Acquires Barretts & Baird Group in UK over 3 years for min IR £7.1m. June 92: aborts negotiations to purchase Williams Group Tullamore. Purchases German Meat Distributor Harzland Fleisch Service for £5.4m. July 92: refinances short term facilities in UK with $50m senior notes 99/2002. August 92: announces 75% interest in Hungarian dairy business for £0.5m. Sept 92: acquires Bennetts Dairies £3.6m. Nov 92: buys Churchfields Dairies & Parkers Dairies £11.6m. Pays £8.5m for 50% Master Pork. July 93: Pays £21.6m for Dairy Crest with milk pool of 39m gallons in Birmingham. Dec 1994: Merger talks with Waterford Foods denied again. Jan 1995: Closed meat plant at Harzland, Germany having closed beef plants of Barretts and Bairds in UK. April 1997: Bids £281m for Waterford Foods. July 1997: Pays £54m for Beni Foods. Aug 1997: Name changes to Avonmore Waterford Group plc. Nov 1997: 900 redundancies announced. March 1998: Sells cheese business in Wisconsin for £26m incurring a loss of £24m. Sells loss-making Waterford Juices in UK for £171.1m. March 1999: Name changed to Glanbia. April 1999: Major shake-up at management level. June 1999: Profits warning. Major u-turn in sale of British liquid milk to Express Dairies for £120.5m and red meat plants in Ireland sold for £10m. Total outcome of both sales is a charge of £66.3m. July 1999: Ned Sullivan puts in place his own management team. April 2000: Cuts Irish milk prices to produc-

ers. June 2000: Opens world's largest cheese factory in Idaho July 2000: Directorate cut to 20. Aug 2000: Leprino Foods buy 29% Glanbia Cheese for £27.5m to attack EU mozzarella marke Sept 2000: Profits warning. Oct 2000: Ned O'Sullivan announce retirement. May 2002: Exits UK cooked meats at Bradford/Milto Keynes. Expects €65m write-off in 2002. July 2002: To se Tamworth chilled foods (t/o £100mstg).

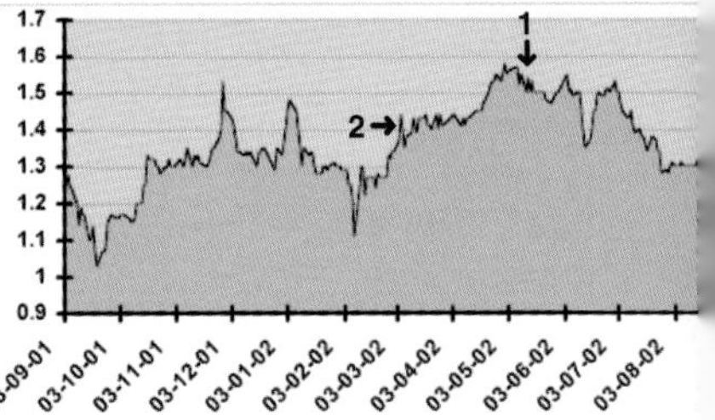

TEN YEAR REVIEW: € m

12 months to December 31	1992	1993	1994	1995	1996	1997	1998	1999	2000	2001
Turnover	1,055.7	1,434.0	1,512.1	1,555.8	1,675.3	3,006.2	2,922.0	2,503.9	2,401.7	2,625.4
Profit (loss) before Tax	31.7	37.1	27.6	40.7	46.3	(149.5) j)	53.6	(34.8) n)	79.5 b)	61.1
Tax	3.6	5.2	4.9	5.7	6.5	11.5	10.9	8.8	5.5	7.5
Profit (loss) after Tax	28.1	31.9	22.7	35.0	39.8	(138.0)	42.7	(43.6)	74.0	53.6
Minority Interest	(1.3)	(0.1)	(0.5)	(0.7)	(1.7)	(0.7)	(0.8)	(0.9)	(0.6)	(0.5)
Pref Dividend	-	-	-	-	-	(12.7)	(12.2)	(12.8)	(13.8)	(13.0)
Available for Shareholders	26.8	31.8	22.2	34.3	38.1	(151.4)	29.7	(57.3)	59.6	40.1
Ordinary Dividend	6.6	7.9	8.3	9.1	10.0	18.1	19.9	20.8	12.6	13.3
Retained Profit (Loss)	20.2	23.9	13.9	25.2	28.1	(169.5)i)	9.8	(70.1)	47.0	26.9
Increase in Reserves	(23.0) f)	(0.7) g)	16.5	24.4	46.5 h)	(225.4)	31.9 a)	50.8 m)	46.5	25.9
Shareholders' Funds	149.4	148.8	165.2	189.6	217.1	14.4	46.4	97.2	142.6	168.6
Ordinary Dividend per Share (€)	0.042	0.045	0.048	0.052	0.057	0.062	0.068	0.071	0.043	0.045
Earnings per Share (€)	0.154	0.183	0.127	0.197	0.218	-	0.10	-	0.204	0.137 k)

(a) Goodwill on disposal +€19.2m; currency gain +€1.9m. b) Includes +€25.9m profits on asset sales. f) Goodwill w/o -€40.8m, currency loss -€2.4m.
g) Goodwill w/o -€19.3m, currency loss -€5.1m. Goodwill transferred to P&L a/c on closure €2.8m. h) Share premium +€19m on conversion of 'B' 20p Ord shares to 5p Ord shares.
i) Goodwill -€29.3m(net); loss on translation of subsidiaries -€26.8m. j) Includes merger & reorganisation costs -€225.8m. (k) Based upon 292.5m shares.
m) Goodwill write-back +€146.1m; currency loss -€14.6m. n) Includes merger costs -€9.0m and loss on sale of operations -€84.2m.

BALANCE SHEET: DECEMBER 31 2001. € m

Share Capital:		Fixed Assets	511.7
		Financial Assets	33.0
292,514,184 Ord. €0.06 shares	17.5	Current Assets	601.3
		Current Liabilities	410.3
Reserves	151.0	Net Current Assets	191.0
		Medium Term Debt	(397.9)
		Pref Shares	(147.8)
		Minorities & Grants	(26.6)
		Net Tangible Assets	163.4
		Intangibles	5.1
Shareholders' Funds	168.5	Net Assets	168.5

Comment:

The surgeon's knife being wielded by John Moloney appears to be straightening out the core business after a period of revenue growth for its own sake. The only cloud going forward is where is the growth going to be generated after the pruning has finished.

GLENCAR MINING plc

(Formerly Glencar Explorations plc)
(Quoted on Exploration Securities Market)

BUSINESS: Mineral exploration particularly in Ghana.
REGISTERED OFFICE: 26 Upper Mount Street, Dublin.
Tel: 01-6619974. Fax: 01-6611205.
HEAD OFFICE: as regd office.
SECRETARY: P. O'Quigley **REGISTRARS & TRANSFER**
OFFICE: Computershare Investor Services (Ireland) Ltd, Heron
House, Corrig Road, Sandyford Industrial Estate, Dublin.
PRINCIPAL BANKERS: Bank of Ireland, Barclays Bank, Irish
Intercontinental Bank. **AUDITORS:** Horwath Bastow Charlton.
SOLICITORS: Whitney Moore & Keller.
STOCKBROKERS: J. & E. Davy, Williams de Broe Plc.
DIRECTORS: H McCullough (Ch Ex - 53), W Cummins (71), S
Finlay (53), P O'Quigley (39), K Harrington (40).
SHARE CAPITAL: Authorised: 130 million Ord €0.031
shares. **Issued:** 97,804,467 Ord €0.031 shares.
STAFF: 300. **SCRIP DIVIDEND:** No

CAPITAL HISTORY:

Incorporated Sept. 1971. 'Rights' issue in 1979 of 1-for-3 at 100p for each Ord. £1 share. 24,785 Ord. £1 shares issued as a result. 1983 'rights' issue of 2-for-3 at 350p for each Ord. £1 share. This raised £221,987 to acquire Rennicks & Bennett plus issue of 55,076 Ord. £1 shares to Sabina Industries Ltd., the vendors. Registered as a public limited company December 1983. 220,306 Ord £1 shares subdivided into 2,203,060 Ord. 10p shares. July 1984 'rights' of 550,765 Ord. 10p shares on the basis of 3 new Ord. 10p shares plus one warrant for every 12 Ord. shares. Classified as a combined unit offered at 159p (Equal to 53p per Ord. share). Warrants allow holder to subscribe for shares at 69p each in Nov. 1985 and 74p each in Nov 1986. £271,000 raised as a result in July 1984. August 1985 'rights' issue of 461,993 Ord. 10p shares at 90p each on the basis of 1-for-6 raising £375,794. In Nov. 1986 170,095 warrants exercised at 74p per Ord. 10p shares raising £125,870. May 1987 244,800 Ord. 10p shares placed at 260p stg. each and as a result £602,160 stg. raised. July 1987 shares split on a 4-for-1 basis to 2.5 shares. May 1988 2,500,000 Ord 2.5p shares placed at 63.5p. Sept. 1993: Placing 5million Ord 2.5p shares at 9p each. Open offer 'rights' to shareholders of 1-for-9 at 9p each-2,033,903 shares taken up (99%). Sept 1994: Placing and open offer (1-for-10) of 9,012,078 Ord 2.5p shares at 33p each. Aug 1995: Placing of 5,750,000 Ord 2.5p shares at 42.5p each. Oct 1996: Placing of 12.6 million Ord 2.5p shares at 53p each and open offer (2-for-7) of 11,593,777 Ord 2.5p shares at 53p each. May 1998: Warrants issued to subscribe for 1.7m shares at 40p each. March 1999: Convertible Loan Note issue $3m by Standard Bank of London Ltd to convert all or part of loan into shares at €0.70 each. July 2000: Rights issue 32,601,489 Ord 2.5p shares (1-for-2) at €0.19 (Ir14.96p/12pstg) fully underwritten (proceeds $5.35m net; expenses $549,000).

COMPANY HISTORY:

Incorporated in 1971. Principal activity up to 1984 was the acquisition of Rennicks & Bennett Ltd. which has a prospecting licence adjoining Tara Mines in Co. Meath. Activity here is centred both at Scallanstown and Liscarton and prospecting is continuing. Joint exploration with Andaman is being carried out in Mayo and gold mineralisation of 530,000 tonnes grading 6gms/tonne has been reported. In November 1986 permission granted to issue American Depository Receipts (ADRs). In May 1987 £670,000 was raised from a placing. These funds applied chiefly to Glencar's overseas exploration activities particularly in Ghana. However Central Bank does not allow Glencar to raise funds here for investment in Ghana. Consequently placement of shares outside Ireland necessary to maintain interest in Ghana. July 1987: D.J. Fay resigned as Director. March 1988: Glencar reduces stake in Teberebie Goldfields from 30% to 27%. May 1988: Share placing raises £1.5m (net). October 1988: Finance for the development of the Teberebie prospect agreed with the Overseas Private Investment Corporation in the U.S. O.P.I.C. to provide loans totalling $9m. April 1989: Glencar sells stake in Teberebie Goldfields for $3.65 million together with an unsecured loan note from Teberebie for $1 million with interest at 2% above LIBOR. October. August 1990: Glencar signs management agreement with Hungarian uranium mining company. June 1991: Discussing possible joint venture in Hungarian uranium mine. July 1992: High Court case in connection with Mayo Co. Co. mining ban. Nov 1992: High Court rules in favour of Glencar in Mayo mining ban. Jan 1994: Subscribed for 1.24m Andaman shares at 10p each. April 1994: Sold 1.1m Andaman shares at 17p each reducing holding to 1.38m shares (5.5%). Sept 1994: Raised £2.86m in placing. Aug 1995: Raises £2.3m from share placing. Sept 1995: Now holds 45% of Wassa Gold Project. Oct 1996: Increases stake in Wassa Holdings by 15.7% to 60.9% costing £7.5m. May 1997: Name changed. Aug 1998: Loses £2m claim for Mayo mining ban. Jan 1999:

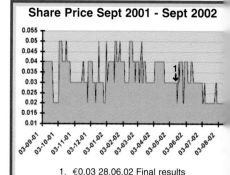

Share Price Sept 2001 - Sept 2002

1. €0.03 28.06.02 Final results

FIVE YEAR SHARE PRICE TREND

1997	High 0.74 (Mar)	Low	0.55 (Feb)
1998	High 0.63 (June)	Low	0.36 (Sept)
1999	High 0.57 (Oct)	Low	0.30 (Jly)
2000	High 0.48 (Jan)	Low	0.11 (Dec)
2001	High 0.16 (Jan)	Low	0.02 (Sept)

FINANCIAL DIARY

Interim Results Announced	06.09.2001
Interim Dividend Payou:	not likely
Final Results Announced:	28.06.2002
Annual General Meeting:	23.09.2002
Final Dividend Payout:	Not likely

INVESTMENT PERFORMANCE

Five year Investment Performance	€ 31
Ten year Investment Performance	€143

Wassa production of gold commences. May 1999: Did Hooper says target production now nearing 11,00 ounces per month. Feb 2000: Underwritten rights issu to raise $7.4m net aborted due to errors in cashflo projections. Shares suspended at €0.36. July 200 75% of rights issue (€5.7m) left with underwriters Dav and Williams de Broe. June 2001: Hopes to sell Wass mine for $28m. Nov 2001: Agrees Wassa sale fo $12m; Standard Chartered Bank to convert loan 24.3m shares (19.8% of equity).

TEN YEAR REVIEW:

12 months to December 31	€'000 1992	€'000 1993	€'000 1994	€'000 1995	€'000 1996	€'000 1997	$'m 1998	$'m 1999	$'m 2000	$'m 2001
Revenue (Interest)	23	5	-	-	-	-	-	26.4	31.1	21.8
Profit (loss) before Tax	(345)	(623)	(264)	(253)	(1,572)	132	(2.79) h)	(61.5)	(21.0)	(19.5)
Tax	-	-	1	7	-	5	-	-	-	-
Profit (Loss) after Tax	(345)	(623)	(265)	(260)	(1,572)	127	(2.79)	(61.5)	(21.0)	(19.5)
Minority Interest	-	-	-	-	(6)	(5)	(0.004)	+32.3	+8.5	+6.7
Available for Shareholders	(345)	(623)	(265)	(260)	(1,568)	122	(2.791)	(29.2)	(12.5)	(12.8)
Ordinary Dividend	-	-	-	-	-	-	-	-	-	-
Retained Profit (Loss)	(345)	(623)	(265)	(260)	(1,568)	122	(2.791)	(29.2)	(12.5)	(12.8)
Increase (Decrease) in Reserves	(347)	(86) b)	3,032 c)	2,296 d)	25,602 e)	3,450 f)	(3.253)	(47.4)	(8.5) a)	(12.8)
Shareholders' Funds	5,763	5,900	9,220	11,703	38,087	41,537	47.074	(0.3)	(7.8)	(20.7)
Ordinary Dividend per Share	-	-	-	-	-	-	-	-	-	-
Earnings per Share	-	-	-	-	-	-	-	-	-	-

a) Share premium +$3.9m. b) Share premium €0.6m. c) Share premium +€3.0m. d) Share premium +€2.8m. e) Share premium +€14.9m; increase in reserves re Wassa +€12.2m. f) Currency profit +€2.5m. h) Mayo project write-off -$2.6m.

BALANCE SHEET: DECEMBER 31 2001 $'m

Glencar
mining
plc

Annual Report and
Financial Statements - 2001

Share Capital:		Tangible Assets	0.06
97,804,467 Ord €0.031 shares 3.4		Current Assets	7.4
		Current Liabilities	54.5
Reserves	(24.1)	Net Current Liabilities	(47.1)
		Minority Interests	+18.8
		Net Tangible Liabilities	(28.3)
		Intangibles	7.6
Shareholders' Funds	(20.7)	Net Liabilities	(20.7)

Auditors Note: *Attention is drawn to certain post balance sheet events including the sale of Wassa and Standard Chartered's loan conversion into Convertible Loan Notes.*

Comment:

Widows and orphans should
look elsewhere.
A truly disastrous investment.

GRAFTON GROUP plc

(Formerly CPI Holdings Plc)

BUSINESS: Builders merchants and DIY stores and manufacturing.

REGISTERED OFFICE: Heron House, Corrig Road, Sandyford Industrial Estate, Dublin. Tel: 01-2160600. Fax: 01-2954470. **HEAD OFFICE:** as regd office.

SECRETARY: C. Rinn **REGISTRARS & TRANSFER OFFICE:** Capita Corporate Registrars plc, Unit 5, Manor Street Business Park, Manor Street, Dublin.

PRINCIPAL BANKERS: Bank of Ireland, Ulster Bank Markets, LloydsTSB Bank, AIB Bank, IIB Bank.

STOCKBROKERS: Goodbody Stockbrokers; ING Barings Charterhouse Securities. **AUDITORS:** KPMG.

SOLICITORS: Arthur Cox ; Lyons Davidson.

DIRECTORS: M Chadwick (Chairman & Ch Exec- 51), K Kilroy (Mng Dir - 63), G Bowler (50), A Collins (63), K Jewson (58), F Malone (60), C. O'Nuallain (49).

SHARE CAPITAL: Authorised: 200m Ord. €0.50 shares. **Issued:** 176,116,140 Ord. €0.50 shares.

STAFF: 3,187   **SCRIP DIVIDEND:** No

CAPITAL HISTORY:

Incorporated 1931. Feb. 1965 went public with issued and fully paid capital of £450,000 in 25p ordinary shares. In Feb 1968 2-for-3 scrip issue, in Oct 71 1-for-3 scrip issue, in August 1976 1-for-1 scrip issue and in March 1979 1-for-2 scrip issue. November 1989: Placed 3,115,000 Ord. 25p shares at 230p each with clawback of 1-for-1 June 1999: Placed 800,000 Ord 25 shares at 528p each (€19.40 each). May 2001: 9-for-1 scrip issue.

COMPANY HISTORY:

Marley Tile acquired one-third of equity in 1948. In 1965 in capital reorganisation Chadwicks Ltd. obtained 432,000 shares by reversing into the company. At that stage Marley had 51%, Chadwicks 24% and Phillip Hill, Higginson Erlangers Ltd. had 25% of equity. In Feb. 1965 Phillip Hill offered their shares to public. Dec 1980 name changed to CPI Holdings Ltd. Accounting period changed to December 31st in 1986.

Aug. 1987: Marley places 6,544,377 shares on Irish management and market. Jan. 1988: Ceased manufacturing of concrete roof tiles. June 1988: Acquires outstanding 75% of associated Co. Sandtex Ireland. July 1988: Name changed to Grafton Group Plc. Nov. 1989: Placing raises £6.9m. March 1990: Acquired MacNaughton Blair, Belfast builders merchants. The consideration to date stg £3.6million. September 1990: Quoted on London S.E. April 1991: Chairman warns of profit decline. May 1991: Acquired MRCB, Belfast. July 1991: Acquired Heatovent Ireland. July 1993: Acquired Bristol Tile Company. Feb 1994: Acquired Bradleys and Nalex in UK for £2.5m stg. May 1994: Changed auditors from Ernst & Young. Nov 1994: Buys Lumley & Hunt for £1.6m stg. Nov 1995: Buys 120,000 own shares from company pension fund at 420p each (held as treasury shares). Jan 1996: Buys R.J. Johnson, Oxford for £4.5m stg and PPS Structural Services, Glasgow for £1m stg. July 1996: Buys Bond & White and Smarts in UK for £1.5m. March 1997: Buys to lease back Holiday Inn Hotel for £6.5m. April 1997: Buys Wessex in UK for £4m stg. Buys FKS Builders Merchants for £2.6m stg and 25% British Dredging for £6.3m stg. April 1998: Buys remaining British Dredging for £25.1m stg. Aug 1998: Sells 50% British Dredging Aggregates for £5.75m stg. Sept 1998: Bought AR Hendricks for £3.9m. Nov 1998: Bought Deben Builders Merchants for £6.8m. March 1999: Buys 4.9% Heiton Holdings for £4.3m (2.3m shares at 187p each). April 1999: Buys Niall Bailey (Building Supplies) Birmingham for £13.5m stg. June 1999: Grafton now holds 12.14% of Heiton. Stake building maybe defensive to stop rival bid. Raises £12.2m from share placing. Nov 1999: Buys J Latham for €12.4m. Feb 2000: Buys E Thompson UK. May 2000: Pays £13.1mstg (cash and loan notes) for Essex Heating Supplies. May 2001: Now holds 18.8% of Heiton Holdings. June 2001: Buys 4 UK builders merchants for €35.4m.

Share Price Sept 2001 - Sept 2002

1. €3.90 04.03.02 Final results

FIVE YEAR SHARE PRICE TREND €

1997	High	1.71 (Oct)	Low	0.89 (Jan)
1998	High	2.45 (May)	Low	1.33 (Oct)
1999	High	2.30 (Nov)	Low	1.49 (Jan)
2000	High	2.56 (Mar)	Low	1.92 (Aug)
2001	High	3.26 (Mar)	Low	2.50 (Sept)

FINANCIAL DIARY

Interim Results Announced:	23.08.2002
Interim Dividend Payout:	none *
Final Results Announced:	04.03.2002
Annual General Meeting:	01.05.2002
Final Dividend Payout:	02.05.2002

*Redeemed redeemable shares @ €0.0375 instead

HALF YEARLY PERFORMANCES: € m

Six months to:	31.12.00	30.06.01	31.12.01	30.06.02
Sales	438.6	469.9	518.9	534.8
Pretax Profit	32.3	29.3	37.9	31.6
Profits % Sales	7.4	6.2	7.3	5.9

SECTORAL ANALYSIS (previous year)

Sales: Merchanting 88% (88%), manufacturing 3% (3%), DIY 9% (9%), R of I 34% (37%), UK 66% (63%).

INVESTMENT PERFORMANCE

Five Year Investment Performance:	€3,998
Ten Year Investment Performance:	€22,438

TEN YEAR REVIEW: € m

12 Months to December 31	1992	1993	1994	1995	1996	1997	1998	1999	2000	2001
Sales	122.4	133.2	169.0	195.7	244.0	327.6	427.6	620.2	830.5	988.8
Profit before Tax	4.9	5.2	10.1	14.0	19.6	23.2	28.2	38.2	52.8	67.2
Tax	1.2	1.1	2.1	2.5	2.9	3.5	3.9	4.6	6.9	8.7
Profit after Tax	3.7	4.1	8.0	11.5	16.7	19.7	24.2	33.6	45.9	58.5
Available for Shareholders	3.7	4.1	8.0	11.5	16.7	19.7	24.2	33.6	45.9	58.5
Ordinary Dividend	1.3	1.4	1.7	2.5	3.5	4.6	5.7	8.2	11.3	14.0
Retained Profit	2.4	2.7	6.3	9.0	13.2	15.2	18.5	25.4	34.6	44.5
Increase (Decrease) in Reserves	1.5 g)	3.6	4.0 d)	7.9	12.8	4.9 e)	37.9 f)	38.1 a)	35.1	47.9
Shareholders' Funds	42.2	45.8	49.8	57.7	70.6	78.6	139.8	181.3	216.5	264.5
Ordinary Dividend per Share (€)	0.008	0.009	0.011	0.016	0.022	0.029	0.035	0.048	0.065	0.080
Earnings per Share (€)	0.236	0.027	0.051	0.073	0.1050	0.123	0.150	0.20	0.266	0.336 b)

a) Share premium +€15.0m. b) Based upon 174.0m shares. d) Goodwill w/o -€2.3m. e) Goodwill w/o -€7.9m. f) Share premium +€7.2m; property revaluation +€35.4m. g) Currency loss -€0.9m. Goodwill write-off -€2.3m.

BALANCE SHEET: DECEMBER 31 2001. € m

Comment:

Loud applause from shareholders as a result of this superb ten year performance.

Further growth in Ireland may be limited but the UK is limitless.

Share Capital:	8.8
176,081,740 Ord €0.50 shares	
Reserves	255.7
Shareholders' Funds	264.5

Fixed Assets		251.5
Financial Assets		33.6
Current Assets	404.5	
Current Liabilities	264.6	
Net Current Assets		139.9
Medium Debt		(223.0)
Net Tangible Assets		202.0
Intangibles		62.5
Net Assets		264.5

GREENCORE GROUP plc

BUSINESS: Processing and distribution of agri-products.
REGISTERED OFFICE: St. Stephen's Green House, Earlsfort Terrace, Dublin Tel: 01-6051000. Fax: 01-6051100.
HEAD OFFICE: as regd office. **SECRETARY:** C Bergin.
REGISTRARS & TRANSFER OFFICE: Computershare Investor Services (Ireland) Ltd, Heron House, Corrig Road, Sandyford Ind Estate, Dublin. **PRINCIPAL BANKERS:** Citibank, Bank of Ireland, Royal Bank of Scotland. **AUDITORS:** PricewaterhouseCoopers.
SOLICITORS: Arthur Cox; Slaughter & May. **STOCKBROKERS:** Goodbodys Stockbrokers; Investec Henderson Crosthwaite.
DIRECTORS: A Barry (Chairman - 68), D Dilger (CEO - 46), J Casey (60), J Kinder (46), R O'Donoghue (60), A Hynes, P Kennedy (33), P Woodall (59), N Chalk (39), N Sullivan (55), D Sugden (52).
SHARE CAPITAL: Authorised: 300 million Ord €0.63 shares. **Issued:** 192,211,908 Ord €0.63 shares. ADRS: 1 ADR = 4 Greencore shares.
STAFF: 13,697. **SCRIP DIVIDEND:** No

Government received £63m. Issue oversubscribed 2.8 times. First day dealings 256p each. June 1991: Discloses 4.2% stake in conjunction with others in Carrs Milling Industries. July 1991: Successfully bid 151p per share for Food Industries; total cost £58m. August 1991: C. Comerford issues proceedings to recover his share (£2m) of proceeds of acquisition of Sugar Distributors. His interest not disclosed at time of flotation. Resignation of Comerford requested and received. Solicitors A & L Goodbody dispensed with. M. Tully, company secretary also resigned. Various Government and High Court investigations undertaken. Nov. 1991: Acquires Food Industries for £36.6m cash plus £19.9m convertible loan stock. Dec. 1991: G. Murphy appointed new C.E.O. Jan 1992: Major management and board changes announced. Feb 1992: Minister for Finance offloads 12.5m shares at 265p each. B. Cahill remains Chairman despite criticism at a.g.m. Sept 1992: R Bolger resigns as Director. March 1993: Archer Daniels Midland shows interest in Government shareholding. G Murphy backs ADM. April 1993: ADM withdraws interest. May 1993: Minister for Finance offloads remaining 30.4% of equity (25m shares) by placing through Davys at 275p each. Major controversy and enquiries relating to Davys handling of placing. Greencore shares temporarily suspended. Eight international investors withdraw from placing. Bank of Ireland forced to absorb 9.6m shares (£26m). July 1993: Bank of Ireland off-load their 9.6m shares, over 50% of which went to US institutions. March 1994: Davy Stockbrokers fined £150,000 by Stock Exchange for their handling of Greencore share sale. May 1994: Buys assets of HDM, Belgium for £2.6m. Dec 1994: J. Wallace resigns as Director. March 1995: G. Murphy resigns as Chief Executive. Nov 1995: Comerford court case settled. ABN Amro suggests Greencore might be likely bid target. Dec 1995: Tully court case settled. Feb 1996: Putnam Investment now hold 10% of equity. March 1996: Pays £6.8m for Williams Group. April 1996: EU states it will fine Greencore for alleged anti-competitive practices. July 1996: Pays £31m for 27% (subsequently diluted to 16%) of Imperial Holly Corp in USA. May 1997: Irish Sugar fined £6.6m (reduced to £787,000) by EC for anti-competitive practices. July 1997: Pays £25.2m stg for 48.5% of Kears. Feb 1998: Buys back 4.9m shares at 380p each (£19.1m). April 1998: Pays £73m for Pauls Malt in UK. Aug 1998: Buys Paramount Foods for £33m. Jan 2000: Greencore stalks Perkins Foods. Feb 2000: D Desmond spends £35m on buying 7.8% of Greencore. £250mstg offer for Perkins Foods aborted. Apr 2000: D Desmond buys more Greencore @ 244p/$3.10; now holds 10.2%. May 2000: Pre-empting a possible bid Greencore dumps NCB and takes on Goodbodys Stockbrokers. June 2000: Desmond mops up more shares @ 217p/$2.75 and now holds 11.1%. Greencore's holding in Imperial Holly worth $1.40 per share (bought originally at $13 in July 1996). July 2000: Decides against MBO. Aug 2000: Desmond's stake now at 14.36%. Buys Roberts

Share Price Sept 2001 - Sept 2002

1. €3.23 29.05.02 Interim results

FINANCIAL DIARY

Interim Results Announced	29.05.2002
Interim Dividend Payout	22.07.2002
Final Results Announced	29.11.2001
Annual General Meeting	07.02.2002
Final Dividend Payout	11.02.2002

FIVE YEAR SHARE PRICE TREND

1997	High	4.95 (Jan)	Low	3.68 (Nov)
1998	High	5.79 (Apr)	Low	2.67 (Oct)
1999	High	4.20 (Jan)	Low	2.40 (Nov)
2000	High	3.23 (Mar)	Low	2.45 (Nov)
2001	High	3.10 (Feb)	Low	2.22 (Nov)

INVESTMENT PERFORMANCE

Five Year Investment Performance:	€ 702
Ten Year Investment Performance:	€1,168

HALF YEARLY PERFORMANCES: € m

Six months to	29.09.00	31.03.01	30.09.01	29.03.02
Turnover	486.1	728.9	1,069.7	936.5
Pretax profit	(25.2)	14.7	(12.6)	4.9
Profit % Sales-	2.0		0.5	0.5

SECTORAL ANALYSIS (previous year)

Sales: Ingredients 30% (54%), frozen 35% (5%), grocery 27% (25%), agribusiness 8% (16%), Rofl 29% (52%), elsewhere 71% (48%). **Profits:** Ingredients 43% (62%), frozen 27% (7%), grocery 22% (17%), agribusiness 8% (14%), Rofl 29% (52%), elsewhere 71% (48%).

Group (UK frozen foods) for €48.1m. Dec 2000: Pays €427m f Hazlewood Foods. Jan 2001: Imperial Holly bankrupt. Feb 200 Shareholders dump Chairman B Cahill. July 2001: Sells Va Heyningen for €25m. March 2002: Sells 25% of Odlum to IAWS May 2002: Sells Grassland Fertilisers to MBO for €28m. June 200 Sells Erin and W Rodgers to Campbell Soups for €27.16m.

CAPITAL HISTORY:

Incorporated February 1991. March 1991: acquired the whole of the issued ordinary share capital of Irish Sugar plc in consideration for the issue of 25 million shares. Applied the sum of IR£40.5 million standing to the credit of its share premium account, resulting from the acquisition of the ordinary share capital of Irish Sugar plc, by issuing 40.5 million bonus shares which were credited as fully paid up. April 1992: Allotted 5,069,336 as part consideration for the acquisition of 50% of the issued share capital of Odlum Group Ltd. Allotted 970,188 shares to holders of loan notes of Irish Sugar plc with a nominal value of IR£2,367,068 in consideration for the surrender of such loan notes. Allotted 76,675 shares in satisfaction of certain debt obligations of Irish Sugar plc arising on the acquisition of James Daly & Sons Ltd. Allotted 12,056,544 shares re its offer for sale. Dec 1995: 7,310,467 Ord £1 shares on conversion of £3.3m 9.5% loan stock. March 1996: Each share subdivided into Ord 50p shares. 12,192,266 Ord 50p shares issued on conversion of 9.5% conv. Unsec. loan stock. July 1997: Issued 3,378,376 Ord 50p shares re purchase of 48.5% Kears Group. Feb 1998: Purchased 4,906,250 own shares on the market at 380p each (held as Treasury shares).

COMPANY HISTORY:

Sugar factory set up Carlow 1926; experienced severe trading difficulties; expanded to Carlow in Carlow; by 1934 sited also at Mallow, Thurles and Tuam. In 1975 acquired 51% of Sums for £17.6m in cash and Loan Notes. 1990 purchased Grassland for £12.2m in cash and loan notes. April 1991 purchased 50% of Odlums for £11.7m cash and 5,069,336 Ord. £1 shares. April 1991: 33m shares offered in flotation at 230p each and 6.5m shares offered to employees and beet growers at 184p each (only half of these discounted shares taken up). Greencore received £22.0m for their shares;

TEN YEAR REVIEW: € m

12 months to Sept. 30	1992	1993	1994	1995	1996	1997	1998	1999	2000	2001
Sales	492.4	500.0	513.6	554.7	582.9	592.8	751.8	862.4	905.9	1,798.6
Profit before tax	39.9	42.8	50.2	59.7	69.4	63.1	73.9	73.0	7.3 j)	2.1
Tax	6.4	6.1	8.5	9.5	10.1	8.7	10.8	6.9	6.5	6.4
Profit after Tax	33.5	36.7	41.7	50.2	59.3	54.4	63.1	66.1	0.8	(4.3)
Minority Interests	(0.6)	(0.8)	(0.9)	(0.9)	(0.6)	(1.1)	(1.5)	(2.6)	(1.7)	(1.4)
Extraordinary Items	(2.4) c)	-	-	-	-	-	-	-	-	-
Available for shareholders	30.5	36.0	40.9	49.3	58.7	53.4	61.6	63.5	(0.9)	(5.7)
Ordinary Dividend	8.5	9.3	10.5	12.8	16.1	18.6	20.2	22.2	23.6	23.7
Retained Profit	22.0	26.7	30.4	36.5	42.6	34.8	41.4	41.4	(24.5)	(29.4)
Increase (Decrease) in Reserves	(2.5) d)	27.5	30.3	33.7	52.0 f)	19.5 g)	(65.8) a)	26.5 b)	10.6 h)	(28.5)
Shareholders' Funds	146.7	174.1	204.8	241.0	302.2	324.8	259.2	285.7	296.4	268.0
Ordinary Dividend per share (€)	0.05	0.056	0.062	0.075	0.086	0.098	0.108	0.119	0.126	0.126
Earnings per Share (€)	0.190	0.216	0.244	0.291	0.321	0.284	0.33	0.34 e)	-	-

a) Goodwill write-off -€83.9m; purchase of own shares -€24.1m. b) Goodwill write-off -€12.3m; currency loss -€2.5m. c) Write-offs -€1.5m; High Court costs -€0.9m.
d) goodwill write-offs -€23.4m; currency loss -€1.1m. e) Based upon 186.8m shares. f) Share premium +€16.9m; goodwill w/o -€7.1m.
g) Share premium +€16.0m; goodwill w/o -€31.5m. h) Goodwill reinstated +€38.9m; currency loss -€3.9m. j) Write-off Imperial Sugar -€71.0m.

BALANCE SHEET: SEPTEMBER 28 2001. € m

Share Capital:			
191,873,109 Ord €0.63 shares	120,991	Tangible Assets	693,872
(Includes 4,906,250 treasury shares)		Financial Assets	9,466
		Current Assets 795,867	
Reserves	146,979	Current Liabilities 712,686	
		Net Current Assets	83,181
		Medium Debt	(857,275)
		Minority	(5,048)
Shareholders' funds	267,970	Net Tangible Liabilities	(75,804)
		Intangibles	343,774
		Net Assets	267,970

Comment:

Shareholders are being paid dividends out of their own reserves for the past 2 years and borrowings are going through the roof - only the goodwill makes the group solvent. The harvest will have to be reaped sometime.

Greencore has been trying desperately to transform itself from a lumbering commodity sugar based business to a more sexy and more broadly based consumer foods grouping carrying a massive amount of debt which it is trying to ameliorate by judicious surgical pruning. From its profit peak of nearly €74 million in 1998 Greencore is now labouring under a mountain of debt after its last year's break-even performance when it paid nearly €58 million in interest to its bankers.

The immediate past history of Greencore does not make for pleasant reading mired in controversy and ending with the Chairman being shown the door in an ignominious but opportune vote at the annual general meeting. But the helm is now under the stewardship of one of the most respected captains of industry, Tony Barry, but unfortunately his stint is short-lived as he has well flagged his departure at the end of this year. It appears that Barry has advised a bit of boardroom spring cleaning with the increase from 10 to 12 chairs around the table to facilitate seven non-executive and five executive directors. The arrival of Ned Sullivan is a welcome non-exec as he is no stranger to wielding the axe having had a few exasperating but worthwhile years in unwinding the mess at Glanbia.

Following a series of acquisitions since it came to the stockmarket, Greencore's business mix is radically different to the early 1990s. The most notable features have been the move into chilled food products and ambient grocery. These products are focused on the UK market, though there is also exposure in mainland Europe and Ireland. Sugar profits, in spite of doubling since flotation (despite recent declines), now represent just over one fifth of total operating profits.

While Greencore has held (or built) market leadership positions in its original businesses of food ingredients and agribusiness, these businesses are now ex-growth. By contrast, the newer divisions covering chilled/frozen and ambient food are considered among the fastest growing food segments in the food industry.

The acquisition of Hazlewood Foods in January 2001 for €588m brought with it pretax profits of £42m stg in 2000 on sales of £760m stg. Any optimistic investor who expected Greencore to turn up with sales in the region €900m + €1.000m or €1,900m the following year producing pretax profits in the region of €73m + €42m - financing cost of, say, €58m totalling €57m had a rude awakening ahead of them. Instead it was excuse after excuse as to why 1+1 never equals 2. Instead they were treated to a balance sheet which would get any banker rushing for the bottle of valium with net intangible assets of €75.8m and a whopping €343m of goodwill keeping the tot on the right side of sanity. One of the problems amongst many at Greencore is that out of a total of earnings attributable to shareholders created over the past few years of €172m they have been paying dividends to shareholders of €108m as if there were no tomorrow. Furthermore, if they could find anyone to underwrite the shares Greencore would have been better to try to pay for the Hazlewood acquisition in paper rather than dig into a bank account that was getting redder by the minute. As the *Financial Times* pointed out at the time "...but the business (Hazlewood) was heading downhill so fast that shareholders were eager to accept or sell in the market yesterday."

Acquisition History		
Date	Company	Cost
Aug '89	Swissco	€5m
1989	James Daly	€5m
'90/'91	Odlums	€53m
Jan '91	Grasslands	€15m
Nov '91	Food Industries	€73m
May '94	Belgomalt	€4m
'94/'97	Kears Bakery	€45m
1995	Williams Group	€9m
Jly '96	Imperial Holly (27%)	€40m
Apr '98	Pauls Malt	€96m
Aug '98	Paramount Foods	€45m
2000	William Rogers	€5m
2000	The Roberts Group	€48m
Feb '00	Hazlewood Foods	€588m

But instead it has developed into a face saving situation having had enough egg on its face over the infamous Imperial Sugar which cost Greencore an eventual write-off of €71m. The old slash-hook has been applied left right and centre. The FH Lee paper business, Rowan ready-made meals and Hillier's pastry business has been given the heave-ho along with two horticultural businesses (VHB and Hectare), the Dutch waffle business (Wafel Janssen), three Dutch and UK fish operations and the Dutch frozen snacks business (Advang). The shutters have been pulled down on the frozen ready meals operation in Dunstable. Gone also are the edible fats business of James Daly and the long-standing but loss making agricultural machinery distributor of Armer Machinery. The bank manager is happier with €100m in his paw. Grassland Holdings with sales of €60m and profits of €2.2m have also been de-ballasted for €19m along with 26% of Odlums. Other bits and bobs have brought the cash coffers €150m so far to date.

So what's left? Well, there are the old stalwarts of sugar processing, malt with its agreement with Interbrew and sundry agribusiness. These are essentially mature commodity businesses where margin and profit growth is dependent on production efficiency. In an environment of cut-throat prices on a household staple such as sugar and higher input costs such as wages, profit improvement will be difficult.

And then there are the new hopefuls. By contrast benefits should be gleaned from the dynamic growing sectors of the food industry which are reflecting changing consumer lifestyles. The need for ready prepared food to satisfy the need for grazing on the hoof such as sandwiches and foods that require little finishing before eating such as ready meals, pizza and quiches or that aid in the preparation of home foods in the form of sauces, underpin the growth profile of these newer Greencore businesses. Sandwiches have been growing at 14%, chilled sauces at 20%, quiches at almost 30% and mineral water at 13%.

The next set of figures will be eagerly awaited to see if there is a decent upward trend in the profits graph to justify the sum paid for Hazlewood and to keep Dermot Desmond, who is sitting on quite a chunk of equity, appeased in the short-term.

(We have reviewed a number of stockbrokers' reports including Goodbodys whose details form the basis of some of the figures quoted above.)

Greencore evolution				
Division	1990 Op Profit €m	%	2002 Op Profit €m	%
Ingredients	17.3	54%	47	39
Chilled & Frozen	0	0	37	31
Ambient grocery	2.8	9	26	21
Agribusiness	11.9	37	11	9
Total	32.0	100	121	100

GREEN PROPERTY plc

BUSINESS: Property development and investment.
REGISTERED OFFICE: Styne House, Upper Hatch St., Dublin.
HEAD OFFICE: as above. Tel: 01-2418400. Fax: 01 2418484. **SECRETARY:** D. McDowell. **REGISTRARS & TRANSFER OFFICE:** Computershare Investor Services (Ireland) Ltd, Corrig Road, Sandyford Ind Estate, Dublin
PRINCIPAL BANKERS: Allied Irish Banks; Bank of Ireland, Barclays Bank, Commerzbank AG, Credit Lyonnais, Dresdner Bank, HSBC Group, Lloyds TSB, NatWest Group, Royal Bank of Scotland, Wurttembergische Hypotheken Bank, Ulster Investment Bank. **AUDITORS:** KPMG. **SOLICITORS:** Arthur Cox .
STOCKBROKERS: J. & E. Davy; Merrill Lynch International.
DIRECTORS: R. MacSharry (Chairman - 64), S. Vernon (Mng Dir - 52), M Cherry (43), R. Hooper (66), D. Kitchen (50), D. McDowell (60), J. McKenna (58), K. Wylie (70), D Twining (61).
SHARE CAPITAL: Authorised: 145m €0.35 Ord. shares.
Issued: 103,079,060 Ord. €0.35 Ord. shares.
STAFF: 55   **SCRIP DIVIDEND:** No

CAPITAL HISTORY:

June 1985: 6,600,000 Ord. 25p shares issued in flotation at 97p each. January 1989: Issued 6,000,000 8% Red Convertible Loan Stock 1995 of £1 at par (conversion terms £16.67 of Ord. shares for every £100, i.e. 150p per share). June 1989: 3,000,000 Ord. 25p shares issued on acquisition of Surelodge at 160p each. Issued 3,000,000 8% Red Convertible loan stock £1 each at 135p. Dec. 1993: Converted Loan Stock by issue of 6,666,666 Ord 25p shares 74 shares for every £100 loan stock (135p per share). Mar. 1994: Issue of 17,536,008 Ord 25p shares in 3-for-4 rights issue at 150p each. Aug 1994: Issues 4,079,999 Ord 25p shares at 150p each part payment for Setanta. June 1996: 1-for-3 rights (15,378,659 Ord 25p shares) at 200p each. Dec 1997: 17,673,333 Ord 25p shares issued by way of rights issue (2-for-7) at 350p each. June 1998: Agrees to issue up to 30,252,371 Ord 25p shares for Trafford Park Estates. March 1,999: Issued 955,410 Ord 25p shares (£4.5m) for United House Realty Ltd.

COMPANY HISTORY:

Green Property commenced operations in 1966 by assembling a site on Hume Street/St. Stephen's Green, Dublin. In 1967 Green Property together with Dublin Corporation, agreed to undertake the joint development of Northside Shopping Centre at Coolock in Dublin.

Other retail projects undertaken were the completion of a shopping arcade in Patrick Street, Cork and the joint development with New Ireland Assurance Company of a shopping centre in Waterford. The assembly of an 88 acre site at Blanchardstown, Dublin was commenced by the Group in 1972. The Group diversified into the Dublin Industrial Property Sector in 1975 by purchasing 25 acres of industrial land at Glasnevin and, subsequently, further land at Bray and Ballymount. January 1988: Purchased shopping centre in Selby, Yorkshire for £5m jointly with United House Realty. January 1989: Placed £6m 8% Red Convertible Loan Stock at par. June 1989: Acquired 18 properties from Surelodge Investments for IR£33.8m. Sold 50% of Northside Shopping Centre for £9.8m. Raised £8.8m by 3m new shares at 160p and 3m, £1 Convertible Loan Stock at 135p. May 1991: Green threatened to suspend Blanchardstown when Quarryvale planning was passed (massive competition for Blanchardstown). June 1991: Bid approaches by two developers but no offer made. July 1993: John Corcoran breaks 5 year service contract and retires as Managing Director. Oct. 1993: Joint venture with PDFM acquires shopping centre in Devon for £10m. Dec 1993: Joint venture with PDFM acquires shopping centre in Middlesbrough. Converted £9m loan notes into shares. Mar. 1994: Purchased Na Mara Investments Ltd for £42m. rights issue raised £25m B. Collins resigns as Director. July 1994: Sells 2 properties for £2.2m. Aug 1994: J. Mc Kenna and D. McDowell sell option shares. Buys Setanta Centre, Dublin for £20m (cash and shares). For £9.9m buys 4 shopping centres in Finglas, Navan, Drogheda and Athlone. Dec 1994: Aborts £9.9m shopping centres purchase. March 1995: Obtains £39m loan to finance Blanchardstown. April 1995: £16m joint purchase with Irish Permanent of IFSC offices. June 1995: Joint off balance sheet venture with GE Capital worth £19.75m in London and Midlands. May 1996: Purchased United Friendly portfolio for £37.1m stg. July 1996: Pays £16.4m for 2 properties in UK. July 1996: 97.8% rights taken up. Nov 1996: Acquired UK property portfolio for £68.5m stg. Feb 1998: Agrees to buy out GE Capital's interest in partnership for £29m stg. July 1998: Bids £156m for Trafford Park Estates. Jan 2000: To invest £50m in 50% joint venture to purchase £400m P&O property portfolio. June 2000: Because of share price discount to NAV may go 'private'. Sept 2000: MBO abandoned. Oct 2000: Treasury Holdings in aborted bid-

talks. Nov 2000: Buys back 6.1m own shares @ €7. each and cancels them (cost €44.5m/£35m). April 200 Buys back and cancels 2,416,097 Ord shares @ €6. each. Nov 2001: Sells 2 London properties for €15.5r July 2002: S Vernon/Merrill Lynch/ICC bid €9.80 ca per share (value €1.05bn) with NAV per share €11.66.

Share Price Sept 2001 - Sept 2002

1. €6.85 07.02.02 Final results
2. €9.65 02.07.02 Bid announced

FINANCIAL DIARY
Interim Results Announced:	02.08.2001
Interim Dividend Payout:	28.09.2001
Final Results Announced:	07.02.2002
Annual General Meeting:	18.04.2002
Final Dividend Payout:	19.04.2002

SECTORAL ANALYSIS
Sales: RofI 34% (28%), UK 66% (72%)
Profits: RofI 35% (31%), UK 65% (69%)

FIVE YEAR SHARE PRICE TREND
1997	High	5.33 (Oct)	Low	3.07 (Jan)
1998	High	7.36 (Apr)	Low	4.31 (Sept)
1999	High	6.09 (Apr)	Low	4.65 (Feb)
2000	High	7.25 (Oct)	Low	5.05 (Feb)
2001	High	8.10 (Mar)	Low	5.90 (Oct)

INVESTMENT PERFORMANCE
Five Year Investment Performance:	€2,199*
Ten Year Investment Performance:	€6,132*

*if the latest takeover offer were considered these investments would increase to €3,343 and €9,201 respectively

HALF YEARLY PERFORMANCES: € m
Six Months to	30.06.00	31.12.00	30.06.01	31.12.01
Rental Income	45.9	47.2	49.8	52.5
Profit before Tax	38.0	28.1	37.2	36.4

TEN YEAR REVIEW: € m

12 months to December 31	1992	1993	1994	1995	1996	1997	1998	1999	2000	2001
Turnover	9.2	13.0	29.8	30.1	26.0	60.6	86.0	142.9	204.8	334.5
Rental Income	5.9	6.2	10.8	12.8	17.4	34.9	57.0	77.7	93.1	102.3
Profits before Tax	2.3	2.7 f)	5.1	8.1	10.8	15.4	27.3	42.2	66.1	73.6
Tax	0.8	0.8	+0.1	0.8	1.3	2.9	6.7	8.0	11.6	9.3
Profits after Tax	1.5	1.9	5.2	7.3	9.5	12.5	20.5	34.2	54.5	64.3
Available for Shareholders	1.5	1.9	5.2	7.3	9.5	12.5	20.5	34.2	54.5	64.3
Ordinary Dividend	0.8	1.1	2.3	2.6	3.3	4.2	8.1	8.9	9.7	11.9
Retained Profit	0.7	0.8	2.9	4.7	6.2	8.3	12.4	25.2	44.8	52.4
Increase (Decrease) in Reserves	(3.9) e)	19.5 g)	40.5 h)	11.7 j)	91.6 i)	143.7 k)	271.8 o)	258.4 a)	206.3 b)	89.8
Shareholders' Funds	36.5	58.4	105.9	117.8	214.4	363.8	645.3	904.1	1,112.0	1,201.0
Ordinary Dividend per Share (€)	0.048	0.051	0.053	0.056	0.058	0.067	0.074	0.08	0.09	0.115
Earnings per share (€)	0.098	0.107	0.116	0.033	0.174	0.202	0.22	0.308	0.491	0.615 n)

a) Property revaluation +€235m. b) Property revaluation +€185.8m; buy-back/cancellation of shares -€44m. e) Property devaluation -€2.2m; currency loss -€3.3m. f) Interest capitalised €1.8m.
g) Share premium re conversion of loan stock and placing +€10.4m, property revaluation +€6.0m, currency uplift +€2.5m. h) Share premium +€32.5m; negative goodwill €2.4m; property revaluation €3.4m.
i) Share premium + €33.3m; asset revaluation + €46.7m; currency profit + €3.2m, j) Asset revaluation +€7.0m. k) Share premium +€71.4m, property revaluation +€59.6m, currency gain +€4.6m.
n) Based upon 104.7m shares. o) Revaluation surplus +€103.0m; share premium +€166.3m.

BALANCE SHEET: DECEMBER 31 2001. € m

Share Capital:				
103,014,674 Ord. €0.35 shares	36.1	Tangible Assets		1,930.9
		Financial Assets		86.5
		Current Assets	60.0	
Reserves	1,164.9	Current Liabilities	92.9	
		Net Current Liabilities		(32.9)
		Long Term Debt		(783.5)
Shareholders' Funds	1,201.0	Net Tangible Assets		1,201.0

Comment:
It's good bye to a solid property company which never got its due praise in a stock market more turned on by dotcoms than solid bricks and mortar. But for those who hung in to Green through the lean years the payoff has been rewarding.

SUPPORTING

EFFECTIVE CORPORATE GOVERNANCE

Accountability and communication are the two essential components for effective corporate governance. Those responsible for the day to day management of a company's affairs need to communicate more transparent and comprehensive information to stakeholders and the capital markets.

We will work with you and your audit committee to help you meet stakeholder expectations by identifying and adopting corporate governance and financial disclosure best practices.

For more information or to find out how we can help please contact either Bill Cunningham or Neil Murphy on (01) 678 9999.

www.pwcglobal.com

TRANSPARENT CORPORATE REPORTING

Businesses today, more than ever before, need to demonstrate transparency and accountability in their reporting practices by:

- Adopting and consistently applying internationally accepted accounting standards; and

- Communicating the structures that the board and its audit committee have put in place to ensure that the organisation is effectively governed and controlled.

Companies are encountering increasingly sophisticated investors who are well informed and moving from a traditionally passive to a more active role. Investors, analysts and other stakeholders expect annual reports to provide clear and credible explanations of business performance. In addition they require information about the future direction of the business, the risks that it is facing and the efforts being taken by the board and management to mitigate these risks. We believe that every company listed on the world's equity markets should, at a minimum, address the following three aspects in their corporate reporting and communications:

1. Reporting Business Performance

Corporate reports deal principally with historical operating and financial performance, but that performance is more easily set in context by including discussion of strategic objectives and external conditions. Shareholders and analysts are better able to assess the performance of the business if the aspirations of the company (both financial and non-financial) are set out for comparison. A good review of business performance should include:

- A comparison of current performance against objectives together with defined targets for the coming year;
- An explanation of the significant features of operating performance highlighting how changes in the industry or external environment have impacted on the business;
- The main market and business risk factors that may affect future results, whether or not significant in the period of review; and
- Capital investments in the current period that will maintain and develop future revenue streams.

The discussion of operating performance should focus on the business overall and on individually important segments.

2. Analysing the Financial Position

The financing structure of the organisation should be explained and details of future financing should also be provided. In commenting on the financial position the following points should be discussed:

- The financial strength of the business, including the debt and equity capital structure;
- Sources of liquidity and the financing implications of capital expenditure plans together with the level and source of borrowings, the maturity profile of debt and the availability of facilities; and
- Policies adopted by the group for managing interest rate, currency and credit risks.

3. Corporate Responsibility

Businesses are recognising their responsibility to explain their activities to an increasingly wider group of stakeholders. As a result we believe that the annual reports of all public interest companies should, as a matter of course, include sections on:

- Corporate governance arrangements, including measures taken by the company to ensure that management decisions are subject to appropriate oversight and that internal control procedures are properly designed, implemented and maintained;
- Business ethics and internal standards of corporate behaviour;
- Employee matters including the measures taken by management to ensure that there is proper communication to employees at all levels in the company;
- Environmental responsibilities and the practical measures taken by companies to protect the environment.

Committed to moving the transparency and accountability debate forward we, at PricewaterhouseCoopers, have developed a framework that encourages businesses to report their performance against previously disclosed financial and non-financial objectives.

We believe that, in the future, companies must provide this wider "information set" to retain stakeholder confidence and to ensure continued access to capital markets.

Bill Cunningham leads PricewaterhouseCoopers' Assurance and Business Advisory Services practice in Ireland where he advises public interest companies on their corporate governance and reporting practices. Bill can be contacted at (01) 704 8549 or via email at bill.cunningham@ie.pwcglobal.com

PRICEWATERHOUSECOOPERS 🔲

GRESHAM HOTEL GROUP plc

(formerly RYAN HOTELS plc)

BUSINESS: Hotel owner/operators.
REGISTERED OFFICE: 23 Upper O'Connell St, Dublin 1.
Tel: 01-8787966.   Fax: 01-8786032.
HEAD OFFICE: as regd office.   **SECRETARY:** E Kenny.
REGISTRARS & TRANSFER OFFICE: Computershare Investor Services (Ireland) Ltd, Heron House, Corrig Road, Sandyford Industrial Estate, Dublin.
PRINCIPAL BANKERS: Allied Irish Banks; Bank of Ireland; Industrial Credit Corp.; Irish Intercontinental Bank; Investment Bank of Ireland; Royal Bank of Scotland.
AUDITORS: PricewaterhouseCoopers.
SOLICITORS: Mason Hayes & Curran; CMS Cameron McKenna.
STOCKBROKERS: Goodbody Stockbrokers; Barclays de Zoete Wedd.
DIRECTORS: P Coyle (Chairman & Ch Ex - 38), R Bastow (35), D Chambers (62), T Byrne, H Soning, A Pickel.
SHARE CAPITAL: Authorised: 91,800,000 Ord. €0.10 shares; 4,200,000 Participating Pref. €0.10 shares; 200,000 Pref. €1 shares. **Issued:** 78,731,102 Ord. €0.10 shares; 4,200,000 Participating Pref. €0.10 shares. Participating Pref. shares are entitled to non-cumulative 9% dividend and, after payment of 22% on ordinary shares, rank for further 3.5%.
STAFF: 703.   **SCRIP DIVIDEND:** Yes

CAPITAL HISTORY:

November 1969 1,664,000 Ord. 5p shares issued for £312,000. April 1969 2-for-3 'scrip' issue. 1970 4,200,000 Participating Pref. 5p shares issued on acquisition of properties. 1972/73/74 2,315,339 Ord. 5p shares issued for Swan Tours. August 1974 750,000 Ord. 5p shares issued for Travel Systems International. January 1979 'rights' of 1-for-6 issued at 17.5p. Feb. 1984 10,750,000 placed in London at 10p (8p stg) which raised £1,019,359. Nov 1988 rights issue (2 for 5) at 32p each to raise £4.6m. July 1989 3,820,000 ord. 5p shares placed at 55p each. April 1991: Rights 4-for-17 at 40p (issues 13,904,994 Ord. 5p shares).

COMPANY HISTORY:

Formed in 1964 to take over Ryans Car Hire Ltd. Went public September 1964. By 1972 had hotels in Sligo, Galway, Limerick and Killarney. 1972 sold car hire to Hertz. Built London Ryan hotel near Charing Cross, London. June 1972 acquired Swan Tours. August 1974 acquired Travel Systems International for £376,042 plus 750,000 shares. May 1977 sold Swan Tours. September 1977 Aer Linte sold its holding in Ryan to Pembroke Investments, a Conor McCarthy/C.P. Bourke investment company. Also in 1977 purchased Gresham Hotel for £1.6m. In 1979 opened Blooms Hotel in Dublin. Purchased Westport Ryan. November 1981 London Ryan sold to Mount Charlotte Investments. March 1983 Pembroke Investments sold 29.9% of its holding in Ryan to UK interests. August 1984 Pembroke Investments acquire 842,282 shares in Ryan. 1984 bid to oust directors by O'Hara/UK consortium fails. July 1984 Belhaven Breweries acquire 14.9% of Ryan Hotels subsequently increased to 23.78%. 1985 Ryan buys Royal Marine Hotel for £1m. August 1985 Belhaven sells stake. Oct. 1987: Sale & leaseback for £4m on Blooms Hotel, annual rental £300,000. November 1988: Purchase of Hotel Le Belson S.A. in Brussels for £2.38m. The Group also took over a £1.1m loan as part of deal. Rights to raise £4.6m. July 1989: Acquired Memphis Hotel, Amsterdam for £1.4m. Share placing 3.92m shares at 55p raised £2.1m. Nov. 1989: Blooms Hotel re-acquired for £4m. May 1990: Disputed Blooms Hotel sale at £4.3m. March 1991: Sold 65% of Blooms and Rosses Point Hotel for £4.25m (net assets). Retained 35% and 1.6m 9% Red. Cum. Pref. £1 shares. 'Put and call' options on pref. shares for 10 years and convert. pref. for 15% of equity. May 1991: Acquired Carat Hotel Hamburg for £6.1m. Rights issue to raise £4.8m. June 1993: Criticism of further write-offs on sale of 3 hotels. July 1993: Sale and leaseback of Hamburg Hotel. Jan 1999: £11m sale and 7-year leaseback of new 96 bedroom Gresham Hotel extension. June 98/Jan/Feb 99: 4 'old' guard retire at Board level (inc. C McCarthy). June 1999: Shareholders criticise share price performance - point out that only 4 out of 9 directors hold shares. July 1999: Pays £25.9m/£21.5mstg for London hotel (188 beds). Pays £7.6m for Metropole Hotel, Cork. May 2000: Red Sea Hotels take Ashdown's 16.6% (at €1.00 per share) stake for €13m. McEniffs buy 5.3% stake (at €0.80 per share) for €4m; subsequently sold. June 2001: Group changes name. Agreed sale and lease back of Dun Laoire hotel for €22m. April 2002: Euro Sea Hotels buy 5.4m shares @ €1.05 each bringing holding to 28.25%. Requests 3 directorships. June 2002: 3 directors ousted. July 2002: McDermott (NCB) led bid rumoured falls through. Aug 2002: Profits warning.

FIVE YEAR SHARE PRICE TREND €

1997	High	0.80 (Oct)	Low	0.51 (Jan)
1998	High	1.27 (Apr)	Low	0.76 (Oct)
1999	High	0.99 (May)	Low	0.74 (Mar)
2000	High	1.21 (June)	Low	0.71 (Feb)
2001	High	1.05 (Jan)	Low	0.65 (Sept)

FINANCIAL DIARY

Interim Results Announced:	27.09.2001
Interim Dividend Payout:	29.11.2001
Final Results Announced:	24.04.2002
Annual General Meeting:	19.06.2002
Final Dividend Payout:	28.06.2002

SECTORAL ANALYSIS: (previous year)

Not provided

HALF YEARLY PERFORMANCES: £m

Six months to:	31.07.00	25.01.01	26.07.01	31.01.02
Sales	20.7	23.6	27.5	27.7
Profit/Loss before Tax	3.2	4.2	(6.0)	1.2
Profit % Sales	15.5	19.1	-	4.3

INVESTMENT PERFORMANCE

Five Year Investment Performance:	€ 1,886
Ten Year Investment Performance:	€ 2,260

TEN YEAR REVIEW: € m

12 months to 31st January	1993 i)	1994	1995	1996	1997	1998	1999	2000	2001	2002
Sales	32.0	27.9	31.1	33.4	34.7	36.1	39.5	46.7	56.3	55.2
Profit (Loss) before Tax	(1.4)	1.5	2.5	3.5	5.1	6.4	7.8	9.0	9.3	(4.8) f)
Tax	0.3	0.3	0.3	0.2	0.3	0.2	0.5	0.9	1.3	0.3
Profit (Loss) after Tax	(1.7)	1.2	2.2	3.3	4.8	6.2	7.3	8.0	8.1	(5.1)
Extraordinary Item	(0.3)	-	-	-	-	-	-	-	-	-
Preference Dividend	-	-	-	-	-	-	-	-	-	-
Available for Shareholders	(2.0)	1.2	2.2	3.3	4.8	6.2	7.3	8.0	8.1	(5.1)
Ordinary Dividend	0.9	0.9	1.1	1.3	1.7	2.1	2.5	2.9	3.3	3.5
Retained Profit	2.9	0.3	1.1	2.0	3.1	4.1	4.8	5.1	4.8	(8.6)
Increase (Decrease) in Reserves	2.9	(0.1)	1.9	2.6	0.6	5.6	46.2	8.3	5.7	9.0 g)
Shareholders' Funds	53.1	52.9	54.6	57.3	58.0	63.6	109.9	118.3	124.1	135.5
Ordinary Dividend per Share (€)	0.013	0.013	0.016	0.019	0.024	0.029	0.034	0.038	0.042	0.045
Earnings per Share (€)	-	0.017	0.03	0.046	0.067	0.09	0.10	0.108	0.104 e)	-

a) Property revaluation +€40.5m. c) Revaluation surplus on properties €14.1m. d) €7.1m share premium; €10.3m property revaluation.

e) Based upon 75.4m shares. f) Includes -€6.0m devaluation in Hamburg hotel. i) 15 months. g) Revaluation of properties +€19.2m.

BALANCE SHEET: JANUARY 31 2002. € m

Share Capital:		Tangible Assets		213.2
78,011,164 Ord. €0.10 Shares	7.8	Current Assets	21.0	
Reserves	127.3	Current Liabilities	17.5	
		Net Current Assets		3.5
		Medium debt		(81.2)
Shareholders' Funds	135.1	Pref shares		(0.4)
		Net Tangible Assets		135.1

Comment:

Property inflation grossed +€78m over the 10 years; after tax profits came to €40m - some indictment on the management over the period. It is not surprising they are under attack in the boardroom.

HEITON GROUP plc

(formerly Heiton Holdings plc)

BUSINESS: Holding company involved in builders providers.

REGISTERED OFFICE: Ashfield, Naas Road, Clondalkin, Dublin. Tel: 01-4034000. Fax: 01-4593696.

HEAD OFFICE: as regd office.

SECRETARY: M. O'Callaghan.

REGISTRAR & TRANSFER OFFICE: Capita Corporate Registrars, PO Box 7117, Dublin.

PRINCIPAL BANKERS: AIB.

AUDITORS: PricewaterhouseCoopers.

SOLICITORS: A & L Goodbody.

STOCKBROKERS: J & E Davy.

DIRECTORS: R Keatinge (Chairman - 55), ? Martin (Gr CEO - 51), J Bourke (66), P Byers (48), ? Hewat (63), P Lynch (36), V O'Doherty (67), P Lynch (58)

SHARE CAPITAL: Authorised: 60m Ord. €0.32 shares, 80,000 6% Cum. Pref. €1.27 shares. **Issued:** 115,658 6% Cum. Pref. €1.27 shares, 49,395,943 Ord. €0.32 shares.

STAFF: 1,581.   **SCRIP DIVIDEND:** Yes

CAPITAL HISTORY:

1965 company floated by offer of 640,000 Ord. 25p shares at 40p each. 1967 533,333 Ord. 25p shares and 80,000 6% Cum. Pref. Shares issued in part consideration for McFerran & Guildford. March 1963 330,000 Ord. 25p shares issued in part consideration for Morgan McMahon & Co. Ltd. 1972 'scrip' issue of 1-for-1. In 1979 'scrip' issue of 1-for-1. Oct. 1985 issue of 300,000 7.5% Conv. Second Pref. £1 shares to institional shareholders. 750,000 converted to Ord. 2.5p shares Oct '87. April 1989, Convertible Pref. shares converted. April 1989: 6,467,231 Ord. 25p shares 3-for-at 58p each. December 1989: issued 300,000 Ord. 25p at 110p each on purchase of Atlantic Homecare in Dublin. March 1994: 4-for-7 rights 16,423,068 Ord 25p shares at 56p each. March 2001: Placed 1,850,000 Ord. €0.32 shares @ €3.80 per share.

COMPANY HISTORY:

Original business established in 1818 in the coal and iron trade. In 1887 J.M. Inglis and W. Hewat trading as Heiton & Co. took over the business. Incorporated in 1896. In 1944 coal merchants J.J. Carroll & Co. were acquired. In 1954 Heitons diversified with minority stake in motor assemblers Booth Poole. In 1960 took minority stake in Smiths Potato Crisps. In 1965 went public by offering 640,000 Ord. 25p shares at 40p each. In 1966 took over McFerran and Guildford and in 1968 took over Limerick based Morgan McMahon. 1971 acquired J. Myles Ltd. Ballyshannon, Co. Donegal (builders providers). In 1973 the solid fuel interests of the Group were merged with those of four other firms. As a consequence Consolidated Holdings Ltd. was established for this purpose. In 1974 company acquired Stephen Stokes & Co. Ltd. Limerick. In 1978 disposed of interest in P. Donnelly (Galway) Ltd. and liquidated the assets of National Oil Co. In 1979 Superwarm Homes Ltd., timber manufacturers, was formed and Heiton's acquired a 25% interest in Oakstead Ltd. an investment company which held a 34% investment in Campus Oil. In 1980 Heitons (26% of equity) and Consolidated Holdings announced plans for £4m timber mill in Fermoy (Home Grown Timber Ltd.) which was subsequently put into receivership in 1983 (cost Heitons £630,000 as extraordinary write-off in 1984). In Sept. 1985 serious financial situation resulted in £2.5m injection by financial institutions. June 1986 purchased coal merchants M. Doherty & Co. Ltd. for £1.58m cash. Doherty held a 26% in Consolidated Holdings Ltd. Subsequently sold 12% of CHL to other CHL shareholders for £855,610 cash. March 1988: Acquired Gilbert T. Bell Ltd. for £1.1mstg in UK. March 1989: Acquired Gloucester Steelstock. April 1989: Rights issue raises £3.6m. November 1989: Purchased McCowen of Tralee for £1m. December 1989: Acquired 3 Atlantic Homecare stores in Dublin for £3.9m in shares and cash. May 1991: Heitons exercises an option to buy Anika, a company which operates two Atlantic stores on the Belgard Road and the Naas Road. March 1992: Swapped 41.5% stake in Consolidated Holdings for 22% of Jubilata. Sept 1993: Pays £156,000 for Cork Atlantic Homecare. March 1994: Buys F & T Buckley for £8.1m. Rights issue to raise £9.2m. May 1996: DCC offloads 25% at 100p per share. July 1996: Bought McCormacks in Gorey. October 1996: Bought Pattons of Monaghan. May 1997: Bought Sam Hire for £5.2m. Sept 1998: Bought Cooper Clarke for max £19.8m stg(min £15.7m stg). Sept 1999: Switches stockbrokers from Goodbody (which also act for Grafton) to Davy. Grafton builds stake to 14.6%. April 2000: Buys Panelling Centre for £6.3m min. July 2000: Buys Tullamore Hardware for €2.7m. May 2001: Grafton buys

Share Price Sept 2001 - Sept 2002

1. €3.05 16.01.02 Interim Results
2. €3.00 03.07.02 Final Results

FINANCIAL DIARY

Interim Results Announced:	16.01.2002
Interim Dividend Payout:	20.03.2002
Final Results Announced:	03.07.2002
Annual General Meeting:	05.09.2002
Final Dividend Payout:	19.09.2002

FIVE YEAR SHARE PRICE TREND €

Year	High		Low	
1997	High	2.76 (Dec)	Low	1.22 (Jan)
1998	High	3.36 (Mar)	Low	1.78 (Sept)
1999	High	3.40 (July)	Low	1.76 (Jan)
2000	High	4.00 (Jan)	Low	2.78 (June)
2001	High	3.95 (Feb)	Low	2.25 (Nov)

INVESTMENT PERFORMANCE

Five Year Investment Performance:	€ 2,741
Ten Year Investment Performance:	€ 7,992

HALF YEARLY PERFORMANCES: €* m

Six months to:	31.10.00	30.04.01	31.10.02	30.04.02
Sales	192.3	176.9	224.8	197.8
Profit(-) before tax	11.8	20.5	10.3	5.2
Profit % Sales	6.1	11.6	4.6	2.6

SECTORAL ANALYSIS (previous year)

Sales: Merchanting 50% (73%), other 44% (20%), steel stockholding 6% (7%). Ireland 81% (85%), UK 19% (15%)

4.88% (@ €3.02 per share) of Heiton bringing its spend on stakebuilding (18.8%) to €25m. Sept 2001: Name changed. Grafton increases stake to 22.5% @ €2.77 each. Nov 2001: Buys and cancels 1.2m own shares @ €2.28 each. April 2002: Buys Cork Builders Providers for €24m. June 2002: Bought 55% of Wright Window Systems.

TEN YEAR REVIEW: €'000

months to April 30	1993	1994	1995	1996	1997	1998	1999	2000	2001	2002
Sales	78,342	85,093	149,844	162,992	178,251	210,406	262,543	318,957	369,246	422,630
Profit (Loss) before Tax	2,220	931	5,092	8,766	10,931	14,008	16,284	19,577	32,297 a)	15,545
Tax	785	699	2,159	3,047	3,708	4,541	4,482	4,571	6,213	2,620
Profit (Loss) after Tax	1,435	232	2,933	5,719	7,223	9,467	11,802	15,006	26,084	12,925
Preference Dividend	10	10	10	10	10	11	11	11	11	11 ?
Available for Shareholders	1,425	222	2,923	5,709	7,213	9,456	11,791	14,995	26,073	12,914
Ordinary Dividend	729	1,012	1,442	1,808	2,291	2,902	3,628	4,766	6,194	6,575
Retained Profit	696	(790)	1,481	3,901	4,922	6,554	8,163	10,229	19,979	6,339
Increase (Decrease) in Reserves	625	8,427 d)	1,609	4,186	5,093	5,319	35,464 e)	11,102	28,138 f)	13,097
Shareholders' Funds	20,768	34,194	35,899	40,230	45,445	50,883	86,518	97,887	126,903	139,672
Ordinary Dividend per Share (€)	0.025	0.025	0.032	0.039	0.050	0.062	0.077	0.10	0.125	0.133
Earnings per Share (€)	0.050	0.008	0.065	0.124	0.156	0.20	0.25	0.32	0.54	0.258 b)

a) Includes profit on sale of property €10.1m. b) Based upon 50m shares. d) Share premium +€5.8m, property revaluation +€3.3m. e) Property revaluation +€26.5m. f) Share premium +€6.6m. g) Property revaluation +€8.6m.

BALANCE SHEET: APRIL 30 2002. €'000

Comment:

Highly geared

and profits sliding.

Share Capital:			Fixed Assets & Investments	131,838
49,395,943 Ord. €0.32 shares	15,954		Current Assets	175,225
Reserves		123,718	Current Liabilities	122,060
			Net Current Assets	53,165
			Medium Debt	(83,724)
			Pref shares	(147)
Shareholders' Funds		139,672	Net Tangible Assets	101,132
			Intangibles	38,540
			Net Assets	139,672

moving forward for greater opportunity

Heiton

HORIZON TECHNOLOGY GROUP plc

(Quoted on ITEQ market)

BUSINESS: Information Technology solutions provider.
REGISTERED OFFICE: 14 Joyce Way, Park West Business Park, Nangor Road, Dublin.
HEAD OFFICE: as regd office. Tel: 6204900. Fax: 6204902
SECRETARY: C O'Caoimh.
REGISTRARS & TRANSFER OFFICE: Computershare Investor Services (Ireland) Ltd, Heron House, Corrig Road, Sandyford Industrial Estate, Dublin.
PRINCIPAL BANKERS: Ulster Bank.
AUDITORS: Ernst & Young.   **SOLICITORS:** William Fry.
STOCKBROKERS: Davy Stockbrokers.
DIRECTORS: S Naji (Chairman & Ch Exec - 40), C Garvey (45), K Melia (55), P Kenny (42), C O'Caoimh (45), P Tierney (53), G Coburn
SHARE CAPITAL: Authorised: 92.3million Ord €0.07 shares. **Issued:** 67,871,857 Ord €0.07 shares.
EMPLOYEES: 556
SCRIP DIVIDEND: No
WEB SITE: www.horizon.ie

COMPANY HISTORY:

Founded in 1988 by S Naji following buyout of Cork based computer systems business. In 1991 opened in Dublin developing open systems and networking systems integration. Group appointed Sun Microsystems partner. In 1992 established knowledge services division providing training courses. In 1993 became a Compaq distributor in Ireland. 1994 opened in London and became a Cisco trainer. 1995 acquired ASAP Ltd, a Surrey based Unix sytems business. Bought Micromuse plc (London) in Sept 1997 for $0.5m. In Feb 1997 bought 70% of 2T in Copenhagen for $819,000. In June 1998 bought Gericmar Ltd,

Samir Naji

a Dublin based Hewlett-Packard and IBM distributor for £3,237,000. In Aug 1998 acquired training business of Ingram Micro (UK) Ltd for £400,000stg. In Nov 1998 raised €6.77m net from private placing. There are 3 divisions - knowledge services, internet infrastructure and distribution services. Oct 1999: Takeover talks with Eircom fail. Dec 2000: Public flotation at 129p. Only 306,860 new shares issued. Naji and Garvey trouser £6.7m from proceeds. First day's dealings reach €4.10 - up 156%. Feb 2000: Raised €28.7m from further share placing. March 2000: Acquires Webfactory for €10m. April 2000: Buys Managed Training Services for €8.3m. Nov 2000: Buys Commerce NTI (UK) for up to €30m. April 2001: K Melia sells 25,000 shares @ €4 each. May 2001: Profits warning, staff layoffs, shares drop 50%. June 2002: Sells Cisco training/HTS Group for max €12m. Directors take pay cuts. Aug 2002: C Garvey resigns as Chief Executive.

CAPITAL HISTORY:

Incorporated June 1988 as private limited company. August 1998 converted A, B, C, D, E and G Ord £1 shares into Ord shares and subdivided them into Ord 5p shares. Allotted 42,832,240 Ord 5p shares 'bonus' to S Naji and C Garvey. Of these 7,856,839 allotted by renouncable letters of allottment, 1,535,000 of such shares renounced in favour of certain executives and family members of selling shareholders with remainder issued to S Naji and C Garvey. Sept 1998: issued 955,000 Ord 5p shares at 45.7p each to K Melia (580,000), P Kenny (150,000), P Tierney (150,000), H Devlin (75,000). Issued 300,000 Ord 5p shares to executives for 45.7p each. Oct 1988: Issued 1,595,000 Ord 5p shares to Horizon ESOP Ltd for 50p per share. Nov 1998: Placed 9,425,000 Ord 5p shares with private investors at 78p each. Dec 1999: Issued 325,400 Ord €0.07 shares @ €3.60 for final 30% of 2T A/S Technology Team each. Dec 2000: Placed 5,526,850 (5.22m from s'holders, 306,860 new) on stock market at €1.638 each. Feb 2000: Placed 2.9m Ord 5p shares at €10.10 each.

Share Price Sept 2001 - Sept 2002

Graph showing share price declining from around 0.8 in Sept 2001 to around 0.2 in Sept 2002

1. €0.50 11.12.01 Profits Warning
2. €0.28 10.06.02 Sales of Cisco Training

FINANCIAL DIARY

Interim Results Announced:	09.09.2002
Interim Dividend Payout:	none
Final Results Announced:	15.03.2002
Annual General Meeting:	28.06.2002
Final Dividend Payout:	none

HALF YEARLY PERFORMANCES: € m

Six months	31.12.00	30.06.01	31.12.01	30.06.02
Sales	183.3	226.2	168.2	192.9
Pretax/(loss) Profits	2.3	(18.7)	(22.9)	(6.2)
Profits % sales	1.2	-	-	

SECTORAL ANALYSIS (previous year):

Sales: RoI 56% (72%), other Europe 44% (28%). Internet services 60% (55%), distribution 40% (45%).

SHARE PRICE TREND: €

1999	High	4.20 (Dec)	Low	3.61 (Dec)
2000	High	14.01 (Feb)	Low	4.20 (Jan)
2001	High	7.50 (Jan)	Low	0.38 (Oct)

FIVE YEAR REVIEW: €'000

12 months to December 31	1997 f)	1998 f)	1999 f)	2000 f)	2001 f)	2001 e)
Sales	56,926	122,654	192,215	296,425	409,528	168,156
Profits Before Tax	1,765	2,832	5,024	11,361	(16,490)	(22,870)
Tax	490	1,228	1,378	3,576	+65	+1,336
Profits After Tax	1,275	1,604	3,646	7,785	(16,425)	(21,534)
Minority Interests	-	(43)	+22	(28)	(4)	-
Pref dividends	5	5	-	-	-	-
Available to Shareholders	1,270	1,558	3,668	7,757	(16,429)	(21,534)
Ordinary Dividend	25	232	-	-	-	-
Retained Profits	1,244	1,326	3,668	7,757	(16,429)	(21,534)
Increase (Decrease) in Reserves	n/a	(2,821)	9,096 d)	42,634 e)	(2,615)	(20,812)
Shareholders' Funds	2,108	(910) b)	11,868	55,127	52,729	32,034
Ordinary Dividend Per Share (€)	0.05	0.05	-	-	-	-
Earnings Per Share (€)	0.028	0.034	0.069	0.134 a)	-	-

a) Based upon 58.0m shares in issue. b) Goodwill write-off -€3.8m. d) Share issue out of reserves -€10.3m net.
e) 6 months to 31 Dec. f) Year ended June 30

BALANCE SHEET: DECEMBER 31 2001 €'000

Share Capital:	4,524	Tangible Assets	11,590
64,626,637 Ord €0.07 shares		Financial Assets	161
		Current Assets	96,920
Reserves	27,393	Current Liabilities	85,850
		Net Current Assets	11,070
		Medium debt	(8,775)
		Minority	(117)
Shareholders' Funds	31,917	Net Tangible Assets	13,929
		Intangibles	17,988
		Net Assets	31,917

Comment:

See

Chairman's Statement

Horizon Technology Group Plc

Horizon
Beats Market Expectations
On Revenue And Earnings

* Diluted adjusted Earnings Per Share was ahead of market expectations at 1.26 cent;

* Excluding discontinued activities, diluted adjusted Earnings Per Share of 3.45 cent provides a solid base for future profitability;

* Revenues of EUR192.9m was up 14.7% on the previous six months;

* Net debt has been reduced from EUR34.7m at 31 December 2001 to EUR3.3m;

* Working capital was reduced from 43 to 11 days generating cash of EUR23.7m;

* EBITDA was a healthy EUR 4.1m. Excluding discontinuing activities, EBITDA was EUR4.7m;

* Several un-profitable and non core businesses were disposed of or discontinued;

* The group has consolidated into four areas of business each of which has been and continues to be profitable and is a market leader in its' area of operation;

* Cost structures have been reduced from a peak quarterly cost of EUR17m in March 2001 to approximately EUR6.8m, a reduction of 60%.

Commenting on the results:

Samir Naji, Executive Chairman of Horizon Technology Group plc said: "The last six months has been a period of significant progress for the group. In a difficult and challenging environment, we have completed a comprehensive and fundamental restructuring of the group's operations and cost base resulting in significant operational efficiencies and bringing the group back to its core and profitable businesses.

We have continued to win new business in our target markets with particular successes in the last six months in the pharmaceutical, retail finance and government sectors - for example, Wyeth Corporation, Bank of Ireland and the Office of the House of Oireachtas. We have gained market share and continue to have an exceptionally high level of customer retention, with over 80% of our business coming from repeat customers.

Chairman's Statement

At the same time, we have produced growth in revenues and positive EBIT and cash flow thereby significantly reducing net debt and risk profile. As a result, the group is now well positioned to deliver growth in earnings going forward."

About Horizon:

Horizon Technology Group plc is an Information Technology Solutions Provider specialising in the design, development and implementation of technical infrastructure and business solutions for the networked economy. Horizon is quoted on the London and Dublin Stock Exchanges.

Samir Naji
Chairman

Samir Naji
Chairman and CEO

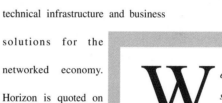

W*e have gained market share and continue to have an exceptionally high level of customer retention, with over 80% of our business coming from repeat customers.*

BUSINESS: Manufacturers and distributors of food products, fertilisers and agricultural products.
REGISTERED OFFICE: 151 Thomas Street, Dublin. Tel: 01-6121200. Fax: 01-6121321.
HEAD OFFICE: as regd office.
SECRETARY: A Lowther. **REGISTRARS & TRANSFERS OFFICE:** Capita Corporate Registrars, P O. Box 7117, Dublin. **PRINCIPAL BANKERS:** Bank of Ireland; Ulster Bank Group.
AUDITORS: Ernst & Young. **SOLICITORS:** L.K. Shields.
STOCKBROKERS: J. & E. Davy.
DIRECTORS: J Moloney (Chairman - 77), P Lynch (Mgr. Dir - 57), D Buckley (57), J Davy (61), P McCarrick (73), N McEniry (71), D Martin (58), W Murphy (68), O Killian (50), D Lucey (66), R McNamee (53).
SHARE CAPITAL: Authorised: 228m Ord shares of 25p each. **Issued:** 122,997,535 Ord 25p shares.
STAFF: 2,020.   **SCRIP DIVIDEND:** No

CAPITAL HISTORY:

Incorporated in May 1988. November 1988: Allotted 2,414,759 'A' Ord. shares of 25p at par for cash. Allotted 66.4m Ord 25p shares to I.A.W.S. Society as for assets of society. Placing of 9.4m Ord. shares of 25p each at 63p per share to raise £5.5m net of expenses. July 1989: Rights 1-for-12 at 77p issued 6,517,900 Ord. 25p shares. August 1990: Allotted 20,436,088 "A" Ord. 25p shares and 14,305,000 8% Subord. Convert. Unsec. £1 Loan Notes. June 1994: Issued 5,220,964 "A" Ord 25p shares on conversion of loan notes.

COMPANY HISTORY:

Established as a society in 1897, reorganised in 1983. 1984: Acquired Townsend Flahavan Ltd. (seed assembly). Commenced grain trading operations, acquisition of Bolands Mills Ltd. 1985: Purchased 30% holding in Goulding Chemicals Ltd. 1986: Acquired remaining shares in Gouldings. 1987: Society agreed to merge the business of Bolands with the milling businesses of Dock Milling and S. & A.G. Davis Ltd. 1988: Acquires entire share capital of Howard Brothers Ltd. July 1988: First overseas acquisition - Sherriffs in Hertfordshire. Acquired James Allen, seed trader for £1.25m. January 1989: Acquires Unigrain Group for £3.25m cash. July 1989: Rights issue raised £4.9m. Sept. 1989: Takes 37.2% stake in First National Bakery for £2.5m. Oct. 1989: Acquired 74% of Shamrock Foods for £0.5m. March 1990: Takes 45% stake in Montross, a hide business for £2m. April 1990: Acquired Independent Fertilisers in UK. August 1990: Acquire R & H Hall for £42.25m in cash and shares. March 1991: IAWS to sell assets including Dower Wood. May 1991: Pays £3.8m cash for remaining 30% Bolands. August 1991: P.I. Meagher resigns as Chairman. Jan 1993: HBP in Hull acquired for rumoured £1m. Feb 1993: Change of auditors. Acquires John Parsons (Yorkshire) Ltd for £650,000 stg. July1993: Acquires Pertwee Holdings in fertilisers in UK. For £1.5m. acquired remaining 26% Shamrock Foods for £0.7m. Feb 1994: Buys Nordos (Fishmeal) for £1.9m. stg. June 1994: Offers 1.2 new Ord shares for each £1 convertible. July 1994: Buys Malting Co of Ireland for £1.5m. Aug 1994: Buys Unifoods or £2.1m. Oct 1994: Bought Yorkshire Malton Fertilisers for £0.7m. Acquires United Fish Products Ltd for £11.3m Jan 1995: Bought Premier & Lisburn By-Products Ltd for £4.2m cash. Feb 1996: Strategic alliance with Cultor of Finland. June 1996: Ir. Agri. W'sale Socy Ltd approve transfer of 10% of equity to individual shareholders reducing its holding to 49.5%. Jan 1997: Bought 45% Group IKEM for £6.7m. May 1997: Buys PB Kent Ltd (UK) for £9m stg and sells Lisburn Proteins Ltd for £8.3m. Oct 1997: Pays £50m for Cuisine de France. June 1998: Sells Suttons for £5.2m. Sept 1998: Sells waterfront property for £8.8m. Nov 1998: Buys 34% Norwegian fish processor for £5.5m. March 1999: Bid for Spillers fails. May 1999: Directors sell shares netting £1m (at approx 319p each). July 1999: Pays total £41m (inc earn-out) for Delice de France. June 2000: Buys Pierre's Food Service for £20.7m/€26.3m. March 2001: Joint venture with Tim Hortons in Canada to invest €75m 50/50 basis. April 2001: Directors net €2.6m from share sales. July 2001: Buys 80% La Brea Bakery (California) for €119m (goodwill €99.1m). May 2002: Ir Agric W'sale Soly transfers 19 million shares to members.

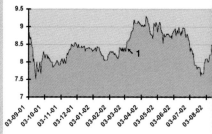

Share Price Sept 2001 - Sept 2002

1. €8.50 07.03.02 Interim Results

FINANCIAL DIARY

Interim Results Announced:	07.03.2002
Interim Dividend Payout:	25.04.2002
Final Results Announced:	22.09.2001
Annual General Meeting:	16.01.2002
Final Dividend Payout:	18.01.2002

FIVE YEAR SHARE PRICE TREND €

1997	High	3.36 (Oct)	Low	2.06 (Jan)
1998	High	4.25 (Apr)	Low	2.10 (Oct)
1999	High	4.80 (Dec)	Low	3.53 (Feb)
2000	High	8.10 (Aug)	Low	4.75 (Jan)
2001	High	8.85 (Sept)	Low	6.70 (Mar)

INVESTMENT PERFORMANCE

Five Year Investment Performance: €4,187
Ten Year Investment Performance: €16,573

HALF YEARLY PERFORMANCES: £'m

Six months to	31.07.00	31.01.01	31.07.01	31.01.02
Sales	540.9	502.0	599.6	580.5
Profits before Tax	33.6	23.3	41.5	16.4
Profits % Sales	6.2	4.6	6.9	2.8

SECTORAL ANALYSIS (previous year)

Sales: Food 48% (44%), Agribusiness 52% (56%). Rofl 57% (55%), elsewhere 43% (45%).

TEN YEAR REVIEW: € m

12 months to July 31	1992	1993	1994	1995	1996	1997	1998	1999	2000	2001
Sales	506.4	510.5	608.9	648.3	703.4	739.9	857.5	849.8	982.2	1,101.6
Profit before Tax	10.0	12.8	16.3	20.5	23.5	32.1	33.3	42.6	56.4 b)	64.8 d)
Tax	1.3	2.5	4.2	4.8	5.1	6.2	7.8	8.9	11.5	13.3
Profit after Tax	8.7	10.3	12.1	15.7	18.4	25.9	25.5	33.7	44.9	51.6
Minority Interest	-	(0.2)	(0.5)	(0.4)	(0.9)	(0.5)	(1.1)	(0.9)	(0.4)	(0.8)
Preference Dividend	-	-	-	0.9	0.9	0.9	0.8	0.6	0.6	0.3
Available for Shareholders	8.7	10.1	11.6	14.4	16.6	24.5	23.6	32.2	43.9	50.5
Ordinary Dividend	1.4	2.0	2.9	3.7	4.1	4.5	5.1	5.9	6.8	8.3
Retained Earnings	7.3	8.1	8.7	10.7	12.5	20.0	18.5	26.3	37.1	42.2
Increase (Decrease) in Reserves	6.4	2.2 f)	11.1	5.1	9.6	13.5 g)	(30.2) h)	27.2	39.8	49.3 i)
Shareholders' Funds	35.7	38.9	57.4	56.8	66.5	80.1	51.1	85.6	118.6	167.5
Ordinary Dividend per Share (€)	0.025	0.027	0.030	0.034	0.037	0.041	0.045	0.052	0.059	0.068
Earnings per Share (€)	0.083	0.095	0.110	0.130	0.150	0.174	0.21	0.28	0.38	0.42 a)

(a) Based upon 119.1m shares. b) Includes net asset disposal profits +€6.6m d) Includes once-off asset profits +€5m. f) Goodwill w/o -€2.8m; currency loss -€2m. g) Goodwill w/o -€10.2m, currency gain +€3.3m. h) Share premium +€2.4m, goodwill written-off -€51.3m. i) Share premium +€6.5m

BALANCE SHEET: JULY 31 2001. € m

Share Capital:		Tangible Assets	232.8
122,085,035 Ord €0.30 shares	36.6	Financial Assets	40.5
		Current Assets	277.4
		Current Liabilities	350.9
Reserves	130.9	Net Current Liabilities	(73.5)
		Medium Term Debt	(183.8)
		Pref. shares, grants, etc	(6.3)
		Minority	(4.0)
Shareholders' Funds	167.5	Net Tangible Assets	5.7
		Intangibles	161.8
		Net Assets	167.5

Comment:

A splendid payoff over the 10 year investment period. Expansion to the New World gives IAWS good scope for further growth.

ICON plc

CAPITAL HISTORY:

Feb 1998: 39,840 Ord 5p shares issued to Corbairt at 5p each. April 1998: Scrip issue of 20-for-1. May 1998: Options exercised by staff over 17,900 Ord 5p shares at 322p each (US$4.63). Issued 3,062,500 ADRs (representing 3,062,500 Ord 5p shares) at $18 each. ADRs first quoted on NASDAQ. Launch quote $18 (1329p). April 1999: Shares first quoted on Irish Stock Market. Jan 2000: Issued 838,828 Ord 5p shares re merger with Pacific Research. Issued 51,387 Ord 5p shares part purchase of YRCR. May 2000: Issued further 24,272 Ord 5p shares re YRCR purchase 'earnout'.

COMPANY HISTORY:

Incorporated in May 1989 to provide clinical research and development to the pharmaceutical and biotechnology industries. It specialises in the management, execution and analysis of complex, multinational clinical trials in most major therapeutic areas. By July 1998 it had 500 staff in 10 offices in 7 countries with clinical trials in 31 countries. Worldwide expenditure on pharmaceutical R&D is approx £36billion of which $17.5billion is of the type offered by the CRO industry and of this $4.4billion is outsourced. The company has serviced over 40 clients and during the year ended May 1998 serviced 30 clients including 11 of the to 20 pharmaceutical companies in the world. During the year serviced 3 biotechnology companies from whom it derived 8% of its revenue. During the year ended May1998 ICON managed 50 clinical trials involving 24,000 patients at 1,700 clinical centres in 30 countries. Net revenues in that year: Nth America 59%, Europe 40% and 1% Asia-Pacific. Competitors include ClinTrials Research Inc, Covance Inc, IBAH inc, Kendle International Inc, PAREXEL, Pharmaceutical Product Development, and Quintiles. March 1999: Share price collapse (from $26.75 down to $10) after warning that profits to May will be down on analysts' forecasts. Announces loss of $5m contract. April 1999: First quoted in Dublin @ €14.81 per share. Jan 2000: Buys Pacific Research Associates for $14m (shares). Bought YRCR (UK) for $1.8mstg cash and shares. March 2000: Bought Protocole for $0.7m. May 2000: Sales were 24% from Pfizer, 18% from Glaxo and 16% from Novartis. June 2000: Bought UCT (US) for max $18m.

Share Price Sept 2001 - Sept 2002

1. €34.00 08.01.02 Second quarter results
2. €34.00 26.03.02 Third quarter results
3. €19.50 30.07.02 Annual results

HALF YEARLY PERFORMANCE: $'m

6 months to	30.11.00	31.05.01	30.11.01	31.05.02
Sales	72.3	79.5	100.3	118.5
Pretax Profits (Loss)	6.2	7.4	9.1	10.2
Profit % sales	8.6	14.9	9.1	8.6

SECTORAL ANALYSIS: (previous year)

Revenue: Asia 1%(2%), Europe 28% (31%), US 71% (67%).

SHARE PRICE TREND €

1999	High 21.26 (June)	Low 12.20 (Oct)
2000	High 22.50 (Oct)	Low 13.03 (Apr)
2001	High 42.40 (Aug)	Low 18.00 (Jan)

TEN YEAR REVIEW: $'000

12 months to May 31	1993	1994	1995	1996	1997	1998	1999*	2000	2001	2002 b)
Sales	8,021	14,984	19,609	28,367	38,569	64,149	94,550	115,087	151,832	218,842
Profits Before Tax	671	2,657	1,471	4,175	1,508	5,988	9,063	9,190	13,595	19,329
Tax	209	900	264	1,618	1,214	1,648	1552	3,122	2,617	5,129
Profits After Tax	462	1,757	1,207	2,557	294	4,340	7,511	6,068	10,978	14,200
Minority Interests	-	-	-	-	-	-	-	-	-	-
Available to Shareholders	462	1,757	1,207	2,557	294	4,340	7,511	6,068	10,978	14,200
Ordinary Dividend	-	-	-	-	-	-	-	-	-	-
Retained Profits	462	1,757	1,207	2,557	294	4,340	7,511	6,068	10,978	14,200
Increase (Decrease) in Reserves	n/a	n/a	n/a	n/a	244	3,637	7,257	5,407	9,559	-
Shareholders' Funds	1,606	3,652	5,129	7,577	9,284	63,009	70,266	77,053	86,580	107,561
Ordinary Dividend Per Share ($)	-	-	-	-	-	-	-	-	-	-
Earnings Per Share ($)	$0.07	$0.25	$0.17	$0.38	$0.04	$0.62	$0.75	$0.55	$0.97	$1.22 a)

a) Based upon 11.7m shares. b) Awaiting Form 20-F. * *These figures seem to be subsequently altered; no satisfactory explanation could be obtained.* These figures are prepared in accordance with US GAAP only.

BALANCE SHEET: MAY 31 2001. $'000

Comment:

Investors in this industry are temporarily wary because of the Elan debacle. Icon is forecasting 20% per annum growth in the medium term which with luck could go to 30%. The current share weakness could present buying opportunities.

Share Capital:	819	Fixed Assets		19,671
11,429,629 Ord €0.06 shares		Current Assets	102,654	
		Current Liabilities	41,507	
		Net Current Assets		61,147
Reserves	85,761	Medium debt		(880)
Shareholders' Funds	86,580	Net Tangible Assets		79,938
		Intangibles		6,642
		Net Assets		86,580

* The May 2002 Balance Sheet was not available at time of going to press.

IFG GROUP plc

(Formerly Credit Finance Bank)

BUSINESS: Financial services conglomerate.
REGISTERED OFFICE: IFG House, Booterstown Hall,
Booterstown, Co Dublin. Tel: 01-2752801,
Fax: 01-2752800. **HEAD OFFICE:** as regd office.
SECRETARY: D Lynch.
REGISTRARS & TRANSFER OFFICE: Computershare
Investor Services (Ireland) Ltd, Heron House, Corrig Road,
Sandyford Industrial Estate, Dublin.
PRINCIPAL BANKERS: Ulster Bank, Anglo Irish Bank, Bank
of Scotland (I) Ltd, Royal Bank of Scotland.
AUDITORS: PricewaterhouseCoopers.
SOLICITORS: O'Donnell Sweeney.
STOCKBROKERS: NCB Stockbrokers Ltd.
DIRECTORS: J Moran (Chairman - 55),
R Hayes (Ch. Exec. - 51), M Bourke, P Gardner-Bougaard,
J Lawrie, D Lynch (54), C Moran (70), V Quigley (52),
T Wacker (56), D Saunderson.
SHARE CAPITAL: Authorised: 83,847,210 Ord €0.12
shares. **Issued:** 64,872,859 Ord €0.12 shares. Warrants to
subscribe for 4.35m Ord €0.12 shares @ €3.75 each up to
2008
STAFF: 536.   **SCRIP DIVIDEND:** No

CAPITAL HISTORY:

5,060,000 Ord. 25p shares in issue by Credit Finance
Bank. Capital restructuring and reverse takeover of
Credit Finance by IFG Securities Ltd. in May 1989 by
issue of 12,000,000 Ord. 10p shares and 8,169 'A'
Ord.£1 shares to IFG Securities and cash offer of 50p
per share for Credit Finance shares. Nov/Dec 1989,
1,988,658 Ord. 10p shares issued for Quigley
Consultants, Bloxham Maguire Quigley and Arthur
Ring & Sons. Dec. 1989 acquired Charles Cain & Co.
for 4,614,275 Ord. 10p shares. March 1990 issued
418,000 ord. 10p shares for Texiana Gas. March
1990: Issued 18,000 Ord. 10p shares at 66p each.
November 1990: Issued 375,000 Ord. 10p shares at
60p stg. each as part consideration for Slater Group.
Dec. 1991: 3,999,605 Ord. 10p shares issued on earn-
outs. July 1992: 2 million Ord 10p shares placed at 22p
each. Dec 1995: Issued 3 million Ord 10p shares to
FNLS (Abbey National Plc subsidiary) at 32p stg each.
8,169 "A" Ord £1 shares converted to 81,690 Ord 10p
shares. R. Hayes allotted 1,960,560 Ord 10p shares at
11.8p each. May 2000: 169,250 Treasury shares cancelled. Oct 2000: Placing and open offer (1-for-3) of
13,509,200 Ord €0.12 shares at €1.625 each.

COMPANY HISTORY:

After failure of Credit Finance Bank, IFG
reversed into 'shell' with net assets of
£400,000 in May 1989. Reverse
takeover of IFG valued IFG at £8.5m
approximately 85 times historic pretax
profits. Nov 1989 purchased Quigley
Consultants, Bloxham Maguire Quigley
and Arthur Ring (a Joe Moran company)
for £1.6m. Dec. 1989 purchased
Charles Cain & Co. in Isle of Man for
£2.8m by way of 4,614,275 new shares
of which 3.4m were placed at 60p each.
March 1990 purchased Texiana Gas for
£0.25m in shares. November 1990:
Acquired the Slater Group UK for £1.0m
plus earn-out of £2.5m. Initial price
shares and loan note. July 1992:
Acquires First National Trustee Co. Ltd.
for £2.47m (£1.1m in cash and balance
in red. pref. shares in IFG Ventures).
Issued warrant for 1.5m 10p Ord. shares
at 30p stg per share to be exercised
before 10.07.97. Placing 2m, shares to
raise £440,000. Sept 1994: Purchased
70% of Lawlink for £35,000. Nov 1994:
Bought 226,000 IFG shares (0.64%) at
21p each (bringing total to 369,000
shares). March 1995: Sold 104,717 IFG
shares. April 1995: Wrote off £5.1m on
overvalued subsidiaries. July 1995: High Court allows
£5m write-off in share premium. Dec 1995: Buys in
1,029,981 Ord 10p shares of its own shares (between
15p and 24p each). Abbey National buys 3 million
shares at 32p each. June 1996: Option to acquire
Financial Tradeline by Sept 1999. December 1996:
Repurchased shares now stand at 1,249,981. June
1997: Reissued 1,249,981 Treasury shares at 47p
each. July 1997: Purchased First American Trustee
UK for £0.3m. Nov 1997: Bought Santhouse
Whittington for £2m plus earn out. Jan 1999:
Repurchased 3m Ord 10p shares from FNLS at 42p
stg; holds them as treasury shares. July 1999: Sells
Arthur Ring for £5,275,000. Sept and Oct 1999:
Repurchased 1,233,684 Ord 10p shares (bringing
total of Treasury shares to 4,233,684 or 10.48% of
equity at average 55.7p/€0.67). Because Directors 'in
concert' held 31.6% Takeover Rules waived. May
2000: Buys remainder (24%) of Tradeline Finance.
Buys Planlife for £2m cash and warrants. Buys P A
Barnes for £1m. Sept 2000: Buys Berkeley Jacobs
(UK) for £4.2mstg/€6.8m in cash plus earn-out up to
£12.3mstg. March 2001: Buys 3 UK financial services
for total £4.275m stg. April 2001: Offloads 2.7m treasury shares @ €3.00 each. Dec 2001: Raise
£10mstg with 7-year notes from Prudential M&G wit
share warrants (1.34m shares @ €4 each to 200S
attached. April 2002: Buys IPS Pensions (UK) for ma
€25.2mstg. June 2002: Announces decision to en
sterling endowment policies business (wort
€65.3m).

Share Price Sept 2001 - Sept 2002

1. €3.10 21.12.01 Major share placing
2. €2.50 25.06.02 Exits sterling policies

FINANCIAL DIARY

Interim Results Announced:	05.09.2002
Interim Dividend Payout:	22.11.2002
Final Results Announced:	03.04.2002
Annual General Meeting:	25.06.2002
Final Dividend Payout:	26.07.2002

FIVE YEAR SHARE PRICE TREND €

1997	High 0.95 (Dec)	Low	0.41	(Jan)
1998	High 1.33 (Jan)	Low	0.93	(Jan)
1999	High 1.05 (Nov)	Low	0.75	(Feb)
2000	High 1.96 (Nov)	Low	0.91	(Jan)
2001	High 3.75 (June)	Low	1.88	(Jan)

HALF YEARLY PERFORMANCE € m

Six months to	30.06.01	31.12.01	30.06.02	30.06.02
Turnover	38.4	43.3	47.3	47.3
Profit (loss)before Tax	5.3	5.2	(21.4)	(21.4)
Profit % Sales	13.8	12.0	-	-

INVESTMENT PERFORMANCE

Five Year Investment Performance:	€ 7,792
Ten Year Investment Performance:	€12,337

TEN YEAR REVIEW: €'000

12 Months to December 31	1992	1993 d)	1994	1995	1996	1997	1998 a)	1999	2000 d)	2001
Turnover	6,298	13,059	15,507	16,099	21,877	28,873	36,596	38,637	51,071	81,717
Profit before Tax	842	929	1,294	1,362	1,977	2,929	4,652	3,044	7,131	10,450
Tax	210	243	137	74	321	455	636	945	1,401	3,100
Profit after Tax	632	686	1,157	1,288	1,656	2,474	4,016	2,099	5,730	7,350
Minority	(67)	(88)	(74)	(2)	(30)	(103)	(137)	(58)	(11)	(94)
Available for Shareholders	565	598	1,083	1,286	1,626	2,371	3,879	2,041	5,741	7,256
Ordinary Dividend	111	136	-	434	295	420	523	641	958	1,446
Retained Profit (loss)	454	462	1,083	852	1,331	1,951	3,356	1,400	4,783	5,810
Increase (Decrease) in Reserves	(2,142)	310	965	1,811 e)	(862) f)	(825) g)	(608) h)	3,447 j)	25,125 k)	34,530 m)
Shareholders' Funds	71	381	1,242	3,684	2,821	1,996	819	4,323	31,282	66,145
Ordinary Dividend per Share (€)	0.003	0.004	-	0.01	0.008	0.01	0.013	0.016	0.019	0.022
Earnings per Share (€)	0.017	0.018	0.031	0.037	0.042	0.06	0.09	0.12	0.13	0.12 b)

a) Subsequently restated b) Based upon 58.5m shares. c) Goodwill written off €7.4m; share premium €2.5m. d) Figures subsequently restated.
e) Share premium a/c +€0.9m. f) Goodwill w/o -€2.4m. g) Share premium +€3.4m, goodwill w/o -€7m. h) Goodwill w/o -€4.1m.
j) Treasury shares -€2.9m; asset disposal +€3.0m; asset revaluation +€2m. k) Share premium +€20.8m

BALANCE SHEET: 31 DECEMBER 2001. € m

Share Capital:		Tangible Assets		15.1
64,627,992 Ord. €0.12 shares,	7.8	Financial Assets		5.7
		Current Assets	131.7	
		Current Liabilities	51.9	
		Net Current Assets		79.8
Reserves	58.3	Medium Debt		(100.7)
		Net Tangible Liabilities		(0.1)
		Intangibles		66.2
Shareholders' Funds	66.1	Net Assets		66.1

Comment:

Investors cannot

complain over the

5 or 10 year

investment period.

INDEPENDENT NEWS & MEDIA plc

(Formerly Independent Newspapers plc)

BUSINESS: Newspaper publishing.
REGISTERED OFFICE: 1/2 Upper Hatch Street, Dublin 2.
Tel: 01-4758432. **Fax:** 01-4752126.
HEAD OFFICE: as regd office. **SECRETARY:** A Donagher.
REGISTRAR & TRANSFER OFFICE: Capita Corporate Registrars plc, Marine House, Clanwilliam Court, Dublin.
PRINCIPAL BANKERS: Ulster Bank Ltd, Bank of Ireland, Bank of America, J P Morgan. **AUDITORS:** PricewaterhouseCoopers.
SOLICITORS: Matheson Ormsby Prentice; McCann FitzGerald.
STOCKBROKERS: Davy Stockbrokers; Merrill Lynch; Goodbody Stockbrokers.
DIRECTORS: A J O'Reilly (Exec Chairman - 67), B Bradlee (82), P Cosgrove, V Crowley (66), C Daly, J Davy (59), B Fallon, J Featherstone (67), V Ferguson (72), J Gilroy (63), B Gleeson, H Hamilton (66), M Hayes (76), L Healy (74), B Hopkins (50), I Kenny (73), J McCarthy (79), B McGuinness (65), A C O'Reilly (39), A J O'Reilly Jnr, G O'Reilly (37), D Palmer (62), J Parkinson (53), J Sanders, B Somers (54).
SHARE CAPITAL: **Authorised:** 700m €0.30 Ord shares.
Issued: 572,875,829 Ord. €0.30 shares.
STAFF: 11,392. **SCRIP DIVIDEND:** Yes.

CAPITAL HISTORY:

Oct. 1973 'B' Ord. 25p shares enfranchised and consolidated with 'A' Ord. 25p shares into one class of Ord. 25p shares. March 1974 50,000 deferred Convertible Shares converted. July 1974 7.5% Cum Pref. shares converted into 10% Loan Stock on the basis of £1 loan stock for each £1 Pref. Share held. Dec. 1977 1 million deferred shares converted. Dec. 1978 900,000 deferred shares converted. Jan. 1979 1-for-2 'scrip' issue. April 1982 350,000 Ord. 25p shares issued as part consideration for Nutley Investments Ltd. July 1983 'rights' issue of 2,987,000 Ord. 25p shares at 118p each on the basis of 1-for-4. April 1986 'scrip' issue of 1-for-2. April 1989: 1-for-2 scrip issue. Issued 677,686 25p ord. shares part purchase of 24% in Buspak. March 1991: Issue of 30,000,000 6% Conv. Capital £1 bonds on basis of 1-for-1.2076 shares. April 1994: 1-for-2 Scrip issue, 39,226,256 Ord 25p shares. Sept 1994: Issues 1.95m Ord 25p shares at 305p each for 6.6% of Jornalgeste. May 1996: Scrip issue June 1996: Rights issue 40,421,403 Ord 25p shares (1-for-3) @€3.43 each. June 2000: Scrip issue1-for-1. Sept 2001: Placed 864,150 Ord €0.30 shares @ €2.02 each.

COMPANY HISTORY:

Incorporated in 1904. Went public in 1937. Acquired the Drogheda Independent in 1967. 1971 purchased the People Newspapers and The Kerryman in 1972. March 1973 Columbia Investments (a company O'Reilly investment company) acquired the 'A' Ord. voting shares for £1.1m. August 1973 enfranchisement of 'B' shares. The result was that Columbia's voting control was reduced to 36% and in turn got deferred shares which would eventually give it rights to 7% of assets and earnings. 1974 acquired Employment Publications Ltd. in UK; January 1978 acquired 58% of Nutley Investments for £843,000 plus 200,000 shares in Independent Newspapers. 1979 bought 80% of Publi-Cites S.A. 1982 acquired 7% of Nutley Investments; closed down David Phillip Printing and Travelwise Publications Ltd. 1986 sold stake in Reuters for £6m and radio stations in US for $10m (net of tax). 1986 acquired 80% of Greater London & Essex Newspapers Ltd. and 87.5% of Presse Edition La Boetie S.A.R.L. Jan. 1987: Invested in Anglo Vision, a company to market television advertising in European hotels; Sept 1987: Competrol sells 0.45 million shares. Dec. 1987: Increased 'goodwill' element of newspapers to £45.4m. Feb. 1988: Increased by 17% stake in Buspak, Australia. June 1988: Bid for Provincial Newspapers (Queensland) in association with Haswell (an O'Reilly Trust company). August 1989: Acquired final 34% in Buspak Australia for A$12.8m in cash (IR£6.4m) and shares. October 1989: Acquired 21% in Golden Grid Plc in UK for £2.64m stg. August 1990: Writes-off £1.5m investment in Golden Grid. Sells remaining Reuters shares for £1.3m surplus. November 1990: Buys 29.9% of Tribune plc for £2.6m (111p per share). March 1991: £30m Bond issue. Nov 1991: Fails in bid for Fairfax Group, Australia. June 1992: US investors inject £15m into Princes Holdings (TV interests) for 50%. July 1992: Buys 21% of Kelsal Pty. from O'Reilly Trust for A$20.5m. May 1993: Buys 10.8% Kelsal Pty. from O'Reilly Trust for A$16.8m. June 1993: Increased stake in APN to 25% (now valued at £38m) by buying shares at A$1.56 each. Nov 1993: Bought 372,500p shares on open market at 400p each. Feb 1994: Paid £23.4m for 29.99% Newspaper Publishing Plc (The Independent in UK). March 1994: Paid £5.8m for 75.1% Capital Newspapers Ltd. June 1994: Buys 150,000 own shares at 275p each; shares cancelled. Bought 116,000 own shares at 285p each; reissued in September. July 1994: Pays £2.6m for 36% Argus Newspapers in South Africa. Aug 1994: Buys 6.6% of Spain's Jornalgeste for £5.9m in shares. Nov/Dec 1994: Bought 1,275,000 own shares at 270p/285p each. March 1995: Now holds 43% of UK Independent. Increases stake in Argus to 58% (total cost £49m). May 1995: Pays (jointly) £121m for 28% New Zealands Wilson & Horton. June 1995: £6.6m out of court settlement in Fairfax case. June 1995: Sold all its own shares at 337p each. July 1995: Increase stake in Wilson & Horton to 33% (total spend £62.4m). Oct 1995: Bought London Recorder and Trindle Newspapers for £1.5m stg cash and shares. Nov 1995: Sells ICA in Australia for £25.5m. Dec 1995: O'Reilly hospitalised. March 1996: increases stake in Jornalgeste to 11.8%. April 1996: Increases stake in Newspaper Publishing to 46.4%. June 1996: Journalgeste confirms having sold its 2% of Independent for £8.9m. Oct 1996: Increased stake in Wilson & Horton (New Zealand) to 62.8% (100% would cost £441.5m). By April 1997 stake had increased to 85.6%. Dec 1996: Offers £10m for Mirror Group stake in lossmaking (-£18.6m) UK Independent. April 1998: Pays £29m for remainder (54%) of UK Independent. Pays £67m for remaining 15% of W & H New Zealand. June/Nov 1998: Bought in 2.3m Ord 25p shares varying between 400p and 220p each. Sept 1998: Sells French outdoor advertising for £60m. March 1999: Bought remaining 25% in INHL (South Africa) for £47m. June 1999: A O'Reilly buys 200,000 shares at $4.70. Jan 2000: A J O'Reilly takes over as Exec Chairman; shares reach $7.25. Buys Internet Ireland. August 2000: Buys Belfast

Share Price Sept 2001 - Sept 2002

1. €2.00 17.04.02 Poor Annual Results

FINANCIAL DIARY

Interim Results Announced:	05.09.2001
Interim Dividend Payout:	02.11.2001
Final Results Announced:	17.04.2002
Annual General Meeting:	05.06.2002
Final Dividend Payout:	06.06.2002

FIVE YEAR SHARE PRICE TREND

1997	High 2.90 (Aug)	Low	1.89 (Jan)
1998	High 3.05 (Jan)	Low	1.33 (Dec)
1999	High 3.25 (Dec)	Low	1.60 (Feb)
2000	High 5.59 (Mar)	Low	2.81 (Dec)
2001	High 3.40 (Jan)	Low	1.51 (Oct)

HALF YEARLY PERFORMANCES: € m

Six Months to	31.06.00	31.12.00	30.06.01	31.12.01
Sales	629.4	713.1	656.0	685.4
Profit before Tax	74.5	80.8	57.6	4.2
Profit % Sales	11.8	11.3	8.8	0.6

SECTORAL ANALYSIS (previous year)

Sales: IRL 28% (25%), UK 18% (16%), Sth Africa 12% (14%), New Zealand 21% (21%), Australia 21% (24%).
Profits: IRL 32% (29%), UK 7% (5%), Sth Africa 10% (11%), Australasia 51% (55%).

INVESTMENT PERFORMANCE

Five Year Investment Performance:	€1,250
Ten Year Investment Performance:	€3,236

Telegraph for $487m. May 2000: Reluctantly implements Accountancy Rule FRS10. June 2000: Princes Holdings buys 51% of Switchcom. Aug 2000: iTouch debut on London market @ 70pstg (valuation $323m); price 'supported' by sponsoring brokers. Nov 2001: Buys 1,075,000 own shares @€1.55/1.57 each. Feb 2002: APN (Australia) and Wilson & Horton (New Zealand) merge with IN&M taking 45% stake. 14m shares traded on Feb 7 at *1.60. June 2002: Buys 1m own shares @ €1.95 each.

TEN YEAR REVIEW: € m

12 months to December 31	1992	1993 b)	1994	1995	1996	1997	1998 a)	1999 b)	2000	2001
Sales	215.7	220.3	344.6	467.1	532.1	760.3	798.8	1,168.2	1,342.5	1,341.4
Profits before Tax	20.3	36.9	47.9	63.5	93.3	127.1	88.9	142.7	155.3 q)	61.8 r)
Tax	3.8	5.3	8.8	12.7	21.2	24.1	13.6	34.2	26.6	23.8
Profit after Tax	16.5	31.6	39.1	50.8	72.1	103.0	75.4	108.5	128.7	38.0
Minority Interest	(1.2)	(3.2)	(9.0)	(12.5)	(24.5)	(30.8)	(13.1)	(38.4)	(47.4)	(34.9)
Available for Shareholders	15.3	28.4	30.1	38.3	47.6	72.2	62.3	70.1	81.3	3.1
Ordinary Dividend	7.4	12.1	13.0	15.3	21.6	24.5	28.8	34.2	38.9	42.9
Retained Profit (Loss)	7.9	16.3	17.1	23.0	26.0	47.7	33.5	35.9	42.4	(39.8)
Increase (Decrease) in Reserves	7.0	40.2 g)	64.6 m)	51.2 h)	97.1 i)	208.4	(90.5)	(447.8) n)	(124.3) d)	(5.9) f)
Shareholders' Funds	182.5	235.6	313.4	365.0	501.9	710.8	621.3	308.8	250.6	257.9
Ordinary Dividend per Share (€)	0.024	0.028	0.032	0.038	0.044	0.05	0.055	0.065	0.075	0.078
Earnings per Share (€)	0.049	0.077	0.076	0.096	0.105	0.145	0.125	0.14	0.158	0.058 e)

a) Year end Dec 18. b) Figures subsequently restated. d) Scrip issue €77.3m; currency losses -€79.4m. e) Based on 532.7m shares. f) Currency loss -€55.2m; share premium +€89m. g) Share premium on bond conversion +€35.0m; scrip issue - €9.9m. h) Share premium +€3.3m, revaluation of reserves +€22.3m. i) Share premium +€101.1m; scrip issue -€25.6m. j) Revaluation of titles +€190.5m; currency loss -€37.7m. k) Currency losses -€129.0m; purchases of own shares -€7.5m; share premium +€5.5m. m) Goodwill revaluation +€44.9m. n) Adjustment to value of titles in 'intangibles' -€449.1m. q) Includes profit on 'deemed' sale of subsidiary +€22.3m. r) Includes -€90.1m in exceptional costs and +€32.5 profit on asset sale to company 40% (now 45%) owned by IN&M.

BALANCE SHEET: DECEMBER 31 2001. € m

Comment:

Despite 1999's balance sheet hoovering with a drop of €449m in goodwill, 'intangibles' are now back up to nearly €1.7 BILLION and 'transparent' borrowings of €1.6 BILLION. This is some exercise in balance sheet leverage.

Share Capital:		
572,078,416 Ord €0.30 shares.	171.6	
Reserves	86.3	
Shareholders' Funds	257.9	

Tangible Assets		395.5
Financial Assets		126.1
Current Assets	647.0	
Current Liabilities	540.7	
Net Current Liabilities		(106.3)
Medium Debt		(1,412.5)
Minority		(638.7)
Net Tangible Liabilities		(1,423.3)
Intangible Assets		1,681.2
Net Assets		257.9

IONA TECHNOLOGIES PLC

BUSINESS: Software for computer network integration
REGISTERED OFFICE: The Iona Building, Shelbourne Road, Dublin.
HEAD OFFICE: as regd office. Tel: 01-6372000
Fax: 01-6372888.
SECRETARY: S Alexander
REGISTRARS & TRANSFER OFFICE: Bank of Ireland, Registration Dept, Hume House, Ballsbridge, Dublin 4
PRINCIPAL BANKERS: Bank of Ireland, Bank of America.
AUDITORS: Ernst & Young
SOLICITORS: William Fry; Testa, Hurwitz & Thibeault
STOCKBROKERS: Goodbodys
DIRECTORS: C Horn (Chairman - 46), S Baker (44), J Conroy (43), B Morris (CEO-40), K Melia (55), I Kenny (73), F Violante (52), J Maikranz (55).
SHARE CAPITAL: Authorised: 150m Ord €0.0025 shares; 101,250,000 Red Pref €0.0025 shares. **Issued:** 32,042,156 Ord €0.0025 shares. One ADR = 1 Ord share.
EMPLOYEES: 907   **SCRIP DIVIDEND:** No

CAPITAL HISTORY:

Aug 1993: 19,998 Ord £1 shares issued at par. Dec 1993: 7,503 Ord £1 shares issued for $600,000. Dec 1993: 408 Ord £1 shares issued to Trinity College Dublin to release certain obligations. Feb 1994: 2,101 £1 Ord shares at par. 202,500 £1 Pref shares issued for £202,500. May 1995: 225 £1 Ord shares issued at par. Sept 1995: 225 Ord £1 shares issued at par. All £1 Ord and Pref shares split 500-for-1. July 1996: 59,375 Ord 0.2p shares issued for $118.75 each. Feb 2001: Issued 908,584 Ord €0.0025 shares re purchase of Object-Oriented Concepts. May 2001: Buys Netfish for 5,036,318 Ord €0.0025 shares @ $55 each plus $30.9m cash. Feb 2002: Placed 4.6m Ord €0.0025 shares @ $15.00 each

COMPANY HISTORY:

Founded in Dublin March 1991 by Chris Horn, Sean Baker and Annrai O'Toole to do research and development and computer consultancy. In July 1993 they released their first product Orbix 1.1, enabling differ-ent incompatible computer systems work together, followed by OrbixDesktop (Dec 1995), OrbixNames (March 1996), OrbixWeb (April 1996), OrbixTalk (Aug 1996), OrbixEnterprise (Jan 1997) and OrbixOTS. Their pricing policy is high volume/low price. Revenue comes from licence fees and service charges. IONA claims over 3,000 customers and 15,000 developers such as Boeing, Motorola, BellSouth, Deutsche Morgen Grenfell, Swisscom, Credit Suisse and Hongkong Telecom. First quoted on NASDAQ Feb 1997 at $18 per share (in ADS form); shareholders pocketed $78m and IONA gained $50m. Nov 1998: Directors sell share tranches to realise £1.2m. Feb 1999: B Morris sells $2.45m worth of shares; other executives realise $1m in sales. March 1999: Panic sales of shares (3.6m on 31.03). April 1999: Profits warning sees share price drop from$37.25 down to $15. July 1999: J Cullinane director resigns. N Toolan (vice-pres marketing) resigns. Q2 profits halve. Oct 1999: Launches IONA iPortal Suite. Intel buys 200,000 shares worth $4.1m/€3.8m. Jan 2000: Strategic partnership with Compaq. Feb 2000: Buys Watershed Technologies for $13.3m. S Baker sells 53,000 shares @ $52.69 each (worth £2.3m/€2.9m) and another 19,000 @ $51 each (worth £787,000). March 2000: On 01.03 Iona joins Nasdaq; shares jump 22% to $84 each. On 20.03 joins FTSE 100 Index. Imprise Corp sues for unfair competition and trademark infringement. RSA Securities and Massachusetts Institute sues for breach of patent license. April 2000: Enterprise Ireland dumps 350,000 shares at £77 each (£27m). C Horn pockets $2.2m after selling 40,000 shares at $55.83 each. May 2000: C Horn resigns as CEO. June 2000 Buys Genesis Development for $24m (€25m). Feb 2001: Buys Object-Oriented Concepts for $3m cash + 908,584 shares. Buys licence rights from Software AG for $10m cash. May 2001: Buys Netfish Technologies for 5.04m Ord shares and $30.9m cash (total cost $294m). Feb 2001: 4.6m shares placed @ $15 each (original plan was to place 5m @ $22 each). April 2002: A O'Toole resigns. May 2001: Cuts staff 15% worldwide. July 2001: Blames amortization charge for H1 loss. July 2002: Major staff cuts to stem losses.

Share Price Sept 2001 - Sept 2002

1. €15.80 17.04.02 Poor results

Interim Results Announced:	17.07.2002
Interim Dividend Payout:	none
Annual Results Announced:	23.01.2002
Annual General Meeting:	18.07.2002
Final Dividend Payout:	none

SHARE PRICE TREND €

1996 High	17.78 (Dec)	Low	16.06 (Dec)
1998 High	36.56 (July)	Low	15.57 (Oct)
1999 High	50.75 (Dec)	Low	11.69 (Sept)
2000 High	106.00 (Mar)	Low	40.63 (Jan)
2001 High	72.43 (Jan)	Low	8.30 (Oct)

SECTORAL ANALYSIS (previous year):

Sales: Orbix + iPortal 65% (69%), conbsultancy 35% (31%). USA 67% (67%), Europe 23% (26%), other 10% (7%).

HALF-YEARLY PERFORMANCES: $'000

6 months to:	31.12.00	30.06.01	31.12.01	30.06.02
Sales:	87,727	94,189	86,515	65,860
Pretax profits/(-)	10,350	(29,799)	(54,469)	(34,589)
Profit % sales	11.8	-	-	-

EIGHT YEAR REVIEW: $'000

12 months to December 31	1994	1995	1996 a)	1997	1998	1999	2000 h)	200
Revenue	2,412	8,636	21,191	48,584	83,627	105,440	153,063	180,70
Profit (Loss) Before Tax	537	2,622	2,317	5,623	9,087	6,547	15,892	(84,268)
Tax	75	398	769	872	1,409	1,088	2,799	+56
Profit (Loss) After Tax	462	2,224	1,548	4,751	7,678	5,459	13,093	(83,500
Preference Dividend	18	19	19	-	-	-	-	
Available for Shareholders	444	2,205	1,529	4,751	7,678	5,459	13,093	(83.500
Ordinary Dividend	-	-	-	-	-	-	-	
Retained Profit	444	2,205	1,529	4,751	7,678	5,459	13,093	(83,500
Increase (Decrease) in Reserves	n/a	2,441	3,573 c)	64,150 b)	7,854	29,741 f)	47,477 g)	224,445 i
Shareholders Funds	1,139	3,550	7,123	71,624	81,978	112,403	159,883	375,76
Net Ordinary Dividend per Share	-	-	-	-	-	-	-	
Earnings per Share ($)	$0.03	$0.14	$0.10	$0.26	$0.40	$0.28	$0.62 d)	

a) Subsequently restated. b) Share premium +$59.6m. c) Stock compensation +$1.9m. d) Based upon 19.8m shares. f) Share premium +$13.1m; unrealized profit on investment +$11.5m g) Share premium +$46m; revaluation reserve -$11m. h) Figures subsequently adjusted. i) Share premium =$313m. j) Includes goodwill write-off -$75.6m

BALANCE SHEET: 31 DECEMBER 2001. $'000

Share Capital:		Fixed Assets	18,789
21,990,324 Ord 0.2p shares	80	Investments	47,998
		Current Assets	102.194
		Current Liabilities	61,932
Reserves	375,686	Net Current Assets	40,262
		Net Tangible Assets	107,049
		Intangibles	268,717
Shareholders' Funds	375,766	Net Assets	375,766

Comment:

Technology industry has lost its shine and Iona is no exception. Revenue graph is on a downward trend and losses are going in the opposite direction.

octagon
Online.ie

Control the Trade

**Octagon Online Services Limited
is authorised by the Central Bank of Ireland
under the Investment Intermediaries Act 1995**

IRISH CONTINENTAL GROUP plc

CAPITAL HISTORY:
Incorporated March 1973. July 1977 authorised capital increased from 4,000 Ord. £1 shares to 10,000,000 Ord. £1 shares. January 1988 shares subdivided into 20,000,000 Ord. 50p shares of which 9,000,000 issued. January 1988 1,018,200 Ord. 50p shares issued to staff at 52p each. March 1988 4,600,000 Ord. 50p shares offered to public at 55p each. March 1989 2,173,102 shares placed at 65p. Jan 1992: 704,687 Ord 50p shares issued to staff at 110p each. April 1994: 3-for-7 rights issue, 7,568,091 Ord 50p shares issued at 400p each.

COMPANY HISTORY:
In October 1987, a number of financial institutions completed the acquisition of the entire issued share capital of the company from Oceanbank at a total cost of £3.7 million. Since 1973, ICG operates passenger and freight ferry services between Rosslare and Le Havre. In 1978, commenced a two ship operation and included a twice weekly service to Cherbourg. In 1983 a service in high season started between Cork and Le Havre. Belfast Ferries was acquired in 1984 and operated between Belfast and Liverpool. The original shareholders in the company included Irish Shipping, Aerlod Teoranta (a C.I.E. company) and two Scandinavian shipping companies. In 1978, Irish Shipping became the majority shareholder. In 1982 Oceanbank acquired the entire issued share capital. Oceanbank is 75% owned by Irish Shipping and 25% owned by A.I.I.B. On 14th November 1984, Irish Shipping went into liqui-

dation and as a result of this Oceanbank sought to sell its interest in the company. This sale was complicated by the fact that the vessels operated by the Group had been financed through partnerships set up in order to make full use of capital allowances available in relation to expenditure on these vessels. In November 1987, the company launched a new corporate identity. 29.5% of offer to public left with underwriters. March 1989: Placing of shares raised £1.4m. Marine Investments purchase 20.7% stake from institutions for £2.3m. or 65p per share. October 1989: Fleet revalued £38.9m. August 1990: Ceased Belfast/Liverpool route. October 1990: Sold St. Colum ship for £6.6m. March 1991: Bids £6.5m for B&I Line. Dec 1991: Discloses £1.8m write-off will be made in '92 accounts for Eurocar Shipping. Marine Investments S.A. sells its 25% stake in ICG for £4.6m. Jan1992: Acquires B & I Line for £8.5m (net assets). May 1993: Official quote Dublin & London. Sept 1993: Acquires 25% of Bell Line for £2.5m. Oct 1993: L. Booth sells 21,809 shares at 215p each. Nov 1993: Buys 'Pride of Bilbao' for £55.5m financed by 10 year loan for £56.9m. April 1994: Rights issue to raise £29.2m - 84.7% take-up. Contracts for new car ferry to be built for £45.6m. Nov 1994: Dumps B & I Line name. Oct 1995: Contracts to build ferry for £60m. March 1996: High Court allows reduction of £121m in Irish Ferries capital. Jan 1997: F. Carey and G. Hickey resign. June 1997: Sell Isle of Inishturk for £6.2m. May 1998: Sells MV Rockabill for £6.3m. July 1998: Contracts to buy new ferry Jonathan Swift for $40m (£28m). May 1999: Bought EuroFeeders Ltd and K-Tron BV for £2.5m. July 1999: Agrees construction of new ferry Ulysses for

Eamonn Rothwell

IRISH FERRIES

Share Price Sept 2001 - Sept 2002

1. €7.40 17.01.02 Good Annual Results

FIVE YEAR SHARE PRICE TREND €			
1997	High 10.92 (Dec)	Low	5.21 (Jan)
1998	High 16.76 (Apr)	Low	9.78 (Oct)
1999	High 13.00 (May)	Low	9.50 (Sept)
2000	High 12.49 (Feb)	Low	4.80 (Nov)
2001	High 8.30 (Feb)	Low	4.87 (Sept)

FINANCIAL DIARY	
Interim Results Announced:	28.06.2001
Interim Dividend Payout:	31.08.2001
Final Results Announced:	17.01.2002
Annual General Meeting:	29.05.2002
Final Dividend Payout:	31.05.2002

HALF YEARLY PERFORMANCES € m				
Six months to	30.04.00	31.10.00	30.04.01	31.10.01
Sales	122.9	191.0	124.3	186.8
Pretax Profit (Loss)	(4.7)	23.7	(7.2)	18.6
Profit % Sales	-	12.4	-	10.0

SECTORAL ANALYSIS (previous year)
Sales: Ferry 62% (62%), other 38% (38%),
Profits: Ferry 90% (100%), other 10% (0%).

INVESTMENT PERFORMANCE	
Five Year Investment Performance:	€1,310
Ten Year Investment Performance:	€5,215

Holyhead route costing £78m/$100m. Aug 1999: Buys 2 travel agents for £4m stg. March 2000: Profits warning. July 2000: Second profits warning, March 2001: Foot & mouth affecting profits. April 2001: Ulysses starts Dublin to Holyhead. May 2001: Isle of Inishmore starts Rosslare to Pembroke. July 2001: Profits warning. Oct 2001: E Rothwell spends €3m buying 584,000 shares. Feb 2002: 5 year charters agreed for Isle of Innishfree and Pride of Bilbao ferries (worth €70m cash over years).

TEN YEAR REVIEW

12 months to December 31	1992 i)	1993 i)	1994 i)	1995 i)	1996 i)	1997 i)	1998 i) g)	1999 i)	2000 i)	2001 j)
Sales	124.7	138.2	148.3	147.8	161.5	176.7	213.3	249.4	313.9	348.5
Profit (Loss) before Tax	5.3	6.0	11.8	14.0	13.4	18.5	22.3	26.8	19.0	9.0
Tax	0.5	-	0.6	0.3	+0.8	(0.2)	0.2	0.4	0.5	-
Profit (Loss) after Tax	4.8	6.0	11.2	13.7	14.2	18.3	22.5	26.4	18.5	9.0
Extraordinary Items	(2.2) e)	-	-	-	-	-	-	-	-	-
Available for Shareholders	2.6	6.0	11.2	13.7	14.2	18.3	22.5	26.4	18.5	9.0
Ordinary Dividend	0.5	0.7	1.2	1.4	1.7	22.2	2.6	3.1	3.8	4.6
Retained Profit (Loss)	2.1	5.3	10.0	12.3	12.5	16.1	19.9	23.3	14.7	4.4
Increase (Decrease) in Reserves	2.9	5.8	41.9 f)	12.4	12.1	18.3	16.9 a)	32.6 h)	26.7 b)	(1.0) k)
Shareholders' Funds	23.3	29.2	75.9	88.3	100.5	119.1	136.3	170.3	197.5	196.6
Ordinary Dividend per Share (€)	0.031	0.038	0.046	0.057	0.069	0.082	0.10	0.118	0.143	0.171
Earnings per Share (€)	0.277	0.343	0.51	0.542	0.561	0.71	0.87	1.01	0.70	0.34 d)

a) Currency loss -€2.9m; goodwill write-off -€1.7m; share premium +€1.8m. b) Currency gain +€11.6m. (d) Based upon 26.51m shares. e) Closure of 50% of interest in Eurocar Shipping Inc. f) Share premium €33.4m. g) Figures subsequently restated. h) Currency gain +€9.1m. i) Year end Oct 31. j) 14 months to Dec. k) Currency loss -€5.6

BALANCE SHEET: DECEMBER 31 2001. € m

	€'m		€'m
Shares Capital: 26.51m €0.65 shares	17.3	Fixed Assets	397.8
		Current Assets 77.1	
Reserves	179.3	Current Liabilities 102.9	
		Net Current Liabilities	(25.8)
		Medium Debt	(175.4)
Shareholders' Funds	196.6	Net Tangible Assets	196.6

Comments:

A superb 10 year investment and maybe current share prices may well prove just as profitable over the next decade.

IRISH LIFE & PERMANENT plc

BUSINESS: Financial services group.
REGISTERED OFFICE: Lr Abbey Street, Dublin.
HEAD OFFICE: as regd office. Tel: 01-7042000.
Fax: 01-7041908.
SECRETARY: S Ryan.
REGISTRARS & TRANSFER OFFICE: Capita Corporate Registrars plc., Unit 5, Manor Street Business Park, Manor Street, Dublin.
AUDITORS: KPMG.
SOLICITORS: A & L Goodbody.
STOCKBROKERS: Davy Stockbrokers; ABN AMRO Stockbrokers Ltd.
DIRECTORS: R Douglas (Chairman - 58), D Went (Gr Ch Exec - 56), G Bowler (50), D Casey (43), P Fitzpatrick (50), M Hilkowitz (62), R Hooper (66), P Kenny (56), B McConnell (56), K McGowan (59), K Murphy (51), P O'Neill (64), M Scorer (55), F Sheehan (65).
SHARE CAPITAL: Authorised: 400 million Ord €0.32 shares. **Issued:** 278,918,907 Ord €0.32 shares.
STAFF: 5,414. **SCRIP DIVIDEND:** No

CAPITAL HISTORY:

March 1994 changed from mutual society to plc. 76,133,300 Ord 25p shares issued of which 45,333,300 issued free to 'members', 20,970,600 held pending claims up to 21.09.1997 and 4,533,330 to be issued free as loyalty bonus in the future. 30,800,000 Ord 25p shares offered at 180p each of which 16.4m went to institutions. Nov 1995: Issued 1,834,400 Ord 25p shares as 'loyalty shares'. November 1996: 1,714,000 Ord 25p loyalty Shares issued. 1,186,000 Ord 25p Shares issued to savers and mortgagors. Nov 1997: Issued free 7,615,000 Ord 25p shares to savers and mortgagors. April 1999: Issues195,042,964 Ord 25p shares worth €2.76 billion (60.85 Ir Life & Perm shares for every 100 Ir Life shares) forming £3billion group. June 2000: Purchased 7,757,954 own shares @ €12.03. Cancelled 2,578,168 shares; holds 5,179,786 as treasury shares.

COMPANY HISTORY:

First registered in 1884 as The Irish Temperance Permanent Benefit Building Society. I940 name changed to Irish Permanent Building Society. In the '80s acquired the Provident, the Cork Mutual and the Munster & Leinster building societies. Since the enactment of the Building Societies Act, 1989, they have engaged in leasing, unsecured lending, life assurance and pensions. June 1991: R. Douglas joins IPBS. April 1993: E. Farrell removed from Chairmanship and executive office. Acrimonious a.g.m. criticises running of Society. May 1993: R. O'Keeffe and P. Kevans resign as Directors. June 1993: E. Farrell issues claim for £5.8m. March 1994: Irish Permanent counter claims £7.5m stg against E. Farrell. May 1994: Flotation deferred to October 1994. July 1994: Buys Prudental Life of Ireland for £32m. Aug 1994: Buys Guinness Mahon & Co for £6.9m. Sept 1994: Depositors given 300 free shares each. Oct 1994: Flotation - dealings reach 220p per share on first day. Abbey National buys 10% of Irish Permanent. Nov 1994: An Post gains injunction against Irish Permanent's Savings Certificates. October 1996: Acquired Capital Home Loans Ltd for £13m stg (included goodwill £2.9m stg). Dec 1997: Litigation with E. Farrell. April 1999: Irish Life plc reverses into Irish Permanent. P Ledbetter's contract terminated; gets £0.7m. Jan 1999: Abbey National sells 9% of Ir Perm at 1088p each (£78m). April 1999: Merger with Irish Life; total market valuation £3.278m/€4,162m. June 1999: Buys Woodchester from GE Capital for £23.6m/€30m. Oct 1999: Offloads €600m/£473m home loans by way of securitisation. April 2000:17 branches to go. May 2000: Aggro at agm over low share price (merged group lost £1billion market value in first year). June 2000: Closes Guinness Mahon. April 2001: Buys TSB Bank for €430m. Sept 2000: To buyback own shares up to €150m. Jan 2001: Criticism by policyholders over Lifesaver policies. South African junket for 43 brokers and partners criticised. May 2001: Major exudus from Boardroom.

To close 20/30 of TSB branches. Oct 2001: Se▮ 2 assurance companies in US for $256.7m. Fe▮ 2002: Sells industrial branch business to Roy▮ Liver for €172m. June 2002: Buys 1.9m ow▮ shares @ €14.90 each.

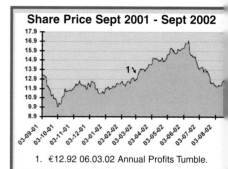

Share Price Sept 2001 - Sept 2002

1. €12.92 06.03.02 Annual Profits Tumble.

FINANCIAL DIARY

Interim Results Announced:	04.09.2002
Interim Dividend Payout:	08.11.2002
Final Results Announced:	07.03.2001
Annual General Meeting:	24.05.2002
Final Dividend Payout:	27.05.2002

HALF YEARLY PERFORMANCES: € m

Six months to	31.12.00	30.06.01	31.12.01	30.06.02
Profit(loss) before tax	157.8	142.8	(63.7)	216.1
Profit(loss) after tax	154.1	115.9	(65.5)	189.4*

* Includes asset sale profit +€98.5m

SECTORAL ANALYSIS: (previous year)

Profits: assurance 65% (80%), banking 35% (20%).

FIVE YEAR SHARE PRICE TREND €

1997	High	7.45 (Dec)	Low	6.22 (Jan)
1998	High	13.13 (Feb)	Low	8.89 (Sep)
1999	High	15.00 (Jan)	Low	9.10 (Sep)
2000	High	13.29 (Dec)	Low	7.30 (Feb)
2001	High	14.25 (June)	Low	9.94 (Oct)

INVESTMENT PERFORMANCE

Five Year Investment Performance: €2,108

TEN YEAR REVIEW: € m

12 months to December 31	1992	1993	1994	1995	1996	1997	1998	1999	2000	2002
Revenue	276.3	301.8	288.5	361.1	368.4	430.7	514.4	4,468.1	4,557.3	7,480.1
Profit before tax	27.3	39.1	44.6	53.8	61.7	69.9	84.7	365.5	311.9	79.1 g
Tax	6.5	10.0	14.1	16.3	18.5	19.9	22.5	69.1	25.7	28.7
Profit after tax	20.8	29.1	30.5	37.5	43.2	50.0	62.3	296.4	286.2	50.4
Minority Interests	-	-	-	-	-	-	-	2.0	2.0	(0.8)
Available for Shareholders	20.8	29.1	30.5	37.5	43.2	50.0	62.3	294.4	284.2	49.6
Ordinary Dividend	-	-	6.1	11.0	13.3	18.2	23.4	101.9	112.8	120.6
Retained Profit	20.8	29.1	24.4	26.5	29.9	31.8	38.9	192.5	171.4	(71.0)
Increase (Decrease) in Reserves	19.9	26.5	36.8a)	24.5	24.9 c)	29.5	40.1	1,481.6	80.7 d)	(108.7) f)
Shareholders' Funds	171.8	198.3	260.0	286.2	312.0	343.9	384.1	1,927.8	2,088.7	1,897.00
Ordinary Dividend per Share (€)	-	-	0.076	0.133	0.156	0.194	0.248	0.350	0.390	0.430
Earnings Per Share (€)	-	-	0.382	0.367	0.423	0.532	0.661	1.022	0.980	0.174 b)

THE FIGURES 1992-1998 ARE IRISH PERMANENT RESULTS ONLY

a) Cost of funding shares -€16.4m; cash to members -€3.3m; goodwill w/o -€5.0m; share premium +€36.9m. b) Based upon 284.6m shares in issue. d) Purchase own shares -€93.2m f) Shares repurchased -€121.6m; resold +€66.9m = -€54.6m net. g) Includes restructuring (banking) costs -€63.0m and loss on sale of US business -€50.0m.

BALANCE SHEET: DECEMBER 31 2001. € m

		Fixed Assets	210.4
		Financial Assets	57.1
Share Capital:	89.3	Long Term Assets	16,962.5
278,918,907 Ord €0.32 shares		Current Assets	5,254.8
		Current Liabilities	11,392.0
Reserves	1,807.7	Net Current Liabilities	(6,137.2)
		Medium Debt	(9,404.1)
		Minority	(12.5)
Shareholders' Funds	1,897.0	Net Tangible Assets	1,676.2
		Intangibles	220.8
		Net Assets	1,897.0

Comment:
International markets are having their adverse impact on insurance companies but the addition of the TSB gives good scope for the group to expand. In the near term there seems to be little weakness in the mortgage market, a sector in which they are expert operators.

(Formerly Irish Wire Products)

BUSINESS: Conglomerate engaged in household, industrial, print products.
REGISTERED OFFICE: 19, Fitzwilliam Square, Dublin.
Tel: 01-6611958. Fax: 01-6611957. **HEAD OFFICE:** as regd office.
SECRETARY: L Ring. **REGISTRARS & TRANSFER OFFICE:**
Computershare Investor Services (Ireland) Ltd, Heron House, Corrig Road, Sandyford Ind Estate, Dublin. **PRINCIPAL BANKERS:** AIB Bank; Barclays Bank, ING Barings, IIB, National Irish Bank, Royal Bank of Scotland. **AUDITORS:** PricewaterhouseCoopers. **SOLICITORS:** Gerrard, Scallan & O'Brien; Trenite Van Doorne **STOCKBROKERS:** Goodbody Stockbrokers; ING Barings Charterhouse Securities.
DIRECTORS: F Plunkett-Dillon (Chairman - 75), J Moran (Ch. Exec. - 67), B Byrne, P Dowling (70), R Hayes (53), L Murray (56), J van der Veer (58), M Colley.
SHARE CAPITAL: Authorised: 96 million Ord 12.5p shares, 55,000 Cum. Pref. £1 shares. **Issued:** 79,591,791 Ord 12.5p shares
STAFF: 4,004. **SCRIP DIVIDEND:** No

CAPITAL HISTORY:

Incorporated November 1935. 1966 Ord. £1 shares subdivided into 25p units and a 'scrip' issue of 1-for-1. 1980 P. Moran granted option to acquire 100,000 share at 80p each up to 31/07/84. April 1980 140,000 Ord. 25p shares placed at 70p each. Nov. 1985 400,000 Ord. 25p share and 409,036 15% Conv. Red. Cum. Pref. £1 shares issued to certain shareholders and lenders on conversion of loans into permanent capital (Foir Teo were the lenders). March 1987 1,200,000 Ord. 25p shares issued to group of investors at par. Capital reduced by cancellation of 409,036 Pref. £1 shares which were converted to 85,000 Ord. 25p shares. July 1987 'rights' issue of 1-for-6 at 45p each (involving the issue of 397,500 shares) and issue of 1,375,000 Ord. 25p shares to Jones/Hayes/Guidex at 45p each. Sept. 1987 4,083,151 Ord. 25p share issued (108,151 placed at 217p) in connection with Tiger Tim. April 1988: 150,000 Ord. 25p shares for cancellation of a contract; 2,997,375 Ord. 25p shares issued re Sanoda; 618,000 Ord. 25p shares placed at 270p; 370,370 Ord. shares of 25p issued re John Cleland. May 1988: 116,743 Ord. 25p shares issued re Silbadora. June 1988: 607,403 Ord. 25p shares issued re Kaarsenfabriek de Toren BV. July 1988: 526,783 Ord. 25p shares issued re Panelling Centre; 400,185 Ord. 25p shares issued re John Cleland. Sept. 1988: 93,937 Ord. 25p shares issued re Panelling Centre. Oct. 1988: 23,622 Ord. 25p shares issued re Sanoda. Nov. 1988: 771,109 Ord. 25p shares issued re William Freeman (Holdings). Dec. 1988: 2,335,514 Ord. 25p shares issued re Reprocentre Group; 4,464,160 Ord. 25p shares issued re Questel plc. Feb. 1989: 594,834 Ord. 25p shares issued re New Era Packaging (Holdings) Ltd. April 1989: 30,561 Ord. 25p shares issued re Belpac Ltd. June 1989: 2,122,320 Ord. 25p shares issued re J. Putzfeld Industrie. Nov 1993: 6 million Ord 25p shares issued to Levendaal Beheer at 308p each. Vendor placing 1,300,000 Ord 25p shares at 315p each. Dec 1995: Issued 235,294 25p Ord shares part payment of Burlington at £4.25p stg each. September 1996: Ord 25p shares split into two Ord 12.5p shares. May 1998: Offers 50 Ord 12.5p shares for every 75 Jeyes shares. Issued 8,109,751 Ord 12.5p shares to Jeyes shareholders.

COMPANY HISTORY:

In 1977 New Ireland Assurance offered its 16.6% shareholding for sale. Irish Base Metals bought and added to its holding bringing it up to 29.6%. In April '80 P.J. Moran arrived into IWP and through a reorganisation DCC acquired a holding, the cost of which they subsequently wrote off. Foir Teo helped the ailing company through the early 80s until a reorganisation which involved D. Jones,(Finance Director of Hazelwood Foods) and R.G. Hayes, another accountant who is Managing Director of IFG plc. Sept. 1987: Acquired Tiger Tim for £11.4m (in cash and shares). April 1988: Acquired Sanoda for £7.8m (cash and shares) plus an additional performance related payment. Acquired John Clelland Holdings for £5m (cash and shares). Bought Technoflex for £0.3m stg. May 1988: Purchase of Sillbodora for £7.5m plus £0.297 in loan repayment through 116,743 share issue. June 1988: Buys Dutch candle maker Kaarsen-Fabriek De Toren B.V. for £1.47m (incl. 0.6m new shares). July 1988: Buys Pannelling Centre for deal worth £3.1m (incl. 526,783 new Ord. shares). Nov 1988: Acquires W. Freeman for £4m stg. (incl. 777,000 new Ord. shares). Purchased CKD for £0.3m cash. Dec. 1988: For £11.6m buys Questel plc and £7.05m bid for Reprocentre. Jan 1989: Purchased New Era Group for £5m cash and shares. April 1989: Acquired Belpac for £700,000 stg. cash and shares. June 1989: Acquired A. Noyek for £450,000 cash. Nov. 1989: Purchased M. Harvey Haircare for £2.3m stg. cash and loan. Dec. 1989: Purchased 33% Rhetorex for $500,000. Jan. 1990: Sold Technoflex for £850,000 stg. cash and loan. Feb. 1990: M.B. Jones, Director, resigns. March 1990: J. Moran assumes role of Chief Executive. May 1990: Purchased additional 17% of Rhetorex Inc for US$500,000 cash. June 1990: D. Jones, Director, resigns. March 1991: J. Walker resigns as Director. May 1991: Purchased Harkwell Cartons Ltd. for £375,000 stg cash. July 1991: Noyek to be sold for £0.5m. April 1992: Acquired DHL Products for £2m stg. May 1992: Acquired Doele Beheer BV for IR£2m. Sept 1992: Looking for buyer of Questel. March 1993: Sold 50% Rhetorex Inc for 875,000 shares in VMX Inc IR£2.1m. June 1993: P Farrell sold 10,000 shares. Nov 1993: Buys Levendaal Beheer (household products) for £50.7m. Jan 1995: Buys Klasema (Dutch, labels) for £5.5m or max £6.67m. Nov 1995: Buys ACME SA and Duurstede Holdings BV (wax polish). Dec 1995: Buys Burlington Holdings (toiletries) for £8.5m stg. March 1996: Sells John Cleland and DM Beheer (cartons) for £10.6m. May 1996: Buys 70% of Polbita in Poland for £2.9m. December 1996: Bought R A Davis (Wales) for £1.4m stg. July 1997: Buys 80% Constance Carroll Holdings for £38.5m stg. Sept 1997: Bought 30% Polbita for £0.5m. May 1998: Pays £60m for Jeyes. Perpetual Plc sells 370,000 IWP shares at 367p stg each worth £1.36m stg. Dec 1998: J Moran buys 1,125,000 shares at 170p each (£2.1m). Feb 1999: Various directors spend £5.3m buying shares at 139p each (Moran 1m, Hayes 1m, Dowling 0.5m, Byrne 0.4m, Popham 0.25m, Murray 0.25m shares). Moran warns of MBO if market does not improve IWP rating. April 1999: Buys Fine Fragrances & Cosmetics for £3mstg min or £8.75m stg max. Dec 1999: Buys back 200,000 own shares @ $1.80/$1.90 each. April 2000: Sells Panelling Centre

Share Price Sept 2001 - Sept 2002

1. €1.70 02.07.02 Sale of household division.

FINANCIAL DIARY
Interim Results Announced:	20.11.2001
Interim Dividend Payout:	02.02.2002
Final Results Announced:	02.07.2002
Annual General Meeting:	24.09.2002
Final Dividend Payout:	11.10.2002

INVESTMENT PERFORMANCE
Five Year Investment Performance:	€731
Ten Year Investment Performance:	€1,613

HALF YEARLY PERFORMANCES: £m
Six months to	30.09.00	31.03.01	30.09.01	31.03.02
Turnover	216.3	230.3	288.0	289.6
Profit before Tax	9.4	6.5	4.7*	(12.5
Profit % Sales	4.3	2.8	1.6	

*after exceptionals of -€6.8m

FIVE YEAR SHARE PRICE TREND €
1997	High 4.19 (Oct)	Low	3.36 (Jan)
1998	High 5.93 (May)	Low	1.90 (Oct)
1999	High 2.54 (Jan)	Low	1.30 (Feb)
2000	High 1.96 (Feb)	Low	1.45 (June)
2001	High 2.10 (Apr)	Low	1.50 (Apr)

SECTORAL ANALYSIS (previous year)
Sales: Household products 51% (50%), labels, etc 27% (21%), healthcare 22% (29%). Rofl 2% (2%), UK 37% (38%), rest 61% (60%). **Profits:** Household products 48% (42%), labels, etc 12% (15%), healthcare 40% (43%).

to Heitons for $9.21m. May 2000: MBO of Irish Wire Products $2.73m. June 2000: Buys back 500,000 own shares @ $1.50 ea J Moran buys 250,000 shares. MBO of 60% Reprocentre for $7.7 More share purchases - 473,214 shares @ $1.45 each. July 200 Sells 65% of household products division (t/o €296m, net aas €86.3m) for €134.2m; will invest €33.2m in purchaser for 35% equity.

TEN YEAR REVIEW: € m

12 months to March 31	1993	1994	1995	1996	1997	1998	1999	2000 k)	2001	200
Sales	120.9	154.1	190.6	211.1	263.6	333.1	476.1	565.1	567.1	577.
Profit (Loss) before Tax	15.0	19.1	21.1	23.0	28.4	32.5	14.6	26.7	20.2	(7.8
Tax	4.1	5.4	6.8	8.0	8.0	8.6	4.3	7.1	5.2	2.
Profit (Loss) after Tax	10.9	13.7	14.4	15.0	20.4	23.9	10.3	19.6	14.9	(10.0
Minority	-	(0.5)	(1.3)	(1.3)	(0.2)	(0.7)	-	-	-	(0.0
Preference Dividend	-	-	-	-	-	-	-	-	-	
Available for Shareholders	10.9	13.2	13.1	13.7	20.3	23.2	10.3	19.6	14.9	(10.0
Ordinary Dividend	2.5	3.3	3.9	4.3	4.8	5.3	6.5	7.2	6.9	6.
Retained Profit	8.4	9.9	9.2	9.4	15.5	17.9	3.8	12.4	8.0	(16.9
Increase (Decrease) in Reserves	3.3 f)	10.7 g)	11.8 h)	(2.7) i)	(3.2) a)	(21.6) b)	41.1 j)	19.3 d)	(3.8) m)	(7.2) n
Shareholders' Funds	26.4	39.5	51.3	48.7	45.5	23.9	66.4	85.7	82.7	72.
Ordinary Dividend per Share (€)	0.046	0.051	0.056	0.062	0.068	0.075	0.082	0.09	0.095	0.09
Earnings per Share (€)	0.202	0.219	0.190	0.197	0.288	0.329	0.133	0.248	0.20 e)	

a) Goodwill w/o -€20.3m. b) Goodwill w/o -€43.3m, currency gain +€7.5m, purchase + cancellation of share warrants -€4.1m. d) Currency gain +€3.2m; goodwill write-back +€3.6m. e) Based upon 76.5m shares. f) Goodwill w/o -€3.8m, currency loss -€1.5m. g) Share premium +€26.5m; goodwill w/o +€26.2m. h) Currency gain +€1.7m. i) Goodwill write-off -€18.9m; goodwill clawback +€6.7m. j) Share premium +€44.2m. k) Figures subsequently restated. m) Currency loss -€5m; purchase of treasury shares -€6.5m. n) Goodwill written back +€9.4m.

BALANCE SHEET: MARCH 31 2002. € m

IWP International plc
Annual Report & Accounts 2002

Share Capital:		Fixed Assets	114.5
79,458,613 Ord. 12.5p shares	12.4	Current Assets	223.4
		Current Liabilities	128.9
		Net Current Assets	94.5
Reserves	60.1	Medium Debt	(206.9)
		Pref Shares	(0.1)
Shareholders' Funds	72.5	Net Tangible Assets	2.0
		Intangibles	70.5
		Net Assets	72.5

Comment:
It's a dire investment over the 5 and 10 year period. Every gimmick has been tried to give the share price a dose of viagara. Directors buying the shares; the company hoovering up excess shares have achieved nothing. The latest sale of the household division is very unclear in its overall corporate strategy. The press release is plentiful in jargon but short in hard facts going forward.

JURYS DOYLE HOTEL GROUP plc

(Formerly Jurys Hotel Group plc)

BUSINESS: Hotel operator.

REGISTERED OFFICE: 146 Pembroke Road, Ballsbridge, Dublin. Tel: 01-6070070. Fax: 01-6605728.

HEAD OFFICE: as regd office.

SECRETARY: S Daly.

REGISTRARS & TRANSFER OFFICE: Computershare Investor Services (Ireland) Ltd, Heron House, Corrig Road, Sandyford Industrial Estate, Dublin.

PRINCIPAL BANKERS: Ulster Bank; Ulster Investment Bank; Industrial Credit Corporation.

STOCKBROKERS: J & E Davy. **AUDITORS:** KPMG.

SOLICITORS: Vincent & Beatty

DIRECTORS: R Hooper (Chairman - 66), W Beatty (69), P McCann (Ch Exec - 51), B Gallagher (43), N Geoghegan (54), D Kennedy (64), P Malone (59), E Monahan (54), C Nelson (65), T Roche (53), E Walsh (68),.

SHARE CAPITAL: Authorised: 85 million Ord €0.32 shares. **Issued:** 62,660,874 Ord €0.32 shares.

STAFF: 4,106. **SCRIP DIVIDEND:** No

CAPITAL HISTORY:

Company incorporated as Irish & Intercontinental Hotels Ltd. in 1960. September 1974 name changed to Jurys Hotel Group. April issued share capital of £4,010,000 which was divided into 3,007,500 'A' shares of £1 each and 1,002,500 'B' shares of £1 each. Were then converted into Ordinary £1 shares and subdivided to 25p shares. Company allotted 5,000,000 25p shares to IBI to facilitate public flotation which at 115p each raised £5.75m. Flotation oversubscribed 6.5 times. May 1990: 1-for-4 rights at 115p issues 5,282,550 Ord 25p shares. July 1995: 1 - for - 4 rights issue 8,674,372 Ord 25p shares at 180p each. May 1999: 14,799,033 Ord 25p shares issued at €8.25 each re acquisition of Thornhill Inc (Doyle Hotels). Feb 2002: Placed 2,850,000 Ord €0.32 shares @ €9.00 each.

COMPANY HISTORY:

In 1972 a group of investors purchase 75% company while Aer Lingus retained 25% holding. After the flotation in April 1986, Aer Linte Eireann held 19.1% and the beneficial and non-beneficial holdings of Directors accounted for a further 33.1%. However, this has since been reduced as a result of significant sales. May 1987: Rockhill Investment Company sells 400,000 shares. June 1987: Nelson interest sells 500,000 shares. August 1987: Nelson interest sells 450,000 shares. February 1987: Rockhill Investments Company sells 100,000 shares. July 1989: Jurys announce 155 Bedroom Hotel in Christchurch, Dublin. January 1990: Purchased Ardree Hotel, Waterford for £2m. May 1990: Acquired Stakis Pond Hotel, Glasgow for £10.3m. Rights issue raises £5.7m. November 1990: Aer Lingus sells its 15% (£4.7m or 118p per share) stake in Jurys to institutions and Cathal Mullan (Chief Exec. Aer Lingus) resigns from Jurys board. Feb 1992: Jurys to lease McDonagh Hotel in Galway. May 1993: Galway and Dublin 'budget' hotels open. Aug 1993: Revealed that Jurys may be called upon to subscribe for £7.75m convertible unsecured loan stock in the landlord of Jurys Christchurch Inn. Nov 1993: Rights issue announced to raise £7.6m. Oct 1993: Bought Onslow Hotel London for £10.3m. Dec 1993: P. Malone and F. Sheehan sell 50,000 shares each. July 1994: Bought Unicorn Hotel Bristol for £6.1m. April 1995: £11m hotel planned to open mid 1996 in IFSC. Nov 1995: Buys 143 Bedroom Cardiff Hotel for £7m stg. May 1996: Plans £9.4m hotel in Belfast. April 1996: Started building Jurys Hotel Pentonville, London costing £12.5m Stg (at £56,800 stg per room). Sept 1996: Opened Jurys Custom House Inn. May 1999: Purchased Doyle Hotels for £194m (£96m in shares and £91m cash+£7m tax debt) including goodwill £63m for 2,087 bedrooms. June 1999: Name changed. Acquires Central Club, London to convert to 170 room hotel for cost of £23m stg. Sept 2000: 170 bed hotel Gt Russell St, London. March 2001:

Share Price Sept 2001 - Sept 2002

1. €9.15 11.01.02 Interim profit fall

INVESTMENT PERFORMANCE
Five Year Investment Performance:	€ 3,234
Ten Year Investment Performance:	€ 7,871

HALF YEARLY PERFORMANCES: € m

Six months to:	31.10.00	30.04.01	31.10.01	30.04.02
Sales	130.0	122.2	137.9	128.5
Profits before Tax	32.8	22.9	28.8	22.2
Profits % Sales	25.0	18.8	20.9	17.3

FIVE YEAR SHARE PRICE TREND €

1997	High	5.84 (Oct)	Low	3.52 (Jan)
1998	High	8.51 (July)	Low	5.23 (Jan)
1999	High	9.00 (Apr)	Low	6.45 (Jan)
2000	High	9.10 (Nov)	Low	6.15 (June)
2001	High	11.10 (Feb)	Low	5.83 (Oct)

FINANCIAL DIARY

Interim Results Announced:	10.01.2002
Interim Dividend Payout:	15.02.2002
Final Results Announced:	09.07.2002
Annual General Meeting:	29.08.2002
Final Dividend Payout:	30.08.2002

SECTORAL ANALYSIS (previous year)

Sales: RofI 53% (58%), UK 37% (32%), USA 10% (10%). **Profits:** RofI 37% (46%), UK 51% (42%), USA 12% (12%).

Bought Chamberlain Hotels Birmingham for £42mstg. Sold part for £8.5mstg. July 2001: Expects £17mstg Croydon hotel to open Jan 2002. Now has 5,454 bedrooms. July 2002: Sold Skylon and Waterford hotels for €14m. Aug 2002: Year end to change to Dec 31.

TEN YEAR REVIEW: € m

Months to April 30	1993	1994	1995	1996	1997	1998	1999	2000	2001 m)	2002
Sales	33.4	42.7	52.5	62.6	73.3	90.7	106.2	219.0	252.2	266.4
Profit before Tax	2.9	4.7	7.6	12.1	17.6	24.8	29.4	50.0	55.7	51.0
Tax	0.4	0.5	0.6	2.2	3.6	5.1	5.3	10.3	9.5	11.2
Profit after Tax	2.5	4.2	7.0	9.9	14.0	19.7	24.1	39.8	46.2	39.9
Extraordinary Item	-	-	-	-	-	-	-	-	-	-
Available for Shareholders	2.5	4.2	7.0	9.9	14.0	19.7	24.1	39.8	46.2	39.9
Ordinary Dividend	1.7	2.1	2.5	3.5	4.1	5.1	6.2	10.2	11.8	13.5
Retained Profit	0.8	2.1	4.5	6.4	9.9	14.6	17.9	29.6	34.4	26.4
Increase (Decrease) in Reserves	(0.3) h)	9.4 k)	4.7	23.4 a)	14.9 b)	97.8	18.4	175.2	22.6 p)	232.7 n)
Shareholders' Funds	81.9	93.8	98.6	125.0	139.9	237.7	256.1	436.1	458.9	674.8
Ordinary Dividend per Share (€)	0.063	0.065	0.073	0.08	0.092	0.11	0.14	0.17	0.199	0.219
Earnings per Share (€)	0.10	0.14	0.20	0.23	24.9p	0.44	0.54	0.68	0.78 f)	0.66 f)

Share premium €17.5m. b) Currency gain +€4.6m. e) Share premium +€118m; currency gain +€34.9m. f) Based upon 60.4m shares. h) Currency loss €1.3m. j) Property revaluation +€78.1m; currency gain +€4.8m. k) Share premium €7.5m. m) Figures subsequently restated. n) Share premium + €25.2m; property revaluation +€182m. p) Currency loss -€8.9m.

BALANCE SHEET: APRIL 30 2002 € m

Comment:

Very well managed and good geographical spread.

Excellent young management well poised for growth going forward. And nearly an 8 fold turn on the ten year investment.

Share Capital:			
62,660,874 Ord €0.32 shares	20.1	Fixed Assets	1,056.1
Reserves	654.7	Current Assets	60.0
		Current Liabilities	103.6
		Net Current Liabilities	(43.6)
		Medium term debt	(393.2)
Shareholders' Funds	674.8	Net Tangible Assets	619.3
		Intangibles	55.5
		Net Assets	674.8

7 OF THE BEST FOR 2003

If you can keep your head when all about you
Are losing theirs and blaming it on the ISEQ;
If you can trust yourself when all men doubt the fundamentals,
But make allowance for their doubting too;
If you can wait and not be tired by waiting,
Or, being misled by exuberance, don't deal in froth,
Or, being ridiculed, don't give way to ridicule,
And yet don't look good, nor talk too wise;

If you can face reality - and not make dreams your master;
If you can think - and not make your thoughts your straitjacket;
If you can meet with triumph and disaster
And treat those two impostors just the same;
If you can bear to hear the truth when spoken by others
Twisted by knaves to make a trap for fools,
Or watch the things you gave your cash to broken,
And stoop and build 'em up with fundamental tools;

If you can make one heap of all your winnings
And risk it on one float of dot.com stocks,
And lose, and start again at your beginnings
And never harbour a grudge about your loss;
If you can force your heart and nerve and sinew
To serve your turn long after they are gone,
And so hold on when there is nothing in you
Except the Will which says to them: "Hold on";

If you can talk with crowds and keep your virtue,
Or walk with beginners - and not lose a balanced view;
If neither foes nor loving loving friends can rock your values;
If all men count with you, but none too much;
If you can fill the unforgiving market
With more than sixty second's worth of trading done-
Yours is the market and everything that's in it,
And - which is more - you'll be a fundamental investor my son!

Who would have thought that over a span of fifteen years we would have experienced two dramatic dips in the Stock Market - Black Monday back in October 1987 and September 11 last year followed by a steady decline in market sentiment fuelled by poor results and a clutch of accounting based corporate scandals. In between there was one helluva party where the bull market of all bull markets made fortunes for the most inept stock pickers. But after every good party comes the hangover and here we are floundering around looking for the quick hangover cure to put us back on feet to face the next bull market face to face.

I was particularly struck by the poem quoted here and taken from *Investor's Week* of some years ago with apologies to Rudyard Kipling:

If you can fill the unforgiving market
With more than sixty second's worth of trading done-
Yours is the market and everything that's in it,
And - which is more - you'll be a fundamental investor my son!

It is only those with Divine Inspiration can predict the immediate future for share prices in this most volatile of times in the market. How many times have we gone to our screens lately to see a hopeful price upswing, only to be dashed the following day by a slide equal to or greater than the previous day's rise.

But the market weakness, in the short term, shows few signs of ending. The recent dip below 4,000 for the Footsie 100 was resisted and it didn't take long for it to haul itself above the 4,000 resistance level. However, the war mongering coming from the other side of the Atlantic means that when the first bomb is hurled at Baghdad the index will no doubt take another dive flamed by further price hikes in oil and its resultant effect on manufacturing costs world-wide.

As that wise old sage Warren Buffet told his shareholders this year, when commenting about 9/11: ' The probability of such mind-boggling disasters, though likely very low at present, is not zero. The probabilities are increasing, in an irregular and immeasurable manner as knowledge and materials become available to those who wish us ill. Fear may recede from time to time, but the danger won't - the war against terrorism can never be won. The best the nation can achieve is a long succession of stalemates. There can be no checkmate against hydra-headed foes'. And of course, every time there is an era of uncertainty, the market is sure to enter a period of jitters. The market always abhors uncertainty.

Let us not forget the other man made trauma of the past year - the accounting problems of the likes of Enron and WorldCom to mention only two. I wonder how many investors have really been assured by the swearing of the SEC-sponsored oaths by the 695 top company executives by the deadline of August 14th last.

Frankly, the cover of the *Economist* magazine spoke for most investors when the cartoon satirised the swearing by quoting: '*I swear.... that to the best of my knowledge (which is pretty poor and may be revised in future), my company's accounts are (more or less) accurate. I have checked this with my auditors (who are cognisant of their consultancy fees) and directors who (I pay to) agree with me.......*' And, of course, anyone familiar with those multitudinous tribunals in this country will easily recall the best legal advice of pleading amnesia when the plaintiff is in an awkward corner. A troupe of grotesque beasts from some American boardrooms have convinced many investors that company bosses are a greedy and dishonest bunch. We certainly welcome the suggestion that the position of auditor should rotate after, say, five years and unless a new cartel arrangement springs up between the auditing practices, this rotation should either flush out or at least act as deterrent for mal-

practices in this area. When con dence in the annual audit disa pears, the investor will surely f sake the market altogether for will then resemble a second-ha car salesman's yard.

So, with renewed faith, let's ho we have seen the last of the expressions of corporate greed.

The job at hand now is to pi the winners for 2003.

In the light of what we have sa the first rule is do not jump into t market without a clear indicati that the worst is over. I would li to see a 10% lift in prices genera ly, so that the Footsie 100 wou rise to 4,400 before I would more certain that the worst is ov If you pick up shares at 10% their bottom and sell 10% off th peak, then you should be ve happy. How many have tried to g in at the lowest price to find it f subsequently. A little patience see that prices had really bo tomed out would have helped co siderably.

The second rule is that these pu chases should be considered the medium-term, say, five yea or more. Most experts today are the opinion that the rise in th market, when it comes, will gradual and will not reflect th short-term exuberance evidence in the last bull market. So mak your choices on the basis of loc ing them away and taking the out for an annual stock-take to se that there have not been any fu damental changes for the worst the management or in the indust sector.

So, in alphabetical order, w select **Abbey**, the Charle Gallagher run house builder. strengths are, firstly the manag ment is young with the Executiv Chairman only 43 years of ag Secondly, the balance sheet without blemish without any gea ing; there are not too many co struction companies are run is th manner. Thirdly, instead of acqu sition for acquisition sake, th company, when flush with cash recent years paid out bonus div dends in 1998 and 1999 instead frittering the money away in acqu sitions they may regret in th future. And as an added bonus th shares are changing hands rolling price earnings ratio of 5. times. For that quality of perfo mance, where pretax profits hav grown over 3 times in 5 years on doubling of sales now producin 26.3% pretax on the most recen six months, a 5.7 times multiple a near steal with a well-covere dividend of 4.4%. The only snag that a takeover of Abbey would b out of the question and therefore sexy rating is out of the equation

Continued on page 119...

BUSINESS: Mineral exploration and development company in Mozambique and Ireland.
REGISTERED OFFICE: Chatham House, Chatham Street, Dublin. Tel: 01-6710411. Fax: 01-6710810.
HEAD OFFICE: as regd office.
SECRETARY: D Corcoran. **REGISTRARS & TRANSFER OFFICE:** Computershare Investor Services (Ireland) Ltd, Heron House, Corrig Road, Sandyford Industrial Estate, Dublin. **PRINCIPAL BANKERS:** AIB Bank, HSBC, Anglo Irish Bank, Irish Nationwide (IOM). **AUDITORS:** Deloitte & Touche. **SOLICITORS:** O'Donnell Sweeney.
STOCKBROKERS: Davy Stockbrokers; Canaccord Capital Europe Ltd
DIRECTORS: C Carvill (Chairman - 74), A Brown (64), M. Carvill (43), I Egan (56), S Farrell (52), T Fitzpatrick (42), D Kinsella (59), T McCluskey (38), P McAleer (60).
SHARE CAPITAL: Authorised: 300million Ord 5p shares. **Issued:** 262,209,123 Ord €0.06 shares + 48,031,467 Def €0.25 Shares
STAFF: 49   **SCRIP DIVIDEND:** No

million Ord 5p shares placed at 31p each. June 1997: 4,673,249 Ord 5p Shares placed at 31p each. Dec 1997: Placed 5,197,120 Ord 5p shares at 12.5p stg each. Also 5,197,120 warrants issued to subscribe for an Ord 5p share at 13.5p stg by 08.12.2001. July 1999: 5.7m Ord 5p shares placed at 7p each with warrants. Dec 1999: Placed 5,741,900 Ord 5p shares at 7.5pstg with warrants. Jan 2000: 5,741,900 Ord 5p shares placed at 7.5pstg with warrants. Feb 2000: Placed 12,732,100 Ord 5p shares @16p each (£2m). Placed a further 25,757,062 Ord shares to finance Moma Titanium Minerals project. Aug 2000: Placed 15,433,333 Ord 5p shares @ 11.25p each. April 2002: Placed 56,950,000 Ord €0.06 shares @ €0.23 each and Open Offer of 23,881,255 Ord €0.06 shares (1-for-8) @ €0.23 each.

COMPANY HISTORY:

CAPITAL HISTORY:

Incorporated July 1972. In January 1983 had issued 561,800 Ord. 25p shares, December 1984 issued 6m Ord. 25p shares to Cluff Oil plc to discharge debt of £650,000 (equal to par). June 1987 issued 6,666,657 Ord. 25p shares for Irish Marine Oil plc. Oct. 1987 500,000 Ord. 25p shares issued to Cluff Oil at par. 13,000 Ord. 25p shares issued to Ransford International. January 1988 500,000 Ord. 25p shares issued to Cluff Oil at part. Sept. 1988 1.8 million Ord. 25p shares issued to investors at 4.25p each. Sept. 1988 100,000 Ord. 25p shares issued to Cluff Oil. April 1989 Ord. 25p shares listed on USM. May 1989 2.9m Ord. 25p shares issued to Cluff Resources at 34.25p each. Nov. 1989, 285,000 Ord. 25p shares placed with Hong Kong institution at 43.5p each. Oct 1991: 1-for-1 3,021,263 Rights of Ord 5p shares at 7.5p each shares split into deferred Ord 20p shares (38,424,000) and Ord 5p shares (19,212,000). June 1993: Placing of 4,073,650 Ord 5p shares at 11.5p each (4,131,650). Oct 1994: Placed 4,095,238 Ord shares at 10.5p each. March 1995: Placed 2.4m Ord shares at 13p each. July 1995: Placed 1.75m Ord shares at 12.5p each. Jan 1996: 3,744,839 Ord shares placed at 24.5p stg each. July 1996: 8.9

February 1987: J.G. Cluff resigned as Director. June 1987: Acquisition of Irish Marine Oil by issue of 26,666,667 Ord. 25p shares on the basis of 2 Kenmare shares for every 3 Irish Marine shares. June 1987: Name changed from Kenmare Oil to Kenmare Resources. November 1987: A. Cluff takes up options on 1 million shares at 25p each while another Cluff company Celtic Basic Oil Exploration sells 3 million shares. March 1989: First gold poured at 49% owned mine in Sudan. May 1989: Cluff Resources pays £1m for 2.9m shares (1.75m shares at 42p each) and placed with institutional investors. November 1990: N. Taher issues $650,000 claim against Kenmare. November 1990: JCI withdraws joint venture in Mozambique. Sells its stake in African Gold plc - 5 million shares standing in balance sheet at £50,000. Oct 1991: Rights issue to raise £3.4m but only £1.7m raised. Oct 1992: Company progressing graphite and mineral sands projects in Mozambique. Aug 1993: Ancuabe Graphite project funding negotiations completed and construction of process commenced. EIC and CDC provide $7m debt finance. March 1994: Bought 75% zinc deposit mine in Bolivia. May 1994: Abandons Bolivian mine. June 1995: J. Teeling sells 1 million shares to African Gold. June 1998: Loans of £7.2m to be converted to Preference

shares. April 1999: D Horgan, finance director, dismissed. High Court action against Kenmare followed. May/June 1999: Major exodus of directors from Board. Oct 1999: Ancuabe graphite mine in Mozambique put on 'care and maintenance basis'. April 2000: Its titanium time in Mozambique to start in 2003 finance cost US$160m. Operating surplus estimated between US$45m and US$72m. Jan 2002: Arranged $280m funding for Moma mine.

Share Price Sept 2001 - Sept 2002

1. €0.22 11.04.02 Annual results; major placing

FINANCIAL DIARY

Interim Results Announced:	05.09.2001
Interim Dividend Payout:	unlikely
Final Results Announced:	11.04.2002
Annual General Meeting:	23.07.2002
Final Divident Payout:	unlikely

FIVE YEAR SHARE PRICE TREND €

1997	High	0.50 (Jan)	Low	0.18 (Dec)
1998	High	0.19 ((Feb)	Low	0.11 (Dec)
1999	High	0.16 (Sep)	Low	0.08 (Mar)
2000	High	0.36 (Mar)	Low	0.12 (Jan)
2001	High	0.35 (Feb)	Low	0.20 (Sept)

INVESTMENT PERFORMANCE

Five Year Investment Performance:	€ 621
Ten Year Investment Performance:	€ 2,300

TEN YEAR REVIEW: €'000

12 Months to Dec 31	1993 d)	1994 d)	1994 f)	1995	1996	1997	1998	1999	2000	2001
Turnover	-	-	-	841	1,779	2,878	3,923	2,705	-	-
Profit/(Loss) before Tax	6	(11)	(53)	(858)	(2,796)	(2,327)	(1,586)	(4,190)	(868)	(990)
Tax	1	-	-	-	-	-	-	-	-	-
Profit/(Loss) after Tax	5	(11)	(53)	(858)	(2,796)	(2,327)	(1,586)	(4,190)	(868)	(990)
Extraordinary Item	-	-	-	-	-	-	-	-	-	-
Minority Interests	-	-	-	245	988	47	-	-	-	-
Available for Shareholders	5	(11)	(53)	(613)	(1,808)	(2,280)	(1,586)	(4,190)	(868)	(990)
Ordinary Dividend	-	-	-	-	-	-	-	-	-	-
Retained Profit (Loss)	5	(11)	(53)	(613)	(1,808)	(2,280)	(1,586)	(4,190)	(868)	(990)
Increase (Decrease) in Reserves	(282)	602 c)	218 e)	(116) g)	1,464 h)	654 i)	1,544	(3,139)	39,617 a)	7,558 j)
Shareholders' Funds	-	-	5,719	6,267	8,545	9,847	8,303	5,891	48,680	56,682
Ordinary Dividend per share	-	-	-	-	-	-	-	-	-	-
Earnings per share	-	-	-	-	-	-	-	-	-	-

a) Share premium +€5m; property revaluation +€35m. c) Share premium +€0.3m; currency uplift +€0.3m d) Year ended 30th April. e) Share premium +€0.3m.
f) Eight months. g) Share premium +€0.9m. h) Share premium +€3.4m; currency loss -€0.3m. i) Share premium +€1.8m; currency gain +€1.1m. j) Share premium +€4.8m, currency gain +€2.4m.

BALANCE SHEET: DECEMBER 31 2001. € m

Comment:

Moma mia is now the flavour

of the day with a lot of money

being borrowed. It will be 2005

before we know if this gamble is

going to pay off.

Share Capital:				
191,050,040 Ord €0.06 Shares	23.5	Fixed Assets		47.2
48,031,467 def ord €0.25 shares		Current Assets	1.5	
Reserves	33.2	Current Liabilities	1.7	
		Net Current Liabilities		(0.2)
Shareholders' Funds	56.7	Medium debt		(3.0)
		Net Tangible Assets		44.0
		Intangible Assets		12.7
		Net Assets		56.6

Auditor's Note: "*In forming our opinion we have considered the adequacy of the disclosures made in the financial statements concerning the valuation of Mineral Interests, Tangible Assets and Investment in Subsidiaries. The realisation of Mineral Interests of €12,637,388 and Tangible Assets of €47,219,811 included in the Consolidated Balance Sheet and Investment in Subsidiaries of €20,078,283 in the Company Balance Sheet is dependent on the successful development of economic ore reserves. We draw attention to further details given in notes 9,10 and 10. Our opinion is not qualified in this respect*"

KERRY GROUP plc

CAPITAL HISTORY:

To facilitate the introduction of outside shareholders Kerry Group plc. was formed. June 1986 Kerry Group acquired the undertaking, property and assets of Kerry Co-Op for the consideration of 89,999,980 'B' Ord. shares. July 1986 10,350,000 'A' Ord. shares placed with existing shareholders at 35p each raising £3.62m. October 1986 8,000,000 'A' Ord. shares placed in public flotation at 52p each. May 1987 6,000,000 'A' shares placed at 85p each. May 1988 placed 3m 'A' Ord. shares at 93.5p per share. August 1988: 15m 'A' Ord. shares placed at 135p each. May 1989: rights issue 1-for-10 involving 13,641,383 'A' Ord. 10p shares at 135p. May 1991: 6,000,000 "A" Ord. 10p shares placed at 182p each. Nov 1994: 7.8 million "A" Ord 10p shares placed at 335p each. Feb 1998: Placed 6.192m A Ord 10p shares with institutions at €10.35 each. March 1998: Placed 2m A Ord 10p shares with employees at €10.41 each.

COMPANY HISTORY:

Kerry Co-Op commenced trading in January 1974 having purchased creameries and other assets in Co. Kerry and having amalgamated with a number of co-op societies in the county owned by farmer milk suppliers. It set about rationalising the various activities of the individual co-ops, streamlined and reorganised the milk collection system, butter production and feed milling operations.

Through shares acquired as a result of the formation of Kerry Co-Op and subsequent acquisitions, the Group owns 83% of North Kerry Milk Products Ltd. which owns the Listowel plant. Between 1974 and 1982 Kerry Co-Op acquired various liquid milk businesses giving it a distribution network in the south and west of Ireland. In 1982 it purchased Dennys, a major pig processing plant in Tralee and Duffys, a meat processing plant in Hacketstown, Co. Carlow. In March 1986 paid £5.76m for the purchase of, through its 80% owned subsidiary, a beef processing plant at Middleton, Co. Cork and a beef burger manufacturer at Tallaght, Co. Dublin. April '87: Purchased food mfg plant in Wisconsin, USA. No price disclosed. May '89: 6 million shares placed at 85p each to raise £5m net. Dec. '87: Purchased South West Meat in Somerset for £4m Stg. March '88: Purchased assets and business of Primas Food Products Inc. USA for $3.75m. May '88: Purchased Grove Farm Ltd. for IR£20m. Sept '88: Acquisition of Beatreme Foods in U.S. for £91m. April '90: Purchased Milac in Germany for £3m. April 1990: Full listing on stock market (188p). May-July '90: Purchased North Yorkshire Lamb; Sykes Meat Processing, Blackpool; A.E. Button & Sons Ltd. East Anglia. Dec '90: Purchased Robirch Ltd. and W.L. Miller & Sons for IR£29m cash. May '91: Purchased Meadow Meats for £2.5m cash. May '91: Placed 6 million "A" Ord. shares with institutions raising £11m (182p per share). July '91: Purchased Dairyland Products Inc for £23.1m cash (half to be paid June '82 and Jan '93). Purchased cold storage, two farms and meat plant in Clones for £8m. July '92 acquired Buxted Duckling. Dec '92 bought Tuam Dairies. Feb '93 £7m acquisition of Malcom Food Specialities (Canada). July '93 £10m stg acquisition of Tingles Ltd (UK). Obtains listing in London. Sept 1993: Raised $155m in senior notes from US institutional investors. Acquired Research Foods in Canada for £5.3m. Jan 1994: Acquired Dermet in Mexico for £14.7m. Nov 1994: Bought Mattesson Walls. Dec 1994: Bought DCA/Margetts for £260m. Dec 1995: Sells Meadow Meats and withdraws from Irish beef processing. Jan 1996: Bought Ciprial SA for £25m. July 1996: Approved Kerry Co-op dilute below 52% to 39%. Nov 1997: Buys SDF Malaysia for €6.6m. March 1998: Buys Dalgety Food Ingredients for £394m cash. Sells Spillers Milling for £108m. Oct 1999: Buys Shade Foods (US) and Specialty Food Ingredients (Europe) for $80m/£59m. Feb 2000: Sells DCA bakery for €101.7m. Oct 2000: Buys Armour Food (US) for €41m. May 2000:

HALF YEARLY PERFORMANCES: € m

Six Months to:	31.12.00	30.06.01	31.12.01	30.06.02
Sales	1,357.1	1,339.7	1,663.1	1,799.8
Profits before Tax	101.8	78.0	111.7	57.3
Profits % Sales	7.5	5.8	6.7	3.2

FIVE YEAR SHARE PRICE TREND €

1997	High	10.73 (Oct)	Low	7.55 (July)
1998	High	14.48 (Aug)	Low	9.27 (Sep)
1999	High	13.00 (Apr)	Low	10.34 (Aug)
2000	High	15.10 (Sep)	Low	11.40 (Feb)
2001	High	14.53 (Oct)	Low	11.80 (Mar)

FINANCIAL DIARY

Interim Results Announced	03.09.2002
Interim Dividend Payout	29.11.2002
Final Results Announced	26.02.2002
Annual General Meeting	27.05.2002
Final Dividend Payout	31.05.2002

SECTORAL ANALYSIS (previous year)

Sales: Ireland 17% (16%), Europe 47% (49%), America & Asia 36% (35%). **Profits:** Ireland 17% (16%), Europe 38% (39%), America & Asia 45% (45%).

INVESTMENT PERFORMANCE

Five Year Investment Performance:	€1,839
Ten Year Investment Performance:	€6,047

Buys various firms in US, Italy, France for €62.6m. Aug 2000: Buys Golden Vale for €245m. Sept 2001: Buy Golden Vale for €238.7m. Jan 2002: Buys 2 firms in US & France for €50m. Feb 2002: To sell Leckpatrick Dairy for €33m. April 2002: Kerry Co-op will 'spin-out' 6.4m c the plc shares to the Co-op members (Co-op holding reduced from 34% to 31%).

TEN YEAR REVIEW: € m

12 Months to December 31	1992	1993	1994	1995	1996 h)	1997	1998 c)	1999	2000	2001
Sales	1,049.7	1,117.2	1,120.8	1,522.5	1,565.9	1,706.7	2,200.0	2,456.4	2,621.9	3,002.8
Profit before Tax	36.5	44.5	50.4	54.8	65.0	99.7	119.2	113.8 a)	173.2	189.7
Tax	5.0	7.6	9.5	6.4	9.0	17.7	24.4	38.4	40.6	46.3
Profit after Tax	31.5	36.9	40.9	48.4	56.0	82.0	94.8	75.5	132.5	143.5
Minority Interest	(0.2)	(0.2)	-	-	-	-	-	-	-	-
Available for Shareholders	31.3	36.7	40.9	48.4	56.0	82.0	94.8	75.5	132.5	143.5
Ordinary Dividend	4.5	5.2	5.9	6.9	8.0	9.1	11.6	13.5	15.6	18.5
Retained Profit	26.8	31.5	35.0	41.5	48.1	72.9	83.2	61.9	116.9	124.0
Increase (Dec.) in Reserves	25.8	42.0 f)	59.3 g)	31.0	46.5	(331.8)	158.1	72.0 b)	178.1 j)	287.1
Shareholders' Funds	26.4	305.8	366.1	397.1	443.6	111.8	271.0	327.3	505.0	793.6 e)
Ordinary Dividend per Share (€)	0.029	0.033	0.036	0.042	0.048	0.056	0.066	0.079	0.09	0.10
Earnings per share (€)	0.201	0.235	0.260	0.30	0.342	0.50	0.56	0.44	0.76	0.817 d)

a) After restructuring costs -€35.4m. b) Currency gain +€10m. c) Figures subsequently restated. d) Based upon 175.7m shares. e) Share premium +€164.2m. f) Currency gains +€13m. g) Share premium +€31.4m. h) Figures subsequently restated; pretax profits increased to +€79.6m. i) Goodwill written back +€66m; goodwill written off -€453.8m. j) Share premium +€3.8m; goodwill write-back +€75m; currency loss -€17.3m. k) Share premium +€82.5m.

BALANCE SHEET: DECEMBER 31 2001. € m

Share Capital:		Fixed Assets	885.8
184,998,845 'A' Ord €0.125 shares	23.1	Current Assets	897.0
		Current Liabilities	775.5
Reserves	770.5	Net Current Assets	121.5
		Medium Term Debt	(862.8)
		Deferred income	(36.8)
		Net Tangible Assets	107.7
		Intangibles	685.9
Shareholders' Funds	793.6	Net Assets	793.6

Comment: Tip top management who have had no fear of leveraging the balance sheet. Shareholders have nothing to complain about over the 10 year investment period but as Kerry has grown so substantially it will probably take a mega deal to impact on earnings at this stage. The dividend is comfortably covered well over 7 times

Head for the light

Capita Corporate Registrars is **big enough** to meet all your share registration requirements yet **small enough** to deliver a personal approach.

Benefit from our exceptional breadth of

- **Expertise**
- **Products**
- **Services**
- **Integrated Solutions**

If you desire unsurpassed service, call Pat O'Donoghue on 01-8102429 or email podonoghue@capitacorporateregistrars.ie

Capita Corporate Registrars Plc
Unit 5 Manor Street Business Park
Manor Street, Dublin 7
www.capitacorporateregistrars.ie

CAPITA

KINGSPAN GROUP plc

BUSINESS: Manufacturers of building components.
REGISTERED OFFICE: Dublin Road, Kingscourt, Co Cavan.
Tel: 042-9698000. Fax: 042-9667501.
HEAD OFFICE: as regd office.
SECRETARY: D Mulvihill. **REGISTRARS & TRANSFER OFFICE:** Computershare Investor Services (Ireland) Ltd, Heron House, Corrig Road, Sandyford Industrial Estate, Dublin.
PRINCIPAL BANKERS: AIB, Ulster Bank Markets, IIB, ABN AMRO, ING Barings, Bank of Ireland, Barclays, Royal Bank of Scotland, ICC, Bayerische Landesbank,Wachovia Bank.
AUDITORS: Grant Thornton.
SOLICITORS: McCann FitzGerald; Macfarlanes.
STOCKBROKERS: Goodbody Stockbrokers, Investec Henderson Crosthwaite.
DIRECTORS: E Murtagh (Chairman & Ch-Exec - 60), R Barr (46), D Kitchen (51), E McCarthy (61), D Mulvihill (53), B Murtagh (57), G Murtagh (31), K O'Connell (65), J Paul (61), R Shiels (42).
SHARE CAPITAL: Authorised: 220m Ord €0.13 shares.
Issued: 167,728,115 Ord €0.13 shares.
STAFF: 3,326. **SCRIP DIVIDEND:** No

CAPITAL HISTORY:

Dec 1984 had issued 405,000 'A' Ord.£1 shares and 95,000 'B' Ord.£1 shares. March 1989: 26,316 'A' ord.£1 shares issued at £30.40 each to IDA. May 1989: issued 26,316 'A' Ord.£1 shares for Kingspan Building Products and Hangar Industrial Doors. May 1989: 'A' and 'B' shares converted to Ord.£1 shares and then subdivided into 10 Ord.10p shares. 3-for-1 scrip issue resulting in the issue of 16,578,960 Ord.10p shares. May 1989 public flotation by placing of 4,342,105 new Ord.10p shares at 76p each. March 1996: Placed 1.32 million Ord 10p shares at 225p each. February 1997: Rights issue (1-for-6) 4,641,941 Ord 10p shares at 440p each. Nov 1997: Scrip issue (4-for-1) of 132,129,024 Ord 10p shares.

COMPANY HISTORY:

Formed in 1970 engaged in machinery installation, mechanical services and structural steel fabrication. In 1976 developed composite panels for roofs and side walls. In late 70s developed thermal insulation boards for roofs and walls. ICC subscribed for 19% of equity in 1980. Losses occurred in 1982-84 and loss making divisions closed in 1984. In 1986 acquired Torvale Insulation Board for £350,000stg. In 1988 acquired 49.9% of Veha, a central heating radiator manufacturer. March 1989: IDA takes 5% investment. May 1989: goes public at 76p and quickly reached 85p. May 1990: announces acqui-

sition of The Thermal Insulation Board Division of B.P.B. for £1.1m. July 1990 announces the acquisition of 50% of Kuiper van der Kooij - a Dutch distributor for £1.6m. Dec 1990: Kingscourt Construction Group issued 100,000 6.5% Cum. Red. Pref. £1 shares at 700p each. Dividend payable on £700,000 Redeemable December 1995. October 1990: Announced joint venture with Partek of Finland to market fibrous cement board in UK and Ireland. January 1991: Purchased Integration AP, Liverpool, manufacturer of architectural panels, for £525,000. Dec 1991: Acquired Coolag in UK for £2m stg. Sept 1993: Riada replaces NCB as brokers. Jan 1994: ICC offloads its remaining shares (total of 13% now sold). March 1994: Bought 50% Kingspan Veha Ltd for £829,000. Subsequently sold 100%. April 1994: E. Murtagh (33.9%) and B Murtagh (16.2%) offload 3m shares at 130p each (£3.9m). June 1995: Revealed that certain Directors had received Tax-Free royalty payments of £1m in 1994, £827,000 in 1993 and £589,000 in 1992. IAIM requests remuneration committee be setup to examine overall payments. Oct 1995: Sells pipe insulation business for £1.65m stg. Feb 1996: Bought S & D Group for £8.6m. Bought remaining 50% Kingspan Nedeland for £2.6m. March 1996: Pays £4.3m tax free to buy-out Directors royalty payments. Aug 1996: Buys Kooltherm in Wales for £9.5m stg. December 1996: Acquires Ward UK and Atlas Germany for max £28.5m. June 1997: E. McCarthy sells 340,000 shares at 525p each. Jan 1998: S. Rusk sells 2 million shares at 240p each. June 1998: 4 Directors sell 8.5m shares at 310p each for £27m. July 1998: Buys Interlink Holdings for £7m. Dec 1998: B Murtagh resigns as Director. Jan 1999: Buys Hewetson plc for £37.8m stg. Buys Entec (Pollution Control) for £2.65m stg. April 1999: Major share selling by ex-director B Murtagh (12.8m shares at 179p each). May 1999: Shareholders query why directors sold 21m shares realising £49.8m during the year. Oct 1999: Buys Flooring Services Group for £4.8mstg. Sells various non-core businesses for £4.5mstg. May 2000: P Molloy resigns as Director. July 2000: Previous qualification in accounts re Canadian venture comes to light. Jan 2001: Bought Tate Global for €112m. June 2001:

Share Price Sept 2001 - Sept 2002

1. €3.00 05.09.01 Interim results
2. €2.90 20.03.02 Annual results

INVESTMENT PERFORMANCE

Five Year Investment Performance: € 2,561
Ten Year Investment Performance: €16,867

FIVE YEAR SHARE PRICE TREND €

1997	High	3.17 (Oct)	Low	2.92 (Nov)
1998	High	4.44 (Feb)	Low	2.18 (Oct)
1999	High	3.00 (Jan)	Low	2.17 (Feb)
2000	High	3.90 (Dec)	Low	2.70 (May)
2001	High	4.80 (Feb)	Low	2.38 (Oct)

FINANCIAL DIARY

Interim Results Announced:	10.09.2002
Interim Dividend Payout:	11.10.2002
Final Results Announced:	20.03.2002
Annual General Meeting:	23.05.2002
Final Dividend Payout:	28.05.2002

HALF YEARLY PERFORMANCES: € m

Six months to:	31.12.00	30.06.01	31.12.01	30.06.02
Sales	337.5	438.3	390.6	360.5
Pretax Profits	36.1	38.0	35.4	28.7
Profit % Sales	10.7	8.7	9.1	8.0

SECTORAL ANALYSIS: (previous year)

Sales: Raised flooring 30% (16%), panels 30% (37%), insulation 12% (13%), other 28%(34%). RofI: 13% (15%), UK 60% (69%), elsewhere 27% (16%).

€375m loan facility arranged. Dec 2001: Bought in and cancelled 1.4m own shares during the year @ €2.82 each. Feb 2002: Heavy share trading ahead of profits warning because of Tate losses. Aug 2002: AIBIM sells 1.2m shares.

TEN YEAR REVIEW: € m

12 Months to December 31	1992 c)	1993	1994	1995	1996	1997	1998	1999	2000	2001
Sales	68.2	77.7	88.9	105.8	160.2	303.5	368.8	532.5	662.6	828.9
Profits (Loss) before Tax	1.5	3.9	6.0	7.8	16.8	38.7	48.0	58.7	67.5	73.4
Tax	0.3	0.4	0.7	1.1	3.1	8.6	11.2	12.9	16.1	17.9
Profits (Loss) after Tax	1,2	3.4	5.3	6.7	13.7	30.1	36.8	45.8	51.4	55.4
Minorities/Associates	(0.2)	(0.2)	(0.4)	(0.4)	(0.5)	(0.7)	(0.3)	(0.1)	(0.2)	(0.02)
Available to Shareholders	1.0	3.2	4.9	6.3	13.2	29.4	36.5	45.7	51.2	55.4
Ordinary Dividend	0.7	0.8	1.0	1.2	1.8	2.4	2.9	4.2	6.1	8.0
Retained Profit	0.3	2.4	3.9	5.1	11.4	27.0	33.6	41.5	45.1	47.4
Increase (Decrease) in Reserves	(0.5)	0.2 d)	4.2	4.4	(1.4) e)	18.7 f)	29.5 g)	49.7 a)	44.8	46.5
Shareholders' Funds	15.6	15.9	20.1	24.6	23.3	59.6	89.3	139.5	184.4	231.0
Ordinary Dividend per Share (€)	0.0055	0.006	0.008	0.009	0.011	0.014	0.017	0.025	0.036	0.047
Earnings per Share (€)	0.008	0.024	0.036	0.046	0.093	0.18	0.22	0.27	0.30	0.33 b)

a) Currency gain +€8.6m. b) Based upon 171.6m shares. c) Subsequently restated. d) Owing to change in accounting policy, goodwill w/o -€2.3m.
e) Goodwill w/o -€17.3m; share premium +€3.7m. f) Share premium +€24.6m; scrip issue -€16.8m; goodwill w/o -€17.4m; currency gain +€1.3m. g) Currency loss -€4.1m.

BALANCE SHEET: DECEMBER 31 2001. € m

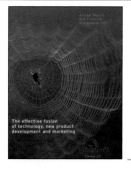

The effective fusion of technology, new product development and marketing

Share Capital:		Fixed Assets		167.5
169,373,115 Ord €0.13 shares	22.0	Current Assets	323.1	
		Current Liabilities	179.8	
		Net Current Assets		143.3
Reserves	209.0	Medium Debt		(240.0)
		Minority		(1.8)
		Net Tangible Assets		69.0
		Intangibles		162.0
Shareholders' Funds	231.0	Net Assets		231.0

Comment:
The problems at Tate should dampen Kingspan's ardour for further acquisitions on the other side of the pond. However, any investor who has been into the share for the long haul cannot complain with the investment performance over the decade.

LAMONT HOLDINGS plc

BUSINESS: Manufacture textile products.
REGISTERED OFFICE: P O Box 28448, Finance House, Orchard Brae, Edinburgh
HEAD OFFICE: Stotts Mill, Bridgefold Road, Rochdale, Lancashire.2LN. Tel: 01706 752055. Fax: 01706 340987
SECRETARY: G Askew **REGISTRARS & TRANSFER OFFICE:** Lloyds TSB Registrars Scotland, P O Box 28448, Finance House, Orchard Brae, Edinburgh.
PRINCIPAL BANKERS: Northern Bank, Bank of Ireland, Lloyds Bank. **AUDITORS:** PricewaterhouseCoopers.
SOLICITORS: n/d **STOCKBROKERS:** Davy Stockbrokers.
DIRECTORS: P Casey (Chairman - 49), W Gleave (Ch Exec - 36), V McGinlay (52), Lord Rathcavan (H O'Neill - 63), R Wilson (55).
SHARE CAPITAL: Authorised: 100m Ord 10p shares. 160,000 4.2% cum pref 50p shares; 500,000 5.6% 2nd cum pref £1 shares; 890,895 10% 3rd cum pref £1 shares. **Issued:** 95,084,959 Ord 10p shares. 160,000 4.2% cum pref 50p shares; 500,000 5.6% 2nd cum pref £1 shares; 890,895 10% 3rd cum pref £1 shares.
EMPLOYEES: 482. **SCRIP DIVIDEND:** No

CAPITAL HISTORY:
Incorporated Feb 1936. Aug 1975 2million Ord 10p shares placed at 25p each. Apr 1986 issued 2,544,597 Ord 10p shares

for Shaw Carpets. May 1992: Rights issue 1-for-4 5,995,471 Ord 10p shares at 280p each. June 2002: Placing and open offer (5-for-4) of 65m Ord shares @ 2pstg each.

COMPANY HISTORY:
Incorporated Feb 1936. Dec 1973: Name changed from J H Lamont & Co to Lamont Holdings having acquired brassfounders Lamont.. Changed to plc in Dec 1981. June 1992 paid £16.3m for A Drew & Sons (fabric printing). May 1993 sold ICS Computing for £1.9m. Oct 1993 paid £6m for Cunningham Johnson Ltd, 50% of Deramore Lamont and 50% Lakefable. April1994 paid £0.6m for Ballievery Ltd and 50% Lakefable. Aug 1994 sells Tatlor & Jones for £0.4m. Dec 1996: Sells Shaw Carpets for £1m. Sept 1997: Sells carpet underlaying business for £2.2m. June 1999: R Wilson (Monaghan Mushrooms) and P Casey through Castlemere Enterprises Ltd hold 15.8% of equity costing £3.1m/*3.9m. Jan 2000: 265 redundancies in yarn and carpets. April 2000: Sells textile business at Hollybank for £0.7m stg. July 2000: Exits carpet production. Sells Killinchy business for £1.1m stg.

FINANCIAL DIARY
Interim Results Announced:	28.09.2001
Interim Dividend Payout:	none
Final Results Announced:	24.05.2002
Annual General Meeting:	19.06.2002
Final Dividend Payout:	none

SHARE PRICE TREND
1997	High	360p (Jan)	Low	135p (June)
1998	High	181p (Feb)	Low	51p (Dec)
1999	High	64p (Mar)	Low	28p (Nov)
2000	High	35p (Apr)	Low	19p (June)

SECTORAL ANALYSIS (previous year)
Sales: UK 75% (73%), other 25% (27%). Fabrics 90% (86%), carpets 10% (14%).

May reinvent itself as investment holding company. Feb 2001: Sells Moygashel for £3.3m stg/*5.2m. Jan 2002: Shares suspended. June 2002 Share placing to raise *1.3mstg. Now left with BFF and Alexander Drew. £15.3mstg in debt to be converted to equity and non-interest loan stock. To leave London & Dublin Stock Exchanges and trade on the AIM in London.

EIGHT YEAR REVIEW: £'000 stg
2 months to December 31	1994	1995	1996	1997	1998	1999	2000	2001
Sales	142,920	125,048	122,002	95,130	83,169	63,879	48,377	32,369
Profits/(Loss) Before Tax	9,081	9,686	(8,637)	7,488	1,599	(20,752)	(20,055)	(13,172)
Tax	2,911	2,815	+2,578	1,346	144	+5,025	+611	+443
Profits/(Loss) After Tax	6,170	6,871	(6,059)	6,142	1,455	(15,727)	(19,444)	(12,729)
Minority Interests								
Preference Dividends	121	121	121	121	121	122	122	122
Available to Shareholders	6,049	6,750	(6,180)	6,021	1,334	(15,849)	(19,566)	12,851
Ordinary Dividend	3,848	3,848	3,852	3,852	1,099			
Retained Profits	2,201	2,902	(10,032)	2,169	235	(15,849)	(19,566)	12,851
Increase (-) in Reserves				n/d	(214)	(18,208) a)	(19,651)	(12,772)
Shareholders' Funds	45,796	48.709	41,998	44,134	44,348	26,141	6,490	(6,282)
Ord Dividend Per Share (pstg)	12.8p	12.8p	12.8p	12.8p	3.65p	-	-	-
Earnings Per Share (pstg)	20.1p	22.5p	-	20.01p	4.43p	-	-	-

a) Goodwill adjustment -£2.4m.

BALANCE SHEET:
DECEMBER 31 2001. £'000

Fixed Assets	18,308
Current Assets	11,673
Current Liabilities	36,263
Net Current Assets	(24,590)
Pref shares	(1,471)
Net Tangible Assets	(7,753)
Share Capital:	
30,084,959 Ord 10p shares	3008
Reserves	(10,761)
Shareholders' Funds	(7,753)

> **Comment:** An unfortunate investment over the years. So it's 'goodbye' to Dublin and 'hello' to the AIM in London.

MARLBOROUGH INTERNATIONAL plc

BUSINESS: Recruitment consultants
REGISTERED OFFICE: 111-113 Grafton St., Dublin. Tel: 01-6173800. Fax: 01-6777546. **HEAD OFFICE:** Arena House, Arena Road, Sandyford, Dublin.
SECRETARY: J Nolan. **REGISTRARS & TRANSFER OFFICE:** Computershare Investor Services (Ireland) Ltd, Heron House, Corrig Road, Sandyford Industrial Estate, Dublin. **PRINCIPAL BANKERS:** AIB Bank.
AUDITORS: Chapman Flood Mazars **SOLICITORS:** A & L Goodbody **STOCKBROKERS:** Davy Stockbrokers.
DIRECTORS: C Brownlee (Acting Chairman - 58), D McKenna (Group Mgr Director - 42), D Richardson (52), I Finan (45).
SHARE CAPITAL: Authorised: 41.5million Ord €0.06 shares. **Issued:** 31,465,000 Ord €0.06 shares **STAFF:** 467. **SCRIP DIVIDEND:** No

CAPITAL HISTORY:
Incorporated April 1984 as Marlborough Recruitment Ltd. January 1992: changed to Marlborough Consulting Ltd. January 1996 changed to Marlborough Investments Ltd. Bonus issue of 8 Ord £1 shares at par, Issued 12 Ord £1 shares to J Nolan and A McGennis for £167 each. July 1997: Subdivided shares into Ord 5p shares. Bonus issue of 597,597 Ord 5p shares at par. August 1997 changed to Marlborough International plc. October 1997: Bonus issue of 9,575,000 Ord 5p share to shareholders. April 1998: Issued 5m Ord 5p shares at 152p stg re acquisition of Walker Hamill.

COMPANY HISTORY:
Marlborough Consulting Ltd was acquired in 1992 by David McKenna

and Brian McCarthy from the liquidator of Marlborough Employment (1) Ltd and started supplying contract and permanent staff to manufacturing, technical, commercial, retail an building sectors. December 1993 bought 60% of Resultants Recruitment specialising in computer and contract staff but has been dormant since December 1994 since transferring its trade to MGL. April 1994 bought The Professional Placement Group Ltd in operation since 1986. November 1995 Brian McCarthy sold his stake in MGL to David McKenna. August 1997 sold its 60% in Resultants Recruitment to David McKenna. October 1997: J Doupe computer divisional head resigns over contract. October 1997: Placed 6.25m shares on Dublin (DCM) and London (AIM) markets at 96p each raising £6m; directors placed 4.2m shares for £4m. Closed first day dealings at 112p each. January 1998: Announces buying Walker Hamill for £21m. April 1998 purchased Walker Hamill Ltd for £17.6m stg. Share quotation reinstated with Full Listing. March 1999: Sold property for £2m. June 1999: Directors Hamill and Walker sell a total of 1,032,445 shares at 158p each. Aug 1999: Buys Ann O'Brien agency for £4.1m. Oct 1999: Paid Irf4.6m/$5.9m for two Scottish agencies. June 2000: Massive 'egg-on-face' when reverse takeover involving E-Pawn.com (A Reynolds an E-Pawn director) aborted when it is revealed E-Pawn involved in fraud allegations. Shares hit $1.90 before the egg broke. Dec 2000: In talks with Spring Group (UK). Talks ended. Feb 2001:

FINANCIAL DIARY
Interim Results Announced:	24.10.2000
Interim Dividend Payout:	none
Final Results Announced:	15.06.2001
Annaul General Meeting:	27.07.2001
Final Dividend Payout:	none

SHARE PRICE TREND
1997	High	171p (Dec)	Low	106p (Nov)
1998	High	400p (Apr)	Low	170p (Jan)
1999	High	236p (Mar)	Low	142p (Oct)
2000	High	205p (Sept)	Low	95p (July)
2001	High		Low	

HALF YEARLY PERFROMANCES:
Six months to	31.08.99	28.02.00	31.08.00	28.02.01
Sales (net)	10,732	13,590	16,051	28,365
Profits/(-) before tax	2,247	2,716	2,536	(3,702)
Profits % sales	20.9	20.0	15.8	-

SECTORAL ANALYSIS: (previous year)
Net Fees: Contracting fees 31% (30%), permanent fees 69% (70%). Rofl 51% (54%), UK 43% (42%), Australia 6% (4%).

Profits warning. May 2001: Chairman N Welch resigns. Profits warning due to bad debts. July 2001: Looking at MBO possibility. Feb 2002: David Hughes of Ernst Young appointed Receiver to the Group. Shares suspended in Dublin and London.

SEVEN YEAR REVIEW:
Months to February 28	£'000 1995	£'000 1996	£'000 1997	£'000 1998	£'000 1999	£'000 2000	£'000 2001	€'m 1999	€'m 2000	€'m 2001
Gross Fee Income	5,057	6,801	10,801	16,948	38,845	56,864	72,789	49.3	77.2	92.5
Net Free Income	2,090	3,078	4,643	8,043	17,022	24,322	44,416	21.9	30.9	36.1
Profits/(Loss) Before Tax	112	125	647	3,068	4,600	4,963 f)	(1,166)	5.8	6.3 f)	(1.4)
Tax	48	54	218	1,110	1,409	1,463	286	1.8	1.9	0.4
Profits/(Loss) After Tax	64	71	429	1,958	3,191	3,501	(1,451)	4.0	4.4	(1.8)
Minority Interest	-	-	(5)	(7)	(5)	(2)	-	-	-	-
Available For S'holders	64	71	424	1,951	3,186	3,499	(1,451)	4.0	4.4	(1.8)
Ordinary Dividend	-	-	-	-	-	-	-	-	-	-
Retained Profits	64	71	424	1,951	3,186	3,499	(1,451)	4.0	4.4	(1.8)
Increase (-) in Reserves	N/A	73	424	7,028 a)	11,359 e)	3,542	(1,174)	14.4	4.5	(1.5)
Shareholders' Funds	(109)	(36)	388	8,349	19,958	23,500	22,242	25.3	29.8	28.2
Ord Dividend per share	-	-	-	-	-	-	-	-	-	-
Earnings Per Share	0.24p	0.27p	1.6p	7.3p	10.3p	11.1p b)	-	&0.13	&0.14 b)	

a) Share premium +£5.1m, property revaluation +£0.6m. b) Based upon 31.4m shares. e) Share premium +£8.0m. f) Includes profit on asset disposal of £360k.

BALANCE SHEET: FEBRUARY 29 2001
	£'000	€'m	€'m		£'000
Share Capital:			4.4	Fixed Assets	3,478
31,465,000 Ord			22.9	Current Assets	18,028
€0.06 shares	1,487	1.9	30.3	Current Liabilities	23,831
Reserves	20,755	26.3	(7.4)	Net Current Liabilities	(5,803)
			(0.1)	Medium debt	(70)
			(3.1)	Net Tangible Liabilities	(2,395)
			31.3	Intangibles	24,637
S'holders' Funds	22,242	28.2	28.2	Net Assets	22,242

> **Comment:**
> It looks as if 'the fat lady has sung'.

NO DEATILS FOR THE YEAR ENDED FEBRUARY 2002 HAVE BEEN RECEIVED

McINERNEY HOLDINGS plc

BUSINESS: Construction company
REGISTERED OFFICE: 29 Kenilworth Square, Rathgar, Dublin. Tel: 01-4962010. Fax: 01-4962055.
HEAD OFFICE: as regd office.
SECRETARY: M. Shakespeare.
REGISTRARS & TRANSFER OFFICE: Computershare Investor Services (Ireland) Ltd, Heron House, Corrig Road, Sandyford Industrial Estate, Dublin.
PRINCIPAL BANKERS: Bank of Ireland, Anglo Irish Bank, Irish Intercontinental Bank, Royal Bank of Scotland, Bank of Scotland, Banco Bilbao Vizcaya Argentaria.
AUDITORS: Deloitte & Touche.
SOLICITORS: Radcliffes Le Brasseur; Wm. Fry.
STOCKBROKERS: Davy Stockbrokers
DIRECTORS: R Ferris (Chairman - 70), B O'Connor (Mng Dir - 48), D McInerney (42), W Riordan (64), P Shortall (64), M Leece (57).
SHARE CAPITAL: Authorised: 45 million Ord €0.125 shares. **Issued:** 32,609,071 Ord €0.125 shares. 850,000 share warrants at 10p each up to Dec 2003
STAFF: 551.   **SCRIP DIVIDEND:** No

CAPITAL HISTORY:

Public flotation Nov. 1971 at 66p per share. Nov. 1971 'scrip' issue of 9,421,148 Ord. 10p shares issued. 1975 1,000,000 Deferred Ord. 10p shares issued at 50p each to McInerney trust companies. June 1979 1,000,000 Ord. 10p shares issued on conversion of the deferred ordinary shares. Nov. 1986 purchased land at Southampton, England financed by 785,886 Ord. 10p shares. June 1987 placing and open offer of 3,054,959 Ord. 10p shares at 236p each (rights on the basis of 1-for-5). July 1990 rights issue (2-for-1) 36,812,172 Ord. 10p shares at 20p each. June 1992: 5,000,000 A Ord shares of 10p each. 60,218,258 C Ord shares of 0.001p each, 6,027,000 10% Cum Red Pref shares of £1 each, 6,927,000 Red Pref shares of £1 each. The 10% Cum Red Pref shares are redeemable in five equal annual instalments commencing 31.12.1996 subject to the company having reserves available to effect the redemption; dividends on these shares accrue from 01.01.'94. The Red Pref shares are redeemable in twelve equal annual instalments commencing 31.12.2002 but subject to the company having reserves available to effect the redemption. The Redemption of the 10% Red Pref shares and the Red Pref shares is secured by the Guarantee of Geufrom Ltd supported by a second charge on that company's shareholding in McInerney Construction (Holdings) Ltd and by guarantees from certain subsidiaries supported by second or third charges on the group's income from its leisure developments in Spain and Portugal. December 1996:

Issued 10p Ord Shares at €0.444 each in McInerney Holdings plc pursuant to restructuring of McInerney Properties plc. Placing and open offer of 16,842,857 McInerney Holdings plc 10p Ord Shares at €0.444 each. Feb 1999: Placing and open offer (1-for-4) 6,498,214 Ord €0.125 shares at €1.485 each.

COMPANY HISTORY:

Incorporated in June 1963. November 1970 paid £150,000 for Kingscourt Bricks. In 1971 purchased Cappincur Joinery for £500,000. Went public in 1971 when £2.5m was raised. Incurred pretax losses of £3m in 1974. Over the period 1971-1975 acquired and disposed of property at Grattan St., Clarendon St., old Fitzwilliam Tennis Club site and office development in Paris. By December 1975 McInerney's debt/equity ratio was over 700%. Finance package arranged whereby Bank of Ireland and Northern Bank Finance purchased development valued at £1.5m and McInerney family trusts injected equity capital. McInerney survived and went on to build in the Middle East, a time-share complex in Portugal and Spain and various projects in the UK. Dec. 1987: Part of consortium awarded Custom House docks development project. Feb. 1988: R. Chenery resigns as Chief Executive. D. McInerney to act as Chief Executive. Dec. 1989: Issues 10m GTD 9.7% Cum. Red. Pref. £1 shares in McInerney Estates plc at 100.28p (redeem 1997) Jan. 1990: S. Cannon appointed Chief Executive. July 1990: Rights issue raised £7m. March 1991: UK operations restructured. Investment in UK properties of £13.1m written off. April 1991: G. Pierse purchases 85% of McInerney Contracting for £4m. Sept. 1991: Barclays Bank appoint receiver over McInerney Homes in UK. Downside limited to £1m sterling guarantee. July 1992: Massive financial restructuring which raised £13m in preference shares, £0.5m in new equity and £2.3m raised from sale of 25% of Custom House Development. Certain Irish operations ring-fenced by being placed in a company called McInerney Construction (Holdings) Ltd. Original shareholders diluted to 44.0% of the company. A. McInerney and T. Hardiman resign as Directors, R. Ferris apptd Chairman. B. O'Connor apptd Director. Aug 1993: Shares suspended ahead of High Court action by an American creditor. Sept 1993: Creditor problem resolved. Share quote restored. Oct 1993: D. Cody resigned. April 1994: Sold Vilamoura resort for £1.65m stg resulting in loss of £2.7m stg. May 1994: S. Cannon resigned. June 1996: Financial restructuring being finalised leading to 'substantial dilution' for existing shareholders and £5m in new equity. December 1996: End of McInerney Properties plc; McInerney Holdings plc rises from the ashes. Feb 1999: 73% take-up of

rights issue. April 1999: D McInerney buys 70,00[0] shares at €1.75 each. Aug 1999: Bought W Hargreave[s] Ltd UK for €18.2m. Dec 1999: Built 600 houses in 199[9] Nov 2000: Harcourt Developments (Pat Doherty) take[s] 10.8% stake in McInerney. Jan 2002: Bought Charlt[on] Group for €13m. May 2002: Buys 294 plots in UK f[or] €5m.

Share Price Sept 2001 - Sept 2002

1. €0.33 Results announced 22.07.02.
2. €2.55 17.05.02 Final results.

FINANCIAL DIARY

Interim Results Announced:	26.09.2001
Interim Dividend Payout:	22.03.2002
Final Results Announced:	17.05.2002
Annual General Meeting:	28.06.2002
Final Dividend Payout:	none

FIVE YEAR SHARE PRICE TREND €

Year	High		Low	
1997	High	1.14 (Oct)	Low	0.44 (Jan)
1998	High	2.35 (July)	Low	0.99 (Jan)
1999	High	1.90 (Feb)	Low	1.50 (Feb)
2000	High	2.82 (Nov)	Low	1.70 (Jan)
2001	High	2.79 (May)	Low	1.20 (Nov)

SECTORAL ANALYSIS: (previous year)

Sales: Housing 70% (71%), Leisure 7% (4%), other 23% (25%).

HALF YEARLY PERFORMANCE: € m

Six months to	30.06.00	31.12.00	30.06.01	31.12.01
Sales	66.7	107.6	68.7	116.5
Pretax profits (-)	7.6	11.5	4.1	14.0
Profit % Sales	11.4	10.7	6.0	12.0

TEN YEAR REVIEW: € m

12 months to Dec.	1991 d)	1992 d)	1993 d)	1994 d)	1995	1996	1997	1998	1999	2000	2001
Sales	43.3	41.7	40.2	47.6	42.8	49.6	66.0	80.9	109.7	174.3	185.2
Profit (Loss) before Tax	(15.0)	(3.4)	(10.8)	0.4	0.4	1.6	4.2	9.0	14.2	19.1	18.1
Tax	+1.3	(1.1)	0.2	0.3	0.1	0.5	1.0	2.6	3.4	4.4	4.2
Profit (Loss) after Tax	(13.7)	(4.5)	(10.6)	0.1	0.3	1.1	3.2	6.4	10.7	14.7	13.9
Minority Interest	(1.4)	-	-	-	-	-	-	-	-	-	-
Extraordinary Items & Pref Div.	+0.4	-	-	0.8	-	-	-	-	-	-	-
Available for Shareholders	(14.7)	(4.5)	(10.6)	(0.7)	0.3	1.1	3.2	6.4	10.7	14.7	13.9
Ordinary Dividend	-	-	-	-	-	-	0.3	0.5	0.8	1.1	1.5
Retained Profit	(14.7)	(4.5)	(10.6)	(0.7)	0.3	1.1	2.9	5.9	9.9	13.6	12.4
Increase (Decrease) in Reserves	(14.5)	(7.0)	(9.9)	(0.7)	1.3	33.2 c)	4.3	6.2	18.7 f)	13.6	12.3
Shareholders' Funds	(12.2)	(18.5)	(28.4)	(29.0)	(27.7)	1.0	5.2	11.4	30.9	44.5	56.9
Ordinary Dividend per Share (€)	-	-	-	-	-	-	0.013	0.02	0.025	0.035	0.045
Earnings per Share (€)	-	-	-	-	0.015	0.044	0.13	0.22	0.353	0.463	0.437 e)

c) Premium on new shares plus compromise with creditors +€11.4m. Remaining difference is due to restructuring into a new McInerney Holding Company. d) McInerney Properties plc. e) Based upon 31.9m shares. f) Share premium +€8.3m.

BALANCE SHEET: DECEMBER 31 2001. € m

Share Capital:				
		Tangible Assets		9.4
		Financial Assets		1.5
32,568,571 Ord. €0.125 shares	4.1	Current Assets	179.8	
		Current Liabilities	88.7	
Reserves	52.8	Net Current Assets		91.1
		Medium Debts		(50.7)
Shareholders' Funds	56.9	Net Tangible Assets		51.3
		Intangibles		5.6
		Net Assets		56.9

Comment:

Continued recovery in line with construction industry.

(Formerly Fishers International plc; originally Celtic Gold plc)

BUSINESS: Insurance and financial services.

REGISTERED OFFICE: 20 St Dunstan's Hill, London.
Tel: 020-73988700. Fax: 020-73988730.

HEAD OFFICE: as regd office.

SECRETARY: I Meier.

REGISTRARS & TRANSFER OFFICE: Computershare Investor Services plc, PO Box 435, 8 Bankhead Crossway North, Edinburgh.

PRINCIPAL BANKERS: Bank of Scotland, Singer & Friedlander Ltd, AIB.

AUDITORS: KPMG Audit plc.

SOLICITORS: Travers Smith Braithwaite.

STOCKBROKERS: HSBC Securities.

DIRECTORS: J Hodson (Chairman - 57), R Horton (52), S Sheridan (60), R Wood (60), M Hughes (Ch Exec - 44), S Anderson.

SHARE CAPITAL: Authorised: 200million Ord 5p shares.
Issued: 164,384,356 Ord 5pstg shares

STAFF: 1,160.   **SCRIP DIVIDEND:** No.

CAPITAL HISTORY:

Incorporated August 1987. Aug 1987: 250,000 Ord 5p shares issued at par for cash. Nov 1987: 1,250,000 Ord 5p shares issued at par of which 1,250,000 were issued for cash and 13million for certain mineral exploration rights and information. Dec 1987: 2,249,993 Ord 5p shares issued for 5p each. June 1989: 2,637,000 Ord 5p shares issued for 30p each. June 1994: Placing and open offer (1-for-6) of 3,397,833 Ord 5p shares at 17p each. Jan 1995: Issued 76,818,181 Ord 5p shares to Vendors of Fishers Group at 11p stg each. June 1997: Issued 11,511,843 Ord 5p shares at 18.5p each for Farrell & Applied Technology. March 1998: Vendor placing 12 million Ord 5p shares at 38p each. Feb 1999: Vendor placing 4m Ord 5p shares at 38p each on acquisition of Pycraft & Arnold. March 1999: 8,968,015 Ord 5p shares issued at 38p each. May 2000: Issues 434,982 Ord 5p shares on acquisition of B Collins Ltd. Issues 3,018,696 Ord 5p shares re Miller Farrell and ATA Group.

COMPANY HISTORY:

May 1994: E Stanley and S Finlay resign as directors. Change of control. Cladagh Gold Ltd sold 11million shares in Celtic Gold (54% of equity) to K Kenny (3.75m/18.4%), Singer & Friedlander (6.1m/29.9%), English Trust (0.5m) and English Trust clients (0.65m). Sold its only subsidiary, Clare Calcite Ltd (net deficit £6,439 after capitalising expenditure of £168,286), for £1 to H Stanley & S Finlay. Announces bid for Coyle Hamilton Group (insurance brokers) to be paid for by 63.9m new Ord 5p shares and £2.65m cash (total valuation £13.5m). June 1994: Reverse takeover of Coyle Hamilton fails as it only had support of 42% of Coyle Hamilton shareholders. Hold option to purchase before 31.01.95 293,637 Coyle Hamilton shares (42%) at £15 each. Jan 1995: Acquired Fishers Group (Insurance) for between £8.45m stg and £11.95m stg. Name changed to Fishers International plc. Oct 1995: High Court approved capital reorganisation of £1,186,000 reduction in share premium account. April 1996: Bought Miller Knight and Robert Bishop for £1.8n with possible earn-out of £1.25m. June 1997: Buys Farrell Group & Applied Technology for £7.1m. March 1997: Purchased NLA Group for £6m (cash and shares). July 1997: Fishers bids £70m for Hambro Insurance Service. Sept 1997: Increases Hambro offer to £84m. Bid rejected. July 1998: D. Farrell sells 3.6m shares at 38.5p stg. Feb 1999: Buys Pycraft & Arnold for £10.8mstg. May 1999: Name changed to Miller Fisher Group plc and domicile to UK. High Court allows write-down of £7.9m in capital. May 2000: Acquires B Collins Ltd (Ireland) for £550,000. Feb 2001: Miller Fisher in bid talks. July 2000: Profits warning. May 2001: Sold Homecare for £4.5m stg. Dec 2001: Ch Exec K Kenny resigns. March 2002: Bank of Scotland to subscribe for

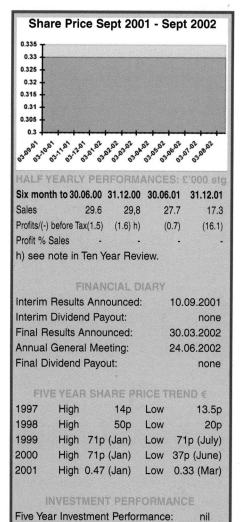

Share Price Sept 2001 - Sept 2002

HALF YEARLY PERFORMANCES: £'000 stg

Six month to	30.06.00	31.12.00	30.06.01	31.12.01
Sales	29.6	29,8	27.7	17.3
Profits/(-) before Tax	(1.5)	(1.6) h)	(0.7)	(16.1)
Profit % Sales	-	-	-	-

h) see note in Ten Year Review.

FINANCIAL DIARY

Interim Results Announced:	10.09.2001
Interim Dividend Payout:	none
Final Results Announced:	30.03.2002
Annual General Meeting:	24.06.2002
Final Dividend Payout:	none

FIVE YEAR SHARE PRICE TREND €

1997	High	14p	Low	13.5p
1998	High	50p	Low	20p
1999	High	71p (Jan)	Low	71p (July)
2000	High	71p (Jan)	Low	37p (June)
2001	High	0.47 (Jan)	Low	0.33 (Mar)

INVESTMENT PERFORMANCE

Five Year Investment Performance: nil

13.12m CRCP shares in return for capitalising £13.25m bank debt (bank debt = £24.8mstg). Chairman Kitson resigns. July 2002: Receiver appointed over Miller Fisher plc - banks had had enough.

TEN YEAR REVIEW

months to Dec 31	IR£'000 1992	IR£'000 1993	IR£'000 1994	Stg £'000 1995	Stg £'000 1996	Stg £'000 1997	Stg £'000 1998	Stg £'000 1999	Stg £'000 2000	Stg £'000 2001
Income	6,184	2,769	23,828	24,033	36,744	40,354	42,958	60,834	59,419	45.0
Profit/(Loss) before Tax	(160,321)	(302,002)	(257,974)	874	1,934	2,957	3,390	2,604	(3,105) h)	(16.8)
	-	428	-	252	420	885	961	269	59	0.7
Profit/(Loss) after Tax	(160,321)	(302,430)	(257,974)	622	1,514	2,072	2,429	2,335	(3,164)	(17.5)
Available for Shareholders	(160,321)	(302,430)	(257,974)	622	1,514	2,072	2,429	2,335	(3,164)	(17.5)
Ordinary Dividend	-	-	-	352	550	798	1,336	1,611	166	-
Retained (Losses) Profits	(160,321)	(302,430)	(257,974)	270	964	1,274	1,093	724	(3,300)	(17.5)
Increase (Decrease) in Reserves	(160,321)	(302,430)	101,744 a)	(3,557) c)	(133) d)	(1,231) e)	5,765 f)	9,344 g)	(2,821)	(17.3)
Shareholders' Funds	1,367,914	1,065,484	1,337,120	2,052	2,200	1,543	16,852	26,300	23,652	6.4
Dividend per Share (p stg)	-	-	-	0.32p	0.5p	0.65p	0.85p	1.0p	0.1p	-
Earnings per Share (p stg)	-	-	-	0.63p	1.38p	1.8p	1.8p	1.51p b)		

a) Share premium +£360,000. b) Based upon 155.0m shares. c) Share premium +£3.8m; goodwill write-off -£8.8m. d) Goodwill -£0.8m.
e) Share premium +£1.5m; goodwill -£4m. f) Share premium +£2.8m. g) Increase in merger reserve +£8.5m. h) Includes one-off costs of £2.2mstg.

BALANCE SHEET: DECEMBER 31 2001. £ m stg

Comment:

Five loss making years out of the last ten - the banks had had enough and the plug was pulled.

Share Capital:		Tangible Assets		5.0
164,017,410 Ord 5p shares	8.2	Current Assets	17.6	
		Current Liabilities	40.6	
Reserves	(1.8)	Net Current Assets		(23.1)
		Medium Debt		(2.1)
		Net Tangible Liabilities		(20.2)
		Intangibles		26.5
Shareholders' Funds	6.4	Net Assets		6.4

millerfisher

Annual Report & Accounts

(Quoted on Exploration Securities Market - formerly Feltrim Mining Plc)

BUSINESS: Natural resources company.
REGISTERED OFFICE: 10 Fitzwilliam Square, Dublin. **HEAD OFFICE:** as regd office. Tel: 01-6613309. Fax: 01-6613119. **SECRETARY:** A. W. Banyard.
REGISTRARS & TRANSFER OFFICE: Computershare Investor Services (Ireland) Ltd, Heron House, Corrig Road, Sandyford Industrial Estate, Dublin.
PRINCIPAL BANKERS: Bank of Ireland. **AUDITORS:** Deloitte & Touche.
SOLICITORS: O'Donnell Sweeney. **STOCKBROKERS:** Davy Stockbrokers; Investec Henderson Crosthwaite.
DIRECTORS: J Metcalfe (Chairman - 63), M Nolan (Ch Ex - 41), M Johnson (53), A Robson (52), D Hall (44), C Lins (59).
SHARE CAPITAL: Authorised: 750 million Ord €0.012 shares, **Issued:** 497,440,590 Ord €0.012 shares.
STAFF: 53. **SCRIP DIVIDEND:** No

CAPITAL HISTORY:

Incorporated as Feltrim Mining plc in February 1988. March 1988: 179,993 Ordinary 20p shares issued at IR40p each. March 1988: 2,320,000 Ordinary 20p shares issued atIR40p each when floated on the Stock Exchange. March 1990: 1,446,799 Ordinary 20p shares issued at IR32p each. March 1990: 6,950,945 Ordinary 20p shares issued re acquisition of Connary Minerals. Shares subdivided into one ordinary 5p share and one deferred share of IR15p each. May 1993: Issued 2,823,863 Ordinary 5p shares at IR5p each by way of an open offer and conversion of debt. June 1993: Every 3 Ordinary 5p shares converted into 1 Ordinary 15p shares. Each Ordinary 15p share was sub-divided into 1 Ordinary 1p share and 1 Deferred Ordinary share of IR14p. 94,985,242 Ordinary 1p shares issued at par by way of a placing open offer to conversion of loan and conversion of debt. March 1994: 2.5 million Ord 1p shares issued at 4p each to buy CDC Landscapes. May 1994: 4.9 million Ord 1p shares placed at 4p each. July 1994: 4 million Ord 1p shares placed at 5p each. 1.25m Ord 1p shares issued at par re options. Sept 1994: 60,000 Ord 1p shares issued at 5p each to A. Lee in lieu of fees. Oct 1994: 100,000 Ord 1p shares issued at 5p each in lieu of fees on Russian projects. Jan 1995: 12,323,117 Ord 1p shares issued in open offer and placing at 2.5p each. Aug 1995: Placed 1,142,858 Ord 1p shares with 2 new Directors (Metcalfe & O'Hanlon) at 1.75p each. Issued 875,000 Ord 1p shares at par in lieu of debts at 2p each. Issued 500,000 Ord 1p shares to M. Nolan for fees at 2.0p each. Issued 3 million to P. Bristol re options. Issued 142,857 Ord 1p shares to E. Lee at 1.75p/2.0p each in lieu of fees. Placed 7,050,000 Ord 1p shares at 1.5p stg each. Jan 1996: Placed 9 million Ord 1p shares at par. Jan/April 1996 1,800,920 Ord 1p shares at 1.25p each in lieu of debts. June 1996: Placed 8m Ord 1p shares with GFM International Investors at 3.25p/3.5p stg each. February 1997: Placed 10,285,741 1p Ord shares at 3.25p stg each. June 1997: 950,000 Ord 1p shares issued at 1.25p re options. 150,000 Ord 1p shares issued at 6p each for Minmet (Bolivia) Ltd. Nov 1997: 20.3m Ord 1p shares placed at 4.5p stg each. 4,076,627 Ord 1p shares issued at 4p to 7p each to Connary Minerals shareholders. July 1998: Offers 2 Minmet for every 3 Connary shares - issue of 39,586,545 new Minmet Ord 1p shares. Nov 1998: 22,849,200 Ord 1p shares placed at 6p stg each. Dec 1998: 7.5m Ord 1p shares issued at 6p stg each for 100% of Anagram Ltd. June 1999: 4.7m Ord 1p shares placed at 6pstg each. July 1999: 25m Ord 1p shares issued at 9pstg each for 100% of Mineradora de Bauxita Brazil. Sept 1999: Placing and open offer of 134,374,609 Ord 1p shares at 8pstg each. Sept 1999: Deferred shares cancelled. May 2000: 7.7m Ord 1p shares issued at 8pstg each re acquisition of Mineradora de Bauxita. March 2001: Issues 680,000 Ord 1p shares re purchase of Mearim, Brazil. June 2001: Placed 23,554,600 Ord 1p shares @ 15.75p stg each. May 2002: Places 1m ord €0.012 shares @ 11p stg each.

COMPANY HISTORY:

The company has acquired interests in licences at Galway and Kerry for the purpose of prospecting for gold. Feltrim is applying for licences for prospecting for precious and base metals at four areas in Kerry. Feltrim has an 80% interest in the Galway exploration with a commitment to spend £10,000 on exploration. J Barniele holds the remaining 20% and will spend £2,500. July 1988: Buys 85% stake in Wild Blue Mining Co. with interests in gold prospects in New Mexico. The consideration being an exploration programme to be funded by Feltrim at a cost of $0.55m. October 1988: Buys 66% stake in Sea Scoop Ltd. Sea Scoop is exploring for coal in the Crataloe Coalfield in Co Limerick. February 1989: Buys a placer mining property in Valdex, Alaska. July 1989: Feltrim suspended on news of Kelly & Fitzsimons acquiring 25% stake with intention of making it a leisure company. Oct 1989: Abandons leisure plans and announced reverse takeover by Pan Andean Resources for £0.9m. Subsequently abandoned. February 1990: Rights issue to raise £450,000. March 1990: Shares reinstated. Opened at 34p compared with 48p at suspension. Acquired Connary Mineral plc for £2.2m in all paper deal of 6.95m shares valued at 32p each. July 1990: Board exodus by N.A. Haughey, S.B. Gibbs, J.P. Shannon, J. O'Connor and J. David. Mr. Fitzsimons appointed to Board. August 1990: Mr. Fitzsimons resigns as Director after one month. Sept. 1990: J. Coleshill and C. Burton resign as Directors. Sept. 1990: Stock Exchange examining share dealings over 12 months to July. Boardroom squabble. March 1992: B. Cahill resigns as Chairman. Name changed to Minmet. Open offer and placing hope to raise £0.6m. Unsuccessful. C F Haughey resigns as Managing Director. June 1992: Shares suspended pending discussion with continental investor. May 1993: Placing of 72.5m shares to raise £700,000, Takeover of Solent Trees for £375,000. June 1992: R F Haughey resigns as Director. Relinquishing all mining licences concentrating on developing non toxic leaching process and other areas within natural resources, mature trees, landscaping and ground maintenance. June 1993: Buys Solent Trees Ltd for £375,000. Oct 1993: Buys CDC Landscaping for £270,000 stg (plus max earn out of £130,000 stg) plus 2.5 million Minmet shares at 4p each. July 1994: Minmet shareholders offered 1 share in Connary Technology at 1p each plus 1 warrant for each 5 Minmet shares held. Minmet placing 5 m shares in Connary at 1p each. If full take up, 31.4m new Connary shares to issue (29.5%) with Minmet holding remainder. Acquired 23% of Gulf Exploration Consultants. Dec 1994: Sold CDC Landscapes at total loss of £704,000. Jan 1995: Open offer of 1 - for - 6 which might have involved issuing 22 million new shares; gets only a 42% response from share-

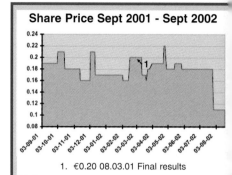

Share Price Sept 2001 - Sept 2002

1. €0.20 08.03.01 Final results

FINANCIAL DIARY

Interim Results Announced:	29.08.2002
Interim Dividend Payout:	not likely
Final Results Announced:	08.03.2002
Annual General Meeting:	25.04.2002
Final Dividend Payout:	not likely

FIVE YEAR SHARE PRICE TREND €

1997	High 0.06 (Apr)	Low	0.04 (Feb)
1998	High 0.15 (June)	Low	0.09 (Oct)
1999	High 0.30 (Nov)	Low	0.09 (Jan)
2000	High 0.75 (Feb)	Low	0.25 (Jan)
2001	High 0.32 (Jan)	Low	5.83 (Oct)

INVESTMENT PERFORMANCE

Five Year Investment Performance: £3,571

holders. Feb 1995: Sold Salisbury Landscapes Ltd at loss of £61,00 Oct 1996: Offers 2,593,476 Ord 1p shares in Crediton Minerals Plc Minmet shareholders at 10p each. October 1996: Minmet ADR's trade New York. February 1997: Increases stake in Connary Minerals 57.6%. July 1998: Offers £4.1m stg for remaining 35% of Connar Minerals. July 1999: Acquired Brazilian bauxite mine for Ir£2.25m $250,000 + 7.7m warrants. Sept 1999: Chairman Metcalfe appears c *Show Me The Money* and share price doubles. Aug 2000: Puff piece i *Daily Mail* ('billions of pounds worth of gold.. in Brazil') sends share pric soaring to €0.55. March 2001: Further investment in Sth America. Ja 2002: Sold Tiger Resources for £0.6m.

TEN YEAR REVIEW: €'000

12 Months to 31 Dec	1992	1993	1994	1995	1996	1997	1998	1999 f)	2000	2001
Sales	55	395	112	130	-	-	-	-	-	-
Profit (Loss) before Tax	(471)	42 a)	(1,427)	(656)	(149)	(123)	(1,114)	(84)	(119)	(438)
Tax	-	-	-	-	2	5	1	8	-	-
Profit (Loss) after Tax	(471)	42	(1,427)	(656)	(151)	(128)	(1,115)	(92)	(119)	(438)
Minority	-	-	-	-	-	-	-	-	+123	-
Available for shareholders	(471)	42	(1,427)	(656)	(151)	(128)	(1,115)	(92)	4	(438)
Ordinary Dividend	-	-	-	-	-	-	-	-	-	-
Retained Profits (Losses)	(471)	42	(1,427)	(656)	(151)	(128)	(1,115)	(92)	4	(438)
Increase (Decrease) in reserves	n/a	2,656 b)	-	(599)	693 c)	1,070 d)	5,594 e)	17,122 g)	1,352	4,924 h)
Shareholders' Funds	(204)	2,011	2,189	1,967	3,050	4,574	11,056	29,309	30,761	36,013
Ordinary Dividend per Share	-	-	-	-	-	-	-	-	-	-
Earnings per share	-	-	-	-	-	-	-	-	-	-

a) Directors emoluments of €28,342 capitalised. b) HighCourt reduced share capital by effectively writing down P & L A/c deficit by €4.6m and by reducing share premium a/c by €1.3m. c) Share premium +€0.6m. d) Share premium +€1.4m; goodwill w/o -€0.3m. e) Share premium +€6.7m. f) Subsequently restated. g) Share premium +€16.6m. h) Share premium +€5.7m.

BALANCE SHEET: DECEMBER 31 2001. € m

Share Capital:		Fixed Assets	0.5
496,356,590 Ord €0.012 shares	6.3	Current Assets	15.0
Reserves	29.7	Current Liabilities	0.6
		Net Current Assets	14.4
		Net Tangible Assets	14.9
		Intangibles	21.1
Shareholders' Funds	36.0	Net Assets	36.0

Comment:

Performs well at handling media exposure but their exploration activities are not quite so successful.

Auditors Note: *"Fundamental uncertainties:....the realisation of intangible assets of IR£16,656,452 in the consolidated balance sheet and of intangible fixed assets and investment in, and loans to subsidiaries of IR£20,657,416 in the company balance sheet .....is dependent on the successful development of the various business activities being pursued by the group....."*

(Formerly Navan Resources plc)

BUSINESS: Mineral exploration and production in Bulgaria, Ireland and Spain.

REGISTERED OFFICE: Norden House, Basing View, Basingstoke, Hampshire, RG21 4HG. Tel 0044 1256 353312. Fax: 0044 1256 335500.

HEAD OFFICE: as regd office.   **SECRETARY:** S. Olsen.

REGISTRARS & TRANSFER OFFICE: Computershare Investor Services plc, P.O. Box 435, Owen House, 8 Bankhead Crossway North, Edinburgh.

PRINCIPAL BANKERS: Deutsche Bank.

AUDITORS: KPMG   **SOLICITORS:** Wm. Fry; Clyde & Co.

STOCKBROKERS: J. & E. Davy; Canaccord Capital (Europe) Ltd

DIRECTORS: R Lockwood (Chairman - 59), P Burnell (61), R Read (56), L Marsland (48).

SHARE CAPITAL: Authorised: 600 million Ord. 15p stg shares. **Issued:** 226,040,109 Ord 15p stg shares.

STAFF: 1,130.   **SCRIP DIVIDEND:** No.

CAPITAL HISTORY:

Navan Mining plc incorporated May 2000 emerged from Mining Resources incorporated in January 1987. November 1987 placed 499,980 Ord. 10p shares at 10p each. November 1987 500,000 Ord. 10p shares divided into 1,000,000 Ord. 5p shares. January 1988 1,000,000 Ord. 5p shares consolidated to 4,000 Ord. 20p shares. January 1988 3,750,000 Ord. 20p shares placed at 20p each. February 1988 500,000 Ord. 20p shares placed at 20p each. February 1988 338,754 Ord. 20p shares issued to I.D. in return for data. 81,300 Ord. 20p shares issued C. Andrew for data. Nov. 1990: 549,450 Ord. 20p shares issued to Realstate AG for 18.2p stg. each. Aug 91: Rights issue; (3-for-2) 7,429,385 Ord 20p shares placed and taken up at 20p. Oct 1992: Offer & placing 18,271,100 loan notes of 25p with warrants raising £4m. April 1993: Private placing of 3,338,000 Ord shares at 27.55p each. Oct 1992/Aug 1993: 3,530,193 Ord 20p shares issued in exchange for 2,930,963 loan notes converted and 599,230 warrants exercised. Dec 1993: 7 million Ord 20p shares issued at 104.23p each. Oct 1994: 4.65 million Ord 20p shares issued at 138p 3,799,955 Ord 20p shares issued in exchange for 668,037 convertible loan notes and 1,131,918 warrants. Aug 1995: Issued 6 million Ord 20p shares to Homestake Mining Co at US $4 each. Issued 508,727 Ord 20p shares in exchange for 672,100 conv. loan notes and 2,836,627 warrents. Aug 1999: 5,730,000 Ord 20p shares placed at 58pstg each. 1million Ord 20p shares issued to bankers in lieu of fees of $1m. 500,000 Ord 20p shares issued at $0.88 each re purchase of 42% Balkan Mineral. July 2000: One Navan Mining Ord 15p stg share replaces each one Navan Resources Ord 20p share. November 2000: 3.1m Ord 15pstg shares placed @ 78pstg each. July 2001: Open offer (2-for-9) 15,333,694 Ord 15pstg shares @ 113p each (only 1.6m acceptances from shareholders). Feb 2002: 83,697,880 Ord 15p shares placed @ 20pstg each; 2-for-1 rights issue of 1,855,875 Ord 15p shares @20pstg each; 41,568,731 Ord 15p shares issued to Deutsche Bank and Hypovereinsbank to convert loans of $11.7m; issued 9,303,505 Ord 15p shares to Canaccord Capital in lieu of commission.

COMPANY HISTORY:

Formed in 1987 by ex-Tara Mines and ex-Ennex geologist Colin Andrew. In 1988 Navan acquired exclusive ownership of a Trinity College research report and data from C Andrew for a cost of £400,000. June 1989: Announced joint venture with Mount Isa Mines for base metals explorations in Ireland (ongoing). November 1989: Gold discovery in Inishturk. Major andalusite discovery on Mount Leinster. Aug 1990: Exploration rights over 255sq km in Scotland. Oct 1990: Acquired 80% interset in exploration in Spain. July 1991: Acquires 100% interest in the Mazarron Zn-Pb-Ag prospect in Murcia Province, Spain. Sept 1991: S Elbe Ltd of Guernsey now owns 48% via three off-shore companies (Bachmann, Guernroy and Fideicommissaires). May 1992: Acquires a controlling 50% in four Hungarian mines, for £3.7m. Aug 1992: Acquires 25% interest and option on a further 26% over the Chelopech Cu-Au mine in Bulgaria. Nov 1993: Acquires 42% of BIMAC AD in Bulgaria for £4.8m. April 1994: Midland Bank Trust, National Nominees and Davy Nominees off-loaded 3.5 million shares (12.9%). April 1996: Fidelity International increases stake to 4.81%. June 1996: Harpendon Ltd sells 10.7% of Navan. Feb 1997: Major management changes. Nov 1997: Homestake invests £20.1m for 51% of Bulgarian Mine. July 1998: Criticism of revised share option scheme. June 1999: Buys 75% of Chelopech EAD (Bulgaria) for $5.05m. Now holds 92% of BIMAK. Raises $34m from Deutsche Bank. Major boardroom changes. July 1999: Increases stake to 92% in Bulgarian mine. April 2000: Homestake sells its 10.5% stake to Gold Mines of Sardinia. July 2000: Changes name; floats on London; opens @52.5pstg/€0.83 each. Feb 2002: Navan runs short of money; major financial restructuring including bank agrees refinance $23.5m to Feb 2005 and creditors to agree extra time. Ch executive resigns. Spanish mine closed. June 2002: Finance Director resigns. Chairman says: "Navan will need more cash".

Share Price Sept 2001 - Sept 2002

1. €0.28 29.04.02 Final results

FINANCIAL DIARY

Interim Results Announced:	25.09.2001
Interim Divident Payout:	unlikely
Final Results Announced:	29.04.2002
Annual General Meeting:	26.06.2002
Final Dividend Payout:	unlikely

FIVE YEAR SHARE PRICE TREND €

1997	High	2.39	Low	0.93
1998	High	1.14	Low	0.38
1999	High	1.08	Low	0.83
2000	High 1.53 (Nov)		Low 0.80 (Aug)	
2001	High 2.31 (May)		Low 0.68 (Nov)	

INVESTMENT PERFORMANCE

Five Year Investment Performance: € 306
Ten Year Investment Performance: € 7,929

SECTORAL ANALYSIS: (previous year)

Sales: Bulgaria 1% (4%), Spain 13% (14%), other 86% (82%).

TEN YEAR REVIEW

months to 31 Dec	£'000 1992 b)	£'000 1993 c)	£'000 1994	$'000 1995	$'000 1996	$'000 1997	$'000 1998	$'000 1999	$'000 2000	$'000 2001
Sales	-	8,328	9,487	25,944	26,777	46,195	47,708	42,321	36,750	31,774
Profit (Loss) Before Tax	(30)	668	1,215	5,666	996	(15,576)	(12,808)	(7,206)	(5.953)	(83,623)
Tax	10	111	81	730	58	597	415	315	4	264
Profit (Loss) After Tax	(40)	557	1,134	4,936	938	(16,173)	(13,223)	(7,521)	(5,957)	(83,887)
Minority	-	(465)	(781)	(2,497)	(437)	+2,701	+765	+153	+206	+850
Available for Shareholders	(41)	92	353	2,439	501	(13,472)	(12,458)	(7,368)	(5,751)	(83,037)
Ordinary Dividend	-	-	-	-	-	-	-	-	-	-
Retained Profit (Loss)	(41)	92	353	2,439	501	(13,472)	(12,458)	(7,368)	(5,751)	(83,037)
Increase (Decrease) in Reserves	(41)	6,179 d)	4,895 e)	25,449 f)	377	(9,635) g)	(10,647)	(1,939) h)	(1.685)	(68,813) i)
Shareholders' Funds	2,632	11,585	18,170	60,418	60,827	51,192	40,545	40,503	34.282	(30,382)
Ordinary Dividend per Share	-	-	-	-	-	-	-	-	-	-
Earnings per Share	-	0.6p	1.16p	4.94 cents	0.8 cents a)	-	-	-	-	-

a) Based upon 57.3 m shares. b) Year end March. c) 21 months. d) Share premium £6.1m. e) Share premium £5.5m; currency loss -£1.2m. f) Share premium +$23.3m. g) Currency loss -$2.2m; goodwill on purchase of Almagrera +$6m. h) Share premium +$4.4m. i) Share premium +$21.4m; negative goodwill -$6m.

BALANCE SHEET: DECEMBER 31 2001. $'000

Comment:

Another exploration company

unsuited to

widows and orphans.

Share Capital:		
87,480,114 Ord 15p stg shares	19,518	
Reserves	(49,900)	
Shareholders' Funds	(30,382)	

Fixed Assets		35,258
Financial Assets		170
Current Assets	4,817	
Current Liabilities	35,305	
Net Current Liabilities		(30,488)
Medium Debt		(36,195)
Minority Interests		(1,107)
Net Tangible Liabilities		(32,363)
Intangible Assets		1,981
Net Liabilities		(30,382)

NAVAN MINING PLC

NORISH plc

CAPITAL HISTORY:

Public placing of 2,220,000 shares in March 1986 at 180p each. 412,000 shares issued as part of acquisition of Keenfoods in December 1986. July 1988 1.1m Ord. 20p shares offered and placed at 286p per share to raise £3.1m. April 1989: Issue of 427,350 Ord. 20p shares on acquisition of 66% of Eirfreeze.

COMPANY HISTORY:

Norish established in 1975 as a joint Irish/Norwegian venture to provide refrigeration and cold storage facilities for the food industry. Built 0.75 million cubic feet cold storage on 50 acre site at Castleblayney. Further expansion in 1978 and 1984 bringing facility there to 2.25 million cubic feet with total investment of £4.0m. In 1985 built 0.75 million cubic feet cold storage at Ballragget, Co. Kilkenny in joint venture with Avonmore Creameries (Norish Kilkenny Ltd. 60% owned by Norish). Also in 1985 built 0.75 million cubic feet cold store at Craigavon. Stage 2 of Norish (Kilkenny) Ltd. was built in 1986 and the extension comprises 750,000 cubic feet of multi purpose chilled and cold store refrigerated

space. November 1986 acquired 75.2% of Keenfoods a frozen food distributor in Northern Ireland for £1m by issuing 412,000 shares and cash payment of £83,000 stg. The balancing 24.9% was acquired in July 1989. June 1989: Purchased Provincial Frozen Foods, Dublin. December 1987: Acquired West Suffolk Public Cold Store for a total of £3m stg. July 1988: Obtains full listing on London S.E. Placing of shares announced; 552,000 shares held by Ostlandske and Smurfit Investment placed at £2.86 per share and open offer of 1.2m shares at £2.86 per share to raise £3.16m. August 1989: Acquired 66.6% of Eirfreeze for £3.7m.1989: Norish took possession of a 2.6 million cubic foot food store in Brierly Hill, West Midlands. Nov 1990: Sold assets of Keenfoods and Provincial Frozen Foods for £1.5m cash. Aug 1992: Acquired 33% Norish (Eirfreeze) for £1m. Jan 1995: £5 million written off assets as Cork, Craigavon and Belfast plants put up for sale. Sept 1995: L. McCauley resigns as Ch. Exec. March 1996: Sells Belfast store. May 1996: Sells its 60% interest in Kilkenny and sells Norish (Eirfreeze) and Frigofreeze for total £3.4m. L McCauley gets £220,000 pay-off. July 1996: B. Joyce buys 43,865 shares at 63p each. Aug 1996: Sells cold store in Castleblayney for £1.65m. August 1997: High Court cancels £1.2m in share premium a/c. May 1999: Buys Belvedere Warehousing Group for £7m stg (cash + loan notes) - imports cocoa/coffee. Sept 1999: Based now in the UK. Added 200,000 sq ft of warehousing to 600,000 sq ft. June 2000: Sells its 30% operation in Castleblayney for £300,000stg. July 2000: Buys warehouse in York for £350,000stg. May 2001: Profits warning from foot & mouth plus low levels of cocoa imports. Feb 2002: J Teeling buys 4.77% for €193.000; T Cunningham buys 5.37%; Kappa Alpha increases stake to 5.4%.

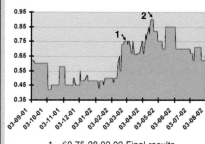

Share Price Sept 2001 - Sept 2002

1. €0.75 28.02.02 Final results
2. €0.90 19.04.02 Bid rumours

TEN YEAR REVIEW

12 months to Dec. 31	1992	1993	1994	1995	1996	1997	1998	1999	2000	200
Sales	13.5	14.0	12.4	12.1	12.2	12.3	12.6	20.3	21.8	21.
Profit (loss) before Tax	3.0	3.4	(1.0)	(8.7)	2.1	3.6	2.9	3.7	3.2	0.
Tax	0.6	0.7	0.8	+1.3	0.4	0.9	0.8	1.1	0.8	0.
Profit (loss) after Tax	2.4	2.7	(1.8)	(7.4)	1.7	2.7	2.1	2.6	2.4	(0.1
Minority Interest	(0.2)	(0.2)	-	-	-	-	-	-	-	
Available for Shareholders	2.2	2.5	(1.8)	(7.4)	1.7	2.7	2.1	2.6	2.4	(.01
Ordinary Dividend	1.2	1.2	0.5	-	-	0.4	0.4	0.5	0.5	0.
Retained Profit	1.0	1.3	(2.3)	(7.4)	1.7	2.3	1.7	2.1	1.9	(0.5
Increase (Decrease) in Reserves	1.6	1.6	(5.2) c)	(7.9)	1.8	3.1	1.3	3.1	1.9	(0.2
Shareholders' Funds	14.5	16.0	10.9	3.0	4.8	7.9	9.2	12.6	14.5	14.
Ordinary Dividend per Share (€)	0.146	0.146	0.057	-	-	0.05	0.05	0.05	0.053	0.05
Earnings per share (€)	0.263	0.295	-	-	0.203	0.319	0.25	0.307	0.28 b)	

b) Based upon 8.5m shares. c) Devaluation of properties -€2.9m.

BALANCE SHEET: DECEMBER 31 2001 € m

Share Capital:		Fixed Assets	16.6	
8,466,230 Ord. 20p shares	2.5	Current Assets	5.3	
Reserves	11.9	Current Liabilities	8.4	
		Net Current Liabilities		(3.1)
		Medium Debt		(5.1)
Shareholders' Funds	14.4	Net Tangible Assets		8.4
		Intangibles		6.0
		Net Assets		14.4

Comment:

Only 348 shareholders including 17 who own 74% of the equity of which 9 are listed with more than 3% of the equity.

It is not surprising to see opportunistic predators hovering around for the kill.

OAKHILL GROUP plc

BUSINESS: Printer.

REGISTERED OFFICE: 2A Sandymount Green, Sandymount, Dublin.

HEAD OFFICE: as regd office. Tel: 01-2401400. Fax: 01-2401450.

SECRETARY: P Kearns.

REGISTRARS & TRANSFER OFFICE: Computershare Investor Services (Ireland) Ltd, Heron House, Corrig Road, Sandyford Industrial Estate, Dublin.

PRINCIPAL BANKERS: Bank of Ireland, Allied Irish Banks, Irish Intercontinental Bank, Ulster Bank Markets.

AUDITORS: PricewaterhouseCoopers.

SOLICITORS: William Fry.

STOCKBROKERS: J&E Davy

DIRECTORS: M Delany (Chairman - 53), P Casey (48), J Jordan (44), R McLoughlin (63), A McGuckian (66), J O'Brien (45).

SHARE CAPITAL: Authorised: 8million Ord €0.10 shares. **Issued:** 56,439,080 Ord €0.10 shares.

STAFF: 647.   **SCRIP DIVIDEND:** No.

CAPITAL HISTORY:

Incorporated Nov 1998 and issued 7 Ord 25p shares. Aug 1999: To facilitate demerger from J Crean plc issued 56,439,080 Ord €0.10 shares (for-1) to Crean shareholders including 287,812 Ord €0.10 shares to James Crean for £9m.

COMPANY HISTORY:

Instigated in mid-1999 to takeover print and packaging divisions of the beleagured James Crean plc. Origins go back to the final acquisition in 1996 of the outstanding 29% in Inishtech

plc which Crean did not own. The demerged operation now consists of Milton Holdings in the USA, Droyhurst Ltd, Bell & Bain Ltd, Speedprint (Horsforth), Plasboard Plastics Ltd, Foam Plus Ltd, Technique Labels Ltd all in the UK and Label Art Ltd in Ireland. Sept 1998: Bought Speedprint (Horsforth) Ltd for £6.9m stg. Prospectus states: *"The Directors intend to adopt a conservative dividend policy which takes into account the long term development of the business and the underlying earnings of OakHill, whilst maintaining an appropriate dividend cover."* Elsewhere:*"Crean does not propose to be a long term shareholder in OakHill in that the intention is to dispose in full of its shareholding ....in the best interests of the shareholders of Crean."*When demerged the shares started at 54p (6/8/99) and dropped to 39p (18/8/99) whilst Crean shares dropped from 91p to 47p. Oct 2000: After 3 months Chairman D Chambers flags his exit after agm. Jan 2000: P Casey buys 3,076,984 shares for about €1m. Dec 2000: Sells packaging division for €16.89m. April 2001: Ch Exec D Hurley departs and G O'Toole. July 2001: Only 2 Directors appear at a.g.m., a very acrimonious affair.

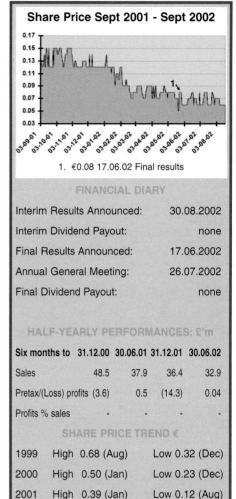

Share Price Sept 2001 - Sept 2002

1. €0.08 17.06.02 Final results

FINANCIAL DIARY

Interim Results Announced:	30.08.2002
Interim Dividend Payout:	none
Final Results Announced:	17.06.2002
Annual General Meeting:	26.07.2002
Final Dividend Payout:	none

HALF-YEARLY PERFORMANCES: £'m

Six months to	31.12.00	30.06.01	31.12.01	30.06.02
Sales	48.5	37.9	36.4	32.9
Pretax/(Loss) profits	(3.6)	0.5	(14.3)	0.04
Profits % sales	-	-	-	-

SHARE PRICE TREND €

1999	High 0.68 (Aug)	Low 0.32 (Dec)	
2000	High 0.50 (Jan)	Low 0.23 (Dec)	
2001	High 0.39 (Jan)	Low 0.12 (Aug)	

SECTORAL ANALYSIS: (previous year)

Sales: Europe 72% (78%), USA 28% (22%).

SIX YEAR REVIEW: € m

12 months to December 31	1996	1997	1998 d)	1999 b)	2000	2001
Sales	72.1	79.0	93.0	110.6	119.0	74.3
Profits/(Loss) Before Tax	3.9	2.1	3.6	5.3	(4.8)	(13.8) g)
Tax	2.1	1.7	2.0	2.6	1.2	+0.7
Profits/(Loss) After Tax	1.8	0.4	1.6	2.7	(6.0)	(13.1)
Minority Interests	-	-	-	-	-	-
Available to Shareholders	1.8	0.4	1.6	2.7	(6.0)	(13.1)
Ordinary Dividend	-	-	-	0.4	0.3	-
Retained Profits	1.8	0.4	1.6	2.3	(6.3)	(13.1)
Increase (Decrease) in Reserves	n/a	(10.6)	40.8	6.3	(5.3)	(11.9) f)
Shareholders' Funds	4.3	(6.4)	43.1	50.4	45.1	33.2
Ordinary Dividend Per Share (€)	-	-	-	0.08	0.05	-
Earnings Per Share (€)	0.03	0.006	0.013	0.022 a)	-	-

a) Based on 56.4m shares in issue. b) Unaudited. d) Subsequently restated. f) Currency gain +€1.1m. g) After 'impairment' provision of €7.1m.

BALANCE SHEET: DECEMBER 31 2001.   € m

Comment:

Borrowing is considerable being 100% of the fixed assets. The company seems to be missing a visionary at the helm and until then the attractions are limited.

Share Capital:			Fixed Assets		21.2
56,439,080 Ord €0.10 shares	5.6		Current Assets	24.2	
			Current Liabilities	23.0	
			Net Current Assets		1.2
Reserves		27.6	Medium debt		(17.3)
			Net Tangible Assets		5.1
			Intangibles		28.1
Shareholders' Funds		33.2	Net Assets		33.2

OGLESBY & BUTLER GROUP plc

BUSINESS: Manufacture of soldering equipment.

REGISTERED OFFICE: Industrial Estate, O'Brien Road, Carlow. Tel: 0503 - 43333. Fax: 0503 - 43577.

HEAD OFFICE: as regd office.

SECRETARY: M Boran.

REGISTRARS & TRANSFER OFFICE: Computershare Investor Services (Ireland) Ltd. Heron House, Corrig Road, Sandyford Ind Estate, Dublin.

PRINCIPAL BANKERS: Allied Irish Banks.

AUDITORS: KPMG.

SOLICITORS: Gerrard Scallan & O'Brien.

STOCKBROKERS: Bloxham Stockbrokers; Davy Stockbrokers.

DIRECTORS: N Dowling (Chairman - 64), A P Oglesby (Ch Exec. - 56), J P Oglesby (56).

SHARE CAPITAL: Authorised: 50,000,000 Ord 10p shares. **Issued:** 12,315,082 Ord 10p shares.

STAFF: 117.   **SCRIP DIVIDEND:** No

CAPITAL HISTORY:

Incorporated March 1984. 15,000 Ord. £1 shares issued at 100p each. July 1984 1,372 Ord. £1 shares issued at 364p each. August 1984 1,006 Ord. £1 shares issued at 497p each. August 1984 915 Ord. £1 shares issued at 546p each. April 1985 5,311 Ord. £1 shares issued at £28.24 each. October 1987 Ord. £1 shares sub-divided into 10p shares and a 'scrip' issue of 36.6-for-1 allotted. October 1987 300,000 Ord. 10p shares offered to the public. Opened on the market at 103p. March 1997: Bought back at 31p and cancelled 124,018 Ord 10p Shares. April

1997: Bought back at 31p/32p and cancelled 276,870 Ord 10p Shares.

COMPANY HISTORY:

Oglesby & Butler commenced in 1984 and raised £105,000 through Hill Samuel Business Expansion Scheme Venture production in Carlow. In September 1987 raised £1 million through a private placing. The company came to the market in September 1987 and initially quoted at 101p each. October 1987 purchased W. Greenwood Electronic and assets of Oryx Electrical in Reading for £1.03m Stg. March 1990: N. Dowling resigns as Chief Executive. D. Flegal and W. Fleming resign as Executive Directors. J. Winterbottom appointed Chief Executive. March 1991: K. Flynn resigns as Chairman. D. Butler and J.D. Murphy resign as Directors. N. Dowling reappointed Chairman. May 1991: 34 made redundant at Carlow. December 1992: J. Winterbottom resigns as M.D. P. Oglesby appointed M.D. March 1992: N. Rose resigns as Director. March 1997: Purchased 124,018 Ord 10p shares at €0.39 each in the market and cancelled them. April 1997: Purchased more shares at €0.39/0.41 each and cancelled them. Aug 2002: "Sales for Q1 have been in line...with same period last year. Margins continue to be adversely affected...."

Share Price Sept 2001 - Sept 2002

1. €0.45 31.07.02 Final results

FINANCIAL DIARY

Interim Results Announced	03.01.2002
Interim Dividend Payout	02.04.2002
Final Results Announced	31.07.2002
Annual General Meeting	28.09.2002
Final Dividend Payout	11.10.2002

FIVE YEAR SHARE PRICE TREND

1997	High	0.50 (May)	Low	0.38 (Feb)
1998	High	0.70 (Nov)	Low	0.44 (Jan)
1999	High	0.72 (Nov)	Low	0.65 (Jan)
2000	High	0.70 (Jan)	Low	0.52 (Nov)
2001	High	0.60 (Jan)	Low	0.38 (May)

SECTORAL ANALYSIS: (previous year)

Sales: Europe 35% (43%), Nth America 50% (43%), elsewhere 15% (15%).

INVESTMENT PERFORMANCE

Five Year Investment Performance: € 1,494
Ten Year Investment Performance: € 3,815

HALF YEARLY PERFORMANCE: €'000

6 months to:	30.09.00	31.03.01	30.09.01	31.03.02
Sales	2,990	2,986	2,955	2,740
Profit before Tax	433	216	348	7
Profit % Sales	14.5	7.2	15.0	-

TEN YEAR REVIEW €'000

12 Months to March 31	1993	1994	1995	1996	1997	1998	1999	2000	2001	200
Sales	3,685	3,890	4,980	5,516	4,829	5,584	5,823	5,327	5,977	5,69
Profit (Loss) before Tax	174	277	479	702	587	794	955	709	649	35
Tax	8	7	3	3	7	31	45	60	57	4
Profit (Loss) after Tax	166	270	476	699	580	763	910	649	592	31
Extraordinary Items	-	-	-	-	-	-	-	-	-	
Available to Shareholders	166	270	476	699	580	763	910	649	592	31
Ordinary Dividend	-	-	-	-	142	284	362	364	392	21
Profit (Loss) Retained	166	270	476	699	438	479	548	285	200	10
Increase in Reserves	166	270	513	701	405 d)	401	1,658 f)	285	200	19
Shareholders' Funds	1,437	1,708	2,183	2,884	3,272	3,638	5,333	5,617	5,920	6,02
Ordinary Dividend per Share (€)	-	-	-	-	0.013	0.025 e)	0.032 e)	0.032 e)	0.032 e)	0.017 e
Earnings per share (€)	0.014	0.023	0.041	0.056	0.047	0.062	0.081	0.056	0.05 c)	0.026 c

c) Based upon 11.2m shares. d) Cancelled shares bought on market -€34,000. e) As the dividend is paid out of royalty income it is tax free. f) Property revaluation +€1.1m.

BALANCE SHEET: MARCH 31 2002. €'000

Share Capital:		Fixed Assets		4,631
12,315,082 Ord 10p shares	1,478	Current Assets	2,521	
		Current Liabilities	1,142	
		Net Current Assets		1,379
Reserves	4,546	Medium Debt		(333)
		Net Tangible Assets		5,677
		Intangibles		347
Shareholders' Funds	6,024	Net Assets		6,024

Comment:

Profits have been on the slide since 1999 and now the dividend has been cut - it does not augur well for the future.

ORMONDE MINING plc

CAPITAL HISTORY:

Nov 1992 3,000 Ord 1p shares issued at 3p each. Dec 1992: 5 million Ord 1p shares issued at 10p each. Feb 1993: 525,000 Ord 1p shares issued at 10p each. June 1995: 3 Ord 1p shares issued to facilitate the consolidation of every 5 Ord 1p shares into one Ord 5p share. The issued share capital was then 6,621,629 Ord 5p shares. Aug 1995: 6,660,000 Ord 5p shares issued re acquisition Adola Gold. 2,486,212 Ord 5p shares issued at 7p each. Feb 1996: Placed 10 million 5p Ord shares at 12p each. Dec 1997: 8 million Ord 5p shares placed at 7p each. Nov 1998: 3.6m Ord 5p shares placed 7p each. March 1999: 3.99m Ord 5p shares placed at 7.5p each. May 2001: Ord 5p shares replaced by Ord 2p shares. Places 24,262,776 Ord €0.025 shares (with clawback of 1-for-8) @ 2p each. May 2002: Placed 5,099,507 Ord €0.025 shares @ €0.06 each.

COMPANY HISTORY:

Originally Burmin Exploration and Development incorporated September 1983. In 1987 publicly quoted as Burmin. In 1993 Burmin was acquired by SIPA Resources, an Australian exploration company. SIPA transferred all the Australian interests to itself and disposed of the non-Australian interests by June 1994. August 1995: Burmin buy-back whereby name changed to Ormonde Mining. 6.66 million Ord 5p shares were issued to acquire Adola Gold (Exploration properties in Tanzania and Mexico - company based in Bermuda owned by D. Burke and M. Donoghue) plus cash £16,549. Also issued 2,486,212 Ord 5p shares for 7p each. Bought Ramone for £10,000. Of these 13.3m shares issued in August, the promoters got 2.66 million at no cost, Directors and others got 6.4 million at 2.3p each, Directors and others got 4.2 million at 4.5p each and finally, the 2.5 million were issued at 7p each. 1997: High Court allowed write-off £3.4m deficit on P & L A/c. Oct 1997: Listed on Vancouver Stock Exchange. May 2001: New Board, new management. Considers abandoning Vancouver Exchange.

NINE YEAR REVIEW : €'000

	1993 a)	1993 b)	1994 c)	1995 c)	1996 c)	1997 c)	1998 c)	1999 c)	2000 c)	2001 g)
Sales	-	-	-	-	-	-	-	-	-	-
Profit (loss) before Tax	(4,649)	-	-	-	(66)	(720)	(218)	(65)	(1,909)	(876)
Tax	+4	-	-	-	-	-	-	-	-	+3
Profit (loss) after Tax	(4,645)	-	-	-	(66)	(720)	(218)	(65)	(1,909)	(873)
Available for S'holders	(4,645)	-	-	-	(66)	(720)	(218)	(65)	(1,909)	(873)
Dividend	-	-	-	-	-	-	-	-	-	-
Retained Profit/(loss)	(4,645)	-	-	-	(66)	(720)	(218)	(65)	(1,909)	(873)
Increase (-) in Reserves	(4,645)	-	-	-	277 d)	(568)	65	141 f)	(1,909)	(857)
Shareholders' Funds	(4,740)	(4,740)	(4,740)	Nil	1,912	1,507	1,949	2,572	664	422
Ordinary Dividend per Share	-	-	-	-	-	-	-	-	-	-
Earnings per Share	-	-	-	-	-	-	-	-	-	-

a) Year end 31 March. b) 3 months 30 June. c) Year end June 30. d) Share premium +£0.6m.
f) Share premium +£163,000. g) 18 months to Dec 31.

BALANCE SHEET: DECEMBER 31 2001. €'000

Share Capital:		Fixed Assets	8
68,180,617 Ord		Current Assets	171
€0.025 shares	3,404	Current Liabilities	138
43,917,841 Def €0.038 shares		Net Current Assets	33
Reserves	(2,982)	Net Tangible Assets	41
		Intangibles	381
Shareholders' Funds	422	Net Assets	422

Auditor's Report: Fundamental Uncertainty *"In forming our opinion we have considered the adequacy of the disclosures made in the financial statements concerning the uncertainty of the valuation of intangible assets of €381,237 in the consolidated balance sheet and financial assets of €380,200 in the company balance sheet .*

Comment: It is start again time for Ormonde under new management (mainly ex-Navan Resources). Now they are Morocco bound including Spain and Tanzania. Only time will tell whether this reincarnation will be any more successful.

OVOCA RESOURCES plc

CAPITAL HISTORY:

Incorporated January 1985. Originally 315,563 Ordinary 10p shares issued at 24p each. April 1986 315,563 Ordinary 10p shares issued at 90p each. Subsequently subdivided into Ordinary 2p shares. Subsequently 540,000 share options exercised. April 1987 trading commenced on the Stock Exchange having been introduced at 90p each. August 1987: Rights issue of 1,231,887 Ord. shares to raise £410,000. June 1988, 1,000,000 Ord. 2p shares issued on placing at 42p each. July 1989: Issued 5,927,508 Ord. 2p shares on acquisition Albannach Ltd. and Barnagapal Ltd. at 47.9p each. July 1990: 500,000 share options exercised. Sept. 1990: 1m Ord. 2p shares allotted at 29.6p each (27p stg.). Dec 1992: Issued 100,000 Ord 2p shares acquiring Emeo Ltd. June 1993: Allotted 254,1176 Ord 2p shares for drilling services; 292,857 Ord 2p shares were allotted for Geophysical services. Issued 2,168,542 Ord 2p shares for X-Ore Ltd. Dec 1993: 1.5 million 2p Ord shares issued at 22p each. 1995: 1,650,000 Ord 2p shares issued at 7p each. 1,535,588 Ord 2p shares issued in lieu of services 1992-1995. Nov 1996: 1,250,000 Ord 2p shares to be issued at 13p each. Oct 1997: Placed 2.1m Ord 2p shares at 15.5p each. July 1998: 2m Ord 2p shares placed at 21.75p each. Jan 1999: Shares placed at 33p each (raised £0.6m). July 1998: Placed 2m Ord 2p shares at 21.75p per share. Jan 1999: Placed 1,890,000 Ord 2p shares at 33p each. June 2001: Placed 1.5m Ord 2p shares with Mercury Holdings @ €0.26 each.

COMPANY HISTORY:

Since its formation Ovoca has prospected in Wicklow, Mayo and Connemara and Longford. They have also prospected in Brazil, Ghana and Northern Ireland. Original Board included J. Teeling, P. Power and Emmet O'Connell who subsequently resigned. April 1987: Public quote on Dublin Stock Exchange (Third Market). November 1987: Public quote on London Stock Exchange. August 1987: Rights issue of 1,231,887 Ord. shares to raise £410,000. June 1988: Placing of 1 million shares to raise £420,000, at 42p per share. June 1989: Acquired Albannach and Barnagapal by issue of 5,927,508 Ord. 2p shares. Sept. 1990: P. Fleming and G. Kennedy resign as Directors. Sept. 1990: Placed 1 million shares raising £300,000. Name change to Ovoca Resources Plc. Nov 1991: A. Kenny resigns as Director. Dec. 1991: Withdraws from Ghana and relinquishes licences in Northern Ireland. Purchases Emeo Ltd for 100,000 Ovoca shares (worth £11,000). 1993: Issues 2.2m shares for X-Ore Ltd. Dec 1993: Placing 1.5m shares at 22p each to fund machinery in respect of Russian (Georgia) deal. July 1997: J. Stanley resigns. Company to be restructured. Oct 1998: 8% of Ovoca equity linked with J Stanley. Oct 1998: Chairman Swithwick predicts shares will climb to 400p in a year - shares move to 60p capitalising Ovoca at £12m. Board distances itself from Chairman's remarks. June 2001: Mercury Holdings takes 5% stake in Ovoca

TEN YEAR REVIEW £'000

	1991 e)	1992 e)	1993 e)	1994 e)	1995 d)	1997	1998	1999	2000	2001
Sales	-	-	-	-	-	-	-	-	-	-
(loss) before Tax	(519)	(7)	(16)	(56)	(21)	(351)	(104)	(145)	(138)	(161)
Tax	-	-	-	-	-	-	-	-	-	+25
(loss) after Tax	(519)	(7)	(16)	(56)	(21)	(351)	(104)	(145)	(138)	(136)
Available for S'holders	(519)	(7)	(16)	(56)	(21)	(351)	(104)	(145)	(138)	(136)
Ordinary Dividend	-	-	-	-	-	-	-	-	-	-
Retained Profits (Losses)	(519)	(7)	(15)	(56)	(21)	(351)	(104)	(145)	(138)	(136)
Increase (-) in Reserves	82	-	275 c)	(56)	190	(173)	152	808	(138)	(119)
Shareholders' Funds	1,120	1,122	1,470	1,414	1,667	1,522	1,717	2,605	2,588	(2,472)
Dividend per share	-	-	-	-	-	-	-	-	-	-
Earnings per share	-	-	-	-	-	-	-	-	-	-

c) Share premium £291,000. d) 14 months to February '96. e) Year end Dec 31.

Comment: Still wondering why the Chairman claimed the shares would be worth £4 by 1999.

Accounts note:
Fundamental Uncertainties: *"In forming our opinion, we have considered the adequacy of the disclosures in note 1 concerning the uncertainties as to: i) The realisation by the group of expenditure on exploration properties of IR£2,351,231 in the consolidated balance sheet and IR£1,306,534 in the company balance sheet, ii) The realisation of the company's investment in subsidiary undertakings of IR£459,338 and advances to subsidiary undertakings of £653,225 in the company balance sheet, which are dependent upon the successful outcome of future exploration and development. In view of the significance of these uncertainties we consider that they should be drawn to your attention but our opinion is not qualified in this respect".*

BALANCE SHEET: FEBRUARY 28 2001. £'000

Fixed Assets		194
Current Assets	90	
Current Liabilities	163	
Net Current Liabilities		(73)
Net Tangible Assets		121
Intangibles		2,351
Net Assets		2,472
Share Capital: 27,583,145 Ord.		
2p shares		552
Reserves		1,920
S'holders' Funds		2,472

LATEST BALANCE SHEET AVAILABLE AT TIME OF GOING TO PRESS

PADDY POWER plc

(formerly Power Leisure plc)

BUSINESS: Betting shops, telephone and on-line betting.
REGISTERED OFFICE: Airton House, Airton Road, Tallaght, Dublin.
HEAD OFFICE: as above. Tel: 01-4045900. Fax: 01-4045901.
SECRETARY: C Kelly
REGISTRARS & TRANSFER OFFICE: Computershare Investor Services (Ireland) Ltd, Heron House, Corrig Road, Sandyford Industrial Estate, Dublin.
PRINCIPAL BANKERS: Allied Irish Banks.
AUDITORS: FArthur Andersen
SOLICITORS: Arthur Cox: Kennedy McGonagle Ballagh.
STOCKBROKERS: Goodbody Stockbrokers
DIRECTORS: S Kenny (Chairman - 51), J O'Reilly (Ch Exec - 52), J Corcoran (73), I Armitage (47), E McDaid (53), D Power (56), I Ross (40), S Thomas (50), F Drury (44).
SHARE CAPITAL: Authorised: 70million Ordinary €0.10 shares **Issued:** 47,144,120 Ord €0.10 shares
EMPLOYEES: 757
SCRIP DIVIDEND: No

CAPITAL HISTORY:

Incorporated April 1958 as Corcoran's Management Ltd. April 1998: 1,254,000 Ord €0.10 shares issued for €0.35/27.6p each re options. May 1999: Repurchased 720,000 Ord €0.10 shares from S Kenny, 600,000 shares from J Mangan, 240,000 shares from B Sheridan. 3,303,000 Ord €0.10 shares issued under Exec share option scheme. Dec 2000: Public flotation. 2,250,000 Ord €0.10 new shares issued @ €1.20 to float; remainder (6,784,981 shares) came from shareholders. @ €2.40 each.

COMPANY HISTORY:

Incorporated April 1958. In 1988 merged Kenny O'Reilly Bookmakers, P Corcoran Bookmakers and a number of Richard Power bookmakers offices.June 1992: Name changed to Power Leisure Ltd. Has 117 betting offices in Ireland (including 4 on-course shops) and one in London. June 2000: Launched *paddypower.com*. Now (June 2001) has 27,000 users. Nov 2000: Shops number 122. Name changed to Power Leisure plc. Telephone betting, *Dial-a-bet*, now has 19,000 users. June 2001: J Corcoran, S Kenny, D Power, Rowan Nominees, Bank of Ireland Nominees and ICC Bank off load 4,305,473 Ord €0.10 shares @ €3.59 each; their remaining holdings locked in till July 2002. March 2002: Bank of Scotland off-load their 11.8% stake for €25m; S Kenny sells 1m shares @ €4.55 each.

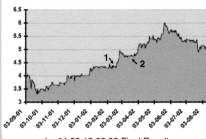

Share Price Sept 2001 - Sept 2002

1. €4.30 19.02.02 Final Results
2. €26.03.02 Bank of Scotland sells stake

FINANCIAL DIARY

Interim Results Announced:	23.07.2002
Interim Dividend Payout:	12.08.2002
Final Results Announced:	21.02.2002
Annual General Meeting:	26.04.2002
Final Dividend Payout:	29.04.2002

HALF YEARLY PERFORMANCE: € m

Six months to	31.12.00	30.06.01	31.12.01	30.06.02
Sales:	188.7	206.5	254.6	319.1
Pretax profits:	5.3	4.3	4.8	9.3
Profits % sales:	2.8	2.1	1.9	2.9

SHARE PRICE TREND:

2000	High 2.90 (Dec)	Low	2.40 (Dec)
2001	High 4.07 (Dec)	Low	2.98 (Jan)

SECTORAL ANALYSIS (previous year)

Sales: betting offices 80% (87%), telephone betting 12% (11%), internet betting 8% (2%).
Profits: betting office 195% (120%), telephone betting 11% (8%), internet betting -103% (-20%).

FIVE YEAR REVIEW: € m

12 months to December 31	1997	1998	1999	2000	2001
Sales	154.9	193.5	169.6	362.8	461.1
Profits Before Tax	4.5	5.6	7.0	11.0	9.1
Tax	1.8	2.0	2.1	2.9	1.8
Profits After Tax	2.7	3.6	4.9	8.1	7.3
Minority Interests	-	-	-	-	
Available to Shareholders	2.7	3.6	4.9	8.1	7.3
Ordinary Dividend	0.4	0.6	1.2	1.8	2.4
Retained Profits	2.3	3.0	3.7	6.3	4.9
Increase (Decrease) in Reserves	n/a	3.3	2.3 b)	9.8 a)	4.6
Shareholders' Funds	10.7	14.1	16.2	26.1	30.7
Ordinary Dividend Per Share (€)	0.008	0.013	0.028	0.04	0.051
Earnings Per Share (€)	0.06	0.08	0.11	0.18	0.15

a) Share premium +£2.6m. b) Repurchase of shares -£1.2m.

BALANCE SHEET: DECEMBER 31 2001. € m

Share Capital:	4.7	Fixed Assets		22.7
47,144,000 €0.10 Ord shares		Current Assets	19.4	
		Current Liabilities	10.7	
		Net Current Assets		8.7
Reserves	26.0	Medium Debt		(1.8)
		Net Tangible Assets		29.6
		Intangibles		1.1
Shareholders' Funds	30.7	Net Assets		30.7

Comment:

Despite the market conditions this share has performed well for punters.

PREMIER OIL plc

BUSINESS: Exploration and production of oil and gas.

REGISTERED OFFICE: Saltire Court, 20 Castle Terrace, Edinburgh EH1 2EN.

HEAD OFFICE: 23 Lower Belgrave Street, London SW1 NR. Tel: 0044-2077301111. Fax: 0044-2077304696.

SECRETARY: S Huddle.

REGISTRARS & TRANSFER OFFICE: Computershare Investor Services plc, Registrar's Dept; PO Box 435, Owen House, 8 Bankhead Crossway North, Edinburgh EH11 8BR. **PRINCIPAL BANKERS:** Barclays Bank, J. Henry Schroder Wagg & Co, Chase Manhattan Bank.

AUDITORS: Ernst & Young.

SOLICITORS: Slaughter & May.

STOCKBROKERS: SG Securities (London) Ltd; Deutsche Bank AG

DIRECTORS: David John (Chairman - 64), C Jamieson (Ch.Exec.- 58), A Alizai (71), R Emerson (56), Gray (64), D Mansor (58), T Marican (50), J Orange (60), van der Welle (47), R Liddell (55), S Dobbie (63), Collins (58), R Mews (46).

SHARE CAPITAL: Authorised: 1,894,043,648 Ord 5p stg shares. 36,214,252 Non-voting Conv shares. **Issued:** 1,552,303,612 Ord 5p stg shares; 36,214,252 Non-voting Conv shares.

STAFF: 488.

SCRIP DIVIDEND: No.

CAPITAL HISTORY:

No background history could be gleaned from the prospectus submitted to the Irish Stock Exchange at the time of obtaining its Irish quotation. February 1995: Issued 407,427,161 Ord 5p shares for purchase of Pict Petroleum. March 1995: Issued 59,872,000 Ord 5p Shares to Amerada Hess Ltd at 33p per Share. Nov1999: Issued 121.0m Ord 5p shares @ 25pstg per share to Amerada Hess. Issued 386.8m Ord 5p shares to PETRONAS International @ 25pstg each; both issues raised £127mstg gross. Issued 3.2m non-voting convertible shares to both parties for £9mstg.

COMPANY HISTORY:

No background history could be obtained from the Irish Quotation Prospectus. In 1993, it had Exploration and Production facilities in the UK, Pakistan and Far East. Its investment policy was 25% for Exploration and 75% for short term cash generation projects. No dividends or bonus share issues were being made. February 1995: Purchased Pict Petroleum. March 1995: Agreed to sell up to 60.04m Ord 5p Shares at 33p each (£18.2m) to Amorada Hess Ltd. October 1996: Acquired Sumatra Gulf Oil for £46.8m Stg. Bought Idemitsu Pakistan Oil Exploration for £23.6m Stg. First quoted on Dublin Market at 32p. December 1996: Bought Discovery Petroleum for £51.4m stg. Oct 1998: Proven oil and gas reserves of 242m barrels of oil equivalent. May 1999: Aggro at a.g.m. Attempts to unseat directors fail. Paladin Resources in talks of a £220m stg reverse takeover; may solve debt problem of about £290m stg. Oct 1999: Strategic alliance with Amerada Hess and Petronas International by share issue. April 2000: Defies British Gov request to leave Burma.

Share Price Sept 2001 - Sept 2002

1. €0.23 12.03.02 Final results

FINANCIAL DIARY

Interim Results Announced:	13.09.2001
Interim Dividend Paid:	None
Final Results Announced:	12.03.2002
Annual General Meeting:	10.05.2002
Final Dividend Paid:	none

HALF YEARLY PERFORMANCES: £m stg

Six months to	30.06.00	31.12.00	30.06.01	31.12.01
Sales	49.4	50.0	75.3	91.5
Profit/(-) before Tax	12.6	4.4	24.8	24.8
Profit % Sales	25.5	8.8	32.9	27.1

SECTORAL ANALYSIS: (previous year)

Sales: Europe 66% (69%), Indonesia 34% (31%). **Profits:** UK 62% (48%), Indonisia 38% (52%).

SHARE PRICE TREND €

1997	High 0.51 (Apr)	Low 0.39 (Mar)
1998	High 0.70 (May)	Low 0.32 (Nov)
1999	High 0.36 (July)	Low 0.17 (Mar)
2000	High 0.25 (Jan)	Low 0.22 (Mar)
2001	High 0.23 (Jan)	Low 0.23 (Jan)

TEN YEAR REVIEW: STG

Months to Dec 31	£'000 1992	£'000 1993	£'m 1994	£'m 1995	£'m 1996	£'m 1997	£'m 1998 k)	£'m 1999 k)	£'m 2000	£'m 2001
Turnover	55,995	45,918	48.9	64.7	138.8	166.2	104.6	83.8	99.4	166.8
Profit (Loss) before Tax	16,760	13,299	14.1	35.6	68.5	71.1	(128.2) j)	(16.7)	17.0	49.6
Tax	4,012	12,043 c)	5.1	10.5	23.2	22.6	9.0	11.0	10.9	29.3
Profit after Tax	12,748	1,256	9.0	25.1	45.3	48.5	(137.2)	(27.7)	6.1	20.3
Available to Shareholders	12,748	1,256	9.0	25.1	45.3	48.5	(137.2)	(27.7)	6.1	20.3
Ordinary Dividend	-	nil	nil	5.1	5.6	6.2	-	-	-	-
Retained Profit	12,748	1,256	9.0	20.0	39.7	42.3	(137.2)	(27.7)	6.1	20.3
Increase (Decrease) in Reserves	n/a	(110)	7.8 d)	106.5 e)	21.1 g)	50.0 h)	(139.8)	86.9 m)	(18.1) a)	21.1
Shareholders' Funds	121,043	122,272	130.1	260.1	281.6	332.0	192.6	308.6	290.5	311.6
Ordinary Dividend per Share (pstg)	-	-	-	0.5p	0.55p	0.605p	nil	nil	nil	nil
Earnings per Share (pstg)	2.76p	0.23p	1.64p	2.63p	4.44p	4.72p f)	-	nil	0.39p	1.28p f)

b) Currency loss -£8.6m; prior year adjustment -£32.8m. c) Includes exceptional charge of £8.8m deferred petroleum revenue tax. d) Currency loss -£1.2m. e) Share premium +£17.5m; merger reserve +£68.2m. f) Based upon 1.58m shares in issue. g) Currency loss -£20.3m. h) Currency gain +£5.2m; share premium +£2.5m. j) After one-off FRS11 charge of £143.3m. k) Subsequently restated. m) Share premium +£106.2m; currency gain +£8.4m

BALANCE SHEET: DECEMBER 31 2001. £ mstg

Comment:

As exploration companies go,

this is one of the better bets

but not exactly appreciated

by Irish investors..

Share Capital: 1,547,784,814	
Ord 5p shares + 36,214,252	79.2
Ord 5p non-voting shares	
Reserves	232.4
Shareholders' Funds	311.6

Fixed Assets		
Oil & Gas Properties		464.3
Other Investments		92.8
Current Assets	192.6	
Current Liabilities	67.6	
Net Current Liabilities		125.0
Medium Debt		(400.9)
Net Tangible Assets		281.2
Intangibles		30.4
Net Assets		311.6

PROVIDENCE RESOURCES plc

(Quoted on Exploration Securities Market)

BUSINESS: Exploration company
REGISTERED OFFICE: 30 Herbert St., Dublin 2
HEAD OFFICE: 60 Merrion Road, Ballsbridge, Dublin 4.
Tel: 01-6675740. Fax: 01-6675743
SECRETARY: M Graham
REGISTRARS & TRANSFER OFFICE: Capita Corporate
Registrars plc, Marine House, Clanwilliam Court, Dublin
PRINCIPAL BANKERS: Allied Irish Bank, ICC Bank.
AUDITORS: Arthur Andersen
SOLICITORS: Matheson Ormsby Prentice
STOCKBROKERS: Goodbody Stockbrokers
DIRECTORS: B Hillery (Chairman - 67), S Carroll,
P Kidney (47), A O'Reilly Jnr (36).
SHARE CAPITAL: Authorised: 1.1billion Ord 1p shares.
Issued: 887,163,460 Ord 1p shares. 10,272,286 $1
unquoted convertible bonds issued by Providence
Resources Capital Ltd.
EMPLOYEES: 6
SCRIP DIVIDEND: No

CAPITAL HISTORY:

287,502,332 Ord 1p shares issued 1-for-1 basis to holders of shares in Arcon International Resources plc as at August 22 1997. Nov 1998: 503,129,413 Ord 1p shares issued at 1p each re 7-for-4 rights issue. June 2000: Issues 12m unquoted convertible bonds $1 each (1 bond-for-65.886 shares). Dec 2000: 96,116,900 Ord 1p shares issued re conv bonds. Dec 2001: 8,672,600 Ord 0.012 shares issued @ €0.02 each on conversion of Bonds.

COMPANY HISTORY:

Incorporated July 1997. Providence was set-up for the purposes of the demerging of the hydrocarbon interests in Arcon Resources. In 1992 Atlantic Resources was 'backed-into' Conroy P&N Resources plc. Name changed to Arcon with focus to develop mineral exploration. Providence was 'spun-off' in Aug 1997 to pursue all exploration and development opportunities. There is a proven production revenue from its interest in the Claymore field. At the outset, resulting from the structure of Arcon, AJF O'Reilly holds 42.8% of the equity, J Bogdanovich 4.2%, Capital Group Co Inc 6% and Goodman & Co Ltd 5.5%. May 1998: V. Caston resigns as Ch. Exec. Dec 1998: Raised £4.8m in rights - 67% take-up. May 1999: A Blankenburgs resigns as Ch Exec. June 2000: Drilling at Helvick oil field commences. Raises €12.6m through convertible bond issue. Jan 2001: Sells Claymore interest for £1.58mstg, the Argo field for £1.86mstg,. June 2001: Decides not to proceed with Helvick oil as a stand alone project. December 2001: 2 more directors leave (S Reihill & P Tracy) Aug 2002: Redemption of Bonds extended to July 2004. Indexia Holdings (A O'Reilly) gives option to S Carroll over 72.5m shares @ €0.006 each up to Feb 2007.

Share Price Sept 2001 - Sept 2002

1. €0.05 28.06.02 Final results

SHARE PRICE TREND €

1998	High	0.032 (Jly)	Low	0.013	(Dec)
1999	High	0.023 (Mar)	Low	0.01	(July)
2000	High	0.06 (Jly)	Low	0.001	(Jan)
2001	High	0.025 (Jan)	Low	0.008	(Apr)

FINANCIAL DIARY

Interim Results Announced	06.09.2001
Interim Dividend Payout	not likely
Final Results Announced	28.06.2002
Annual General Meeting	09.08.2002
Final Dividend Payout	not likely

SIX YEAR REVIEW: €'000

12 months to December 31	1995 b)	1996 b)	1998 d)	1999	2000	2001
Sales	1,802	2,073	1,845	1,713	2,868	1,021
Profit (Loss) before Tax	(329)	122	(2,410)	419	(20,740)	(571) f)
Tax	-	-	(5)	23	184	13
Profit (Loss) after Tax	(329)	122	(2,415)	396	(20,924)	(584)
Available for Shareholders	(329)	122	(2,415)	396	(20,924)	(584)
Ordinary Dividend	-	-	-	-	-	-
Retained Profit (Loss)	(329)	122	(2,415)	396	(20,924)	(584)
Increase (Decrease) in Reserves	-	-	1,833c)	1,141	(9,555) e)	950
Shareholders' Funds	-	2,606	11,871	12,798	4,463	4,901
Ordinary Dividend per share (€)	-	-	-	-	-	-
Earnings per share (€)	-	-	-	-	-	-

b) Year ended Aug 31 as part of Arcon. c) Share premium +€4.1m. d) Figures subsequently restated. e) Issue of convertible bonds +€11.6m. f) Includes profit on asset sales +€956,000.

BALANCE SHEET: DECEMBER 31 2001

	€'m		€'m
Share Capital		Fixed Assets	20
895,420,913 Ord €0.012 shares	10,746	Current Assets 1,168	
		Current Liabilities 844	
		Net Current Assets	324
Reserves	(5,845)	Medium debt	(1,726)
		Net Tangible Liabilities	(1,382)
		Intangibles	6,283
Shareholders' Funds	4,901	Net Assets	4,901

Comment:

Five years, as many chief

executives and still

no profitable exploration.

One has to query why it was ever

spun off from Arcon.

(formerly Qualceram plc)

BUSINESS: Manufacture bathroom suites.
REGISTERED OFFICE: South Quay, Arklow, Co Wicklow
Tel: 0402-31288. Fax: 0402-31292.
HEAD OFFICE: as regd office.
SECRETARY: A. Clince.
REGISTRARS & TRANSFERS OFFICE: Computershare
Investor Services (Ireland) Ltd, Heron House, Corrig Road,
Sandyford Industrial Estate, Dublin.
PRINCIPAL BANKERS: Bank of Ireland; ICC Bank, Ulster
Bank.
AUDITORS: BDO Simpson Xavier.
SOLICITORS: Matheson Ormsby Prentice; Pinsent Curtis
Biddle.
STOCKBROKERS: Davy Stockbrokers; Teather &
Greenwood.
DIRECTORS: S. Henneberry (Chairman - 62),
. O'Loughlin (Ch Exec - 45), J. Byrne (46), T. Byrne (51),
. Donnelly (58), D. Swords (33), B Whooley (56).
SHARE CAPITAL: Authorised: 30 million Ord 10p shares.
Issued: 21,998,625 Ord 10p shares.
STAFF: 999.   **SCRIP DIVIDEND:** Yes

CAPITAL HISTORY:

Company incorporated Feb 1997. Seven Ord
10p Shares issued. April 1997: Qualcor declare
dividend of £250,000 to its shareholders
(Qualcor now a subsidiary holding patents).
,090,281 Ord 10p shares issued on acquisition
Quality Ceramics Arklow. 2,037,462 Ord 10p
shares issued on acquisition of Qualcor. 530,517
Ord 10p shares issued to ICC Bank for
95,775. Issued 1,309,483 Ord 10p shares to
assist public flotation. Sept 2000: Issued
983,875 Ord 10p shares (clawback 1-for-2) @
.40 each re acquisition of Shires. April 2002:
Placed 1,047,000 Ord 10p shares @
£1.45 stg each.

CORPORATE HISTORY:

Commenced business in Arklow in
1988 when Armitage Shanks (Irl) Ltd
ceased manufacturing there. From a
base of 5 vitreous china pieces in
1988 the Group produces 52 vitreous china pieces in 1997 incorporat-
ing 10 bathroom suites and a com-
plementary range of acrylic baths.
Production has increased from
3,100 pieces per month in 1989 to
22,400 pieces per month in 1996.
Ireland accounts for 53% of turnover
in 1996, the UK accounts for 45%
and there is a growing market in
France and Holland. Its marketing is aimed at the
luxury sector. First quoted on Dublin market April
1997 at 150p per share. English Trust sold 4.3m
shares and founder shareholders sold 3 million.
July 1998: Joint venture with Turkish ceramics
firm in Arklow. Sept 1999: Buys Noritake property in Arklow for £300,000. June 2000: Buys
Shires for €50.8m. Shares temporarily suspended @ €2.20 each. Sept 2000: Rights issue raises
£7.6m. Name changed. March 2002:
Rationalised Selecta (showers) in UK. July 2002:
68 redundancies in UK.

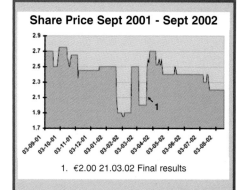

Share Price Sept 2001 - Sept 2002

1. €2.00 21.03.02 Final results

Sales: Ireland 40% (54%), UK 54% (41%),
other 6% (5%). Mfg products 70% (64%),
subcontract 2% (9%), agency 28% (27%).

HALF YEARLY PERFORMANCE: € m

Six months to	31.12.00	30.06.01	31.12.01	30.06.02
Sales	31.4	56.7	49.4	51.2
Pretax/(Loss) profits	(0.2)	3.7	(1.4)	1.5
Profit % sales	-	6.5	-	2.9

FINANCIAL DIARY

Interim Results Announced:	30.08.2002
Interim Dividend Payout:	none
Final Results Announced:	21.03.2002
Annual General Meeting:	06.06.2002
Final Dividend Payout:	27.09.2002

SHARE PRICE TREND €

1997	High	2.22 (May)	Low	1.90 (Apr)
1998	High	2.79 (Mar)	Low	2.07 (Jan)
1999	High	2.30 (Sep)	Low	1.76 (May)
2000	High	2.60 (Apr)	Low	2.10 (Apr)
2001	High	3.20 (Feb)	Low	2.35 (Nov)

EIGHT YEAR REVIEW: € m

months December 31	1994	1995	1996	1997	1998	1999	2000	2001
Sales	6.3	7.1	9.3	11.1	13.4	15.5	41.7	106.1
Profit before Tax	1.1	1.8	2.0	2.2	2.7	3.1	1.5	2.3 f)
Tax	0.1	0.1	0.2	0.2	0.3	0.2	0.2	0.4
Profit after Tax	1.0	1.7	1.8	2.0	2.5	2.9	1.3	1.9
Available for Shareholders	1.0	1.7	1.8	2.0	2.5	2.9	1.3	1.9
Ordinary Dividend	0.2	0.3	0.3	0.5	0.6	0.7	0.9	1.1
Retained Profit	0.8	1.4	1.5	1.5	1.9	2.2	0.4	0.8
Increase (Decrease) in Reserves	n/d	1.4	1.8	2.6	1.9	6.4 b)	13.5 d)	0.6
Shareholders' Funds	3.4	4.9	6.6	10.1	12.0	18.4	32.8	33.4
Ordinary Dividend per Share (€)	0.016	0.022	0.022	0.038	0.038	0.048	0.05	0.053
Earnings per Share (€)	0.08	0.134	0.137	0.151	0.178	0.206	0.08	0.09 a)

a) Based upon 21.0m shares. b) Property revaluation +€4.2m. d) Share premium +€13.1m. f) Includes exceptional write-offs of €1.8m.

BALANCE SHEET: DECEMBER 31 2001. € m

Comment:

The acquisition of

Shires is taking time

to bed down.

Share Capital:				
20,951,625 Ord 10p shares	2.7	Fixed Assets		57.9
		Current Assets	49.6	
		Current Liabilities	34.9	
Reserves	30.8	Net Current Assets		14.7
		Medium debt		(51.0)
		Net Tangible Assets		21.6
		Intangibles		11.8
Shareholders' Funds	33.4	Net Assets		33.4

(Quoted on DCM)

BUSINESS: Design and manufacture computer technology.
REGISTERED OFFICE: Pottery House, Pottery Road, Dun Laoire, Co Dublin. Tel: 01-2350279. Fax: 01-2350361.
HEAD OFFICE: as regd office
SECRETARY: J Caldwell
REGISTRARS & TRANSFER OFFICE: Computershare Investor Services (Ireland) Ltd, Heron House, Corrig Road, Sandyford Industrial Estate, Dublin.
PRINCIPAL BANKERS: Allied Irish Banks
AUDITORS: PricewaterhouseCoopers
SOLICITORS: Binchys
STOCKBROKERS: Dolmen Butler Briscoe.
DIRECTORS: P McDonagh (Chairman - 51), J Caldwell (52), M Newton, B O'Sullivan (CEO), C Molloy.
SHARE CAPITAL: Authorised: 40million Ord €0.125 shares. **Issued:** 23,126,686 Ord €0.125 shares
STAFF: 16.
SCRIP DIVIDEND: No

CAPITAL HISTORY:

Incorporated Sept 1997 with seven subscribers of Ord £1 shares. Then issued 29,993 Ord £1 shares at par (quarter paid). June 1998: 18,180 Ord 10p shares issued at £5.05p each. Dec 1995: 7,353 Ord 10p shares issued at £34 each. Oct 1996 'A' red conv 2% cum pref 10p shares converted into 19,116 Ord 10p shares (creating a premium of £648,088). Then 13,976,226 Ord 10p shares issued out of the Premium A/c. Feb 1997: 531,939 Ord 10p shares were issued at 85p each. April 1997: 2,058,824 Ord 10p shares issued at 34p each. June 1997: 1,069,503 Ord 10p shares issued at 85p each. 500 pref 10p shares redeemed at par. Nov 1997: shares in Feltscope were exchanged 1-for-1. Ord £1 shares were split into 10 Ord shares. 300,000 Ord 10p shares converted into 300,000 redeemable pref 10p shares (to be redeemed out of the Placing). RTG purchases Feltscope for 17,776,666 Ord 10p shares. Dec 1997: Public flotation on DCM - placed 4,205,607 Ord 10p shares at €1.36. May 1999: Placed 1,099,163 Ord 10p shares at €1.27 each.

COMPANY HISTORY:

Group established in 1988 to develop PC peripheral products and software management systems for the EPOS market. Initial holding company was Feltscope with RTI developing and marketing, Feltscope owning the technology and patents of DataCat and RTI Inc selling in USA. In 1990 group changed emphasis to licensing its POS technology to Hugin Sweda and Omron Japan. 1993 began development of easier input techniques for computers and have sold 3,000 units of PasKeyboard by Dec 1997. Manufacture of DataCat is done by HE of Germany. Joint venture with HEMI in which RTI has invested (by loan) £383,000. Dec 1997: receives £4m from public flotation. Dec 1998: "Hoping for profit in 2000". Feb 2000: Close to IBM deal. Shares reach €4.50. Nov 2001: Major changes at management and director level.

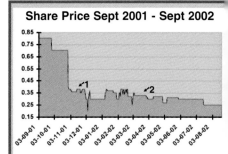

Share Price Sept 2001 - Sept 2002

1. €0.38 19.11.01 Final Results
2. €0.33 27.03.02 Interim Results

FINANCIAL DIARY

Interim Results Announced:	27.03.2002
Interim Dividend Payout:	none
Final Results Announced:	19.11.2001
Annual General Meeting:	08.02.2002
Final Dividend Payout:	unlikely

HALF YEARLY PERFORMANCES: €'000

Six months to	30.06.00	31.12.00	30.06.01	31.12.01
Sales	583	896	766	1,713
Loss before tax	(727)	(998)	(1,995) g)	(911)
Profit % sales	-	-	-	-

g) see 8 year review.

SHARE PRICE TREND

1997	High	1.52 (Dec)	Low	1.75 (Dec)
1998	High	1.42 (Jan)	Low	0.94 (Nov)
1999	High	4.41 (Dec)	Low	0.88 (Jan)
2000	High	4.90 (Mar)	Low	1.05 (Dec)
2001	High	1.85 (Feb)	Low	0.20 (Dec)

EIGHT YEAR REVIEW: €'000

12 months to June 30	1994 a)	1995 a)	1996 a)	1997 d)	1998	1999	2000	2001
Sales	747	236	208	1,053	260	309	991	1,662
Profits (loss) before Tax	(125)	(1,101)	(1,468)	(1,331)	(1,991)	(2,661)	(1,945)	(2,933) g)
Tax	+1	-	-	-	-	-	-	-
Profit (loss) After Tax	(124)	(1,101)	(1,468)	(1,331)	(1,991)	(2,661)	(1,945)	(2,933)
Associate Company	-	-	-	(1)	-	-	-	-
Available To Shareholders	(124)	(1,101)	(1,468)	(1,332)	(1,991)	(2,661)	(1,945)	(2,933)
Ordinary Dividend	215	32	-	-	-	-	-	-
Retained Profit (loss)	(339)	(1,133)	(1,468)	(1,332)	(1,991)	(2,661)	(1,945)	(2,933)
Increase (Decrease) in Reserves	n/a	(1,133)	(518) b)	(358) c)	(1,809)	(1,488) f)	(1,903)	(2,933)
Shareholders' Funds	(65)	(1,197)	(1,713)	171	3,068	1,719	(178)	(3,111)
Ordinary Dividend Per Share (€)	21.42	3.17	-	-	-	-	-	-
Earnings Per Share (€)	-	-	-	-	-	-	-	-

a) Year end Aug 31. b) Share premium +€0.95m. c) Share premium +€1m. d) 10 months. f) Share premium +€1.1m.
g) Includes exceptional charges -€0.7m

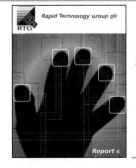

Rapid Technology group plc
RTG

Report &

BALANCE SHEET: JUNE 30 2001. €'000

Share Capital:		Fixed Assets		324
23,126,683 Ord 10p shares	2,937	Current Assets	1,941	
		Current Liabilities	5,574	
		Net Current Liabilities		(3,634)
Reserves	(6,048)	Net Tangible Liabilities		(3,310)
		Intangibles		199
Shareholders' Funds	(3,111)	Net Liabilities		(3,311)

Comment:

Will new management put some 'oomph' into this computer company. So far it has been a major disappointment for investors.

READYMIX plc

BUSINESS: Manufacturers and suppliers of ready mixed concrete, and allied products.

REGISTERED OFFICE: 5/23 East Wall Road, Dublin. Tel: 01-8658700, Fax: 01-8556595.

HEAD OFFICE: as regd office.

SECRETARY: M.O. Egan.

REGISTRARS & TRANSFER OFFICE: Capita Corporate Registrars plc, P. O. Box 7117, Dublin.

PRINCIPAL BANKERS: Allied Irish Banks; Bank of Ireland; Ulster Bank Markets Ltd.

AUDITORS: PricewaterhouseCoopers.

SOLICITORS: McCann FitzGerald.

STOCKBROKERS: Davy Stockbrokers

DIRECTORS: M Rafferty (Chairman - 70), McNerney (M.D. - 58), J Doyle (48), O Egan (58), B Fitzgerald (56), R Kells (64), W McCann (58), N Beale, Newell (52), P Young (64), M Foster (50), F Lynch (45).

SHARE CAPITAL: Authorised: 130m Ord. €0.12 shares. **Issued:** 107,937,096 Ord. €0.12 shares.

STAFF: 1,024.

SCRIP DIVIDEND: No

CAPITAL HISTORY:

May 1972 875,000 shares offered to the public at 5p each. April 1973 'rights' of 1.4 million shares 90p each on basis of 2-for-5. April 1976 'scrip' issue of 1-for-2. November 1977 'rights' issue of 391,346 shares at 46p each on the basis of 3-r-10. May 1978 1-for-3 'scrip' issue. May 1979 for-3 'scrip' issue. November 1981 1-for-3 'rights' issue 6,352,080 shares at 40p each on asis of 1-for-3. September 1984 'rights' issue of for-2 at 16p each to raise £2m. May 1996: acing and open offer of 13,281,617 Ord 10p ares at 97p each (1-for-3). May 1998: Scrip sue of 53,500,200 Ord 10p shares (1-for-1)

COMPANY HISTORY:

UK operators Ready Mixed Concrete Ltd. set up in Ireland in 1965 acquired various plants and built their own - Dublin 1966, Castlemungret 1970, Waterford 1971, Donegal 1972, Durrow 1972, Sligo 1972, Longford 1973, Tullamore 1973, Monaghan 1974, Kilkenny 1974, Ballymahon 1974, Carrigtwohill 1976, Ovens 1977. Because of recession in the industry some small plants in marginal markets were closed in 1982. The 1984 'rights' was underwritten by RMC Group which at that time held 67.7% of the equity. Of the 4.1 million shares available to the remaining shareholders 654,000 were taken up resulting in Readymix Holdings moving up to 76.9% of the equity. November 1988: Acquired business of Wm. Ellis & Sons Ltd. at Rossmore, Carrigtwohill, Co. Cork. June 1990: acquired concrete pipes division of Spollen Concrete Ltd. Dec. 1990: Acquired Ballykilmurray Tarmac. Both June and December purchases totalled £2.5m in cash. April 1996: Purchases RMC Catherwood Nth Ireland and IOM for £22.8m. Arising from placing/open offer RMC Group to dilute to 63%. April 1999: Buys Meath Concrete. Aug 1999: Buys O'Mahony Sand & Gravel, Cork. Acquires Finlay Concrete (Nth Irl) for £10mstg (Ir£11.87m).

Share Price Sept 2001 - Sept 2002

1. €1.25 28.02.02 Final Results
2. €1.40 14.08.02 Interim Results

FINANCIAL DIARY

Interim Results Announced:	14.08.2002
Interim Dividend Payout:	04.10.2002
Final Results Announced:	28.02.2002
Annual General Meeting:	01.05.2002
Final Dividend Payout:	03.05.2002

FIVE YEAR SHARE PRICE TREND €

1997	High	1.48 (Dec)	Low	0.74 (Jan)
1998	High	2.29 (Mar)	Low	1.27 (Dec)
1999	High	1.80 (Dec)	Low	1.00 (Feb)
2000	High	1.80 (Jan)	Low	1.21 (May)
2001	High	1.73 (Mar)	Low	1.15 (Nov)

HALF YEARLY PERFORMANCES: € m

Six Months to:	31.12.00	30.06.01	31.12.01	30.06.02
Sales	110.9	112.5	106.7	101.7
Profit before Tax	12.7	13.7	12.0	12.0
Profit % Sales	11.4	12.2	11.2	11.8

INVESTMENT PERFORMANCE

Five Year Investment Performance:	€2,074
Ten Year Investment Performance:	€4,386

SECTORAL ANALYSIS: (previous year)

Sales: RoI 57% (55%), Nth Ir +IOM 43% (45%).

TEN YEAR REVIEW: € m

months to Dec	1992	1993	1994	1995	1996	1997	1998	1999	2000	2001
Sales	39.1	40.3	45.5	52.1	99.7	140.9	156.2	182.3	228.5	219.2
Profit before Tax	3.8	3.0	4.1	6.0	11.1	16.0	18.4	21.7	25.4	25.7
Tax	0.5	0.4	0.5	0.7	1.8	2.7	2.9	3.4	4.4	4.7
Profit after Tax	3.3	2.6	3.6	5.3	9.3	13.3	15.5	18.3	21.0	21.0
Available for Shareholders	3.3	2.6	3.6	5.3	9.3	13.3	15.5	18.3	21.0	21.0
Ordinary Dividend	1.5	1.5	1.7	1.9	2.9	3.6	4.2	5.0	5.8	6.6
Retained Profit (Loss)	1.8	1.1	1.9	3.4	6.3	9.7	11.3	13.3	15.2	14.4
Increase (Decrease) in Reserves	1.9	1.1	1.9	3.4	13.2 c)	10.7	3.8 d)	17.0 f)	14.8	16.5
Shareholders' Funds	23.5	24.6	26.5	29.9	44.8	55.5	66.2	83.2	98.0	113.8
Ordinary Dividend per share (€)	0.019	0.019	0.020	0.023	0.027	0.034	0.04	0.047	0.053	0.061
Earnings per Share (€)	0.041	0.032	0.044	0.066	0.095	0.124	0.145	0.171	0.196	0.196 a)

a) Based upon 107.2m shares. c) Share premium +€14.1m; goodwill w/o -€7.9m. d) Scrip issue -€6.9m. f) Currency gain +€3.6m.

BALANCE SHEET: DECEMBER 31 2001. € m

Comment:

Last year's profit plateau

is the only blemish on

an otherwise superb

10 year growth.

Share Capital:				
107,200,000 Ord. 10p Shares	12.9	Fixed Assets		119.9
		Current Assets	72.2	
Reserves	100.9	Current Liabilities	49.3	
		Net Current Assets		22.8
		Medium Term Debt		(39.6)
Shareholders' Funds	113.8	Net Tangible Assets		103.1
		Intangibles		10.7
		Net Assets		113.8

BUSINESS: Property investment
REGISTERED OFFICE: No 1 Seaton Place, St Helier, Jersey.
HEAD OFFICE: c/o Treasury Holdings, 35 Barrow Street, Dublin. Tel: 01-6188388. Fax: 01-6188389.
SECRETARY: Aberseen Asset Managers Jersey Ltd.
REGISTRARS & TRANSFER OFFICE: Capita IRG (Offshore) Ltd, 44 The Esplanade, St Helier, Jersey.
PRINCIPAL BANKERS: Bank of Scotland, Royal Bank of Scotland International, HSBC Bank International, HVB Real Estate Capital Ltd.
AUDITORS: KPMG.
SOLICITORS: A&L Goodbody, Bedell Crispin; Herbert Smith.
STOCKBROKERS: NCB Stockbrokers.
DIRECTORS: R Horney (Chairman - 66)), R Barrett (49), J Cogswell (47), C Fishwick (41), K Jenkins (60), J Jenkinson (52), G Milne (60), D Moon (62), P Reed (61), M Richardson (55), J Ronan (49), P Teahon (57).
SHARE CAPITAL: Authorised: 600m Ord 1p shares. 300m 'ZDP' 1p shares. **Issued:** 220,248,058 Ord 1p shares, 63,124,500 zero div. pref. 1p shares ('ZDP'), 125m Convert. Unsecured 7.5% £1 Loan Stock ('CULS' - to be converted into one Ord 1p share). (At redemption May 2011 ZDPs are to be repaid 235.51pstg per share)
EMPLOYEES: none
SCRIP DIVIDEND: No

CAPITAL HISTORY:

Incorporated in Jersey March 2001 as a public close-ended investment company. Aug 2001: Had issued 282,308,493 Ord 1p shares re acquisitions of properties and 75m ZPD 1p shares and 124,434,688 re CULS. June 2001: Share buy-backs 4m Ord 1p shares @ 91pstg each. July 2001: Share buy-backs for cancellation 11,042,346 Ord 1p shares @ 82.5pstg/91.0pstg each (in these cases share price was at a dis-count to NAV; therefore the buy-backs were asset enhancing). May 2002 Share buybacks for cancellation - 27,750,000 Ord 1p shares @30pstg each and 5m ZDP shares @ 59.75pstg each.

COMPANY HISTORY:

Incorporated May 2001 to acquire Jermyn Investment Properties, CMH Group and public flotation in June 2001. The company has a planned life to May 2011. Commenced with gross assets of £804m being Ir£358m of Irish properties owned by CMH, £111m worth of UK, Guernsey and Isle of Man properties owned by Jermyn Group*, £84m portfolio of new investment properties and £326m in an Income Portfolio. Flotation of 300m Ord 1p shares @ 100p each, up to 75m zero dividend pref 1p shares @ 100p each ('ZDP') and £125m convert. unsec. loan stock. Out of the proceeds of flotation, bank and loan stock to be repaid, secondly to satisfy ZDP holders of 235.51p on winding-up date and thirdly to provide ordinary shareholders with expected dividend yield of 8.8% p.a. and capital appreciation on winding-up. *In the process Jermyn was taken over by REO by offering 596 REO shares for every 100 Jermyn shares; the 50% of CMH not owned by Jermyn was satisfied by the issue of Ir£97.5m of Ord shares and loan stock in REO.

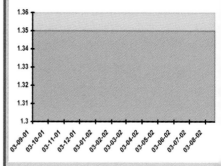

Share Price Sept 2001 - Sept 2002

FINANCIAL DIARY

Interim Results Announced: 06.09.2002
Interim Dividend Payout: Paid quarterly 20.11.02; 28.02.03; 31.05.03; 30.08.03
Final Results Announced: 27.05.2002
Annual General Meeting: 09.07.2002
Final Dividend Payout: see Interims.

HALF YEARLY PERFORMANCE: £'m stg

Six months to	30.06.02
Income	22.9
Pretax (Loss)	(65.1)

Jan 2002: M Harte resigned. July 2002 Suspends second interim dividend payment Sept 2002: Buys and cancels 36m Ord shares @13.5p stg each.

ONE YEAR REVIEW: £'000stg

9 months to December 31	2001
Revenue on Investments	26,322
Profits/(Loss) Before Tax	(49,159)
Tax	337
Profits/(Loss) After Tax	(49,496)
Preference dividend	3,494
Minority Interests	(257)
Available to Shareholders	(53,247)
Ordinary Dividend	12,538
Retained Profits	(65,785)
Increase (Decrease) in Reserves	277,205
Shareholders' Funds	280,806
Ordinary Dividend Per Share	4.4p
Earnings Per Share	-
Net Assets per Ord Share	71.0p a)

a) Net Asset Value at launch (June 2001) 94.34pstg.

BALANCE SHEET: £'000 STG DECEMBER 31 2001

Share Capital:		Fixed Assets		379,059
284,961,886 Ord	3,600	Investments		244,690
1p shares		Current Assets	147,979	
75m 'ZPD' shares		Current Liabilities	22,484	
		Net Current Assets		125,495
Reserves	277,205	Medium debt		(344,260)
		Loan stock		(124,435)
		Minorities		257
Shareholders' Funds	280,806	Net Tangible Assets		280,806

Comment:
The principal directors/ shareholders are property gurus with very deep pockets and long term objectives. Investors should assess the potential in that light especially when you see dividends of £12.5m not even being covered by earnings!.

RIVERDEEP GROUP plc

BUSINESS: Educational software.

REGISTERED OFFICE: Apollo House, Tara Street, Dublin.

HEAD OFFICE: Styne House, Upper Hatch St, Dublin.

Tel: 01-6707570. **Fax:** 01-6707626.

SECRETARY: D Mulville

REGISTRARS & TRANSFER OFFICE: Computershare Investor Services (Ireland) Ltd, Heron House, Carrig Road, Sandyford Industrial Estate, Dublin.

PRINCIPAL BANKERS: Allied Irish Banks

AUDITORS: Ernst & Young

SOLICITORS: McDermott, Will & Emery.

STOCKBROKERS: Davy Stockbrokers.

DIRECTORS: B O'Callaghan (Chairman & CEO - 34), P McDonagh (52), K McLaughlin (58), T Keaveney (57), L Dayton (60), J Levy (63), A Lucki (55), G Pierson (51).

SHARE CAPITAL: Authorised: 1 billion Ord. $0.10 shares, 100 million conv pref $0.10 shares. **Issued:** 225,543,000 Ord $0.10 shares (including 37,757,000 ADS's) 1 ADS = 6 shares.

EMPLOYEES: 381 **SCRIP DIVIDEND:** No

CAPITAL HISTORY:

Nov 1997: Issued 86,321,014 Ord $010 shares for £1,484. May 1998 Issued 7,331,494 Ord $0.10 shares for $130. Oct 1998 Issued 879,915 Ord $0.10 shares at $0.34 each. Nov 1998: 82.7885-for-one share split. (Previous figures reflect this split retroactively). Sept1999: Issued 11,111,110 Ord $0.10 shares as 'golden handshake' to B O'Callaghan (valued at $1.125 each). Oct 1999: Placed 13,333,330 Ord $0.10 shares for $15m ($1.125 each). Feb 2000 Riverdeep Group Ltd took over from Riverdeep Interactive Learning Ltd and exchanged 10 Riverdeep Group $0.10 Ord shares for one Riverdeep Interactive Learning Ltd Ord 1p share. March 2000: Global Offering of 39.2m shares at $3.33/€3.48 per share or $20 per ADS. Values Riverdeep at $546m. Aug 2000: Issues 4.6m ADS (value $85m) to IBM representing 14% of Riverdeep for Edmark Corp. Oct 2001: Reed Elsevier buys 1.39m ADSs @ $18 per ADS.

COMPANY HISTORY:

Incorporated in Dec 1995 as Riverdeep Interactive Learning Ltd. Riverdeep provides web-based courseware for US schools, *Destination Math*, for use on CD-ROM or online which was launched in early 1999. July 1999: Acquired Logal software for $4.51m. Will pay $1m + $0.5m to SimPlayer (formerly Logal and now connected with P McDonagh) for development of online version of coursework. By end 1999 Riverdeep products were licensed to 5,216 US schools and used by 600,000 students. By mid 2000 908,000 subscribed with average revenue per new subscriber of $9.32. Licenses are sold at $200 per workstation with a typical 2 course/30 workstation order worth $12,000. Jan 2000: License agreement with ED Vantage Software for $1.4m. Rumoured approach by Pearson offering to buy Riverdeep ahead of IPO for $300m turned down. Feb 2000 Riverdeep Group Ltd tookmover from Riverdeep Interactive Learning Ltd and exchanged 10 Riverdeep Group $0.10 Ord shares for one Riverdeep Interactive Learning Ltd Ord 1p share. March 2000: Global Offering of 36.5m shares (with additional 5.475m shares for 'orderly market') at $20 ADS (equals $3.33/€3.48 per share). Proceeds paid off P McDonagh's loan of $3.5m and remainder $86m to fund company. First day's dealing saw shares close at €9.20 each. June 2000: Agreement with AOL@SCHOOL. Aug 2000: Issues 4.6m ADS (value $85m) to IBM representing 14% of Riverdeep for Edmark Corp. P McDonagh sells 29.4m shares. July 2001: Bloomberg reveal Credit Suisse First Boston staff bought up to $25m worth of shares in Riverdeep before flotation; subsequent 'glowing' reports emerge. CSFB forbid analysts from trading on their own account. Aug 2001: Continues 'lock-up' deals with McDonagh/O'Callaghan for another year. IBM sells 12m shares @$3.87 each. Sept 2001: Buys education assets of The Learning Company for $42.9m.

Share Price Sept 2001 - Sept 2002

1. €3.65 12.10.01 Reed Elsevier Investment
2. €3.45 31.01.02 Interim results

Interim Results Announced:	31.01.2002
Interim Dividend Payout:	none
Final Results Announced:	31.07.2002
Annual General Meeting:	to be announced
Final Dividend Payout:	none

HALF YEARLY PERFORMANCE: $'000

Six months to	31.12.00	30.06.01	31.12.01	30.06.02
Sales	16,700	35,164	70,817	98,434
Pretax Profit/(Loss)	(34,928)	(17,787)	(2,041)	13,265
Profit % sales	-	-	-	13.5

SHARE PRICE TREND €

2000 High	8.25 (Mar)	Low	3.05 (June)
2001 High	5.80 (June)	Low	2.40 (Sept)

Oct 2001: Collaborative agreement with Reed Elsevier who buys 1.39m Riverdeep ADSs @ $18 per ADS. Aug 2002: Buys Broderbund for €58m. Sept 2002: Share lock-up arrangements for O'Callaghan and McDonagh till 08/03. Gores Group sells 11.7m shares @ €2.23 each.

SIX YEAR REVIEW: $'000

12 months to June 30	1997	1998	1999	2000	2001	2002*
Sales	nil	1	363	8,312	51,884	169,251
Profits/(Loss) Before Tax	(1,167)	(2,767)	(7,110)	(35,170)	(52,712)	11,224
Tax	-	-	-	58	-	2,451
Profits/(Loss) After Tax	(1,167)	(2,767)	(7,110)	(35,228)	(52,712)	8,773
Minority Interests	-	-	-	-	-	-
Available to Shareholders	(1,167)	(2,767)	(7,110)	(35,228)	(52,712)	8,773
Ordinary Dividend	-	-	-	-	-	-
Retained Profits/(Losses)	(1,167)	(2,767)	(7,110)	(35,228)	(52,712)	8,773
Increase (Decrease) in Reserves	n/a	(2,534)	(7,077)	78,384 a)	106,574 b)	100,761 d)
Shareholders' Funds	(1,250)	(3,782)	(7,889)	102,105	180,714	283,481
Ordinary Dividend Per Share ($)	-	-	-	-	-	-
Earnings Per Share ($)	-	-	-	-	-	0.23

a) Share premium +$145.6m. b) Share premium +$124.5m. d) Share premium +$88,851. *** Unaudited**

Comment:

Eureka - Riverdeep has achieved *profitable* sales!

Their profit target now is $50m.

BALANCE SHEET: JUNE 30 2002. $'000

Share Capital:		Fixed Assets	9,321
225,543,000 Ord $0.10 shares	22,554	Current Assets	139,887
Reserves	260,927	Current Liabilities	66,963
		Net Current Assets	72,924
		Medium/long debt	(1,656)
Shareholders' Funds	283,481	Net Tangible Assets	80,589
		Intangibles	202,892
		Net Assets	283,481

RYANAIR HOLDINGS plc

BUSINESS: Airline.
REGISTERED OFFICE: Dublin Airport, Co. Dublin.
HEAD OFFICE: as regd office. Tel: 01-8121212. Fax 01-8121213. **SECRETARY:** H Millar.
REGISTRARS & TRANSFER OFFICE: IRG Capita plc, Unit 5, Manor Street Business Park, Manor Street, Dublin.
PRINCIPAL BANKERS: Bank of Ireland; Barclays Bank.
AUDITORS: KPMG.
SOLICITORS: A & L Goodbody; Cleary, Gottlieb Steen & Hamilton.
STOCKBROKERS: Davy Stockbrokers.
DIRECTORS: D Bonderman (Chairman - 58), R MacSharry (62), M. O'Leary (Ch.Exec -40), J Osborne (52), D Ryan (37), T Ryan (65), R Schifter (47), M Horgan, K McLaughlin, P Pietrogrande.
SHARE CAPITAL: Authorised: 840 million €0.0127 Ord shares. **Issued:** 755,030,716 €0.0127 Ord shares.
STAFF: 1,547.
SCRIP DIVIDEND: No.

CAPITAL HISTORY:

Incorporated June 1996 as Glyndon Ltd with 2 £1 Ord Shares; shareholders M O'Leary and T A Ryan. August 1996: 1 million Ord £1 shares issued to Irish Air L.P., 899,999 Ord £1 shares to Garnham Ltd (MI O'Leary), 774,999 Ord £1 shares to T.A. Ryan, 775,000 Ord £1 shares to D. Ryan, 775,000 £1 shares to C. Ryan, 775,000 Ord £1 shares to S. Ryan. October 1996: Glyndon Ltd changed to Ryanair Holdings Ltd. May 1997: All £1 Ord shares subdivided into 25 Ord 4p shares. 33,333,905 Ord 4p shares issued to facilitate flotation at 195p each. Ryanair Ltd has in issue 140,000,020 Ord 10p shares which were acquired by Ryanair Holdings on August 1996. July 1998: Issued 9,090,909 Ord 4p shares re London placing at IR550p each. Feb 2000: Ord 4p shares split into 2 Ord 2p shares. March 2000: Placing 15.3m Ord 2p shares @ €8.00 each. Feb 2001: Placed 11.0m shares @ €11.60 each. Feb 2002: Placed 30m Ord €0.025 shares @ €6.25 each (3 times oversubscribed).

COMPANY HISTORY:

In 1985 Ryanair began scheduled flights between Waterford and Gatwick. In 1986: Dublin to Luton launched and then Cork to London and Knock to London. Passenger volume grew between 1985 and 1991. But encountered losses and significant cash flow problems in 1990. New management and new strategy of low fares and no frills combined with the closure of unprofitable routes achieved profitability. Emphasised key routes Dublin to Stanstead with routes to major UK cities. Standardised its fleet to Boeing 737-200's. Grew from 650,000 passengers in 1991 to 3.1 million in 96/97. Has 21 Boeings principally 1980/82 models. In 1996/97 revenue consisted of 88% from fares with the remainder coming from charters (30%) and in flight sales (45%). In 1997 reduced agents commission to 7.5%. Launched Ryanair Direct which handles 25% of bookings. May 1997: Public flotation of 54,167,596 Ord 4p shares at 195p each. Jan 1998: 2 months industrial dispute with ground handling staff. June 1998: J. Osborne sells 200,000 shares at £5 each. Orders 25 Boeings for £845m. July 1998: 21m shares placed in London (9m new 12m old) at 550p each (466p stg). June 1999: 20.8m shares offloaded by Ryan family at 660p each (£137.3m); M O'Leary sells 2.5m shares, Irish Air General Partnership sells 5.2m shares. Aug 1999: Annual Accounts reveal all directors sold shares. Significant changes in 1998 accounts disclosed. March 2000: Raises £96m in share placing. O'Leary sells 6m shares (£37.8m); Irish Air GenPar L.P. sells 2.7m shares. June 2001: Closes Rimini route. February 2001: M O'Leary sells £27.6m Ryanair shares. July 2001: Head-on clash with Go airline on Edinburgh & Glasgow routes. T Ryan, C Ryan and D Ryan sell €21.2m Ryanair shares. Nov 2001: T Ryan sells €21.3m Ryanair shares (now holds 1.84%). Feb 2002: Orders 100 Boeing 737-800s for €5bn. June 2002: T Ryan and M O'Leary sell 28m shares @ €6.70 each.

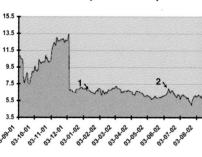

Share Price Sept 2001 - Sept 2002

1. €6.50 17.01.02 Fund raising rumours
2. €6.65 10.06.02 Annual results

FINANCIAL DIARY

Interim Results Announced:	05.11.2001
Interim Dividend Payout:	none
Final Results Announced:	10.06.2002
Annual General Meeting:	25.09.2002
Final Dividend Payout:	none

SHARE PRICE TREND

1997	High 1.29 (Oct)	Low	0.92 (Oct)
1998	High 1.97 (July)	Low	0.98 (Oct)
1999	High 2.69 (Nov)	Low	1.34 (Jan)
2000	High 3.47 (Feb)	Low	1.70 (Feb)
2001	High 6.71 (Dec)	Low	3.23 (Dec)

SECTORAL ANALYSIS (previous year)

Sales: UK 57% (61%); other 43% (39%).

HALF YEARLY PERFORMANCE: € m

6 months to:	30.09.00	31.03.01	30.09.01	31.03.02
Sales	265.9	221.6	344.2	279.9
Profit before Tax	78.9	44.6	102.4	70.0
Profit % Sales	29.7	20.1	29.8	25.0

EIGHT YEAR REVIEW: € m

12 months to March 31	1995 a)	1996 a)	1997	1998	1998 i)	1999	2000	2001	2002
Sales	109.4	139.7	173.2	231.9	231.9	295.8	370.1	487.4	624.1
Profit before Tax	19.9	26.1	30.1	47.2	61.4	75.8	90.1	123.4	172.4 h)
Tax	4.6	9.1	10.6	11.2	15.9	18.3	17.6	18.9	22.0
Profit after Tax	15.3	17.0	19.5	36.0	45.5	57.5	72.5	104.5	150.4
Available for Shareholders	15.3	17.0	19.5	36.0	45.5	57.5	72.5	104.5	150.4
Ordinary Dividend	-	-	-	-	-	-	-	-	-
Retained Earnings	15.3	17.0	19.5	36.0	45.5	57.5	72.5	104.5	150.4
Increase (Decrease) in Reserves	n/a	n/a	n/a b)	107.0 c)	107.0	117.0	190.0	228.2 g)	332.0 j)
Shareholders Fund	23.3	40.3	3.9	112.6	133.5	251.0	441.4	669.9	1,002.3
Ordinary Dividend per Share (€)	-	-	-	-	-	-	-	-	-
Earnings per Share (€)	0.024	0.032	0.042	0.059	0.065	0.087	0.108	0.148	0.206 e)

a) Ryanair Ltd figures up to 23.08.1996; thereafter Ryanair Holdings plc. b) Due to certain financial engineering prior to the flotation these figures would be meaningless. c) Share premium +€71.1m. e) Based upon 740.0m shares. f) Share premium +€117.5m. g) Share premium +€123.7m. h) Capitalised interest €5m. i) Subsequently adjusted. j) Share premium +€181.6m.

BALANCE SHEET: MARCH 31 2002. € m

Share Capital:		Fixed Assets		951.8
755,030,716 €0.0127 Ord shares	9.6	Current Assets	937.8	
		Current Liabilities	308.2	
Reserves	992.7	Net Current Assets		629.6
		Medium Debt		(67.4)
		Long Debt		(511.7)

Comment: It is interesting M O'Leary draws the analogy of supermarket trading when revealing the latest annual results - he did not point out however supermarkets increase earnings by opening new outlets on a regular basis. Now that the Easyjet/Go combination is here to give Ryanair real competition, how soon will they both run out of new European destinations. In the meantime Ryanair's performance is very impressive.

SHERRY FITZGERALD GROUP plc

BUSINESS: Estate agents and auctioneers
REGISTERED OFFICE: Ormonde House, 12/13 Lr Leeson St, Dublin. Tel: 1-6399200. Fax: 01-6399298. **HEAD OFFICE:** as regd office.
SECRETARY: M Hurley **REGISTRARS & TRANSFER OFFICE:** Computershare Investor Services (Ireland) Ltd, Heron House, Corrig Road, Sandyford Industrial Estate, Dublin. **PRINCIPAL BANKERS:** AIB Bank.
AUDITORS: PricewaterhouseCoopers. **SOLICITORS:** McCann FitzGerald.
STOCKBROKERS: Goodbody Stockbrokers.
DIRECTORS: D Chambers (Chairman - 61), M FitzGerald (CEO - 45), C Cullinan (40), L English (40), R McParland (41), J Meagher (41), P Sherry, M Hurley, J Walsh.
SHARE CAPITAL: Authorised: 25million Ord $0.12 shares. **Issued:** 13,589.938 Ord $0.12 shares.
EMPLOYEES: 323   **SCRIP DIVIDEND:** No

CAPITAL HISTORY:

Sherry FitzGerald' incorporated June 1972 as private unlimited company. May 1984 name changed to Sherry FitzGerald & Partners. Oct 1988 Sherry FitzGerald re-registered as limited company. 2 IR£1 Ord shares issued. Dec 1998 issued 941,416 IR£1 Ord shares on acquisition of Sherry FitzGerald. March 1999 issued 10,520 £1 Ord shares at £9.51 per share. Share split 10-for-1 into IR10p Ord shares. Issued 227,967 Ord $0.12 each to 82 employees at €1.99 each. April 1999 2,638,275 Ord $0.12 shares *privately* placed at $1.99 each. April 2000: Issued 126,974 Ord €0.12 shares re purchase of Cork agency.

COMPANY HISTORY:

Company derives from merger in 1982 of FitzGerald & Partners and Sherry & Sons. Between 1996 and 1998 doubled its branch network from 6 to 12. Oct 1998 claimed 15.6% of second-hand residential auction market in Dublin and 26% of residential Dublin market. Fee on sales are typically 2%. In April 1998 the Group's commercial division entered into an equity-based alliance with Debenham Tewson & Chinnocks Holdings whereby DTZ Sherry FitzGerald issued to DTC 2,000 £1 Ord shares for £192,500 plus 305,546 Ord 5p shares in DTC plus capital contribution to DTZ Sherry FitzGerald IR£157,500. April 1999 Placing raises £2.73m net of which £0.6m is repaid to directors. Flotation value £20m. First day dealings reach €2.35. Signs up 11 provincial autioneering franchises bringing total to 13. Sept 1999: Buys 80% of Ross McParland for €5.7m. April 2000: Bought 80% Burton Crowley Flynn for €3.6m. April 2001: 3 directors and management sell 941,203 shares @ €1.70 each. Dec 2001: Profits warning. January 2002: 3 Directors resign.

Interim Results Announced:	05.09.2001
Interim Dividend Payout:	
Final Results Announced:	28.03.2002
Annual General Meeting:	30.05.2002
Final Dividend Payout:	none

SECTORAL ANALYSIS (previous year)

Sales: residential 50% (50%), commercial 32% (34%), new houses 18% (16%).

SHARE PRICE TREND

1999	High	2.30 (Apr)	Low	1.85 (June)
2000	High	2.45 (Sept)	Low	1.90 (Jan)
2001	High	2.30 (Jan)	Low	0.83 (Oct)

HALF YEARLY PERFORMANCES: £'000

Six months to	30.06.00	31.12.00	30.06.01	31.12.01
Sales	12.8	14.4	13.7	9.1
Pretax profits	3.9 d)	2.2	2.6	(1.1)
Profits % sales	30.4	15.5	19.0	-

d) See Five Year Review.

SIX YEAR REVIEW: €'000

12 months to December 31	1996a)	1997b)	1998	1999	2000	2001
Sales	5,144	9,658	11,528	17,356	27,232	22,844
Profits Before Tax	213	349	2,272	3,265	6,127 d)	1,544 f)
Tax	137	263	592	1,045	1,236	648
Profits After Tax	76	86	1,680	2,220	4,891	896
Minority Interests	-	-	(92)	(245)	(603)	(275)
Available to Shareholders	76	86	1,588	1,975	4,288	621
Ordinary Dividend	70	166	-	486	543	136
Retained Profits/(Losses)	6	(80)	1,588	1,489	3,744	485
Increase (Decrease) in Reserves	n/a	182	1,960	6,435	4,003	485
Shareholders' Funds	535	837	2,910	9,839	13,837	14,322
Ordinary Dividend per Share (€)	n/a	n/a	-	0.038	0.04	0.012
Earnings per Share (€)	0.009	0.009	0.157	0.159	0.168	0.046 c)

a) Year ended Aug 31. b) 16 months to Dec 31. c) Based on 13.6m shares in issue. d) Includes property sale profit +€2m. f) Includes profit on sales of investments/property €1.2m.

BALANCE SHEET:
DECEMBER 31 2001. € m

Share Capital:		Tangible Assets	2.3
13,589,938 Ord		Financial Assets	1.4
€0.12 shares	1.6	Current Assets	11.6
Reserves	12.7	Current Liabilities	7.6
		Net Current Assets	4.0
		Medium debt	(-)
		Minority	(1.1)
S'holders' Funds	14.3	Net Tangible Assets	6.6
		Intangibles	7.7
		Net Assets	14.3

Comment: Massive drop in profits and a significant cut in the dividend does not augur well for the short term.

SMF TECHNOLOGIES plc

BUSINESS: Measurement instruments for electrical utilities.
REGISTERED OFFICE: 9 Technological Park, Castletroy, Limerick **HEAD OFFICE:** as regd office. Tel: 061-330799. Fax: 061-330812 **SECRETARY:** M McCormack. **REGISTRARS & TRANSFER OFFICE:** Computershare Investor Services (Ireland) Ltd, Heron House, Corrig Road, Sandyford Industrial Estate, Dublin. **PRINCIPAL BANKERS:** AIB, ICC. **AUDITORS:** PricewaterhouseCoopers. **SOLICITORS:** O'Donnell Sweeney.
STOCKBROKERS: Dolmen Butler Briscoe.
DIRECTORS: W Henebry (Chairman), J O'Donovan (47), M O'Donoghue (57), J McDonnell, B Smyth, B Chambers.
SHARE CAPITAL: Authorised: 50million Ord €0.12 shares
Issued: 6,821,171 Ord €0.12 shares
STAFF: 18   **SCRIP DIVIDEND:** No

CAPITAL HISTORY:

Incorporated Oct 1997 as Wiseview Holdings Ltd; name changed in March 1998 to SupaRule plc. March/April 1998 issued 1,716,537 Ord 20p shares to shareholders of Holdings on acquisition of that company. Issued 116,013 Ord 20p shares for £2.20 or £1.80p. At this stage the issued capital was £366,511 being 1,832,555 Ord 20p shares. July 1998 165,000 Ord 20p shares issued on conversion of loan. June 1998 each Ord 20p was split into 2 Ord 10p shares. March 2000: 548.000 Ord 10p shares placed at €0.825 each.

COMPANY HISTORY:

SupaRules was incorporated in 1987 to carry out R&D. In 1989 SupaRules Systems commenced manufacture of the CHM and in 1984 the ROM was launched. The Group designs and manufactures precision ultrasonic measuring instruments for the telecommunications, electrical utility and railway industries. Products have approved and/or used by Electricite de France, Tokyo Electric Power, British Telecom and Australia's New South Wales Railways. 1996 major breakthrough in EMF technology using electromagnetic field analysis to enable the non-invasive measurement of electrical current in multiple core cable. As a result in March 1997 they launched the Flexiclamp with over 12,000 units sold by June '98. July 1998 floated on stock market at 115p each raising £1.8m for the company and valuing the group at £5.9m. Jan 1999: Buys Reyrolle Industrial, South Africa for £330,000. April 1999: Profits warning of loss of £400,000 for the year to March 1999. Flexiclamp being redesigned. June 1999: S Young (sales) resigns as Director. Oct 1999: Launches voltage/resistance/current tester in Taiwan venture. March 2000: Writes-off Flexiclamp Mark 1 at cost of £132,000. Incurs £69,000 costs of aborted private equity placing and NASDAQ quotation. Sept 2000: Changes name to SMF Technologies plc. Closes UK distribution. Will license technology in future.

Interim Results Announced:	09.11.2001
Interim Dividend Payout:	none
Final Results Announced:	18.07.2002
Annual General Meeting:	16.10.2002
Final Dividend Payout:	none

HALF YEARLY PERFORMANCES: €'000

Six months to	30.09.00	31.03.01	30.09.01	31.03.02
Sales	1,030	980		
Profit (-) before tax	(395)	(583)	(278)	5
Profit % sales	-			

SHARE PRICE TREND €

1998	High	1.55 (July)	Low	1.08 (Nov)
1999	High	1.18 (Jan)	Low	0.80 (Sep)
2000	High	1.80 (Mar)	Low	0.85 (Jan)
2001	High	1.60 (Feb)	Low	0.40 (Nov)

SEVEN YEAR REVIEW: $'000

12 months to March 31	1996	1997	1998	1999	2000	2001	2002
Sales	589	654	1,143	1,122	1,597	2,010	2,269
Profit (Loss) before Tax	(142)	(183)	39	(532)	(1,049)	(978)	(274)
Tax	-	-	-	-	-	-	-
Profit (Loss) after Tax	(142)	(183)	39	(532)	(1,049)	(978)	(274)
Minority Interests	(12)	(3)	-	-	-	-	-
Finance costs	-	-	(20)	-	-	-	-
Available to Shareholders	(130)	(180)	19	(532)	(1,049)	(978)	(274)
Ordinary Dividend	-	-	-	-	-	-	-
Retained Profit (Loss)	(130)	(180)	19	(532)	(1,049)	(978)	(274)
Increase (-) in Reserve	n/a	n/a	n/a	1,314	(687) b)	(463)	(160)
Shareholders' Funds	41	(138)	(160)	1,449	655	455	261
Ord Dividend per Share (€)	-	-	-	-	-	-	-
Earnings per Share (€)	-	-	0.01	-	-	-	-

a) Share premium +€1.8m. b) Share premium +€0.4m

BALANCE SHEET: MARCH 31 2002

Share Capital:		Fixed Assets	134
6,031,361 Ord		Current Assets	811
€0.12 shares	819	Current Liabilities	341
Reserves	(558)	Net Current Assets	470
		Medium debt	(343)
Shareholders' Funds	261	Net Assets	261

Notes to Accounts:
The Accounts have been prepared on the going concern basis.

THESE ACCOUNTS WERE UNAUDITED AT TIME OF GOING TO PRESS

Comment: This fledgling company is still trying to find its profitable niche.

JEFFERSON SMURFIT GROUP plc

BUSINESS: Print and packaging.
REGISTERED OFFICE: Beech Hill, Clonskeagh, Dublin 4. Tel: 01-2027000. Fax: 01-2694481.
HEAD OFFICE: as regd office.
SECRETARY: M O'Riordan.
REGISTRARS & TRANSFER OFFICE: Capita Corporate Registrars plc, Marine House, Clanwilliam Court, Dublin.
PRINCIPAL BANKERS: Various.
AUDITORS: Ernst & Young.
SOLICITORS: William Fry.
STOCKBROKERS: Davy Stockbrokers.
DIRECTORS: MWJ Smurfit (Chairman & CEO - 66), G W McGann (52), P Gleeson (56), H Kilroy (67), R Mac Sharry (64), J Malloy (75), J O'Dwyer (56), M Rafferty (70), M Redmond (52), A Reynolds (70), A Smurfit (39), D Smurfit (58), P Smurfit (60), J Thompson (66), P Wright (61).
SHARE CAPITAL: Authorised: 1,401,214,000 Ord. €0.30 shares. **Issued:** 1,188,390,540 Ord. €0.30 shares. (I American Depositary Receipt = 10 Ordinary shares).
STAFF: 26,751. **SCRIP DIVIDEND:** No

Share Price Sept 2001 - Sept 2002

1. €2.48 20.02.02 Final Results
2. €3.22 10.05.02 Takeover Talks Announced

CAPITAL HISTORY:

Incorporated 1934. Publicly floated 1964. 1967: small 'scrip' of 1-for-5. 1969: 'rights' of 1-for-4 at 125p per share. 1970 acquired Brown & Nolan for shares and cash. Acquired Hely Group for shares and cash. Sept. 1970 'scrip' 1-for-1. 1972 acquired Jefferson Smurfit (Packaging) Ltd. for shares. Acquired Henry Jackson Ltd. for shares. Acquired W.J. Noble & Sons for shares. 1,111,422 "B" Ord. shares issued to Continental Can Co. 1973 1-for-3 'rights' issue at 160p. June 1974 'scrip' issue of 1-for-1. "B" shares redesignated Ord. shares. July 1976 'scrip' 1-for-3. July 1977 1-for-3 'scrip' issue. June 1979 'rights' issue 1-for-6 at 150p per share. May 1981 'rights' of 1-for-6 at 170p. August 1981 'scrip' issue of 1-for-1. July 1982 796,000 7% Red. Cum. Pref. 25p shares converted into Ord. 25p shares. June 1985 'scrip' issue of 1-for-2. June 1985 771,287 Ord. 25p shares issued on acquisition of TMG Group. January 1989: Issue of £115,103,226 9.75% convertible loan notes. Sept. 1992: Scrip issue 1-for-1. Oct 1994: Rights issue 48,763,470 Ord 25p shares 1-for-10 at 330p each. June 1995: 1-for-1 scrip issue. June 1998: Redeems preference shares at par.

COMPANY HISTORY:

Originally formed as General Box Makers in Dublin in 1934. Purchased by late Jefferson Smurfit in 1938. 1942 name changed to Jefferson Smurfit and Sons Ltd. 1964 stock market quotation. In Oct 1981 purchased 70% interest in Clearprint Australia. Sept 1982 acquired 50% of Diamond International and 100% in April 1983. April 1983 bought 50% of Diamond Match. June 1982 bought 50% of Quality Packaging Materials. Obtained controlling interest in Southern Fibre Corp. July 1982 formed Smurfit Paribas Bank (50%). Feb. 1983 closed Smurfit Corrugated at St. Helens. Sept. 1983 reorganised US operations under Jefferson Smurfit Corp. Nov. 1983 issued 2,100,000 shares in Smurfit Corp. at $24 each netting $46m. Oct. 1983 UK corrugated interests merged with MacMillan Bloedel. In 1984 bought remaining 50% of Diamond Match. In 1986 purchased 80% of Publishers Paper Co. for $133m. Oct. 1986 purchased 50% interest in Container Corporation of America (other 50% Morgan Stanley Leveraged Equity Fund) through Jefferson Smurfit Corp ("GSC") for $1.1 billion. January 1987 acquired CCA's European interests £21m. Oct. 1987: Purchased Venezuelan subsidiaries of Container Corp. for £19m. July 1988: Acquires remaining 51% holding in Sonofit Containers from Sonoco. September 1988: Acquisition of a 19.9% stake in PCL Industrials from Unicorp Canada for consideration of $8.584m. Dec. 1988: Purchases 1.37m shares in Scott Robertson plc to bring stake to 16.1%. Acquisition of Industrial Cortonera SA in Spain for £68m cash. March 1989: J.S. Corp. joint venture with Tembec Inc. at a cost of £156m. J.S. Group purchased Rolex Paper Co. June 1989: J.S. Group acquired Mexican and Colombian interests of CCA for £107.1m. Dec 1989: SIBV/MS Holdings Inc, ("SIBV/MS") a newly formed company owned 50% by a Smurfit subsidiary and 50% by the Morgan Stanley Leveraged Equity Fund II and others acquired all the common stock of J.S. Corp, those held by the public at $43 per share and those held by Smurfit at $41.75 per share. As part of the restructuring JSC acquired the 50% of CCA it did not already own. Smurfits and MSLF each put in $200m equity, Smurfit Group put in $100m Preference and the balance was debt funded. SIBV/MS holds 100% of JSC & CCA. June 1990: Acquires 49% in Smurfit Corrugated in U.K. for £17.5m stg. Jan. 1991: Acquired 95% Lestrem Group in France for £28m. Jan 1992: Acquires 52% Finlay Packaging (total value £4.2m). Oct 1992: M. Smurfit and D. Smurfit sell 7.9m shares for £14m.

May 1994: Difficult flotation of SIBV/MS in US Stock price eventually got away at $13 (not $2 as hoped) with more stock (19.25m shares being made available. Additionally JS Group too up 11.54m shares. Smurfit Group ends up wi 46.5%, Public and Morgan Stanley 36.2%. Au 1994: Announces purchase of Cellulose Du P for £684m. Intends paying £20.5m for 27.5% Nettingsdorfer (Austria). May 1995: Buy Limousin for £56m. June 1996: Pays £68m fc 29% of Munksjo (Sweden). Aug 1995: Purchase 25 million own shares at 200p each. Sept 199 M. Smurfit buys 520,000 shares at 192p each June 1997: Pays £17m for Celulosa de Coron Suarez and Asindus in Argentina. Aug 199 Pays £30m for 2 German corrugated box plant Dec 1997: Holds 25m Treasury shares at 202.5 each. May 1998: Announces merger of J Corporation with Stone Containers (Stone to g 99 JS Corp shares for every 100 Stone shares Smurfit will own 33% of SSCC Smurfit buyin 50% of Morgan Stanleys 36% stake in JS Cor for $500 million. Smurfit shares reach 277p. Ju 1998: Increases stake in Nettingsdorfer (Austri to 75% for £54m. Sept 1998: Buys 50 MacMillan Bathurst (Canada) for £83m. No 1998: JSC Corp and Stone Container merge $2billion deal. Dec 1999: Bids £12m for 70% c Norcor Holdings. July 2000: Buys Neopa (Denmark) for €30m/£23.6m. Sept 2000: Spend $13m on Argentinian companies. Dec 200(Pays £43.2m for remaining 25% Nettingsdorfe Papierfabrik. Pays $21m for 25% of Leefung Asco Hong Kong. May 2001: Shareholders crit cise Chairman's remuneration package. Au 2002: €3.6bn offer from Madison Dearbon (€2.15 per share) + one SSCC share for every 1 JSG shares; total value €3.18 per JSG share Shareholders approve spin-off of SSCC.

TEN YEAR REVIEW: € m

12 months to 31 Dec	1993 a)	1994 a)	1994	1995	1996	1997	1998	1999	2000	2001
Sales	1,599.4	1,863.5	2,171.4	3,850.9	3,293.8	3,264.4	3,666.9	3,688.6	4,565.2	4,511.7
Profit before Tax	121.3	60.7	402.6 b)	533.4	255.3	190.7	217.2 q)	263.3	442.3	325.0 e)
Tax	37.4	6.7	25.5	138.5	77.8	52.2	39.5	125.5	169.0	120.4
Profit after Tax	83.9	54.0	377.1	394.9	177.5	138.5	177.6	137.8	273.3	204.6
Minority Interest	(15.2)	(9.5)	(7.7)	(15.1)	(8.5)	(5.1)	(7.1)	(16.2)	(30.8)	(37.0)
Extraordinary Item	(24.5)	-	-	-	-	-	-	-	-	-
Preference Dividend	0.6	-	-	-	-	-	-	-	-	-
Available for Shareholders	43.6	44.5	369.4	379.8	169.0	133.4	170.5	121.6	242.5	167.6
Ordinary Dividend	36.1	24.8	35.6	53.6	56.1	22.6	65.7	109.1	75.2	79.0
Retained Profit (Loss)	7.5	19.7	333.8	326.2	112.9	110.8	104.8	12.5	167.3	88.6
Increase (-) in Reserves	(11.4)	(23.0) j)	494.6 k)	1.3	72.1 u)	178.7 d)	107.5 n)	187.0 f)	241.2 c)	159.0 h)
Shareholders' Funds	1,068.5	1,045.5	1,556.6	1,729.9	1,802.5	1,988.5	2,096.1	2,263.9	2,505.2	2,664.5
Ordinary Dividend per share	0.039	0.025	0.034	0.051	0.053	0.021 r)	0.061	0.101	0.069	0.073
Earnings per share	0.050	0.046	0.107	0.356	0.160	0.124	0.157	0.112	0.224	0.155 g)

a) Year end Jan 31. b) includes one-off clawback profit of +€287m. c) Currency uplift +€72.4m. (d) Share premium +€22.5m; goodwill w/o -€44.4m; currency gain +€89.8m. e) Includes one-off charges -€61.3m. f) Currency gain +€154.9m. g) Based upon 1,083.8m shares (excluding 25m treasury shares). h) Currency gain +€64.4m. j) Goodwill w/o -€34m, accountancy adjustment -€13.2m, currency uplift +€3.9m. k) Share premium +€188.6m (net); currency loss -€19.3m. n) Goodwill write-back +€11.4m, currency loss -€9.9m. q) Profit on disposals +€200.9m. r) No final dividend. u) Goodwill w/o -€16.4m; foreign currency loss -€26.5m.

HALF YEARLY PERFORMANCES: € m

months to 31.12.00	30.06.01	31.12.01	30.06.02
Sales	2,359.2	2,325.5	2,186.2	2,363.4
Pretax Profit	266.9	175.3	149.7	148.3
Profit % Sales	11.3	7.5	6.8	6.3

FINANCIAL DIARY

Interim Results Announced:	06.08.2002
First Interim Dividend Payout:	none
Final Results Announced:	28.02.2002
Annual General Meeting:	26.04.2002
Final Dividend Payout:	03.05.2002

FIVE YEAR SHARE PRICE TREND €

1997	High	3.05 (Oct)	Low	1.96 (Apr)
1998	High	3.52 (Oct)	Low	1.12 (May)
1999	High	3.00 (Dec)	High	1.43 (Feb)
2000	High	3.35 (Jan)	Low	1.74 (June)
2001	High	2.55 (Dec)	Low	1.82 (Mar)

INVESTMENT PERFORMANCE:

Five Year Investment Performance:	€ 1,226
Ten Year Investment Performance:	€ 1,488

SECTORAL ANALYSIS: (previous year)

Sales: Europe 67% (67%), Nth America 15% (16%), Sth America 18% (17%). **Profits:** Europe 47% (36%), Nth America 33% (51%), Sth America 20% (13%).

BALANCE SHEET: DECEMBER 31 2001. € m

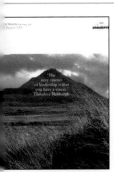

Share Capital:		
1,109,724,639 Ord. €0.30 shares	332.9	
(including 25m treasury shares)		
Reserves	2,331.6	
Shareholders' Funds	2,664.5	

Tangible Assets		2,088.0
Financial Assets		1,743.9
Current Assets	1,948.2	
Current Liabilities	1,413.4	
Net Current Assets		534.9
Medium debt		(1,683.4)
Minority		(175.3)
Net Tangible Assets		2,508.1
Intangibles		156.4
Net Assets		2,664.5

Comment:
A very disappointing investment over the short or medium term and despite claiming the shares were undervalued the eventual take-out by Madison Dearborn (which was uncontested by any other bidder) did not reward investors for their patience. The end of an era!

TRINITY BIOTECH plc

BUSINESS: Production of diagnostic kits.
REGISTERED OFFICE: IDA Business Park, Bray, Co Wicklow. Tel: 01-2769800 Fax: 01- 2769888
HEAD OFFICE: as regd office. **SECRETARY:** M Hickey.
REGISTRARS & TRANSFER OFFICE: Computershare Investor Services (Ireland) Ltd, Heron House, Corrig Road, Sandyford Industrial Estate, Dublin.
PRINCIPAL BANKERS: Allied Irish Banks; Morgan Stanley Dean Witter, Investec Bank (UK) Ltd.
AUDITORS: Ernst & Young. **SOLICITORS:** O'Donnell Sweeney; William Fry; Carter, Ledyard and Milburn.
STOCKBROKERS: Goodbody Stockbrokers.
DIRECTORS: R O'Caoimh (Chairman & CEO - 47), B Farrell (President - 55), M Hickey (42), J Walsh (44), D Burger (59), P Coyne.
SHARE CAPITAL: Authorised: 75million A Ord $0.0109 shares and 700,000 B Ord $0.0109 shares. **Issued:** 39,016,746 A Ord $0.0109 shares and 700,000 B Ord $0.0109 shares.
STAFF: 332. **SCRIP DIVIDEND:** No.

CAPITAL HISTORY:

Incorporated Jan 1992 as Glavron Ltd. July 1992 name changed to Trinity Biotech plc. As at Jan 1 1996 there were 14,615,817 A Ord 1p shares issued of which 589,211 were options and 393,821 warrants exercised at prices between $0.50 and $3.75. During 1997 issued 175,548 A Ord 1p shares to Forbairt; options exercised over 4,440,965 shares at prices between $0.50 and $2.10. and 396,065 warrants at $3 each. Feb 1997: Issued 1,427,142 A Ord shares part payment of Clark Laboratories. Issued 153,202 A Ord shares re purchase of CLI Oncology Inc. June 1997 Private placing of US$3million 4% convert debentures. 1998: US$2.5m of the debentures were converted resulting in the issuance of 1,989,677 A Ord shares at prices between $0.79 and $1.78. During 1998 868,461 Ord A 1p shares were issued on exercise of options at between $0.5 and $1.90. 280,352 A Ord 1p shares were

issued to Forbairt at 134p per share and 436,702 A Ord 1p shares to Forbairt at 86p per share. Oct 1998 675,773 A Ord 1p shares issued to Eastridge Foundation for £1.15 each in consideration for 90,103 shares in Selfcare Inc. At 31.12.1998 there were 1,279,151 Class B warrants outstanding. May 1999: Floated on Irish Stock Market @ 154p ($1.95). 1999: US$500,000 4% Conv Debenture converted into 498,291 A Ord 1p shares @ $1 per share. Private placement of $3.5m 7.5% Conv Deb; conversion rights into A Ord shares by Dec 2002 @ $1.80 per share. Dec 1999: private placement of 1,334,805 A Ord 1p shares @ US$1.50 each. Jan/June 2000: 2.2m Ord 1p shares issued exercise of options. March 2000: 558,000 Ord 1p shares issued on acquisition of MarDx. April 2000: Placed 4m Ord 1p shares at US$3.35 each. 1.041,667 Ord 1p shares issued @US$1.80 on conversion of debenture. May 2001: Ord 1p shares changed to Ord $0.0109 shares.

COMPANY HISTORY:

Founded in 1992 to develop, manufacture and market rapid diagnostic kits used for the clinical laboratory, point-of-care and over-the-counter segments of the diagnostic market primarily for the infectious and auto-immune diseases. The product portfolio comprises more than 100 products which are sold in 75 countries through 130 distributors world-wide. Oct 1994: Bought Disease Detection International Inc which held marketing and manufacturing rights for Trinity's products in US, Canada and South America. Dec 1994: Acquired remaining 50% of FHC Corp, supplier of home pregnancy tests. Dec 1995: 5-year agreement to sell most of its American products to Wampole Laboratories.; cost US$6.7m ($1,9m cash and $4.8m in Trinity A Ord shares). Feb

FINANCIAL DIARY

Interim Results Announced:	26.07.2002
Interim Dividend Payout:	none
Final Results Announced:	30.04.2002
Annual General Meeting:	14.06.2002
Final Dividend Payout:	none

SHARE PRICE TREND

1999	High 1.96 (May)	Low 1.46 (Nov)
2000	High 7.66 (Mar)	Low 1.71 (Jan)
2001	High 3.30 (Jan)	Low 1.58 (Oct)

HALF YEARLY PERFORMANCE: $m

Six months to	31.12.00	30.06.01	31.12.01	30.06.02
Sales	15.4	17.7	19.4	23.2
Pretax (loss) profits	1.9	2.1	(0.4)	2.8
Profits % sales	12.3	11.9	-	12.1

SECTORAL ANALYSIS: (previous year)

Sales: USA 68% (58%), other 32% (42%).

1997: Bought Clark Laboratories Inc. for US$8.4m. June 1997: Bought Centocor UK Holdings Ltd for US$6.3m. June 1998: Paid US$2.1m for Microzyme (for drugs of abuse). Sept 1998: Paid US$1.9m for a heart disease predictor. Sept 1998: Paid US$4.3m for HIV diagnoses. Purchased MicroTrak (for sexually transmitted diseases) for US$13m. Oct 1998: Sold its US OTC pregnancy test business. Dec 1999: Sells HQ (sale and leaseback) for $5.85m/$5.7m. Jan 2000: Receives FDA approval for Uni-Gold (ulcer and cancer drug). Also FDA approves heart disease drug.. Shares reach $3.25 in US. Feb 2000: Buys MarDx Diagnostics (California) for $4m/$4.2m. Oct 2000: Buys 33% HiberGen for $1.37m. Dec 2000: Bought Bartels for $9.5m. Dec 2001: Bought Biopool for $6.3m. Relocation of various production facilities costs $2.9m. Feb 2002: Increases stake in HiberGen for $3.1m.

SIX YEAR REVIEW: US$'000

12 months to December 31	1996	1997	1998	1999	2000	2001
Sales	6,799	17,832	23,169	26,105	29,743	37,065
Profits (Loss) Before Tax	(753)	1,280	2,551	4,916	4,947	1,655 c)
Tax	-	-	-	-	124	206
Profits (Loss) After Tax	(753)	1,280	2,551	4,916	4,823	1,449
Minority Interests	-	-	-	-	-	-
Available to Shareholders	(753)	1,280	2,551	4,916	4,823	1,449
Ordinary Dividend	-	-	-	-	-	-
Retained Profits (Loss)	(753)	1,280	2,551	4,916	4,823	1,449
Increase (Decrease) in Reserves				8,063	31,714 b)	1,489
Shareholders' Funds	10,573	7,105	14,624	22,723	55,043	56,532
Ordinary Dividend Per Share ($)	-	-	-	-	-	-
Earnings Per Share ($)	-	0.07	0.10	0.175	0.13	0.04 a)

a) Based on 40.4m shares. b) Share premium +$27.4m. c) Exceptional charges $3.7m.

BALANCE SHEET: DECEMBER 31 2001. US$'000

Share Capital:		
39,016,746 A Ord		
$0.0109 shares	606	
+ 700,000 B Ord		
$0.0109 shares		
Reserves	55,925	
Shareholders' Funds	56,531	

Fixed Assets		5,967
Financial Assets		1,351
Current Assets	29,309	
Current Liabilities	12,692	
Net Current Assets		16,616
Medium debt		(7,805)
Net Tangible Assets		16,129
Intangibles		40,402
Net Assets		56,531

Comment:
Steady progress in an exciting industry.

TULLOW OIL plc

BUSINESS: Production of oil and gas and exploration for hydrocarbons.
REGISTERED OFFICE: 5th Floor, 30 Old Burlington Street, London W1S 3AR. Tel: 0044 2073336800. Fax: 0044 2073336830.
HEAD OFFICE: London Office: as above. **Dublin Office:** 5th Floor, Block C, Central Park, Leopardstown Dublin 18 Tel: 01-2137300. Fax 01-2930400. **SECRETARY:** T Hickey. **REGISTRARS & TRANSFER OFFICE:** Computershare Investor Services (Ireland) Ltd, Heron House, Corrig Road, Sandyford Industrial Estate, Dublin. **PRINCIPAL BANKERS:** CIBC World Markets plc; National Westminster Bank, Bank of Scotland. **AUDITORS:** Robert J. Kidney & Co; Deloitte & Touche **SOLICITORS:** Wm. Fry; Dickson Minto W.S. **STOCKBROKERS:** Davy Stockbrokers; Investec Henderson Crosthwaite.
DIRECTORS: P Plunkett (Chairman - 51), Aidan Heavey (Mng Dir - 49), R Courtney (54), E Maleki (51), G Martin (48), M O'Donoghue (58), T Hickey (34), J Lander (58), C Spottiswoode (49), S McTiernan (51).
SHARE CAPITAL: Authorised: 1 billion Ord 10p stg shares. **Issued:** 358,474,570 Ord 10p stg shares.
INVESTOR RELATIONS: Wendy Goodbody (01-2137300)
STAFF: 87. **SCRIP DIVIDEND:** No
WEB SITE: www.tullowoil.com

CAPITAL HISTORY:

August 1985 incorporated. 7 £1 Ord. shares issued at par. Dec. 1985 29,993 Ord. £1 shares issued 25p paid. March 1986 75p per share balance called up. April 1986 'scrip' issue of 57-for-1. Dec. 1986 350,000 Ord. £1 shares issued at 100p (conversion of loan). April 1987 1,234,739 Ord. £1 shares issued at 100p. Sept. 1987 2,223,160 Ord. £1 shares at 128p by 'rights' and placing Nov. 1987 £1 shares subdivided into 10p units. March 1988 7,000,000 Ord. 10p share at 23p by way of placing. Dec 1988: issued 1,750,000 Ord. 10p shares at 27p for acquisition of Moseley Petroleum Ltd. Jan 1989: Issued 1,000,000 Ord. 10p shares at 19p for acquisition of U.K. licences for Pict. Petroleum plc. March 1989: issued 28,407,899 Ord. 10p shares at 16p by way of placing. April 1990 issued 300,000 Ord. 10p shares at 22.5p per share in part consideration of the purchase by the company from Pict of a 30% net profits interest in certain United Kingdom Licences. May 1990: Rights issue 31,345,630 Ord. 10p shares at 13p per share (8-for-24) with warrants. March 1991: 7,217,744 Ord. 10p shares issued to Enterprise Oil at 15p each . May 1991: 11,754,611 Ord. 10p shares issued to warrant holders at 18.5p each. May 1992: Places 2.15m Ord. 10p shares at 14.3p. Oct 1993: 1 million Ord 10p shares issued re options at 13.27p each. Nov 1993: 446,667 Ord 10p shares issued re options at 13.4p each. April 1994: Placing and open offer (1-for-16) of 27,346,971 Ord 10p shares at 22p each. Oct 1995: Issued 4,375,000 Ord 10p shares to Centrotrade at 20p stg each on exercise of option. Aug 1996: 1-for-5 rights issue (37,905,993 Ord 10p shares) at 77.75p each. June 1998: $10m 10% Secured Redeem Convert Loan Notes 1998 converted into 6,378,218 Ord 10 shares at 109.56p

per share. Dec 1999: Placing and open offer (1-for-22) 38,461,538 Ord 0.13 shares at 52p stg. Aug 2000: Share placing and open offer (1-for7 rights) of 77m Ord $0.13 shares @ 57.5p stg each to raise £41.8m stg to buy producing assets from BP Amoco costing £201m stg/$324.9m.

COMPANY HISTORY:

In 1985 licensed to explore 874 sq. kms. in Castlecomer on which company spent £0.6m by Dec. '87. March 1986 joint venture to explore 3,470 sq. kms. in Dakar, Senegal. 3 wells had produced 17,000 barrels of oil by Feb '88. Gas production commenced Nov. '87 and by Feb. '88 grossed 23 million cu. ft. In 1987 acquired stakes in 6 exploration permits in Italy. Company obtained 15 mineral prospecting licenses in Wexford, Cavan, Louth & Meath. Acquired land drilling rig in December '87 for use in Senegal. Senegal Wells produced 19,222 barrels of oil in 1988, gas production grossed 332m cu. ft. in 1988. Acquired 19 U.K. onshore licences in

Aidan Heavey

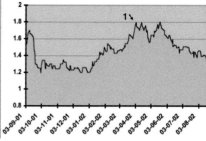

1988 and 1989 including the Kirby Misperton, Malton gas fields. The Marishes 1 well in Yorkshire added to the Kirby Misperton and Malton reserves. Feb. 1989: Raised £4.5m by way of placing. May/June 1990: Rights issue raises £5.9m (69% take-up). March 1991: Buys UK onshore interests of Enterprise Oil for approx £0.8m. May 1991: Second part of 1990's rights issue raises £2.17m, 11.7m shares at 18.5p each. July 1991: Production commenced on onshore UK oilfield - circa 200 bbls per day. Tullow share 43%. June 1992: Sold Yemen interest for cash phased payment of $5.25m and royalties. April 1993: Dian Niadio East well drilled in Senegal. Initially tested 17 million standard cubic feet per day of gas, put on production at 3.5 million standard cubic feet per day. June 1993: Signed initial agreement with Czech MND management and technical services.Oct 1993: A. Heavey exercises 1 million share option at 13.27p each and then places shares with Centrotrade Corp. of Panama at 27p stg each. May 1995: Kalu-1 in Pakistan abandoned. June 1995: High Court cancels £7.4m shares premium with P & L deficit. July 1995: Power generation deal announced in Pakistan which could generate $18m by April 1996.March 1996: Through Tullow Pakistan (D) Ltd issued $10 million 10% red. conv. loan notes. Sept 1996: Takeover rumours abound.

Share Price Sept 2001 - Sept 2002

1. €1.79 04.04.02 Final results

FIVE YEAR SHARE PRICE TREND

1997	High 2.12 (Dec)	Low	1.08 (Jan)
1998	High 2.48 (Feb)	Low	0.58 (Oct)
1999	High 1.33 (Mar)	Low	0.62 (Jan)
2000	High 1.49 (Mar)	Low	0.72 (May)
2001	High 1.70 (Sept)	Low	0.92 (Jan)

SECTORAL ANALYSIS: (previous Year)

Sales: Oil & Gas 87% (82%), other 13% (18%), Europe 94% (38%), Asia 6% (62%).

FINANCIAL DIARY

Interim Results Announced:	03.09.2002
Interim Dividend Payout:	None
Final Results Announced:	04.04.2002
Annual General Meeting:	30.05.2002
Final Dividend Payout:	None

HALF YEARLY PERFORMANCES: £ m stg

Six months to	31.12.00	30.06.01	31.12.01	30.06.02
Sales	4.1	27.1	49.5	55.0
Pretax Profit (Loss)	(0.2)	6.6	9.5	12.6
Profit % Sales	-	24.4	19.2	22.9

INVESTMENT PERFORMANCE

Five Year Investment Performance: € 1,111

Large buying in London. March 1997: Gets 25% interest in Medus Oil. July 1998: Schroder Investment Management now holds 17.8% Tullow. Dec 1999: Rights issue raises £18.9mstg/$29.3m net. Ja 1999: Increases stake in North Yorkshire gas fields to 60%. April 200 Board downsized - 4 retire. April 2000: Decides to domicile in UK. Ju 2000: Announces share placing (inc 1-for-7 rights) of 77m Ord $0.1 shares @ 57.5p stg each to raise £41.8m stg to buy producing asse from BP Amoco costing £201m stg/$324.9m. March 2001: Buys 30° Algerian oilfield.

TEN YEAR REVIEW

Year to 31st December	Ir£'000 1992	Ir£'000 1992g)	Ir£'000 1993	Ir£'000 1994	Ir£'000 1995	Ir£'000 1996	Ir£'000 1997	Ir£'000 1998	Ir£'000 1999	£ m stg 2000	£ m stg 2001
Revenue	1,304	1,304	3,424	3,621	5,308	5,870	6,178	4,998	6,580	7.8	76.6
Profit (Loss) before Tax	(677)	1,633	1,076	1,159	1,186	2,347	(222)	(18,041)	(15,181)	0.8	16.0
Tax	-	-	-	-	-	168	48	+51	-	-	6.7
Profit (Loss) after Tax	(677)	1,633	1,076	1,159	1,186	2,178	(270)	(17,990)	(15,181)	0.8	9.3
Exceptional Item	2,310 f)	-	-	-	-	-	-	-	-	-	-
Available for Shareholders	1,633	1,633	1,076	1,159	1,186	2,178	(270)	(17,990)	(15,181)	0.8	9.3
Ordinary Dividends	-	-	-	-	-	-	-	-	-	-	-
Retained Profits (Losses)	1,633	1,633	1,076	1,159	1,186	2,178	(270)	(17,990)	(15,181)	0.8	9.3
Increase (Decrease) in Reserve	(9,667)	462	1,092	4,115 i)	2,292	26,281 j)	1,008	(11,644) k)	2,756 a)	34.2	12.1 m)
Shareholders' Funds	8,514	8,514	9,751	16,753	20,024	50,488	51,580	40,629	47,937	79.4	92.0
Ordinary Dividend per Share	-	-	-	-	-	-	-	-	-	-	-
Earnings per share	-	1.12p	0.73p	0.69p	0.66p	1.07p	-	-	-	0.26p	2.61p h)

a) Share premium +£19.1m. b) Currency loss -£1.6m. e) Share Premium £1.2m. f) Sale of licence interest. h) Based upon 356.5m shares.
i) Share premium +£3.0m. j) Share premium +£24.4m. k) Share premium +£6.6m. m) Share premium +£2.0m stg.

BALANCE SHEET : DECEMBER 31 2001. £ m stg

Share Capital:		Fixed Assets		175.2
358,474,570 Ord 10pstg Shares	35.8	Current Assets	67.3	
Reserves	56.2	Current Liabilities	58.6	
		Net Current Assets		8.7
		Medium Debt		(124,4)
		Net Tangible Liabilities		(59.5)
		Intangible Assets		32.5
Shareholders' Funds	92.0	Net Assets		92.0

Comment:

See

Chairman's Statement.

Tullow Oil plc

Chairman's Statement

The first six months of 2002 have shown a steady continuation of the transformation of Tullow.

Strong production continues from our UK Southern North Sea ("SNS") assets and a number of interesting new exploration and development opportunities are being assessed in this area. On our international acreage, we have benefited from first oil production in Cote d'Ivoire. Turnover for the period was Stg £55.0 million, double that of the corresponding period in 2001. Operating profit before exploration costs of Stg £16.8 million was 50% ahead of 2001, leading to a pre tax profit of Stg £12.6 million. Operating Cash Flow of Stg £36.9 million was 120% ahead of the corresponding figure in 2001.

This strong SNS performance demonstrates both the quality of the UK assets and the effectiveness of Tullow's forward sales programme for uncontracted gas.

UK

The full production income from our SNS assets is included as turnover during the period in contrast to 2001, when income was included on a phased basis as completion of the acquisition of the SNS assets occurred in stages.

Our principal SNS project has been the ongoing development of the Caister Murdoch System III ("CMS III") which is a unitised development of five natural gas fields. Substantial progress was made during the period; drilling commenced in April and new offshore facilities were installed in May. The Hawksley well successfully tested at 150 mmscfd of gas and the second CMS III development well is currently being drilled. Elsewhere in the CMS complex the Boulton F well tested gas at approximately 55 mmscfd. We look forward to more success throughout the remainder of the development programme.

Since the end of the period, Tullow added to its SNS portfolio through the award of a total of seven blocks in the recent 20th offshore licensing round.

International Assets

Cote d'Ivoire

The first phase of development work on the Espoir Field, offshore Cote d'Ivoire, is nearing completion. First oil was produced on 4th February 2002 and the field is currently producing approximately 14,000 bopd gross from 3 producing wells. Gas sales from Espoir commenced on 10 August and are expected to reach 20 mmscfd by the end of the year.

One of the key attractions of Espoir is the substantial potential for additional reserves - the next well in the schedule is the Emien exploration well in October while the Acajou prospect is now scheduled to spud early in 2003.

Pakistan

The Sara and Suri wells have continued to perform at an average rate of approximately 32 mmscfd to date in 2002 and are currently producing 38 mmscfd. In addition, a successful development well and workover have led to plans to double field production in the near future, subject to Government approval.

Bangladesh

Tullow commenced work on Block 9 and during the period undertook a seismic survey over targeted regions of the Block. We are optimistic that the results will be of assistance in selecting optimal drilling locations later this year.

India

During 2001, Tullow negotiated a farmout agreement with Reliance Industries in relation to 5 of its licences in India. We anticipate that the first well to be drilled by Reliance, on the GK-OSJ-1 licence, will spud in October. Tullow has entered into arrangements to dispose of its two other Indian licence interests.

Algeria

Geological and geophysical work continued on the Agip-operated 222b licence with the objective of selecting a drillable prospect. We now anticipate drilling will occur in early 2003. Elsewhere in Algeria, Tullow applied for stakes in two field redevelopment projects, where the bid process is ongoing.

Egypt

Tullow has drilled two wells on the North Abu Rudeis licence in 2002. The first well failed to produce oil in commercial quantities. The second well was plugged and abandoned. Tullow is, however, continuing to seek new opportunities in Egypt.

Romania

Following completion of the 2002 seismic programme, work continues on both blocks EPI-3 and EPI-8 with a view to defining a prospect and location for drilling in 2003.

Business Development

Tullow retains an active focus on new exploration and development opportunities in the Group's existing core areas of the UK SNS, West Africa and Pakistan.

We are delighted with the recent award of new licences in the 20th UK licensing round. The blocks include two undeveloped gas discoveries. We are confident that a number of new exploration or appraisal prospects will materialise which, if successful, could form the nucleus for a future CMS IV development. In addition, Tullow was awarded its first acreage in the oil-rich sector of the Central North Sea, and we hope this will be the start of a new core area for the Company. We remain focused on expanding the Group's operations through suitable acquisitions and exploration new ventures.

Conclusion

The first half of 2002 has been a period of continued progress for Tullow. Our UK and Cote d'Ivoire developments continue to gather momentum, each with major scope for both increased revenue and reserves while our UK and Pakistan assets also continue to produce strong cashflows. Over the coming six months the Group will embark on a period of intensive exploration in the UK, Cote d'Ivoire, Bangladesh, India and Algeria; we are hopeful that some of these projects will form the basis of a new value creation area for Tullow over the coming years.

I look forward to the remainder of 2002, which will be an interesting period in the development of the Group.

Pat Plunkett
Chairman

Patrick Plunkett
Chairman

The first six months of 2002 have shown a steady continuation of the transformation of Tullow.

ULSTER TELEVISION plc

BUSINESS: Telecasting in Northern Ireland on behalf of the Independent Television Commission.

REGISTERED OFFICE: Havelock House, Ormeau Road, Belfast. Tel: 01232-328122. Fax: 01232-246695.

HEAD OFFICE: as regd office.

SECRETARY: J Downey.

REGISTRARS & TRANSFER OFFICE: Computershare Investor Services Ltd, 19 Bedford Street, Belfast.

PRINCIPAL BANKERS: Northern Bank Ltd.

AUDITORS: Ernst & Young LLP.

SOLICITORS: G L MacLaine & Co; Theodore Goddard; Arthur Cox.

STOCKBROKERS: Dresdner Kleinwort Wasserstein.

DIRECTORS: J McGuckian (Chairman - 63), J McCann (Mng Dir - 49), R.C. Bailie (59), H. McClure (47), A. Bremner (56), J Downey (56).

SHARE CAPITAL: Authorised: 100m Ord 5p shares.
Issued: 52,546,600 Ord 5p shares.

STAFF: 281

SCRIP DIVIDEND: No

CAPITAL HISTORY:

Incorporated Feb 1959. July 1961: non-voting A Ord 25p shares placed at 105p. June 1984: 1-for-1 scrip issue resulted in 365,000 Ord 25p shares issued and 2,045,000 non-voting A Ord 25p shares. Dec 1986: 88,750 Ord 25p shares issued in 1-for-8 scrip. Non-voting A Ord 25p shares redesignated into Ord 25p shares and 4,888,750 Ord 25p shares issued in 1-for-1 scrip. June 1996: Ord 25p shares subdivided into 5 Ord 5p shares.

COMPANY HISTORY:

Incorporated February 1959. In July 1991 floated on the non-voting A Ord 25p shares on the market at 105p each. Up to 1991 UTV suffered a Government levy on revenue in excess of £15mstg @ 10% which was subsequently reduced to 2.5% in excess of £25mstg in 1992. This levy was replaced in 1993 when UTV successfully bid unopposed for the Northern Ireland franchise at a cost of £1,027,000 per annum indexed in line with inflation. This is renewable at UTV's option in 1999 for a further ten-year period. April 1992: An independent company TSMS appointed to sell advertising airtime which is 94% of total revenue. Nov 1992: Quoted on Dublin Stock Exchange at 242p per share. March 1994: J McGuckian highlighted that after consolidation of commercial television licensees in UK & Nth Ireland, four companies control 80% of ITV ad revenues with 7 companies controlling the balance. Sept 1995: Plans to get involved in TV3 in R of I. Feb 1996: Shares soar to £13 on bid rumours. Mercury Asset Management now holds 14%. April 1996: Fidelity sells 356,570 shares at £13 each. August 1996: Venture in TV3 aborted. Nov 1996: Mercury Asset Mgt sells 1.62m shares. Oct 1997: Scottish Media Group holds 18.2%. CanWest buys 2.7% (1.4m shares) for £3.5m. Feb 1998: CanWest now holds 29.99% after acquiring Scottish Media's holding (paid 250p per share). Sept 1998: Gained £2.5m stg from sale 17% of SES. Dec 1999: Agrees new 10-year ITC licence (5% of qualifying revenue + annual £0.55m cash; total £2.2m in first year). Feb 1999: Pays special one-off interim dividend of 35p stg. Feb 2000: Sells S.E.S. for profit of £13.4m. March 2000: Buys Direct Net Access for £4.25m. Feb 2001: Agrees to buy 60% County Media in Cork for €21.6m with option on further 40%. Dec 2001: Joins Absolute Radio UK to bid for UK radio licences. April 2002: Buys Limerick Live 95FM for €15.7m. Buys other 40% County Cork Media for €14.2m.

Share Price Sept 2001 - Sept 2002

1. €5.87 18.03.02 Final results

FINANCIAL DIARY

Interim Results Announced:	17.09.2001
Interim Dividend Payout:	05.10.2001
Annual Results Announced:	18.03.2002
Annual General Meeting:	31.05.2002
Final Dividend Payout:	05.06.2002

SHARE PRICE TREND

	High		Low	
1997	High	3.03 (Sep)	Low	1.71 (Sep)
1998	High	3.66 (Apr)	Low	2.63 (Sep)
1999	High	3.97 (Dec)	Low	2.34 (Mar)
2000	High	3.40 (Nov)	Low	3.09 (Mar)
2001	High	5.72 (Jan)	Low	3.72 (Nov)

HALF YEARLY PERFORMANCES: £'m

Six Months to	30.06.00	31.12.00	30.06.01	31.12.01
Sales	20.4	20.4	20.9	22.1
Pretax Profit	20.4 b)	6.6	6.4	5.5
Profit % Sales	100.0	32.4	30.6	24.9
b) See Ten Year Review				

TEN YEAR REVIEW: £'000stg

12 months to Dec 31	1992	1993	1994	1995	1996	1997	1998	1999	2000	2001
Turnover	28,786	27,961	31,413	34,170	34,473	34,779	37,164	38,340	40,818	42,973
Profit before tax	4,180	5,068	7,486 d)	8,196	9,017	8,272	12,478	7,814	27,013 b)	11,884
Tax	1,637	1,728	2,425	2,755	2,987	2,555	4,030	2,213	7,933	3,778
Profit after tax	2,543	3,340	5,061	5,441	6,030	5,717	8,448	5,601	19,080	8,106
Extraordinary Items	-	-	-	-	-	-	-	-	-	-
Available for Shareholders	2,543	3,340	5,061	5,441	6,030	5,717	8,448	5,601	19,080	8,106
Ordinary Dividends	1,051	1,576	2,102	12,874 e)	2,679	2,991	3,310	22,332 f)	4,572	4,835
Retained Profits	1,492	1,764	2,959	(7,433)	3,351	2,726	5,138	(16,731)	14,508	3,271
Increase (Decrease) in Reserves	1,496	1,764	2,959	(7,433)	3,351	2,726	5,138	(16,731)	14,508	3,212
Shareholders' Funds	13,093	14,857	17,816	10,383	13,734	16,460	21,598	4,867	19,375	22,587
Ordinary Dividend per Share (p stg)	2.0p	3.0p	4.0p	24.5p e)	5.1p	5.7p	6.3p	42.5p f)	8.7p	9.2p
Earnings per Share (p stg)	4.84p	6.4p	9.64p	10.4p	11.5p a)	10.9p	16.1p	10.7p	36.3p	15.4p a)

a) Based upon 52.5m shares. b) Includes profit on sale of investments +£13.4mstg. d) Includes investment profit £862,000. e) Payment of excess funds by way of one-off 20p dividend. f) Includes Special dividend of £18.4m (35p per share).

BALANCE SHEET: DECEMBER 31 2001. £'000 stg

Share Capital:		Fixed Assets		7,266
52,546,600 Ord 5p shares	2,627	Current Assets	22,859	
Reserves	19,960	Current Liabilities	30,509	
		Net Current Liabilities		(7,650)
		Medium debt		(4,045)
		Net Tangible Liabilities		(4,429)
Shareholders' Funds	22,587	Inangible Assets		27,016
		Net Assets		22,587

Comment:
Well managed but because of the big payout to shareholders in 2000 the balance sheet is looking a tad undernourished instead of looking like the cash cow that it has been over the years. However the revenue and profits rose in a year in which there was nothing but whingeing from its southern competitor, RTE.

UNIDARE plc

BUSINESS: Engineering group.
REGISTERED OFFICE: Unidare House, Richview Office Park, Clonskeagh, Dublin. Tel: 01-2837111. Fax: 01-2603177. **HEAD OFFICE:** as regd office.
SECRETARY: K Gallen.
REGISTRARS & TRANSFER OFFICE: Capita Corporate Registrars, P.O. Box 7117, Dublin.
AUDITORS: PricewaterhouseCoopers.
STOCKBROKERS: NCB Stockbrokers Ltd.
DIRECTORS: J Hayes (Chairman - 68), P Duggan (Ch Exec - 43), K Gallen (41), J McGuckian (63).
SHARE CAPITAL: Authorised: 30million Ord. €0.30 shares, 200m 'A' Ord 0.1pstg shares. **Issued:** 19,782,858 Ord. €0.30 shares and 19,782,858 'A' Ord 0.1p stg shares
STAFF: 817. **SCRIP DIVIDEND:** No

CAPITAL HISTORY:

August 1963 1-for 5 'scrip' issue. Sept. 1976 1-for-3 scrip issue. Sept. 1978 1-for-5 'scrip' issue. January 1986 reorganisation of capital wherein preference shares redeemed. June 1989: Placing of 3,000,000 Ord. 25p shares at 515p each. April 1993: rights of 1-for-2 (6,408,419 shares) at 265p each

COMPANY HISTORY:

Incorporated in November 1947 as Aberdare Electric Co. Aberdare Cables Ltd. in UK held one third equity. Name changed to Unidare in Feb. 1957. Capital considerably increased between flotation and 1963. In March 1963 Pye of Cambridge Ltd. acquired 76.5% of equity. On the same date Pye sold one-third of its newly acquired holding to Alcan Aluminium the principal supplier of aluminium to Unidare. Pye then had 51% of Unidare. Pye subsequently taken over by N.V. Philips and in December 1970 paid £1.5m for Pye's 51% of Unidare. Right up to 1986 76.5% of Unidare held in two blocks. Philips 51% and Alcan 25.5%. In March 1986 Alcan decided to place all its shares on the market and Philips put a substantial part of its holding on the market retaining 10.5%. Placing price 55p each raising £11m for the two major share-holders. Dec. 1987: Universal Welding Alloys Ltd. Ltd. Hobert Bros (GB) Ltd. acquired. Dec. 1987: purchased remaining 50% of Unidare Cables for £3m. Dec. 1987: F. Werdmolder resigns as

Chairman. J.P. Culliton appointed Chairman. Jan. 1988: Major redundancy programme leading to loss of 100 jobs. Sept. 1988: Acquisition of E. & E. Kaye Ltd. July 1989: Placed 3m shares at 515p each raising £15m. July 1989: Acquired Daalderop BV in Netherlands for Fl8.2m. Nov. 1989: Acquired Centrajet for £1.6m. Apr. 1990: Acquired Southborough for £1.4m. June 1990: Disposed of cable division of Unidare Cables for £5.9m. July 1991: Purchases Hoek Loos (HLL) for £1.5m. Sept. 1991: In talks to acquire Spanish welding company. Dec. 1991: Acquires Berry Magicoal for £1m stg. July 1992: Merger talks with Jones Group aborted. March 1993: announced £32m bid for Nasco. Rights issue to raise £16.2m. (97% Take-up). June 1994: Wire division offered for sale. July 1994: Decides to pay maximum earnout now of £7.3m for Nasco. Dec 1994: D. Rutledge resigns as Ch. Exec. May 1995: Plastics division for sale. Sells Finglas industrial estate for £5.25m. Sept 1995: Sells Unidare Environmental to Glen Dimplex for £6m stg. March 1996: IIU (D. Desmond) builds 5.3% stake at about 225p per share. July 1996: IIU reveals 8.3% stake (180p to 220p each). Aug 1996: Sells plastics division for £5.3m stg. Profits warning issued. Sept 1996: IIU now holds 13.1% (at around 175p). J. Culliton resigns as director. Feb 1997: Buys Eland Electrical for £2.65m stg. July 1997: IIU now holds 18.7%. March 1998: IIU sells out at 260p per share. Sept 1998: Sells Southborough for £5.1m. Feb 1999: J McGuckian buys 4% at 116p each. J Hayes bought 200,000 shares 116p each. P Duggan and K Gallen bought 30,000 shares each at 116p. Alliance Capital the seller. March 1999: J McGuckian buys 970,561 shares at 169p each (now holds 8.99%). D Desmond & P Casey acquire 26.6% at about 189p per share (costing £9m). Claim against Unidare by buyer of Southborough. Profits warning. May 1999: Announces purchase of Oklahoma Rig & Supply for max $60.1m. June 1999: Tirade from Beechworth (Desmond & Casey) against Board and purchase of ORS at e.g.m. Cites 3 profits warnings in 1996 plus 2 in last 4 months. Proposal to buy ORS narrowly passes (51.7% to 48.3%). July 1999: IIU (Desmond) buys 470,368 shares now holding 29.1% with Beechworth.

Share Price Sept 2001 - Sept 2002

1. €1.35 05.12.01 Final Results
2. €1.18 25.04.02 Interim Results

SECTORAL ANALYSIS: (previous year)

Sales: Distribution 89% (89%), manufacturing 11% (11%); Irl & UK 13% (15%), other 87% (85%). **Profits:** Distribution 44% (69%), manufacturing 56% (31%).

INVESTMENT PERFORMANCE

Five Year Investment Performance:	€ 896
Ten Year Investment Performance:	€ 856

HALF YEARLY PERFORMANCES: € m

Six months to:	30.09.00	31.03.01	30.09.01	31.03.02
Sales	146.1	146.1	164.1	129.9
Profits/(-) before tax	6.0	1.5	- *	(0.9)
Profits % Sales	4.1	1.0	-	-

*Includes charges -€9.5m disposal/closure/goodwill

FIVE YEAR SHARE PRICE TREND €

1997	High	3.17 (Dec)	Low	2.16 (May)
1998	High	3.81 (Apr)	Low	2.16 (Dec)
1999	High	2.76 (Apr)	Low	1.49 (Feb)
2000	High	2.65 (May)	Low	2.01 (Feb)
2001	High	2.45 (Feb)	Low	0.99 (Oct)

FINANCIAL DIARY:

Interim Results Announced:	25.04.2002
Interim Dividend Payout:	none
Final Results Announced:	05.12.2001
Annual General Meeting:	20.03.2002
Final Dividend Payout:	none

TEN YEAR REVIEW: €'000

months to September 30	1992 e)	1993 f)	1994	1995	1996	1997	1998	1999	2000	2001
Sales	144,726	132,938	215,778	192,393	166,371	159,080	176,772	171,741	281,104	293,990
Profit(loss) before Tax	6,896	5,704	(1,856) h)	10,329	5,638	8,729	10,393	8,545	10,870	1,516
Tax	1,054	1,236	92	1,958	1,887	2,374	2,772	2,354	3,395	1,942
Profit (loss) after Tax	5,842	4,468	(1,948)	8,371	3,751	6,355	7,621	6,191	7,475	(416)
Minority Interest	(465)	(368)	(137)	(382)	(231)	(273)	(318)	(45)	+128	+60
Available for Shareholders	5,377	4,100	(2,085)	7,989	3,520	6,082	7,303	6,146	7,603	(356)
Ordinary Dividend	2,555	2,466	3,577	4,257	4,235	4,370	4,545	4,748	4,847	593
Retained Profit	2,822	1,634	(5,662)	3,732	(715)	1,712	2,757	1,398	2,756	(949)
Increase (Decrease) in Reserves	(2,084)	876	(11,661) g)	4,718	(744)	1,813	4,265	4,138 a)	10,238 c)	(2,871)
Shareholders' Funds	42,371	45,281	33,689	38,542	37,798	39,611	43,875	47,718	57,956	55,085
Ordinary Dividend per Share (€)	0.199	0.128	0.184	0.214	0.214	0.221	0.23	0.24	0.245	0.03
Earnings per Share (€)	0.420	0.248	-	0.404	0.178	0.307	0.37	0.31	0.384 b)	-

a) Currency gain +€2.4m. b) Based upon 19.8m shares. c) Currency gain +€7.5m. d) Currency loss -€4.3m, asset profits +€4.7m, grants -€1.5m e) Year end December. f) Nine months to Sept. g) Property devaluation -€0.9m; currency loss -€1.7m; goodwill net -€4.4m. h) -€9.7m write-off re wire closure.

BALANCE SHEET: SEPTEMBER 30 2001. € m

Comment:

A dreadful investment over 5 or 10 years.

D Desmond must be waiting patiently for something to improve.

Share Capital:			Fixed Assets		14.5
19,782,858 Ord. 25p shares			Current Assets	94.5	
and 19,782,858 "A" Ord			Current Liabilities	46.2	
0.1p stg shares		6.0	Net Current Assets		48.3
Reserves		49.1	Medium Debt		(33.2)
			Minority		(1.4)
Shareholders' Funds		55.1	Net Tangible Assets		28.2
			Intangibles		26.9
			Net Assets		55.1

UNITED DRUG PLC

BUSINESS: Pharmaceutical wholesaling.
REGISTERED OFFICE: James' Street, Ballina, Co. Mayo.
HEAD OFFICE: United Drug House, Belgard Road, Dublin.
Tel: 01-4598877. Fax: 01-4596893.
SECRETARY: A Ralph.
REGISTRARS & TRANSFER OFFICE: Computershare
Investor Services (Ireland) Ltd, Heron House, Corrig Road,
Sandyford Ind Estate, Dublin.
PRINCIPAL BANKERS: ABN-AMRO Bank, Ulster Bank
Group, Bank of Ireland, First Trust Bank.
AUDITORS: KPMG.
SOLICITORS: Arthur Cox. **STOCKBROKERS:** J & E Davy.
DIRECTORS: M Rafferty (Chairman - 70), L Fitzgerald
(Ch Exec - 38), P Caffrey, P Delany (69), P Digan (46),
M Durcan, D Egan (69), R Kells,
K McGowan, B McGrane, S Simms (50).
SHARE CAPITAL: Authorised:
30,000,000 25p Ord. shares. **Issued:**
28,971,901 Ord 25p shares and
2,225,438 redeemable Ord 25p shares
(treated as treasury shares).
STAFF: 1,445
SCRIP DIVIDEND: Yes
WEB SITE: www.united-drug.ie

UNITED DRUG PLC

CAPITAL HISTORY:

November 1985 scrip issue 1,251,830 Ord.
50p shares. 1,606,190 Ord. 50p shares

Martin Rafferty

issued to BWG in clearance of loans of £1.6m.
2,163,000 Ord. 50p shares offered in Dec. 1985 at
100p each. February 1989 allotted 297,934 Ord.
50p shares at 100p to certain Directors. February
1989 Ord. 50p shares subdivided into Ord. 25p
shares. February 1989 placing of 2,583,470 Ord
25p shares on stock market at 107p each. Nov.
1990: Issued 312,500 Ord. 25p shares part payment Trinity Instruments. Nov 1992: Issues
2,823,654 Ord. 25p shares for Alchem at €2.35
each. May 1993: 2,730,405 Ord 25p shares offered
by way of 1-for-5 rights at €2.20 each. June 1994:
Issues 333,710 Ord 25p shares re purchase of
Smith & Co Derry at €2.60p each. Aug 1995:
Issued 350,000 Ord 25p shares at €3.17 each part
payment for Novapath and Vector. December 1996:
Rights issue (1-for-4) 4,456,376 Ord 25p shares at

€3.68 each. Dec 1997: 3,657,888 Ord
25p shares to be issued re Dublin
Drug. May 2000: Issued 224,085 Ord
25p shares @ €7.62 per share re purchase of Ashfield Healthcare.

COMPANY HISTORY:

Incorporated 1948. Originally purchased
by BWG Group in the 70's which itself in
1984 was acquired by Irish Distillers. In
January 1986 management bought out
United Drug from IDG. In Dec. 1987 purchased Ulster Anaesthetics. In January
1988 bought Nuns Island
Pharmaceuticals. Feb. 1989 placing on
stock market at 107p raises £2.52m.
April 1989: IDG placed 20% of equity
with institutions. July 1989: B. Rogan

resigns as Director. Oct. 1990: Acquired Trinity
Instruments for cash and Loan Notes for £775,000.
Nov. 1990: Acquired Irish Photo Marketing Ltd. (Ilford
and Canon) for nominal consideration. March 1992:
Achieves full listing on Stock Exchange. Sept. 1992:
Bid 13 United Drug shares for every 8 Alchem shares
and 3p stg. loyalty bonus for holding United Drug
shares for at least 3 months. Valued Alchem at £5.2m.
March 1993: Full listing in London and Dublin. May
1993: Rights issue raises €5.6m (80% acceptances).
June 1994: Buys R. Smith & Co (Derry) for €2.2m stg
shares and cash. Aug 1995: Buys Novapath Supplies
and Vector Scientific for €2.7m. July 1997: Buys Dublin
Drug for €19.2m. Dec 1997: Joint venture with Co-
operative Animal Health for veterinary medicines. May
2000: Buys Ashfield Healthcare (UK) for €21m. April
2002: Buys New Splint (UK) for €11.4m. Sept 2002:
Buys Intraveno Healthcare for €13.3m.

Share Price Sept 2001 - Sept 2002

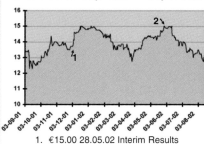

1. €15.00 28.05.02 Interim Results
2. €13.80 04.12.01 Final Results

FINANCIAL DIARY

Interim Results Announced:	28.05.2002
Interim Dividend Payout:	02.08.2002
Final Results Announced:	04.12.2001
Annual General Meeting:	13.02.2002
Final Dividend Payout:	13.02.2002

FOUR YEAR SHARE PRICE TREND €

1997	High	5.54 (July)	Low	4.06 (Jan)
1998	High	7.87 (July)	Low	5.26 (Jan)
1999	High	7.22 (Jan)	Low	6.01 (July)
2000	High	10.89 (Dec)	Low	6.89 (July)
2001	High	15.00 (Dec)	Low	10.90 (Jan)

HALF YEARLY PERFORMANCES € m

Six months to:	30.09.00	31.03.01	30.09.01	31.03.02
Sales	367.8	407.2	436.0	475.5
Profits before Tax	10.0	10.2	11.8	12.4
Profit % Sales	2.7	2.5	2.7	2.6

SECTORAL ANALYSIS

Sales: R of I 67% (65%), UK 33% (35%).

INVESTMENT PERFORMANCE

Five Year Investment Performance:	€ 3,703
Ten Year Investment Performance:	€ 7,926

TEN YEAR REVIEW: € m

12 months to 30 Sept	1992	1993	1994	1995	1996	1997	1998	1999	2000	2001
Sales	97.069	173.381	214.290	271.384	314.357	383.422	515.8	600.9	720.547	843.248
Profit before Tax	3.923	4.367	5.594	6.419	7.626	9.299	11.1	14.9	18.065	22.038
Tax	1.445	1.243	1.891	2.155	2.383	3.033	2.6	3.5	3.934	4.439
Profit after Tax	2.478	3.124	3.703	4.264	5.243	6.266	8.5	11.4	14.131	17.599
Minorities	(1)	-	-	-	-	-	-	-	-	-
Available for Shareholders	2.477	3.124	3.703	4.264	5.243	6.266	8.5	11.4	14.131	17.599
Ordinary Dividends	0.919	1.627	1.609	1.790	2.034	2.871	3.4	4.0	4.825	5.971
Retained Profit	1.558	1.497	2.094	2.474	3.209	3.395	5.1	7.4	9.306	11.628
Increase (Decrease) in Reserves	1.554	9.569	2.258	(0.691) e)	3.998	20.381 f)	6.9 g)	12.1 a)	17.0 h)	16.6 i)
Shareholders' Funds	13.255	24.597d)	27.023	26.525	30.616	52.502	60.8	73.2	90.547	107.399
Ordinary Dividend per Share (€)	0.085	0.089	0.095	0.103	0.114	0.126	0.14	0.159	0.183	0.219
Earnings per Share (€)	0.22	0.21	0.216	0.243	0.286	0.293	0.35	0.455	0.54	0.65 b)

(a) Share premium +€2.5m. (b) Based on 26.9m shares (2.2m treasury shares are excluded. d) Share premium €10.5m, goodwill w/o -€3m. e) Goodwill w/o €4.2m.
f) Share premium +€15.4m; currency gain +€1.8m. g) Share premium +€11.8m, goodwill w/o -€7.6m, treasury shares purchased -€11.7m. h) Share premium +€5.1m. i) Share premium +€4.3m

BALANCE SHEET: SEPTEMBER 30 2001. € m

Share Capital:		Fixed Assets	53.9
29,521,592 Ord		Financial Assets	3.6
€0.32 shares (incl		Current Assets	247.6
2,225,438 treasury shares)	9.4	Current Liabilities	188.8
Reserves	98.0	Net Current Assets	58.8
		Medium Debt	(31.4)
Shareholders' Funds	107.4	Net Tangible Assets	84.9
		Intangibles	22.5
		Net Assets	107.4

Comment:

An excellent 5 and 10 year track
record; the dividend has increase
by 2.8 times and the earnings pe
share have grown by 3.25 times
over the 10 year period. This type
of investment would do wonders t
a pension portfolio.

The first six months of the 2002 financial year has seen another strong performance by United Drug. All business divisions - Pharma Wholesale, Contract Distribution and Contract Sales Outsourcing - reported further progress during the period.

United Drug Plc

In total, turnover increased by 16% to €569 million for the six months with operating profits increasing by 2% and pre-tax profits (before goodwill amortisation) of €12.97 million are 20% ahead of the first half of the 2001 financial year. Fully diluted earnings per share (before goodwill amortisation) are up by 5% to 37.48 cent and an interim dividend of 7.0 cent per share has been declared – a 14% increase on the 2001 interim dividend.

This strong performance has been driven by a number of factors including: continuing growth of the Irish pharmaceutical market; market share gains in United Drug Wholesale; reduction in operating cost ratios following investment in infrastructure and technology; a strong contribution from our medical & scientific business unit; and further progress by Ashfield Healthcare in the contract sales market in the UK. The combination of these factors has ensured that United Drug has continued its development, both financially and strategically.

Pharma Wholesale

There were a number of elements combining to drive our wholesale business forward in the period.

Government spending on health and drugs in the Republic of Ireland continues to lag behind average EU spend per capita. However, health spending now has a strong cross-political focus and looks set to substantially increase in coming years to close that gap.

To enable us to meet this growing demand for our services, we have invested significantly in our infrastructure. Last year saw the commissioning of our new automated warehouse in Magna Park in Dublin. In the current year, we have constructed and commissioned a 30,000 square foot semi-automated warehouse facility in Ballina.

In Northern Ireland, Sangers maintained its clear market leadership position. Sales growth was in line with the market, in a market with different growth characteristics to the Republic of Ireland market. Sales increases and expenses held at the same level as last year have collectively resulted in a satisfactory improvement in profits.

Sangers Distribution and Pemberton also performed strongly during the period with good growth in both turnover and profits.

Contract Distribution Outsourcing

Our Contract Distribution Outsourcing (CDO) business in Ireland, United Drug Distributors, continues to grow strongly on the back of very healthy overall market growth. Sales and profits were at record levels and this was achieved whilst investing in a major re-engineering process in our main Dublin facility.

UniDrug, our CDO joint venture in the UK market, increased its turnover during the period by 9% due to growth in the pharmaceutical market and new business. Pre-tax profits for the period advanced by 3%, below the growth in turnover, due to additional investment in quality procedures to meet and exceed all manufacturers expectations and also increased insurance costs in the aftermath of September 11. These cost factors will not be as significant in future months and new contracts signed will contribute to the second half of the year, so a stronger full year performance is expected.

Our consumer distribution businesses, Pemberton Marketing and Blackhall Pharmaceuticals, recorded good growth in turnover and profits during the period under review. Significant progress has been made in operational efficiency and business development.

Our medical & scientific business - trading as Unitech in the Republic of Ireland and Ulster Anaesthetics in Northern Ireland - made significant progress during the period on a number of fronts. Our core business has considerably exceeded last year's results in terms of both sales and profits.

In April, United Drug announced the acquisition of New Splint Limited. Based in Hook in Hampshire, New Splint provides marketing, selling and distribution support to international manufacturers of medical device products, mainly orthopaedic implants, to the UK market. Consideration for the acquisition is Stg. £7 million, paid on completion,

plus an additional consideration of up to Stg. £1 million payable on achievement of agreed profit targets for the 12 months to 31 March 2003. Strategically, the acquisition of New Splint gives United Drug a foothold and vital infrastructure in the UK.

Contract Sales Outsourcing

Ashfield Healthcare, our Contract Sales Outsourcing company, continues to be the second largest and fastest growing contract sales outsourcing company in the UK market and has put in a very strong performance and further increased its market share during the period. During the last six months new contracts were won with Eli Lilly, Fujisawa, Schering Plough, BMS and Roche.

The demand for contract sales outsourcing services from pharmaceutical manufacturers worldwide is forecast to grow steadily over the coming years. We will continue to look at opportunities to grow our business in new markets and further develop our international contract sales outsourcing activities.

Conclusion

It is very pleasing to be able to report good progress in all areas of the business, a strong financial performance and the further implementation of our strategic development during the first half of the 2002 financial year. These achievements leave United Drug well positioned to continue its development for the remainder of the 2002 financial year, and beyond. The achievement of this performance has only been brought about through the skill, determination and enthusiasm of management and staff throughout the United Drug organisation. To all of these people I would like to express my thanks and admiration for their efforts over the last 6 months.

Liam Fitzgerald
Chief Executive

Liam Fitzgerald
Chief Executive

I t is very pleasing to be able to report good progress in all areas of the business, a strong financial performance and the further implementation of our strategic development during the first half of the 2002 financial year.

UNITED DRUG PLC

VIRIDIAN GROUP plc

(Formerly NORTHERN IRELAND ELECTRICITY plc)

BUSINESS: Procurement, transmission, distribution and supply (but not generation) of electricity in Northern Ireland.
REGISTERED OFFICE: P.O.Box 2, Danesfort House, 120 Malone Road, Belfast BT9 5HT.
HEAD OFFICE: as above. Tel: 028 90661100.
Fax: 028 90663579. **SECRETARY:** I Thom.
REGISTRAR & TRANSFER OFFICE: Capita IRG plc, Bourne House, 34 Beckenham Road, Beckenham, Kent BR3 4TV.
PRINCIPAL BANKERS: Bank of Ireland.
AUDITORS: Ernst & Young LLP.
SOLICITORS: Cameron McKenna.
STOCKBROKERS: Credit Suisse First Boston de Zoete & Bevan; UBS Warburg; Goodbody Stockbrokers. A low cost share dealing service is offered by Barclays Stockbrokers Ltd; contact The Shareholder Relations Dept. at Viridian plc head office.
DIRECTORS: P Rogerson (Chairman - 58), P H Haren (Ch Exec - 52), H McCracken (53), L Rouse (55), D Smyth (53), P Bourke (46), D Lewis (52).
SHARE CAPITAL: Authorised: 216 million Ord 25p shares; one special rights Red. Pref. £1 share. **Issued:** 132,106,291 Ord 25p shares; one Special share.
STAFF: 3,139. **SCRIP DIVIDEND:** No

CAPITAL HISTORY:

Incorporated October 1991. Feb 1992 49,998 Ord £1 shares (25p paid) issued at par to Dept of Economic Development. June 1993 these shares were fully paid up. 50,000 £1 Ord shares subdivided into 200,000 Ord 25p shares. 164,400,000 Ord 25p shares allotted at par to Dept of Ec. Dev. Share flotation of 164.6m shares at 220p stg each. Aug 1995: Bought Back 24,532,158 Ord 25p shares at 397p each and cancelled them. Dec 1997: NIE cancel 131,009,784 Ord 25p shares; consideration was £186.6m stg; For every 10 NIE Ord 25p shares 9 new Viridian Ord 25p shares plus 10 Viridian loan notes of 47.4p each (redemption 2003).

COMPANY HISTORY:

The first commercial supply of electricity in Northern Ireland was provided by a private company in 1982. Prior to 1931 the industry was operated by numerous local authorities and private companies using a variety of technologies. Existing undertakings were acquired by the Electricity Board for N.I. following the Electricity (Supply) Act (N.I.) 1931. The existing undertakings of the Belfast Corporation and the Londonderry Corporation were not affected by this legislation. In 1948 the N.I. Joint Electricity Committee was set up to co-ordinate generation and the supply of electricity. It was superseded in 1967 by the N.I. Joint Electricity Authority. In 1973 the Service was established to replace the 4 predecessor undertakings and in 1986 assumed the name Northern Ireland Electricity. Between April 1981 and March 1990 electricity tariffs in Northern Ireland were linked to those in Great Britain. Since then there has been a move towards fully cost-reflective tariffs. April 1992 4 N.I. power stations sold to private sector creating current structure whereby Northern Ireland Electricity is not responsible for generation but is responsible for procurement, transmission, distribution and supply. June 1993: Offer 3.9 times oversubscribed. First day of dealing in partly paid (100p) shares closed at 126p. 51m shares traded. May 1995: Flotation strongly criticised being priced too cheaply and that NIE not well served by its financial advisers headed by NM Rothschild. Floated at 220p per share, valued at £362m, shares now sell at 342p valuing NIE at £563m. Aug 1995: Bought back 24.53 million NIE shares at 397p each being 14.9% of equity for £97.4m. Shares cancelled. Institutional holdings now 41%. Aug 1996: Proposal by Ofreg to reduce electricity cost in Nth Ireland by 6%. July 1997: Windfall budget tax to cost £44m stg. Aug 1997: NIE to oppose Ofreg price cuts of 29%. Aug 1997: Sells appliance retailing business. Jan 1998: Shareholders get £67m cash bonus in Loan Notes. Feb 1998: Changes name to Viridian Plc. Nov 1998: Buys site (joint venture with CRH) at Huntstown Quarry, Co Dublin for gas power plant. Dec 1998: £9m goodwill payments suffering storm supply difficulties. Jan 1998: Discussions with Canatxx (US) re gas pipeline Ireland/Britain. March 1999: Viridian moves into telecoms (with Energis) - shares jump 52p on the news. April 1999: Viridian accuses ESB of 'abusing its dominant position'. ESB eyes major Nth Ireland customers. May 1999: NIE to connect to Scottish Power (costing about £100mstg net). Jan 2000: Permission for power station granted in North Dublin (Viridian/CRH venture). May 2000: Acquires First Software and Specialist Computer Programming in UK. August 2000: Buys Derry insurance broker. Sept 2000: Buys Birmingham insurance broker. Nov 2000: Buys CRH's 49.9% of Huntstown. Feb 2001: Turkish company to build Viridian power plant at Huntstown. Jan 2002: DOE to examine clawback of value of former assets in NIE which resulted in privatisation proceeds of £774m stg (£356mstg from power stations and £418m stg from flotation). March 2002: Takes 'hit' of £26m stg impairment in Sx3 and £22.3m in Stentor. April 2002: Sells Open+Direct for £111.4m stg.

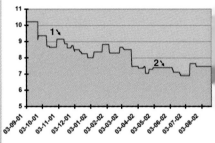

Share Price Sept 2001 - Sept 2002

1. €9.13 13.11.01 Interim Results
2. €7.40 16.05.02 Final Results

FINANCIAL DIARY

Interim Results Announced:	13.11.2001
Interim Dividend Payout:	28.03.2001
Final Results Announced:	16.05.2002
Annual General Meeting:	05.07.2002
Final Dividend Payout:	01.10.2002

SECTORAL ANALYSIS: (previous year)

Sales: Power procurement 36% (34%), distribution 18% (19%), supply 46% (47%).
Profit: Power procurement 5% (6%), distribution 85% (82%), other 10% (12%).

SHARE PRICE TREND €

1998 High	10.42 (Nov)	Low	8.96 (Apr)
1999 High	10.92 (Mar)	Low	8.90 (Sep)
2000 High	12.95 (Oct)	Low	9.20 (Jan)
2001 High	11.35 (June)	Low	8.00 (Dec)

HALF YEARLY PERFORMANCES: £'m stg

Six months to	30.09.00	31.03.01	30.09.01	31.03.02
Turnover	241.9	360.9	305.3	424.7
Pretax (loss) profit	40.9	44.3	26.7	(34.2)
Profit % Sales	16.9	12.3	8.7	-

TEN YEAR REVIEW: £'m stg

12 months to March 31	1993 c)	1994	1995	1996	1997	1998 c)	1999	2000	2001 c)	2002
Turnover	452.4	481.9	497.7	524.7	560.9	500.4	512.2	566.3	602.8	730.0
Profit /(Loss) before tax	64.1	74.9	86.8	107.4	59.8 e)	76.7	86.6	89.5	85.2	(7.5) b)
Tax	15.0	14.5	19.3	20.2	29.5	57.9 f)	16.2	12.2	11.6	15.1
Profit/ (Loss) after Tax	49.1	60.4	67.5	87.2	30.3	18.8	70.4	77.3	73.6	(22.6)
Extraordinary Items	-	-	-	-	-	-	-	-	-	-
Available for Shareholders	49.1	60.4	67.5	87.2	30.3	18.8	70.4	77.3	73.6	(22.6)
Ordinary Dividend	16.5	18.8	22.1	24.3	29.3	29.7	33.0	36.3	40.0	41.4
Retained profit (loss)	32.6	41.6	45.4	62.9	1.0	(10.9)	37.4	41.0	33.6	(64.0)
Increase (Decrease) in Reserves	n/a	(28.4)	45.5	(29.1) d)	1.3	(66.3) g)	37.6	41.0	34.6	(61.7)
Shareholders Funds	326.2	297.8	343.3	308.1	309.4	240.8	288.3	329.3	363.9	234.5
Ord Dividend per Share (p stg)	10.02p	11.39p	13.4p	19.0p	20.9p	23.0p	25.3p	27.8p	30.61p	31.42p
Earnings per Share (p stg)	27.8p	36.7p	41.0p	58.8p	21.6p	13.4p	54.6	59.4p	56.4p a)	-

a) Based upon 130.5m shares. b) Includes various 'impairment' charges of £48.3m stg. c) Figures subsequently restated. d) Purchase and cancellation of own shares -£98.2m. e) After charging exceptional restructuring costs £50.6m. f) Includes Windfall Tax of £42.7m; issue of loan notes -£69m.

BALANCE SHEET: MARCH 31 2002. £ m stg

Share Capital:		Tangible Assets		1,030.0
		Financial Assets		1.4
131,386,206 Ord 25p shares	33.0	Current Assets	329.0	
		Current Liabilities	390.8	
		Net Current Liabilities		(61.8)
Reserves	201.5	Deferred income		(199.5)
		Medium debt		(595.5)
		Net Tangible Assets		174.6
		Intangibles		59.9
Shareholders' Funds	234.5	Net Assets		234.5

Comment:

Deviating from the core business of electricity has cost Viridian dearly and the balance sheet has suffered accordingly. It will take some effort to get back up to the profitability level of 1996 especially with Ofreg breathing down their necks.

VISLINK plc

(Formerly Silvermines Group plc)

BUSINESS: Manufactures electrical components.
REGISTERED OFFICE: Marlborough House, Charnham Lane, Hungerford, Berkshire.
HEAD OFFICE: as above. Tel: 0044 (0) 1488685500.
Fax: 0044 (0) 488685501. **SECRETARY:** J Trumper.
REGISTRARS & TRANSFER OFFICE: Computershare Investor Services plc, PO Box 82, The Pavilions, Bridgewater Road, Bristol. **PRINCIPAL BANKERS:** Barclays Bank.
AUDITORS: PricewaterhouseCoopers. **SOLICITORS:** Whitney Moore & Keller; Anderson Legal, Garretts. **STOCKBROKERS:** Investec Henderson Crosthwaite; Davy Stockbrokers.
DIRECTORS: A Morton (Chairman - 61), I Scott-Gall (Ch Exec - 54), J Trumper (41), E Walters (58), T Trotter (44).
SHARE CAPITAL: Authorised: 126 million Ord. 2.5p shares. **Issued:** 102,072,848 Ord. 2.5p shares.
STAFF: 541. **SCRIP DIVIDEND:** No

CAPITAL HISTORY:

In 1973 capital reduced by writing down the Ord. 5p shares to Ord. 2.5p shares. Total number of shares in issue remained unchanged. Sept. 1973 240,000 issued to Jan Badeni in return for his holding in Newbridge Holdings. June 1980 'rights' issue of 20-for-7 at 100p (4m shares issued). March 1985 'scrip' issue 1-for-4. Oct. 1986 3,826,531 Ord. 2.5p shares issued re acquisition of PGM Holdings Ltd. June 1987 placing 725,000 at 99p each Ord. 2.5p shares re acquisition of 50% of Irish Cold Stores. August 1987 placing of 500,000 Ord. 2.5p shares at 195p each re acquisition of property. Feb. 1988 placed 1 million Ord. 2.5p shares at 165p each re purchase of Burdon & Miles. Placing of 7.5m new Ord. 2.5p shares at 142.5p each to raise £11m. Rights issue of 7,051,728 (1 for 10) Ord. share at 142.5p each to raise £7m. April 1989: issued 415,856 Ord. 2.5p shares as additional consideration re acquisition of PGM Holdings Limited. January 1990, 1,552,381 Ord. 2.5p shares issued for Muirhead Vactric. June 1992: Issued 494,545 Ord 2.5p Ord shares to for Elequip at 36.97p each. June 1993: Issued 183,908 Ord 2.5p shares part payment for Norcroft Dynamics. Feb 1994: Issued 11,114,859 Ord 5p shares for Molynyx. March 1994: 20,348,972 Ord 5p shares issued in placing and open offer (5-for-8) at 55p each. Jan 1996: Placed 3,201,100 Ord 2.5p shares at 61.5p each. Nov 1996: Placed 16,805,775 Ord 2.5p shares at 78p each. Dec 1997: 7,617,850 Ord 2.5p shares issued re purchase of Active Image Plc. Issued 19,995 warrants to preference shareholders to purchase 80p up to 31.12.99. April 2000: Issued 1.2m Ord 2.5p shares @ 135pstg each on purchase of Advent Communications Ltd. July 2000: 7,759,000 Ord 2.5p shares placed @ 58pstg each. Dec 2000: 101,376,768 Ord 2.5pstg shares issued (1-for-1) on relocating as a UK co.

COMPANY HISTORY:

Incorporated in 1948 and name changed to Silvermines in 1968. Formed originally to acquire mineral bearing properties at Silvermines, Co. Tipperary. 1964 Silvermines obtained 25% stake in Mogul of Ireland. Mining of lead/zinc concentrates commenced in 1968. Jan 1973 first dividend paid. 1977 acquired 26% of Anglian Windows for £496,000. 1981 acquired 24.7% interest in overriding Royalty on Marathon acreage. 1981 Silvermines halved its holding in Aran Energy to 9.45%, earning a capital profit of £2.05m. April 1983 disposed of its remaining 6.05 million shares in Aran realising £750,000. June 1983 acquired 9.7% of Falcon Resources (1 million shares at 25p stg). Feb. 1984 acquired 12.3% of Tuskar Resources. Oct. 1984 sold 500,000 shares in Falcon Resources; held on to 1 million shares. Acquired 5% of Falcon-Andrau Energy Co. 1984 Drilling Programme for 1 million dollars. 1985 acquired a 35.5% interest in Ardmore Petroleum. Sold stake in Anglian Windows for a total of £10.2m. Acquired 10% interest in PGM Ballscrews for £365,000. Oct. 1986 acquired 100% of PGM Ballscrews (the 90% cost £4.2m plus a further £600,000 stg in 1988).1987: Acquired W.E. Sykes (1986) Ltd. for Stg£1.1m. 1987: Acquired a 75% interest in Solid State Induction for stg£75,000 and Elequip Limited for stg£1.65m. June 1987: Purchased 50% of Irish Cold Stores for £1 million stg. August 1987: Purchased Dolphin House for £1.6m. Jan. 1988: Purchased Johnson Precision Ltd. of Nottingham for IR£952,000. Feb. 1988: Acquired Burdon & Miles for IR£1.65m. June 1988: Complete takeover of Detroit based National Broach & Machine Co. for $27m., payment to be phased over three years. August 1988: Acquires J & T Electrical Controls in the U.K. for stg £0.533m. February 1989: T.P. Mahoney resigns from board. April 1989: Sell 5m shares in Tuskar Resources. April 1989: K. Baker appointed Chief Executive. May 1989: Acquires Marine House, Dublin 2 for £5.5m cash. Nov. 1989: F. Traynor resigns as Mgr. Dir. Jan. 1990: Purchase Muirhead Vactric for £3.3m. Feb. 1990: Sold 12.5% interest in Marathon Royalty. April 1990: Sold Stillorgan property. August 1990: Sold 24% of Marathon producing Royalty; sold interest in Irish Cold Stores. September 1990: Sold Tallaght property. Dec. 1990: F. Traynor resigns as Director. March 1991: Sold St. Clair Industries and National Broach & Machine for $36m (IR£21.2m). Profit after costs and exchange rate variation approx. £1m. Aug 1991: Bid feelers received. Dec 1991: Takeover talks aborted. May 1992: Dalney and Sykes sold for £0.6m stg. Aug 1992: Sold PGM Group for £3.1m stg. Dec 1992: Sold Burdon & Miles for £0.9mstg. June 1993: Acquires Norcroft Dynamics for £400,000 in cash and shares. Sept 1993: EGM wrote off £6.2m in P&L A/c against Share Premium A/c. Nov 1993: Sold Traffic Controls for £1.8m. Jan 1994: Sold Dolphin House for £1.9m. May 1994: Acquires Molynyx for £5.1m. Jan 1996: Bought Falcon Equipment and Pickering Controls for £1.75m. Feb 1996: Marine House sold for £4.4m. Nov 1996: Bought Continental Microwave Group for £10.3m. April 1997: Took 49% interest (for £3.7m) in Automotive Motion Technology Ltd and sells £5.6m of related business to it. July 1997: Bought Hunting Aviation for £2.2m. Oct 1997: Bought Deakin Davenset Rectifiers for £1.05m. Dec 1997:

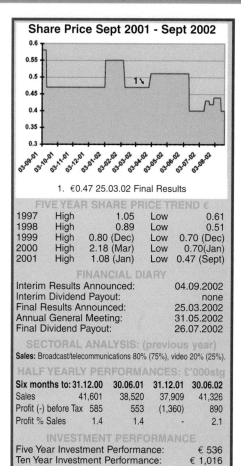

Share Price Sept 2001 - Sept 2002

1. €0.47 25.03.02 Final Results

FIVE YEAR SHARE PRICE TREND €

1997	High	1.05	Low	0.61
1998	High	0.89	Low	0.51
1999	High	0.80 (Dec)	Low	0.70 (Dec)
2000	High	2.18 (Mar)	Low	0.70(Jan)
2001	High	1.08 (Jan)	Low	0.47 (Sept)

FINANCIAL DIARY

Interim Results Announced:	04.09.2002
Interim Dividend Payout:	none
Final Results Announced:	25.03.2002
Annual General Meeting:	31.05.2002
Final Dividend Payout:	26.07.2002

SECTORAL ANALYSIS: (previous year)

Sales: Broadcast/telecommunications 80% (75%), video 20% (25%).

HALF YEARLY PERFORMANCES: £'000stg

Six months to:	31.12.00	30.06.01	31.12.01	30.06.02
Sales	41,601	38,520	37,909	41,326
Profit (-) before Tax	585	553	(1,360)	890
Profit % Sales	1.4	1.4	-	2.1

INVESTMENT PERFORMANCE

Five Year Investment Performance:	€ 536
Ten Year Investment Performance:	€ 1,016

Bought Active Imaging for £4.3m. May 1998: Riada replaced by Davys as stockbrokers. July 1998: Bought Multipoint Communications for £0.85mstg. July 1998: Profits warning issued. April 1999: Unconfirmed MBO offer at 50p per share rejected. C Jansen exits. Nov 1999: TT Holdings offloads its 6% holding. Sept 1999: Sells aerospace business for £13.9m. Sells its electrical division for £5.5mstg. Oct 1999: Further asset sales bring total to £28.1mstg. Dec 1999: Changes name to Vislink plc. April 2000: Buys Advent Communications for £13.3mstg. July 2000: Buys Microwave Radio Communications for $18.9m/£12.5mstg. Dec 2000: Changed to UK based company.

TEN YEAR REVIEW: £'000 stg

months to December 31	1992	1993	1994	1995	1996	1997	1998	1999	2000	2001
Sales	36,765	27,204	44,549	54,009	65,278	87,739	114,178	82,153	61,045	76,429
Profit (Loss) before Tax	(3,233)	1,571	2,560	3,514	4,144	5,569	(726)	(21,170) k)	1,007	(807) c)
Tax Charge	177	566	367	828	1,000	1,350	(770)	679	245	+76
Goodwill	130	-	-	-	-	-	-	-	-	-
Profit (Loss) after Tax	(3,540)	1,005	2,193	2,686	3,144	4,219	(1,496)	(21,849)	762	(731)
Extraordinary Item	(6,480)	-	-	-	-	-	-	-	-	-
Available for Shareholders	(10,020)	1,005	2,193	2,686	3,144	4,219	(1,496)	(21,849)	762	(731)
Ordinary Dividend	324	163	640	763	1,033	1,219	1,377	275	405	101
Retained Profit	(10,344)	842	1,553	1,923	2,111	3,000	(2,873)	(22,124)	357	(832)
Increase (Decrease) in Reserves	(8,537) f)	(1,668) g)	5,002 j)	2,126	10,792 h)	(1,516) a)	(3,107)	(2,161) m)	6,524 b)	(717)
Shareholders' Funds	16,557	14,894	20,683	22,397	33.688	32,339	29,233	27,072	33,596	32,879
Ordinary Dividend per share (p stg)	1.0p	0.5p	1.0p	1.15p	1.3p	1.45p	1.5p	0.3p	0.4p	0.10p
Earnings per share (p stg)	-	3.1p	3.8p	4.2p	4.52p	5.02p d)	-	-	0.8p d)	-

Share premium +£3.2m; goodwill w/o -£7.4m. b) Merger reserve +£5.4m. c) Includes stock write-down -£2.2mstg. d) Based upon 96.6m shares. f) Goodwill transfer +£3.2m; currency loss -£1.5m. g) Goodwill w/o -£3.7m; currency uplift +£1.1m. h) Share premium +£14m; goodwill w/o -£4.6m. j) Goodwill -£6.8m; share premium +£10.8m; currency loss -£0.6m. k) Includes loss on sale of businesses -£20.3m. m) High Court approves write-down of goodwill £23.8m.

BALANCE SHEET: DECEMBER 31 2001. £'000 stg

Comment:

It always seems to be 'jam tomorrow but never jam today' for Vislink. The electronic hardware for television these days seems to be intertwined with the digital versus analogue war.

The changeover by 2010 in the UK does not seem to be practically attainable from today's realistic viewpoint.

Share Capital:		Fixed Assets		6,047
101,376,768 Ord. 2.5p Shares	2,534	Current Assets	34,850	
		Current Liabilities	18,828	
Reserves	30,345	Net Current Assets		16,022
		Medium Debt		(11,155)
		Net Tangible Assets		10,914
		Intangibles		21,965
Shareholders' Funds	32,879	Net Assets		32,879

WATERFORD WEDGWOOD plc

BUSINESS: Manufacture of Waterford Crystal, Wedgwood china, All-Clad cookware.
REGISTERED OFFICE: Kilbarry, Waterford. Tel: 051-73311. Fax: 051-74052. **DUBLIN OFFICE:** 1/2 Upper Hatch Street, Dublin. Tel: 01-4781855; Fax: 01-4784863. **SECRETARY:** P Dowling. **REGISTRARS & TRANSFER OFFICE:** Capita Corporate Registrars plc, Manor Street, Dublin.
PRINCIPAL BANKERS: Bank of Ireland. **AUDITORS:** PricewaterhouseCoopers. **SOLICITORS:** William Fry.
DIRECTORS: Sir A J F O'Reilly (Chairman - 67), P R O'Donoghue (President & CEO - 60), R Barnes (55), G Dempsey (75), L Glucksman, P Goulandris (55), C Johnson (63), O Kusel (52), C McGillivary (56), K McGoran (68), S Michaels, R Niehaus (48), Lady O'Reilly (53), A O'Reilly Jnr (39), B Patterson (59), D Sculley (57), A Wedgwood (66), Lord Wedgwood, J Foley, P Cameron.
SHARE CAPITAL: Authorised: One billion Ord. €0.06 shares. **Issued:** 758,304,732 Ord. €0.06 shares. There are also income shares arising out of the acquisition of Wedgwood.
Authorised: One billion income shares of 1p sterling each. **Issued:** 758,163,220 income shares of 1p sterling each. One ADR = 10 W'ford W'wood stock units.
STAFF: 9,743. **SCRIP DIVIDEND:** Yes
WEB SITE: www.waterfordwedgwood.com

Bottle Co. Floated off separately in 1966. 1970 acquired J. Aynsley & Sons for approx £1m. July 1971 took 60% of Switzers Group. In 1971 Waterford acquired John Hinde. In 1974 acquired Smith Group. 1982 purchased remaining 40% of Waterford-Wuidart Ltd., its UK distributor for £905,000. Sold its 25% stake in Memory (Ire) Ltd. for £870,000. August 1984 McGrath interests sell their 20% holding in Waterford to Globe Investments. July 1986 raised £29.2m from American Depositary shares. Oct. 1986 completed sell off of Smith Group. Nov. 1986 successfully bid for Wedgwood at a cost of £256.1m Ir. in a share or cash offer. July '87: Trent Sanitaryware sold for IR£26.5m; 2,000 acre Ranton Estate sold IR£2.8m; Facilities sold in Australia IR£2.4m. Sept. '87: Redundancies at Waterford for 1,005 workers. Dec. '87: Aynsley China sold to management for £19.7m. August '88: Sells J. Hinde for £5.7m cash.

Sir Anthony O'Reilly

WATERFORD WEDGWOOD

CAPITAL HISTORY:
Jan. 1967 Waterford Glass went public at 165p per Ord. 25p share. March 1969 'rights' of 1-for-12 at 200p each. April 1969 'scrip' issue of 1-for-2. June 1970 85,415 shares issued on acquisition of John Aynsley & Sons (Longton) Ltd. March 1971 Ord. 25p shares subdivided into 5p shares; 1-for-1 'scrip' issue. July 1971 4,220,750 shares issued on acquisition of Switzer & Co. April 1972 1-for-3 'scrip' issue. March 1973 1-for-3 'scrip' issue. 1974 6,624,446 Ord. 5p shares issued on acquisition of Smith Group. 1975: 5,186,087 10% Cumulative Preference £1 shares issued by way of 'rights' on the basis of 1-for-17 Ord. held. May 1977 1-for-3 'scrip' issue. July 1979 1-for-2 'scrip' issue. June 1986 21,400,000 Ord. 5p shares issued in the form of 2,140,000 American Depositary shares at US$20.04 per ADS. Dec. 1986 156,814,214 Ord. 5p shares issued as part consideration of Wedgwood. April 1990 212 million Ord. 5p shares plus income shares issued to Shuttleway at 37.5p each. Rights issue 1-for-5 new stock units 82,793,024 issued at 27.5p each. July 2001: Issues 9,331,733 Ord 5p shares @ €1.20 for Ashling Capital

COMPANY HISTORY:
Incorporated in 1947 and became a subsidiary of the Irish Glass

November '88: Sells 45 acre site in California for US$24.8m. January '89: Announces weakness in management accounting at Waterford Glass. Oct. '89: Name changed to Waterford Wedgwood plc. April '90: Shuttleway (Morgan, Stanley, Fitzwilton) invests £79.5m in Waterford Wedgwood at 37.5p per stock unit (212m stock units). Waterford Wedgwood rights issue at 27.5p raises £22.8m. July '90: 14 week strike ends. Oct. '90: To source crystal glass from abroad. March '91: Waterford and Wedgwood Boards clearly separated. Sept. '92: 500 job cuts at Waterford. Dec 92: Closes one Wedgwood plant; 160 lose jobs. Jan 1995: Wedgwood closes factory in Stoke-on-Trent. July 1995: Acquires Stuart Crystal for £4.7m. Dec 1995: Albany Trust (O'Reilly/Goulandris) pay 69p per share for 26.5 million WW shares from Morgan Stanley. April 1997: Goulandris pays £23m for 3.6% of WW. Feb 1998: Buys Rosenthal for £75m. Oct 1998: Bought back 8 million own shares at €0.74 each (€6m). May 1999: Buys All-Clad Inc (US cookware) for £82m. Sells 8m own shares back to the market at $1.08 each (having bought them at $0.75). Nov 1999: Buys 14.9% Royal Doulton @ 90pstg costing $17.6m. Aug 2000: Buys Hutschenreuther

(Germany) for €10.2m. June 2001: Buys 5.2% of Rosenthal f €5.3m. July 2001: Buys 86.5% Ashling Corp (linens) for $9.5m shares. March 2002: Increases Royal Doulton stake to 20.6%. close 40 concession shops and Stourbridge (UK) plant; €5.7 write-off Stuart Crystal; €16.2m write-off Royal Doulton. W change year end to March 31. July 2002: To push for more L investors.

Share Price Sept 2001 - Sept 2002

1. €0.85 12.09.01 Interim Results

INVESTMENT PERFORMANCE
Five Year Investment Performance: €1,324
Ten Year Investment Performance: € 2,449

HALF YEARLY PERFORMANCES: € m

Six months to:	30.06.00	31.12.00	30.06.01	31.12.01
Sales	446.9	637.4	462.3	549.7
Profits (-) before Tax	15.5	64.1	14.0	(57.3) b)
Profit % Sales	3.5	10.1	3.0	-

b) See 10 year review

FIVE YEAR SHARE PRICE TREND €

1997	High	1.26 (Aug)	Low	0.95 (Nov)
1998	High	1.57 (Apr)	Low	0.67 (Dec)
1999	High	1.05 (July)	Low	0.63 (Feb)
2000	High	1.46 (Nov)	Low	0.90 (Mar)
2001	High	1.37 (Feb)	Low	0.55 (Sept)

FINANCIAL DIARY
Interim Results Announced:	12.09.2001
Interim Dividend Payout:	03.12.2001
Final Results Announced:	06.03.2002
Annual General Meeting:	25.07.2002
Final Dividend Payout:	06.09.2002

SECTORAL ANALYSIS: (previous year)
Sales: Chinaware 47% (44%), crystal 36% (40%), cookware/other 17% (16%).
Profits: Chinaware 19% (17%), crystal 48%(63%), cookware/other 33% (20%).

TEN YEAR REVIEW: € m

12 months to Dec. 31	1992	1993	1994	1995	1996	1997	1998 k)	1999	2000	200
Sales	347.4	405.3	412.7	437.4	477.8	529.7	730.5	879.6	1,084.4	1,012.
Profit (Loss) before Tax	(21.6)	12.8	28.7	35.7	44.3	15.5 f)	18.9	65.5	79.6	(43.3) b)
Tax	2.5	1.4	2.5	5.1	7.5	7.4	2.5	9.4	11.0	1.
Profit (Loss) after Tax	(24.1)	11.4	26.2	30.6	36.8	8.1	16.4	56.1	68.6	(44.8
Minority Interest	-	-	-	-	-	-	(0.3)	+0.9	(0.8)	(0.4
Available for Shareholders	(24.1)	11.4	26.2	30.6	36.8	8.1	16.1	57.0	67.8	(45.2
Ordinary Dividend	-	-	7.2	11.2	12.8	14.1	16.1	19.1	22.9	23.
Retained Profit (Loss)	(24.1)	11.4	19.0	19.4	24.0	(6.0)	nil	37.9	44.9	(68.8
Increase (Decrease) in Reserves	(47.7) c)	25.9 d)	13.3	18.5	29.0 e)	(16.0) g)	(17.1) j)	55.9 m)	59.9 a)	(54.9) r
Shareholders' Funds	128.5	154.5	168.4	187.8	217.1	201.5	184.6	236.0	293.7	239.
Ordinary Dividend per Share (€)	-	-	0.01	0.013	0.018	0.02	0.023	0.027	0.0306	0.03
Earnings per Share (€)	-	0.016	0.04	0.043	0.051	0.011	0.022	0.078	0.092 h)	

a) Sale of treasury shares +€8.6m. b) Once-off charges: Stuart Crystal -€5.7m, inventory -€17m, redundancy -€39.1m, Royal Doulton investment -€16.2m (total -€78m). c) Devaluation of properties -€13m; currency loss -€10.4m. d) Currency uplift +€14.5m. e) Currency gain +€2.8m. f) Restructuring charge -€35.3m. g) Goodwill w/o -€35m, currency gain +€22.1m. h) Based upon 737.1m shares. j) Purchase of own shares -€6m; currency loss -€11.4m, goodwill w/o -€3m.k) Figures subsequently restated. m) Currency gain +€16.5m. n) Share premium +€12m.

BALANCE SHEET: DECEMBER 31 2001. € m

Share Capital:		Fixed Assets	264.6
758,063,220 Ord. €0.06 shares,		Financial Assets	8.1
758,063,220 1p stg. Income shares	55.3	Current Assets	582.8
		Current Liabilities	244.4
Reserves	184.4	Net Current Assets	338.4
		Medium Debt	(491.4)
		Minorities	(3.4)
		Net Tangible Assets	116.3
		Intangibles	123.4
Shareholders' Funds	239.7	Net Assets	239.7

Comment:
See Chairman's Statement.

Waterford Wedgwood plc

At the time of our year end results announcement on 6 March 2002, the Group reported its decision to change its financial year end to 31 March, in order to create a more even flow of financial information and to improve its business planning process. Under a calendar year system, sales and profits were weighted to the second half of the year. With a March year end, a more even split between the two halves of the year is achieved. The period reported in these accounts allows the Group to start its new financial year on 1 April 2002.

The January to March period is cyclically the quietest of the year in terms of sales and profits, as our fixed cost base is spread consistently throughout the year despite changing sales patterns. 2002 was no exception, but sales showed an upwards trend compared with the final quarter of 2001.

Turnover of €207.2 million was 6.5% below 2001, but level with 2000, which in turn was up 8.1% on the previous year. The operating loss of 8.8 million was in line with our expectations.

The US market continues to be challenging although All-Clad and our linens business, Ashling Corporation, have started the year well. After a long period of difficulty, we are again seeing growth for Wedgwood in the all-important Japanese market. The European market, particularly Germany, remains tough.

Cash flow from trading was significantly improved from prior year with a net outflow of €20.4 million compared with €58 million during the same period in 2001. Closing net debt was €390.2 million, €11.8 million lower than 31 March 2001. Inventory traditionally increases in the January-March period but we succeeded in maintaining inventories close to December 2001 levels. Capital expenditure was 18% below 2001 levels.

The restructuring programme announced in November is well under way and on track to deliver on-going annual savings of €43 million from 2003 onwards. The Stourbridge, West Midlands, crystal plant has been closed. Our Group workforce of around 10,000 is being reduced by some 1,400; slightly over half of this planned manpower reduction has already been accomplished.

Operations Update

The Group is pleased to report that sales in May equalled May 2001 levels. The Group's strategy remains to increase sales through marketing initiatives, the development of new product ranges, enhanced overseas representation and by diversifying into associated new product categories. We have achieved good progress in all these areas since the start of the year.

In February, Rosenthal launched the first collection of its Andy Warhol range, to great acclaim. Rosenthal has secured the worldwide licence for reproduction of the entire Andy Warhol collection in ceramics and crystal.

In April the Vera Wang at Wedgwood collection was launched in the US and initial orders have exceeded expectations. In May, Wedgwood announced its first ever alliance within the interior design sector, with the appointment of Kelly Hoppen to design a gift collection "The Art of Giving" for Wedgwood, to be launched in the UK in 2002 and internationally in 2003.

Jasper Conran at Wedgwood, following its success in Europe, is due to be launched shortly in the US, and John Rocha's new ranges for Waterford continue to increase sales.

On 7 May the Group announced that it had acquired certain assets - including, notably, the Spring brand - of Spring AG, a Swiss luxury cookware company which is one of Europe's leading luxury cookware brands.

Spring is an ideal European complement to the Group's existing luxury cookware business, All-Clad. We intend to establish a new company in Switzerland to handle sales, marketing and customer service, employing some of Spring's existing employees. This company will form the basis of expansion for Waterford Wedgwood's luxury cookware business throughout Europe and beyond.

In April, the US celebrity chef, Emeril Lagasse, appeared for 2 hours on the US shopping channel QVC, promoting the All-Clad product range. This resulted in $4 million of sales during the two hour period which is a cookware record for QVC. We will continue to pursue similar marketing initiatives.

Christopher Johnson, Group Technical and Manufacturing Director, retired from this role and from the Board, in April 2002. Chris has made a highly significant contribution to manufacturing efficiency during his long career with our Group and we wish him well in his retirement.

Outlook

Although trading conditions remain difficult, it is fair to say that some 'green shoots' are beginning to appear; for example, worldwide sales in May equalled, for the first time since August 2001, the same month in the prior year. A combination of a continuing improvement in economic conditions and leaner retailer inventories, together with our creative marketing, new product development and new distribution strategies will, we believe, generate improving earnings and cash performance as the year progresses.

Sir Anthony O'Reilly
Chairman
5 June 2002

Sir Anthony O'Reilly
Chairman

> *The Group's strategy remains to increase sales through marketing initiatives, the development of new product ranges, enhanced overseas representation and by diversifying into associated new product categories*

P. Redmond O'Donoghue
Group Chief Executive Officer

"*Waterford Wedgwood remains committed to its objective of doubling the business within the next five years*" was the concluding comment from Chairman Sir Anthony O'Reilly with the last Annual Report. That probably means, therefore, turnover by 2006 reaching €2 billion but let us hope it means a substantially better performance than the loss shown on the €1 billion of sales last year. The last time we read of such a forward commitment was from Don Panoz in Elan who also promised to top the £2 billion mark in sales by 2000 and about which we commented at the time 'turnover is for vanity, profits are for sanity'. We doubt if this may happen with Waterford.

Once again we turned to the Form 20-F which we find more revealing than all those glossy photos which adorn the WW annual communication to shareholders. The pretax loss of €43.3m which was the bottom line according to Irish accounting practice grew to €54.1m if drawn up in US generally accepted regulations.

It is up to shareholders to make up their own minds which system throws up the truer picture. It appears that in Irish accounting rules, goodwill may either be written off immediately on completion of the acquisition against shareholders' equity or capitalized in the balance sheet and amortized through the profit and loss account on a systematic basis over its useful life. Going back over the history of Waterford, the acquisition of Wedgwood in November 1986 which gave rise to goodwill of a whisker under €200 million on consolidation was offset against the share premium outstanding at that time and agreed to by the High Court. In December 1997 they paid €35 million over the net asset value ('goodwill') for 61.5% holding in Rosenthal and this too has been offset against reserves and not capitalized.

In January 1998 the Irish accountancy body ruled that goodwill must be capitalized and amortized through the income statement on a systematic basis over its useful life, subject to a recommended write-off period of 20 years thus bringing to end any chance of massaging the all important earnings per share yardstick. In early 1998 Wedgwood increased its stake in Rosenthal up to 84.6% for €23

million thus giving rise to further goodwill of €18.4 million which was capitalized and is being written-off over 20 years. The same happened when they increased their hold on Rosenthal by another 5.2% in August 2001 creating more goodwill of €4.4 million. In June 1999 WW paid a whopping €88 million in goodwill for the All-Clad acquisition and this, similarly, was capitalized in both the Irish and US accounting methods to be amortized over 20 years.

In August 2000 Hutschenreuther was acquired with goodwill of €2 million which is being written-off over 20 years. Then in July 2001 the group acquired 86.5% of Ashling Corporation for €10 million over its net assets and capitalized under Irish and US accounting but is only being amortized under Irish principles over 20 years because in January 2002 the US regulation on amortization is now governed by FAS 142 which suspends the amortization of goodwill. So, in the case of Rosenthal, All-Clad, Hutschenreuther and Ashling no amortization has been allowed under US GAAP since the beginning of 2002. This has given rise to an extra charge of €6.6 million. Two other major differences have shown up between Irish and American practice in the area of pensions where €9.2 million has been charged and in the area of 'available for sale securities' the US system has credited €16.2 million. One other item with which the Americans do not agree is the method of inventory valuation. WW changed its method of stock valuation by including transportation, warehousing and storage and these amounted to €7.8 million. But the Yanks have said 'whoa, not on' and as a result they have charged this amount to the bottom-line.

Over the years WW has been trying to cut costs and at the same time expand its product range qualitywise and pricewise. Much emphasis has been laid on the positioning of its brands. The brand repositioning strategy pursued in recent years has resulted in a marked shift in sales patterns away from

stemware toward giftware, to the extent that giftware is now the single most important category. At the same time an increasing proportion of annual sales is represented by new product introductions within the previous twelve months. The key element in the brand re-positioning strategy was the creation in 1991 of the Marquis brand which is out sourced from lower cost producers in East Europe and as a result they are more competitively priced creating a new market segment of consumer to offset the expensive premium image which Waterford Crystal was achieving.

New products have been instrumental in driving annual sales growth. The US continues to be by far the largest market for Waterford's crystal products. New crystal product introductions accounted for 14 per cent of 2001 sales. However, the Millennium Collection linked to the turn of the century launched in 1996 achieved net sales in 2001 of €9.6 million and signalled the end of its life which then resulted in the expensive write-down of its unsold millennium product and other items by a significant €17 million.

Looking at the return to shareholders over the past five years, one has to admire the way the group has looked after its investors. In the years 1997-2001 the group has made a cumulative €136.2 million in pretax profits out of which they have fed the Revenue Commissioners just short of €32 million. This has left €104.4 million to be shared out between the shareholders and reinvested in the business. Tony O'Reilly has considered it better to look after the investors than worry too much about retained earnings. Therefore the shareholders have done well by extracting €95.8 million to line their pockets.

What should WW be returning by way of pretax profits when the turnover reaches the magic €2 billion level? Way back in 1996 when the group was a fraction of its current size WW returned 9.3% pretax profits which actually rose to 9.5% the following year before they had another reorganisation charge of €35.5 million. A performance therefore of anything up to 10% profit before tax on sales of €2 billion would be very satisfactory and no doubt ensure that Chief Executive Redmond O'Donoghue will be able to profitably exercise his 2,500,000 share options which have an unattractive option price today of €1.00 per share. There are five years to achieve this golden egg which at the price of €1 per share (remember they have been as high as €1.46 in November 2000 and €1.37 in February 2001 per share) would give a capital gain of 72% based on today's buying price - that's a compound growth rate of 11.5% and on top of this you would get an annual dividend of at least 5.3% gross - now that's better than putting money on deposit these days!

(We have taken much of the detail from the Form 20-F and we have reviewed the reports from Davys and Morgan Stanley.)

Segment	Sales 2001	%	Profits* 2001
Crystal	369m	36%	29.2m
Ceramics	473m	46%	11.3m
Cookware	170m	18%	20.2m
	1,012m	100%	60.7m

* before exceptional charges

Continued from page 82...

Allied Irish Bank is our second choice. The bank has been through the mill over the past few months and the share price reflects this. So I would not be surprised to hear you say why choose this bank! Well our belief is that financial shares are not great of late no matter which institution you favour. I would tend to steer away from one that has a serious proportion of its business in the assurance business. I also feel that after the Rudnick debacle the AIB management has got a 'tap on the shoulder' and is, in the short-term at least going to see that banana skins are avoided. Having got away lightly with Allfirst mess the out-turn for 2002 should produce pretax profits of €1.5billion. 57-year-old Michael Buckley will be praying for that outcome or the next a.g.m. won't be a vicar's teaparty.

Our third choice is **CRH**, another company in the construction industry. What attracts us to this share is that it has fallen back to about to two-thirds of its peak of last year when it tipped a high of €21.51 mid year. We are strong believers in backing management and the 56-year-old Liam O'Mahony is chiselled from the same granite as Tony Barry and Jim Culliton who ran the group very well over the years. These are tough times for this sector of the construction industry where there is heavy reliance on both public and private sector spending. Over the medium term I cannot see this faltering significantly and their diversification into Central Europe having made plenty of headway in the States should see the Group through any geographical weaknesses.

DCC is my fourth selection. It was only when we were doing our review of the best performers in the dividend payout department did we then realise how well shareholders have been looked after for the past ten years - their dividend stream has increased by a magnificent 28% compound per annum. If you were fortunate enough to receive €1,000 by way of a dividend from DCC in 1992, in 2001 you would be receiving €9,220 - seeing that inflation has only gone up by 3% per annum during that time, anybody holding these shares in their pension portfolio must be deliriously happy. Jim Flavin's DCC conglomerate of investments is well placed for growth going forward. Furthermore, Jim is a significant shareholder himself and has not been shedding stock.

Our next choice is **Jurys Doyle Hotels**. We are dependent on the tourist business in this country and the performance of Jurys has been excellent even though there was a small dip last year Once again the youthful management of Peter McCann (51) is in the Peter Malone mould who has the credit for introducing the 'Inn' brand of lower priced accommodation to the Group. It is also interesting to see that when Walter Beatty handed over the Chairman's baton to Dick Hooper his first action was to go into the market and buy additional shares. If that isn't a vote of confidence in the future I don't know what is, because the ex-Chairman is hardly short of a few shares owning about €7m worth already.

A holding in the agribusiness sector is a good cornerstone in any portfolio. We therefore choose **Kerry Group** as our next investment. This choice is not cheap as it currently changes hands at about 23 times the rolling price earnings ratio. Normally I would balk at moving into the 20s in the p/e ratio area and a pretax profit of 3.2% on sales in the latest interim results was not greeted with wild enthusiasm by the market. It is up to 58-year-old Hugh Friel to squeeze more profit out of these sales to prove he is a worthy incumbent in Denis Brosnan's chair. Unfortunately the dividend yield while we wait is paltry. This is the only choice I am wavering over.

My next choice is **United Drug**. You could hardly overlook the healthcare industry in the medium term and as the 38-year-old Liam Fitzgerald's charge is primarily in the agency distribution business you don't have the sleepless nights associated with competitive products and patent protection which are inherent in the Elan type operations. This is one industry sector which I thought was as dull as dish water with vicious price controls but under Martin Rafferty and Jerry Liston I was proved wrong. Again at current levels United's shares don't come cheap but the dividend income is luxuriously covered and if it does as well over the next five years as it has done in the last five, we'll be happy.

So let's lick our wounds and start rebuilding those portfolios. We have just been through a reality check - there will no doubt be many more to come - now is the time to avail of a great buying opportunity but you should also realign your target timespan for profitability. All indications are that the timespan for the next peak will be some way off. In the meantime, pick wisely and sleep soundly.

Companies Providing 'Scrip' Dividends

Allied Irish Banks

Anglo Irish Bank Corp

Ardagh

Aviva*

CRH

Gartmore*

Gresham Hotel

Heiton

Independent News & Media

Qualceram Shires

United Drug

Waterford Wedgwood

*Dividend Reinvestent Plan

SHARE WEIGHTINGS ON ISEQ INDEX

Bank of Ireland	20.37%
Allied Irish Banks	20.15%
CRH	13.45%
Ryanair Noldings	7.55%
Irish Life & Permanent	6.09%
Kerry Group	4.69%
Anglo Irish Bank	3.53%
Galen	2.32%
Viridian	1.82%
Elan	1.81%
IAWS	1.65%
DCC	1.47%
Independent News	1.46%
Grafton Group	1.19%
First Active	1.18%
All Others	11.27%

ISEQ INDEX HIGHS & LOWS

2002 HIGH 5,714 (Jan 17)

2002 LOW 3,926 (July 25)

TAX DEADLINES 2002 AND 2003

Income Tax and Capital Gains Tax

31 October 2002

Pay preliminary income tax for 2002
Pay capital gains tax for 2001
Pay balance of income tax for 2001
Last date for election to defer payment of income tax on
share options exercised in 2001
Last date for payment of retirement annuities for 2001
Last date for filing 2001 tax return

31 December 2002

Last day of 2002 tax year;
Last date for payments to Additional Voluntary
Contribution (AVC) schemes and Permanent Health
Insurance (PHI) plans for 2002

31 October 2003

Pay preliminary income tax for 2003
- Pay balance of income tax for 2002
- Pay capital gains tax for 2002
- Last date for filing 2002 tax return
- Last date for election to defer payment of income tax
  on share options exercised in 2002
- Last date for payment of retirement annuities for 2002

CAPITAL GAINS TAX (CGT)

Rates:

Development Land	20%
Foreign Life Assurance policies and offshore funds	40%
All Other Assets	20%

Individuals, trusts, and unincorporated bodies are chargeable to CGT: capital gains of companies are chargeable to Corporation Tax (except for gains arising on the disposal of development land in which case the gain is subject to Capital Gains Tax)

Married Couples : a transfer of assets between husband and wife does not give rise to a disposal for capital gains tax purposes. The recipient is deemed to have made the original acquisition. (the same rules apply to transfers following the issuing of a decree of divorce or between separated spouses).

Main Exemptions

Individuals: the first €1,270 of chargeable gains are exempt: Disposal of interest in private residence and grounds of up to one acre; Irish Government Securities, National Saving Schemes, Betting winnings, personal injury compensations; transfer of land to children (value not greater than €254,000); for construction of residence; disposal by individual over 55 of business or farm where the consideration is less than €476,250 and where the individual must have owned the assets for a minimum period of 10 years prior to disposal

Indexation (see over)

Indexation tables are available commencing from values on 6 April 1974 when assets are deemed to have been acquired at their market value on that date

STAMP DUTY

Residential Property

There are specific definitions for "First Time Buyer" and "Other Owner Occupiers" on which advice should be sought.

New Residential Properties

Additional rules apply for owner occupiers of new residential properties.

- Stamp duty is not payable if the property is under 125sq.m (where certain other conditions are met).
- Properties over 125sq.m will qualify for a reduced amount of stamp duty. (where certain conditions are met).

Stamp Duty is payable on the acquisition of a property.

From 6 December 2001, stamp duty rates are as follows:

Rates of Stamp Duty for Residential Property:

Market value	First time occupiers	Other owners	Investors buyers new/ 2nd hand houses/apartments
Up to €127,000	Nil	Nil	Nil
€127,001 €190,500	Nil	3.00%	3.00%
€190,501 €254,000	3.00%	4.00%	4.00%
€254,001 €317,500	3.75%	5.00%	5.00%
€317,501 €381,000	4.50%	6.00%	6.00%
€381,001 €635,000	7.50%	7.50%	7.50%
Over €635,000	9.00%	9.00%	9.00%

Transfer of Shares

Where shares in a company are being transferred, duty is payable at the rate of 1% on the open market value of the shares.

The main exemptions and reliefs are:

- A transfer of any property between spouses*.
- A transfer of any property between a divorced couple where the transfer is made on foot of certain specified court orders*.
- A transfer to an Owner Occupier of a new house/apartment up to 125sq.m in size, where a Floor Area Certificate has been issued by the Department of the Environment and Local Government*.
- Certain Financial Instruments used in the Financial Services Industry*.
- Certain conveyances, transfers or leases of land to a body established for charitable purposes.
- A transfer of land to a Young Trained Farmer, where certain conditions are met.
- A transfer or lease of a site to a child, the purpose of which is for the child to build their own home, where the market value of the site does not exceed €254,000 and where other conditions are met

MISCELLANEOUS TAX BASED INVESTMENTS

Business Expansion Schemes Qualifying investments (subject to a minimum of €250 and a maximum of €31,750) are deductible from total income.

Film Scheme Investments Qualifying investments subject to a maximum of €31,750 are deductible from total income but are restricted to 80% of the investment amount or 80% of the maximum limit, whichever is the lower.

Tax Incentives for investments in Irish industry and businesses include:
- relief for 'seed capital' investment by new entrepreneurs (including redundant workers;
- relief for additional 'own capital' investment by original entrepreneurs:
- relief for investment in research and development projects

Investments in a company or a partnership

Tax relief may be available to:
- directors or employees of certain companies for interest paid on loans to acquire an interest in the company;
- individuals acquiring an interest in a partnership

Relief for Donations to Sports Bodies

Relief will be available for personal and corporate donations made to sports organisations on or after 1st May 2002 for capital projects, provided certain conditions are met.

Property Development Incentive Schemes

Tax relief from Income Tax and Corporation Tax was introduced in respect of the redevlopment of certain specified areas within the cities of Dublin, Cork, Galway, Limerick, Wateford, and have been, extended by various tax acts to most large towns in the country.

There are many conditions to be satisfied in order for expenditure to qualify for this relief, not least of which is the qualifying period in which expenditure relief is claimed.

VALUE ADDED TAX (VAT)

Rates:

Rate	Main Items
10%	Relates to certain agreements (mainly construction of domestic dwellings, car hire, holiday and hotel lettings) entered into prior to 25 February 1993
12.5%	Hotel and holiday accommodation; newspapers and magazines; meals, theatre and entertainment admissions
21% (Standard Rate)	Adult clothing, sports and personal goods, drink, most building materials, most services, including professional services
zero	Childrens clothing, most food and drink for human consumption, certain books and booklets, certain medical equipment
Exempted activities	Admission to sports events, medical services, educational and certain child-care services

Thresholds:

Supply of Goods: €51,000 (90% of receipts must derive from supply of taxable goods
Supply of Services: €25,500
Cash Basis: €635,000 (or where not less than 90% of turnover derives from sales to unregistered persons)

INCOME TAX

Tax rates and thresholds:

Rate	Single/widowed	Single parent	Married Couple (one income)	Married Couple(*) (two incomes)
20%	First €28,000	First €32,000	First €37,000	First €56,000*
42%	Balance	Balance		Balance

(*)Transferable between spouses up to a maximum of €37,000 for any one spouse

Personal credits	Short Tax "Year" 2001	2002
	€	€
Single	1034	1520
Married couple	2067	3040
Widowed - in year of bereavement	2067	3040
Widowed - no dependent child	1221	1820
Widowed with dependent child/children	1034	1520
Age credit - Single or Widowed	151	205
Age credit - Married	302	410
Dependent Relative credit	42	60
Dependent Relative - Income limit	6335	9352
Incapacited child credit	302	500
PAYE credit	376	660
Home carers credit (Max.)	564	770
Carers Income limits - for full credit	3758	5080
- for reduced credit	4886	6620

Rent Allowance Credits 2002	Under 55 €	55 or over €
Single	254	508
Married	508	1016
Widowed	508	1016

Mortgage Interest relief (^)(Maximum allowable) for 2002	First mortgage (Taken on or after 6/4/98)	Mortgage taken prior to 6/4/98
	€	€
Single	3175	2540
Married/Widowed	6350	5080

(^): Relief is granted at the standard rate of Income Tax (20%) and is granted at source

Marginal rate allowances	2001 Allowance €	2002 Allowance €
Revenue Job Assist - basic allowance Year 1	3810	3810
- for each child (Year 1)	1270	1270
Blind - Additional allowance for guide dog	611	825
Employment of carer for incapacitated person(Max)	9396 (Max)	30,000

CAPITAL GAINS

TAX (Indexation Tables)

Year expenditure incurred	Y/e 5 April 2001	Short Y/e 31 Dec 2001	Y/e 31 Dec 2002
1974/75	6.582	6.930	7.180
1975/76	5.316	5.597	5.799
1976/77	4.580	4.822	4.996
1977/78	3.926	4.133	4.283
1978/79	3.627	3.819	3.956
1979/80	3.272	3.445	3.570
1980/81	2.833	2.983	3.091
1981/82	2.342	2.465	2.554
1982/83	1.970	2.074	2.149
1983/84	1.752	1.844	1.911
1984/85	1.590	1.674	1.735
1985/86	1.497	1.577	1.633
1986/87	1.432	1.507	1.562
1987/88	1.384	1.457	1.510
1988/89	1.358	1.430	1.481
1989/90	1.314	1.384	1.434
1990/91	1.261	1.328	1.376
1991/92	1.229	1.294	1.341
1992/93	1.186	1.249	1.294
1993/94	1.164	1.226	1.270
1994/95	1.144	1.205	1.248
1995/96	1.116	1.175	1.218
1996/97	1.094	1.152	1.194
1997/98	1.077	1.134	1.175
1998/99	1.059	1.115	1.156
1999/00	1.043	1.098	1.138
2000/01	-	1.053	1.091
2001	-	-	1.037

Example: Use the Multiplier as follows:
£10,000/€12,697 worth of shares were purchased in Aug 1974 and sold in March 2001 for £80,000/€101,579.
£12,697 x 6.582 = €83,571.
£101,579 - €83,571 = €18,008 constitutes your taxable gain @ 20% = €3,601.

NOTE: In the expenditure column, and for all years to 2000/2001 inclusive, a year means 1 12 month period commencing on 6 April and ending on the following 5 April. The year 2001 covers the period 6/4/2001 tp 31/12/2001. Indexation is not available on expenditure incurred within 12 months prior to the date of disposal.

PERSONAL RETIREMENT

SAVINGS ACCOUNT (PRSA)

Long-term personal retirement account introduced by the Pensions Act, 2002 and should be available from early 2003. It is designed to enable people, especially those with no pension provision, to save for retirement in a flexible manner. A PRSA will be a contract between an individual and a PRSA provider in the form of an investment account. Subject to age-based limits, tax relief will be given for contributions to a PRSA. Contributions paid into a PRSA will benefit from tax relief at an individual's marginal income tax rate. There will also be relief from PRSI and the health levy for employees. Where PRSA contributions are deducted by an employer, the net pay arrangement will apply

Maximum allowable contributions:

Age	% of Net Relevant Earnings
Under 30	15%;
30-39	25%;
40+	30%

Different tax limits apply for AVCs

Net relevant earnings are relevant earnings less losses, capital allowances and certain payments which reduce a person's income for tax purposes such as tax effective covenants.

Except in the case of an employee who is a member of an occupational pension scheme or of a statutory pension scheme, a taxpayer is entitled to tax relief on a contribution of €1,525 paid even if this exceeds the normal income-based limit

An earnings cap of €254,000 will apply also to PRSAs as is the case with Retirement Annuity Contracts [RAC] for the purposes of tax relief. Thus, for example, where a person is aged over 40, the maximum tax relieved contribution is €254,000 x 30% = €76,200 per year

PAYE will apply to all annuities and other withdrawals from a PRSA other than

● a tax free lump sum [25% of the fund],
● a transfer to an ARF/AMRF,
  or,
● a transfer to another PRSA, to an occupational pension scheme or to a statutory scheme.

CORPORATION TAX

Rates of Tax

	Standard Rate	Higher Rate	Lower Rate
y/e 31/12/2002	16%	25%	12.5%
From 1 January 2003	12.50%	25%	N/A

The 12.50% rate of tax applies from 1 January 2001 to companies with annual trading income of less than €254,000 (£200.000).
There is marginal relief during 2002 on profits between €254,000 and €317,500
Form 1st January 2003 all trading income is taxable at Standard Rate
Non-Trading Income includes foreign income, interest on government securities, bank deposit interest, royalties, rental income from land and building in the State, income from mining and petroleum activities and dealing in non-residential land.

Payment of Corporation Tax
Preliminary tax
The payment date will be brought forward by seven months to one month before the year-end. There will be a transition period of 5 Years, during which preliminary tax is payable in two instalments.
In the transition period the percentage of preliminary tax payable one month before the end of the accounting period is the lower of the following:

For Accounting periods ending	% of previous year's liability (*)	% of Actual year's liability
2002	20	18
2003	40	36
2004	60	54
2005	80	72
2006	100	90

(*)Where total liability was less than €50,000
The 2nd instalment is payable within 6 months of the end of the accounting period but no later than the 28th day of that month or the 20th day if the month is December
The balance of the tax due (i.e.10%) will be payable one month after the issue of the notice of assessment.

CAPITAL ALLOWANCES AND TAX INCENTIVE SCHEMES
Motor Vehicles
The car value threshold for the restriction of capital allowances is increased to €22,000 (£17,326).These changes apply to expenditure incurred in accounting periods that end on or after 1 January 2002.(The previous restriction on the tax deduction for motor tax running expenses is abolished from 1 January 2002)

EMPLOYEE SHARE INCENTIVE SCHEMES

The most common schemes in operation in Ireland are:

1). Unapproved Share Option Schemes
Can be offered to employees on a selective basis. Income Tax payable on difference between option price and market price at time of exercise of option. I.T. liability can be deferred until date of disposal or seven years after exercise whichever is the earlier. CGT is payable, subject to exemption of €1,270, on any gain on disposal of shares (credit given for I.T. already paid)

2) Revenue Approved Share Option Schemes
Employees will not be chargeable to Income Tax on the exercise of the option. Instead they will be chargeable to Capital Gains Tax on the full gain (i.e. difference between the amount paid for shares and disposal proceeds), provided certain conditions are met.

3) Revenue Approved Save As You Earn' Share Option Schemes
Period of savings set at commencement of scheme. Regular monthly savings plan with qualifying financial institutions from after-tax income: min.€12;max.€30. Share options granted on basis of savings only. No I.T. payable on savings or at grant of exercise (unless option is exercised within 3 years of date of grant). Costs of establishing scheme are allowed for CT purposes

4) Approved Profit Sharing Schemes
Employee trust must be established.Employees given right to convert profit sharing bonus into shares. Employee apply % (not more than 7.5%)of gross salary; Shares must be fully paid-up non-redeemable ordinary shares in either company or its parent; maximum of €12,700 allocation per employee in any year; no I.T. if not disposed of within 3 years

5) Restricted Stock Schemes
Patriciant given/acquires shares at discount in company or parent on condition that shares be held for fixed period: Shares are held by trust: Initial I.T. liability is reduced due to restrictions: - ultimate I/T. liability depends on restriction period (min.10% to max. 55% abatement); CGT payable upon disposal;

6) Share Subscription Schemes (Revenue Approved)
Employee entitled to I.T. deduction to maximum lifetime of €6,350 for subscription in newly issued fully paid-up non-redeemable ordinary shares in employer which must be Irish trading or holding company. The shares must not be sold for 3 years or relief will be lost; For CGT purposes base cost of shares will be reduced by IT deduction

Common aspects of approved schemes: All employees and full-time directors who have been employed for minimum period (which can be set by employers and of not less than 3 years) must be eligible.

GIFT AND INHERITANCE TAX

Category	Threshold	Includes
Threshold 1	£381,000	A child, a step child, a foster child in certain circumstances and to a grand child under the age of 18 of the donor whose parent is dead, and to an inheritance taken by parent where certain conditions are met;
Threshold 2	£38,100	Brothers, sisters, nephews and nieces
Threshold 3	£19,050.	This applies to a successor who does not come under Threshold 2 Threshold 3

These thresholds can be reached either by a single gift or inheritance or by a collection of a number of gifts and inheritances over a period of years. Only prior gifts and inheritances to which the same group threshold apply are aggregated (added together) for the purposes for calculating tax.
The thresholds are index linked and increased inline with inflation since 2001. (Indexation factor for year 2002 is 1.108)

The rates of tax are as follows -
The threshold amount Nil
Excess 20%

Main exemptions

1). Inheritances taken by spouses after 29 January 1985 and gifts taken by spouses after 30 January 1990 .
2). Gifts/Inheritances for public or charitablepurposes
3). Gifts/Inheritance of a dwelling-house taken on or after 1 December, 1999 provided certain conditions are fulfilled
4). Pictures, prints, books or other items which are of national, scientific or artistic interest provided certain conditions are fulfilled

A return on a form I.T. 38 must be lodged when an inheritance/gift either by itself or when aggregated with prior benefits taken by the successor, exceeds 80% of the relevant tax-free amount This should be done within 4 months of the valuation date (the date on which the benefit is retained or set aside for the benefit of the successor). The tax must be paid within 4 months of the valuation date

For inheritances taken on or after 5 December 2001 only prior gifts and inheritances taken after 5 December 1991, to which the same threshold applies, are aggregated for the purposes of calculating a liability to tax.

R V KEARNS & ASSOCIATES

18 Terenure Road North, Dublin 6W
Tel: 00353-1-4923790. Fax: 00353-1-4923791
E-mail: rvkearns@eircom.net

ABBEY:
Gallagher Holdings 28.83%, Bank of Ireland Nominees 20.48%, Jupiter Split Trust 8.36%, FMR Corp 6.68%, Allied Irish Bank 4.85%, Clerical Medical Investment Group 4.62%.
(**2001:** Gallagher Holdings 28.84%, Bank of Ireland Nominees 18.56%, Allied Irish Bank 10.93%, Ulster Bank Markets 4.87%, Jupiter Split Trust 8.36%, Clerical Medical Investment Group 4.47%, Quinn-Direct Insurance 3.99%. No shareholder profile published.)

ALLIED IRISH BANKS:
The Capital Group Companies Inc 7.1%, AIB subsidiaries 4.0%. 93,353 shareholders of which 348 holders have 63% of equity; 63% of equity held overseas.
(**2001:** Bank of Ireland Asset Management Ltd 4.9%, Irish Life Assurance 4.1%, AIB subsidiaries 5.5%.)

ALPHYRA GROUP:
Bank of Ireland Nominees 22.72%, Citibank Nominees 4.64%, Chase Nominees 5.71%, Clydesdale Bank 7.79%, Quinn Direct Insurance 4.51%, Bank of New York (Nominees) 4.59%, De La Rue International Ltd 3.38%, J Nagle 5.1%.
(**2001:** Bank of Ireland Nominees 14.93%, Citibank Nominees 7.17%, Chase Nominees 6.04%, Clydesdale Bank 5.57%, Nortrust Nominees 5.14%, Quinn Direct Insurance 5.34%, AIB Custodial Nominees 4.67%, Bank of New York (Nominees) 3.41%, J Nagle 5.1%, M Healy 2.5%.)

AMINEX:
International Finance Corporation 8.35%, Eurogulf Investments Ltd 5.32%, Zarubezhneft 4.91%, Solestar Corp 5.31%, Credit Suisse First Boston Equities Ltd 4.75%, East West Oil Ltd 4.73%, Bank of England Pension Fund 3.74%, Channel Hotels & Properties 3.44%, F Tughan 1.6%, B Hall 1.3%. No shareholder profile published.
(**2001:** International Finance Corporation 9.85%, Zarubezhneft 5.78%, Solestar Corp 6.26%, Credit Suisse First Boston Equities Ltd 5.6%, East West Oil Ltd 5.58%, Phaseone Investments Ltd 5.27%, Bank of England Pension Fund 4.41%, F Tughan 1.5%.)

ANGLO IRISH BANK CORPORATION:
Bank of Ireland Nominees 5.8%, Zurich Financial Services Group 6.7%, Fidelity Investments 3.6%. 13,719 shareholders of which 59 have 74.1% of equity. Non-Irish hold 35.8%.
(**2001:** Bank of Ireland Nominees 8.7%, Zurich Financial Services Group 7.0%, Morgan Stanley Group 5.7%, Fidelity Investments 3.8%, Scottish Provident 3.8%.)

ARCON INTERNATIONAL RESOURCES:
Sir A O'Reilly 44.1%, Capital Group Companies Inc 5.5%, J Bogdanovich 4.2%.
(**2001:** Sir A O'Reilly 44.1%, Capital Group Companies Inc 5.5%, J Bogdanovich 4.2%.)

ARDAGH:
Rowan Nominees 30.83%, Yeoman International Holdings S.A. 22.65%, Davy Nominees 3.68%, Bank of Ireland Nominees 3.17%. No shareholder profile published.
(**2001:** Rowan Nominees 31.29%, Yeoman International Holdings S.A. 19.31%, Bank of Ireland Nominees 3.36%, ESB Pension Funds 3.33%.)

ARNOTTS:
Arnotts Staff Pension Fund 12.38%, FMR Corporation 10.1%, Art plc 9.9%, Bank of Ireland Asset Management 9.84%, Aberdeen Asset Management (I) Ltd 3.78%, M.G.O'Connor 3.51%. No shareholder profile is provided.
(**2001:** Arnotts Staff Pension Fund 12.65%, FMR Corporation 9.99%, Art plc 9.76%, Bank of Ireland Asset Management 9.89%, Aberdeen Asset Management (I) Ltd 4.16%, M.G.O'Connor 3.39%.)

AVIVA:
Legal & General 3.08%. There are 956,663 shareholders of which 432 hold 75.75% of the equity. Only 14% are individuals - the rest are institutional.
(**2001:** No shareholder had a 'notifiable interest'.)

AIB no longer holds notifiable interest in Bank of Ireland; Fidelity now a significant player

BANK OF IRELAND:
Bank of Ireland Asset Management Ltd 6.2%, Fidelity International & Subsidiaries 4.3%. There are 61,406 shareholders of which 134 hold 73.1% of equity. 59% of equity is non-Irish assuming 'private' are Irish.
(**2001:** Bank of Ireland Asset Management Ltd 6.8%, AIB plc & subsidiaries 3.1%. There are 67,929 shareholders of which 128 hold 72.4% of equity. 55% of equity is non-Irish.)

Bank of Ireland Nominees get rid of half their Barlo holding.

BARLO:
Bank of Ireland Nominees 14.6%, AIB & subsidiaries 7.1%, Aberdeen Asset Management 5.4%, A Barlow 3.06%, Syden/A Mullins 3.3%, IIU Ltd 4%, Ennismore Fund Management 4%, Friends First 3.4%, Standard Life 3.3%.
(**2001:** Bank of Ireland Nominees 29%, AIB & subsidiaries 9.5%, Standard Life Ass 6.0%, Aberdeen Asset Management 5.6%, A Barlow 3.06%, Syden/A Mullins 3.3%.)

BULA RESOURCES (HOLDINGS):
Channel Nominees (Deutsche Bank) 3.83%, Chamonix Nominees 3.29% (which are in the process of being extinguished), A Reynolds 1.85%.
(**2001:** Channel Nominees (Deutsche Bank) 6.1%, Chamonix Nominees 3.5%.)

CELTIC RESOURCES:
K Foo 10.0%, RAB Capital 9.52%, Resources Investment Trust 6.4%, Family Investments 6.21%, L&B Hannen 6.08%, Gartmore Investment 4.2%, Neil McDermott 5.4%.
(**2001:** Dragon Oil plc 11.88%, Neil McDermott 8.91%, Millennium Projects Ltd 5.52%, Family Investments Ltd 5.33%, K Foo 15.75%.)

CONDUIT:
E Kerr 21%, L Young 21%, The Capital Group Companies 6.96%, Bank of Ireland 5.56%.
(**2001:** E Kerr 21%, L Young 21%, Sonera Media Holding BV 9.98%, The Capital Group Companies 7.18%.)

CPL RESOURCES:
A Heraty 40.96%, P Carroll 40.96%, J Hennessy 1.73%. 3 shareholders own 83.7% of the equity.
(**2001:** A Heraty 40.96%, P Carroll 40.96%, J Hennessy 1.73%. 3 shareholders own 83.7% of the equity.)

AIB & Irish Life fall off the radar screen at CRH

CRH:
Bank of Ireland Nominees 5.50%, Putnam Investment/Putnam Advisory 6.43%, The Capital Group Companies Inc 5.01%. There are 24,165 shareholders, of which 55 hold at least 1million shares
(**2001:** Allied Irish Banks & subsidiaries 4.69%, Bank of Ireland Nominees 5.38%, Irish Life Assurance 5.47%, Putnam Investment/Putnam Advisory 7.35%, The Capital Group Companies Inc 4.72%.)

DATALEX:
N Wilson 15.73%, other directors and executive officers 4.4%, ICC Bank 8.25%, Atraxis AG 7.07%, IIU Nominees 6.53%, AIB & Subsidiaries 7.08%, Parnib NV 3.1%.
(**2001:** N Wilson 19.9%, other directors and executive officers 9.9%, ICC Bank, 9%, Atraxis AG7.2%, IIU Nominees 6.9 Skerries Nominees 5.4%, Parnib NV 3%, L.H. Nominees 3.2 Enterprise Ireland 1.23%, J Vecchione 1.8%.)

DCC:
FMR Corp & subsidiaries 12.3%, Bank of Ireland Nomine 9.8%, Merril Lynch Inv Mgrs 6.8%, Allied Irish Banks & su sidiaries 4.8%, J Flavin 2.6%. There are 3,110 shareholders which 37 own 84% of equity or 67 own 90%.
(**2001:** FMR Corp & subsidiaries 10.7%, Bank of Irela Nominees 10.4%, Merril Lynch Inv Mgrs 5.2%, Allied Iri Banks & subsidiaries 5.0%, 3i Group 3.8%, Aberdeen Ass Managers 3.1%, J Flavin 2.6%.)

Friends First Exit From Donegal Creameries

DONEGAL CREAMERIES:
Bank of Ireland Nominees 6.38%, Merrion Stockbroke Nominees 3.09%, G Vance 1.7%, D Gregg 2.0%, J Keon 1.6 P Kelly 1.2%.
(**2001:** Friends First 5.21%, Merrion Stockbrokers Nomine 3.41%, G Vance 1.7%, D Gregg 2.0%, J Keon 1.6%, P Kelly 1.2°)

DRAGON OIL:
Emirates National Oil Co Ltd 66.7%.
(**2001:** Emirates National Oil Co Ltd 69.4%.)

Dunloe Ewart: N & A Smyth 22.5%, P Monahan 6.74 Vantive Holdings 27.3%.
(**2001:** N & A Smyth 22.5%, P Monahan 6.75%, Vanti Holdings 27.3%.)

ELAN:
Capital Research Management 9.7%, Fidelity Manageme 8.9%, Franklin Resources 6%, Directors 2.4%.
(**2001:** Capital Research Management 8.0%, Fidel Management 6.0%, Directors 1.9%..)

Nominee companies rush for the door at Enne

ENNEX INTERNATIONAL:
N Y Nominees 8.73%, J Craven 5.44%, M Roche 5.44%, Wrafter 5.44%, Puma Nominees Ltd 3.25%, B Cusack 1.6%, McCarthy 2.3%, C Schaffalitzky 1.4%.
(**2001:** Endeavour Capital Corp 14.95%, Winterflood Securiti Ltd 4.14%, Linoff Securities 3.86%, Norwest Holdings L 3.61%, Pershing Keen Nominees 3.51%, B Cusack 2.5%, McCarthy 3.6%, C Schaffalitzky 2.1%.)

FBD HOLDINGS:
Farm Business Developments plc 39.7%, KBC Insuran 22.6%, FBD Trust Co Ltd 7.1%, Hibernian Investme Managers 4.0%.
(**2001:** Farm Business Developments plc 39.7%, KB Insurance 22.7%, FBD Trust Co Ltd 7.1%, Hiberni Investment Managers 4.0%.)

FIRST ACTIVE:
Irish Life Investment Managers 3.09%. There are 157,31 shareholders of which 6 hold 17% of equity; 96.06% of shar holders are Irish.
(**2001:** First Active Share Account (No 1) Ltd 5.84%, Fir Active Share Account (No 2) Ltd 5.53%, First Active Sha Account (No 3) Ltd 5.67%, First Active Share Account (No Ltd 5.61%, First Active Share Account (No 5) Ltd 5.52%, Fir Active Share Account (No 6) Ltd 3.38%, AIB Custod Nominees 3.12%. There are 164,211 shareholders of which 2 hold 16% of equity; 94.82% of shareholders are Irish.)

FYFFES:
Balkan Investment Co & related parties 11.6%, Bank of Irelar Nominees 10%/15%, Fidelity Investments 3%/5%, AI Custodial Nominees 3%/5%, Marathon Asset Manageme 3%/5%, Fyffes plc treasury shares 3%.
(**2001:** Balkan Investment Co & related parties 11.4%, Bank

...and Nominees 10%/15%, AIB Custodial Nominees & Gartrath Asset Management 5%/10%, Aberdeen Asset Management 3%/5%. Lambent Ltd 2.5%, Fyffes plc treasury shares 3%.

GALEN HOLDINGS:
J McClay 17.2%, J A King 7.6%. Elan International Services Ltd 3.8%, R G Elliott 2.8%.
(2001: A J McClay 24.0%, J A King 12.6%. Elan International Services Ltd 4.5%, R G Elliott 4.0%, Galen Trustees 3.1%.)

What does Jupiter know about Gartmore that the rest of us don't know...

GARTMORE IRISH GROWTH FUND:
Jupiter Asset Management 22.8%, Friends Provident 65%, Exeter Asset Management 7.14%, East Riding Pension Fund 5.08%, Clients of Gartmore Investment Ltd 9%, Aurora Investment Trust 4.33%, Bank of England Pension Fund 3.46%, Deutsche Bank 3.46%.
(2001: Exeter Asset Management 14.03%, Friends Provident 10.74%, Jupiter Fund 5.33%, East Riding Pension Fund 5.10%, Clients of Gartmore Investment Ltd 0%, First Friends Life Ass 4.72%, Aurora Investment Trust 4.64%, Anson Fund - Guernsey 4.49%, Bank of England Pension Fund 3.71%, Boston Safe Deposit 3.34%.)

Institutional Investors Fight Shy of Glanbia

GLANBIA:
Glanbia Co-operative Society Ltd (formerly Avonmore-Waterford Co-op Socy) 54.79%.
(2001: Glanbia Co-operative Society Ltd (formerly Avonmore-Waterford Co-op Socy) 54.79%.)

GLENCAR MINING:
Stanlife Nominees 9.86%, Williams de Broe 7.26%, Bank of Ireland Nominees 5.02%, Willbro Nominees 4.64%.
(2001: Stanlife Nominees 9.86%, Williams de Broe 26%, Bank of Ireland Nominees 5.02%, Willbro Nominees 5.01%.)

GRAFTON GROUP:
Bank of Ireland Nominees A/c NRI 25.19%, Nortrust Nominees 6.85%, Bank of Ireland Nominees A/c NRS 82%, Citibank Nominees 5.44%, Scottish Provident Irish Holdings 3.28%, Clydesdale Bank Nominees MGG A/c 3.12%, M Chadwick 10.25%.
(2001: Bank of Ireland Nominees A/c NRI 27,85%, Nortrust Nominees 4.74%, Citibank Nominees 6.63%, Scottish Provident Irish Holdings 3.94%, Clydesdale Bank Nominees MGG A/c 3.16%, M Chadwick 10.25%.)

Merrill Lynch, Irish Life and Scottish Provident Exit Greencore

GREENCORE GROUP:
Bank of Ireland Asset Management Ltd 14.4%, D Desmond 15.6%, Sprucegrove Invest Managers 5.3%, Allied Irish Banks & subsidiaries 4.6%, Standard Life Assurance 3.9%. There are 12,483 shareholders of whom all own 76.1% of the company.
(2001: Bank of Ireland Asset Management Ltd 14.4%, D Desmond 14.4%, Merrill Lynch 10.9%, Irish Life Investment Managers 5.2%, Allied Irish Banks & subsidiaries 4.6%, Scottish Provident Institution 4.1%, Standard Life Assurance 3.9%.)

AIB, Eagle Star, Canada Life get their timing wrong at Green; Jupiter gets it right.

GREEN PROPERTY:
Jupiter Asset Management 9.97%, Morgan Stanley 54%, Bank of Ireland Nominees 6.17%, Fidelity Investments 5.72%, ESB Pension 4.11%, Scottish Provident 3.9%.
(2001: Bank of Ireland Nominees 10.08%, Eagle Star Life Assurance Co 7.76%, Fidelity Investments 7.32%, Morgan Stanley 6.9%, Allied Irish Bank 4.67%, Scottish Provident 3.94%, Canada Life 3.28%.)

GRESHAM HOTEL GROUP:
Euro Sea Hotels BV 17.51%, Irish River Holdings 6.88%, I Isley 4.48%.
(2001: Euro Sea Hotels BV 17.95%, Bank of Ireland Nominees 7.17%, Clydesdale Bank Nominees 4.6%, Popular Investments 3.33%.)

Big Stakeholders Grow Larger At Heitons

HEITON HOLDINGS:
Grafton Group plc 23.81%, Allied Irish Banks & Subsidiaries 7.57%, Mr EC Johnson/Fidelity International Ltd/FMR Corp 13.01%, Bank of Ireland Asset Management Ltd 8.88%, Jupiter Asset Management 2.73%, R Hewat 1.0%. There are 3,495 shareholders with 18 of them owning 71.2% of the equity.
(2000: Grafton Group plc 18.78%, Allied Irish Banks & Subsidiaries 10.53%, Mr EC Johnson/Fidelity International Ltd/FMR Corp 9.54%, Bank of Ireland Asset Management Ltd 5.23%, Scottish Provident 3.72%, Jupiter Asset Management 3.04%, R Hewat 1.0%.)

HORIZON TECHNOLOGY GROUP:
S Naji 49.4%, C Garvey 4.8%, Horizon ESOP Ltd 5.04%.
(2001: S Naji 44.9%, O. Sheehan (Mrs Naji) 6.7%, C Garvey 5.1%, K Melia 1%.

IAWS:
Irish Agricultural Wholesale Society Ltd 40.53%, FMR Corporation/Fidelity International 8.21%.
(2001: Irish Agricultural Wholesale Society Ltd 42.47%, FMR Corporation/Fidelity International 7.94%.)

ICON:
J Climax 23.1%, R Lambe 23.1%, Capital Guardian Trust 8.5%, Merrill Lynch 7.9%. All executives and directors account for 47.4%.
(2001: J Climax 23.7%, R Lambe 23.7%.)

Gartmore sells and CGNU takes 6% of IFG

IFG:
Jupiter Asset Mgt 10.28%, Fidelity Investments 10.02%, CGNU 5.93%, Scottish Provident 3.73%, Newpark Holdings 3.09%, N Moran 3.69%, J Moran 7.8%, R Hayes 7.2%, C Moran 2.8%, V Quigley 1.3%.
(2001: IFG Group treasury shares 6.88%, Jupiter Asset Mgt 10.76%, Fidelity Investments 8.86%, Gartmore Investment Managers 4.76%, Dresdner RCM European Smaller Co Trust 4.12%, Scottish Provident 4.09%, N Moran 3.69%, J Moran 7.8%, R Hayes 7.2%, C Moran 2.8%, V Quigley 1.8%.)

INDEPENDENT NEWS & MEDIA:
The Capital Group Companies Inc 5%/10%, Bank of Ireland Nominees 5%/10%, Irish Life & Permanent plc 5%/10%, FMR Corporation & Fidelity International Ltd 5%/10%, A O'Reilly 27.0%
(2001: The Capital Group Companies Inc 5%/10%, Bank of Ireland Nominees 5%/10%, Irish Life & Permanent plc 5%/10%, Standard Life Assurance Co 3%/5%, FMR Corporation & Fidelity International Ltd 3%/5%, A O'Reilly 27.0%)

Baker & O'Tooles' holdings in IONA drop off the notifiable screen.

IONA Technologies: Guaranty Nominees Ltd (representing the ADRs in US) 79.4%, C Horn 6.5%.
(2001: Guaranty Nominees Ltd 67.7%, C Horn 9.7%, A O'Toole 6.9%, S Baker 6.3%.

Merrill Lynch and Salomon Smith Barney sell out of ICG

Irish Continental Group: Allied Irish Banks 13.2%, FMR Corp 12.1%, Citigroup 8.2%, Zurich Financial Services 4.4%, KBC Asset Management 5.7%, Canada Life 3.7%, E Rothwell 3.7%.
(2001: Allied Irish Banks 13.1%, FMR Corp 11.1%, Merrill Lynch Investment Mgrs 9.8%, Salomon Smith Barney Inc 7.4%, Zurich Financial Services 7.0%, KBC Asset Management 4.4%, E Rothwell 1.8%.)

IRISH LIFE & PERMANENT:
Capital Group 9%, Fidelity International Ltd 4%, Zurich Financial Services 4%, Bank of Ireland Asset Management 4%, Standard Life 4%, Scudder Kemper Investments Inc 3%.
(2001: Fidelity International Ltd 8%, Zurich Financial Services 6%, Bank of Ireland Asset Management 6%, Standard Life 4%, Scudder Kemper Investments Inc 3%.)

IWP INTERNATIONAL:
P J Moran 11.0%, Bank of Ireland Asset Management 10.3%, Prudential 9.4%, Scottish Provident Institution 5.7%, Anstalt Fur Investition 4.4%.
(2001: Bank of Ireland Asset Management 11.53%, P J Moran 8.96%, Schroders 6.12%, Scottish Provident Institution 5.72%, Prudential 5.47%, Anstalt Fur Investition 4.4%, Foundation Pour Les Antres (PLA) 3.14%, Airspace Investment Ltd 4.9%.)

Major Shareholders (Aberdeen, BofI and Royal & Sun) Exit from Jurys

JURYS DOYLE HOTEL GROUP:
W Beatty 7.2%, F M R Corp 4.1%, Canada Life 3.1%, E Monahan 8.3%, A Roche 8.3%, B Gallagher 8.3%.
(2001: W Beatty 7.2%, Aberdeen Asset Managers 5.6%, F M R Corp 3.7%, Royal & Sun Alliance 3.2%, E Monahan 8.3%, A Roche 8.3%, B Gallagher 8.3%, Bank of Ireland Asset Management 10.3%.)

KENMARE RESOURCES:
Chase Nominees 7.33%, State Street Nominees 4.14%, Bank of Ireland Nominees 3.91%, Nutraco Nominees 3.73%, Bank of New York Nominees 3.46%, BNY GIL Clients 3.38%, Nortrust Nominees 2.96%, BNY (OCS) Nominees 2,91%, C Carvill 2.15%. There are 5,475 shareholders of which 39 hold 65% of equity. 37% of shareholders are Irish.
(2001: Gartmore Investment Management Ltd 9.4%, Clydesdale Bank 6.5%, Nutraco Nominees 5.2%, Capital Group 4.6%, Nortrust Nominees 4.2%, Bank of New York Nominees 3.5%, C Carvill 2.9%. There are 4,928 shareholders of which 32 hold 55% of equity. 43% of shareholders reside in Rupublic of Ireland.)

KERRY GROUP:
Kerry Co-op Creameries 31%, Bank of Ireland Asset Mgt 5%, AIB Investment Managers 4%, AIM Funds 4%.
(2001: Kerry Co-op Creameries 37%, Bank of Ireland Nominees 6%, AIB Investment Managers 5%, AIM Funds 4%.)

Fidelity, Chase and Hibernian head for the door at Kingspan

KINGSPAN GROUP:
E Murtagh 24%, Jupiter Asset Management 7.6%, Invesco Perpetual 3.3%, Bank of Ireland Asset Management 4.4%, AIB Asset Managers 7.2%, B Murtagh 3.8%, E McCarthy 1.8%.
(2001: E Murtagh 24%, Citibank Nominees 9.9%, Bank of Ireland Nominees 9.1%, Allied Irish Banks 8.2%, Fidelity Investments 7.9%, Chase Nominees 6.0%, Nortrust Nominees 5.8%, Hibernian Investment Managers 3.5%, B Murtagh 3.8%, E McCarthy 1.8%.)

LAMONT HOLDINGS:
Castlemere Enterprises (Casey/Wilson) 63.6%, Lord Rathcavan 36.5%, lending institutions 9.2%.
(2001: Castlemere Enterprises (Casey/Wilson)15.81%, Prudential Corp Group 4.8%, Scottish American Investment Co 3.3%.)

Significant Changes at McInerney

MCINERNEY HOLDINGS:
ICC Venture Capital Partners 19.06%, Bank of Ireland Asset Management 11.23%, Harcourt Developments 10.52%, Merrill Lynch Investment Managers 9.06%, ICC Bank 6.29%, D McInerney Snr 6.12%, Standard Life 5.55%, Norwich Union Life 4.7%, Irish Life 3.09%, B O'Connor 4.14%.

(2001: ICC Venture Capital Partners 19.58%, Harcourt Developments 10.81%, Mercury Asset Management 9.0%, Standard Life 8.85%, ICC Bank 6.46%, D McInerney Snr 6.12%, Bank of Ireland Asset Management 5.96%, Norwich Union Life 4.83%, Irish Life 3.17%, B O'Connor 2.2%, J McNamara 2.4%.)

MARLBOROUGH INTERNATIONAL:
D & E McKenna 44.4%, Merrill Lynch Investment Managers 9.95%, Quinn Direct Insurance 6.48%, Sean Dunne 4.73%, UBCS Gartmore Irish Growth Fund 4.46%, HSBC Global Custody 3%/5%, AIB Custodial Nominees 10%/15%, J Nolan 3.2%, Bank of Ireland Nominees 3%/5%.
(2000: D & E McKenna 44.5%, J Nolan 3.2%, A McGennis 3.2%, AIB Custodial Nominees 15%/20%, Bank of Ireland Nominees 5%/10%, Mercury Asset Management 13.88%, Quinn Direct Insurance 4.82%, Ulster Bank Markets 3%/5%, HSBC 3%/5%.)

MILLER FISHER:
D Farrell 6.1%, Mr & Mrs Gunn 3.1%, K Kenny 3.1%.
(2001: Newton Investment Management 9.4%, Merrill Lynch Investment Management 5.7%, M & G Investment Management 4.4%, Gerrard Investment Funds 3.7%, Dresdner RCM Global Investors 3.6%, Fidelity International 3.5%, K Kenny 3.14%, S Pyatt 1.52%.)

MINMET:
Mercury Asset Management 9.26%, The Capital Group Companies Inc 4.36%, A Robson 1.2%.
(2001: Mercury Asset Management 8.94%, The Capital Group Companies Inc 5.53%, A Robson 1.3%.)

Big Players Arrive At Navan

NAVAN MINING:
Henderson Investors 17.31%, RAB Capital 10.71%, Capital Group 7.7%, Deutsche Bank 7.7%, Invesco Asset Management 7.05%, Jupiter Asset Management 4.61%, Matopos Holdings 4.31%, Nutraco Nominees 4.14%, Middlemarch Partners 3.94%.
(2001: Henderson Investors 19.17%, Equitable Life Assurance 8.76%, Gold Mines of Sardinia 8.05%, Invesco English & International Trust 5.46%, Abbey Pensions 4.02%, Jupiter High Income 3.22% Fleming Mercantile Investment Trust 3.21%.)

NORISH:
Standard Life Assurance 8.56%, Friends First 8.0%, T B Mantor A/S 8.49%, Friends First 8.09%, ESB Superannuation 6.22%, W L McCauley 6.13%, Kappa Alpha 5.41%, T Cunningham 5.37%, J Teeling 4.77%, 2Ms Special Pension 4.13%, B Joyce 1.8%. There are 348 shareholders of which 17 hold 74.1% of the equity.
(2001: Aberdeen Asset Managers 12.73%, Standard Life Assurance 9.15%, Friends First 8.0%, T B Mantor A/S 8.49%, ESB Superannuation 6.22%, W L McCauley 6.13%, 2M's Special Pension Fund 4.13%, Kappa Alpha 3.04%, B Joyce 1.8%.)

OAKHILL:
Bank of Ireland Nominees Ltd 4.5%, P Lynch 8.3%, P Casey 5.7%, R McLoughlin 29.3%.
(2001: James Crean plc 20.0%, Bank of Ireland Nominees Ltd 4.5%, P Lynch 8.3%, P Casey 5.6%, R McLoughlin 9.2%.)

OGLESBY & BUTLER:
Bank of Ireland Nominees Ltd 8.67%, Nortrust Nominees Ltd 5.89%, A Oglesby 20.3%, J Oglesby 15.4%, D Scott 4.1%.
(2000: Bank of Ireland Nominees Ltd 8.67%, Ulster Bank Dublin Nominees Ltd 5.89%, A Oglesby 22.6%, J Oglesby 16.5%, D Scott 4.3%.)

Major changes in Ormonde shareholdings

ORMONDE MINING:
Viadacos Nominees 11.67%, D & A Burke 6.81%, Davy Nominees 4.54%.
(2001: Alana Investments (M Donoghue) 12.48%, AIB Custodial (2 accounts) 11.97%, D & A Burke 8.16%.)

OVOCA:
Davy Nominees 5.47%, Mercury Holdings 5.16%, Darford Ltd 4.27%, F Buckley 1.1%, D Alexander 1.4%, D Dobson 2.7%, P Smithwick 1.3%.

(2001: Darford Ltd 4.52%, Scoti Co Ltd 4.52%, K Milner 3.37%F Buckley 1.1%, D Alexander 1.4%, D Dobson 2.7%, P Smithwick 1.3%.)

POWER LEISURE GROUP:
J Corcoran 14.7%, S Kenny 7.4%, D Power 10.4%, Bank of Ireland Nominees 9.4%, SKC Nominees 5.3%.
(2001: J Corcoran 14.8%, S Kenny 7.4%, D Power 10.8%, Rowan Nominees 6.7%, Bank of Ireland Nominees 7.6%, ICC Bank 4.3%, SKC Nominees 5.3%.)

PREMIER OIL:
Amerada Hess Ltd 25%, Petronas International Corp 25%.
(2001: Amerada Hess Ltd 25%, Petronas International Corp 25%, Keppel Corp 3.02%.)

PROVIDENCE RESOURCES:
A J F O'Reilly 38.63%.
(2001: A J F O'Reilly 39.05%.).

Framlington and Gartmore exit from Qualceram

QUALCERAM:
ICC Bank plc 9.82%, ICC Equity Partners 8.23%, RSTB Nominees 7.94%, Nortrust Nominees 7.77%, HSBC Global 4.77%, Scottish Provident (Irish Holdings) Ltd 3.41%, J O'Loughlin 14.31%, J Byrne 14.31%, T J Byrne 14.31%.
(2001: Framlington 1000 Smallest Companies Trust 7.16%, ICC Bank plc 9.82%, ICC Equity Partners 8.23%, RSTB Nominees 7.03%, Gartmore Irish Smaller Companies Investment Trust 4.62%, Scottish Provident (Irish Holdings) Ltd 3.74%, Bank of Ireland Nominees 3.0%, J O'Loughlin 14.31%, J Byrne 14.31%, T J Byrne 14.31%.

RAPID TECHNOLOGY:
Kirconnell Ltd 8.7%, Barfield Nominees 4.9% R Bannon 10.4%, J Barry 10.8%, J Caldwell 4.6%, R Dickinson 4.6%, P McDonagh 26.1%.
(2001: Kirconnell Ltd 9.5%, AIB Custodial Nominees 5.1%, R Bannon 10.2%, J Barry 10.7%, J Caldwell 4.8%, R Dickinson 4.8%, P McDonagh 27.3%.)

READYMIX:
Readymix Holdings UK 62.0%, AIB Bank Securities Services 4.97%, Bank of Ireland Securities Services13.17%.
(2001: Readymix Holdings UK 62.6%, AIB Bank Securities Services 5.4%, Bank of Ireland Securities Services14.38%, Irish Life Assurance Nominees 3.7%.)

REAL ESTATE OPPORTUNITIES LTD:
Treasury Holdings Ltd 27.32, Jupiter Asset Management 5.83%, BC Asset Management 5.40%, Framlington Investment Management Ltd 4.76%, Morley Fund Management 4.17%, Friends Provident 4.15%, JP Morgan Fleming 3.9%. There are 371 shareholders of which 85 holdings account for 98.42% of the equity.

Big Changes in Riverdeep Holdings.

RIVERDEEP:
P McDonagh 23.1%, IBM 7.1%, B O'Callaghan 5.5%,
(2001: P McDonagh 48.6%, B O'Callaghan 6.6%, E Wallace 4.1%, P Burke 2.1%, S Lunt 2.1%.

RYANAIR:
Fidelity International 13.8%, Putnam Investments 9.3%, Janus 9.3%, Capital Group Companies 5.01%, Wellington Management 4.4%, M O'Leary 5.9%, C Ryan 1.6%, D Ryan 3.5%, T Ryan 2.3%, B Bonderman 1%.
(2001: Fidelity International 12.6%, G Gagnon 9.9%, Putnam Investments 7.3%, Wellington Management 4.6%, Janus 4.6%, Shane Ryan 3.5%, M O'Leary 7.2%, C Ryan 3.5%, D Ryan 3.5%, T Ryan 2.3%, B Bonderman 1%.)

SHERRY FITZGERALD:
Bank of Ireland Nominees 13.26%, M FitzGerald 11.47%, J Meagher 5.36%, K O'Higgins 5.1%, P Sherry 5.02%, G Gill 5.02%, S Ensor 5.02%, G Byrne 3.5%, C Cullinan 3.9%. There are 352 shareholders of which 26 hold 8% of the equity.
(2001: M FitzGerald 11.7%, J Meagher 6.09%, K O'Higgins 5.1%, P Sherry 5.02%, G Gill 5.02%, S Ensor 5.02%, D Lewis 5.02%, G Byrne 3%/5%, Bank of Ireland Nominees 3%/5%.)

SMF TECHNOLOGIES:
M Meehan 2.39%, J O'Donovan 3.79%, M O'Donogh 35.68%, Beacon Investment Fund 8.27%, Bank of N York Nominees 8.22%, Ulster Bank Markets Nomine 6.61%, B Boland 6.37%.
(2001: M Meehan 2.39%, J O'Donovan 3.79%, O'Donoghue 35.68%, Beacon Investment Fund 8.27 Bank of New York Nominees 8.22%, Ulster Bank Mark Nominees 6.61%, B Boland 6.37%.)

SMURFIT GROUP, JEFFERSON:
M Smurfit 6.8%, Bank of Ireland Asset Managem 6.4%, Capital Group 6.1%, Wellington Management LLP 7.9%, Franklin Resources 5.0%, MFS Investm Management 3%/5%. There are 16,947 shareholders whom 142 hold 500,000 or more shares.
(2001: M Smurfit 6.8%, P Gleeson 1.3%, Bank of Irela Asset Management 8.0%, Smurfit Pension Fund 3.1 AIB & subsidiaries 3%/5%, Capital Group 3%/5 Wellington Management Co LLP 7.8%, Frank Templeton 3%/5%.)

TRINITY BIOTECH:
R O'Caoimh 4.3%, B Farrell 1.8%, J O'Connell 1.9% Walsh 2.4%, D Burger 1.4%, Forfas 4.2%.
(2001: R O'Caoimh 4.3%, B Farrell 1.8%, J O'Conr 1.9%, J Walsh 2.4%, D Burger 1.4%, Forfas 4.2%.)

Schroder and Enterprise Oil reduce stakes in Tullow

TULLOW OIL:
Prudential Corporation 13.92%, Schroder Investme 10.72%, Fidelity International 5.95%, Capital Gro 5.01%, Centrotrade Corporation 3.52%, A Heavey 1.7%
(2001: Schroders 16.78%, Prudential Corporati 14.19%, Fidelity International 5.71%, Capital Gro 5.07%, Centrotrade Corporation 4.7%, Enterprise 3.35%, A Heavey 2.0%.)

ULSTER TELEVISION:
CanWest Global Communications Corp 29.99% Milestone Trust Ltd (McGuckian related) 8.80%.
(2001: CanWest Global Communications Corp 29.99% Milestone Trust Ltd (McGuckian related) 8.80%.)

UNIDARE:
Beechworth International (D Desmond) 26.63%, Dill Investments 12.35%, Tweedy Browne Co 7.09%, Bank Ireland Asset Management 6.90%, Mercury Ass Management 3.56%, General Motors Investme Management 3.31%, Securities Trust 3.24%, I Nominees (D Desmond) 2.38%.
(2000: Beechworth International (D Desmond) 26.63% Dillon Investments 12.35%, Tweedy Browne Co 7.09% Bank of Ireland Asset Management 6.90%, Mercu Asset Management 3.56%, General Motors Investme Management 3.31%, Securities Trust 3.24%, I Nominees (D Desmond) 2.38%.)

UNITED DRUG:
Fidelity International Ltd 14.9%, Nortrust Nomine 7.58%, Bank of Ireland Nominees 13.1%, Citiba Nominees (I) Ltd 3.82%, M Rafferty 2.9%.
(2001: Fidelity International Ltd 13.31%, Nortru Nominees 10.24%, Scottish Provident (Irish Holdings) L 4.11%, Bank of Ireland Nominees 3.92%, M Rafferty 2.8%

VIRIDIAN GROUP:
Fidelity Investments 7.06%.
(2001: Fidelity Investments 6.73%.)

VISLINK:
Edinburgh Fund Managers 11.86%, A Morton 5.94% Venaglass 3.70%.
(2000: Edinburgh Fund Managers 12.85%, A Morto 5.7%, Venaglass 3.45%.)

WATERFORD WEDGWOOD:
Shuttleway 17.0%, Bank of Ireland Asset Manageme 12.0%, Lazard Asset Management 8.4%, Araquip International 3.6%, Albany Hill Ltd 3.5% .
(2001: Shuttleway 16.09%, Bank of Ireland Nominee 15.46%, Bank of Ireland Asset Management 9.99% Allied Irish Bank & subsidiaries 3.81%, Araquip International 3.65%, Albany Hill Ltd 3.60%.)

COMPANY NAME	Price € Sept 9 2002	High € 2001	Low € 2001	Shares in issue millions	Market Value €'m	Dividend per share €	Dividend yield %	Dividend cover	Earnings per share €	Price/ earnings ratio	Net tangible assets per share €	Rolling* p/e for 2002 €	COMPANY NAME
Abbey	4.45	5.30 21/5	3.65 30/1	34.1	152	0.20	4.4	3.9	0.784	5.7	4.19	5.7	Abbey
Allied Irish Banks	12.38	15.70 15/5	10.92 24/7	895.5	11,086	0.438	3.3	1.3	0.56	23.6	5.17	11.3	Allied Irish Banks
Alphyra	0.95	4.00 8/1	0.81 29/8	32.7	31	-	-	-	-	-	2.00	-	Alphyra
Aminex	0.30	0.45 1/3	0.27 1/7	90.2	27	-	-	-	-	-	0.44	-	Aminex
Anglo Irish Bank	6.24	7.05 28/5	4.30 2/1	325.0	2,028	0.104	1.6	3.9	0.42	15.4	1.26	13.4	Anglo Irish Bank
Arcon Int Resources	0.03	0.04 4/1	0.01 23/7	1,581.3	47	-	-	-	-	-	-	-	Arcon
Ardagh	1.00	1.30 5/6	0.90 19/7	34.6	35	0.037	4.1	1.0	0.075	12.0	0.05	12.0	Ardagh
Arnotts	10.65	10.75 25/6	6.90 2/1	17.9	191	0.32	3.0	2.6	0.826	13.1	11.12	11.9	Arnotts
Aviva	13.47	13.47 2/1	13.47 2/1	2,255.7	30,384	0.59	4.4	-	0.011	1,347.0	0.73	-	Aviva
Bank of Ireland	11.10	14.05 11/6	9.90 22/3	1,008.6	11,195	0.33	3.0	2.7	0.89	12.5	3.89	12.5	Bank of Ireland
Barlo	0.21	0.31 24/1	0.20 12/4	175.1	37	-	-	-	-	-	0.34	-	Barlo
Bula Resources	0.025	0.029 5/4	0.017 3/4	223.6bn	56	-	-	-	-	-	-	-	Bula Resources
Celtic Resources	0.20	0.31 31/5	0.17 9/1	231.8	46	-	-	-	-	-	-	-	Celtic Resources
Conduit	2.12	2.92 2/1	2.01 4/6	17.4	37	-	-	-	-	-	2.20	-	Conduit
CPL Resources	0.48	0.50 20/6	0.20 10/1	36.2	17	0.01	2.1	8.8	0.11	4.4	0.22	7.1	CPL Resources
CRH	14.55	20.40 2/4	13.90 5/8	523.0	7,610	0.23	1.6	4.9	1.15	12.7	6.85	12.7	CRH
Datalex	0.28	0.48 7/1	0.26 14/5	65.6	20	-	-	-	-	-	0.82	-	Datalex
DCC	9.90	13.25 30/4	9.40 1/8	83.6	911	0.245	2.5	3.7	0.903	11.0	3.27	11.0	DCC
Donegal Creameries	2.15	2.50 4/1	1.80 5/6	10.0	21	0.108	5.0	3.7	0.404	5.3	3.0	5.3	Donegal Creameries
Dragon Oil	0.25	0.43 14/1	0.19 12/7	362.2	98	-	-	-	-	-	-	-	Dragon Oil
Dunloe Ewart	0.33	0.34 28/6	0.26 9/2	387.9	109	-	-	-	-	-	0.44	-	Dunloe Ewart
Elan Corp	2.65	50.27 20/6	1.55 3/7	350.1	928	-	-	-	-	-	1.51	-	Elan
Ennex Inter	0.013	0.03 1/2	0.01 27/6	282..0	4	-	-	-	-	-	-	-	Ennex
F.B.D. Holdings	5.90	5.90 5/9	4.50 25/2	41.0	242	0.195	3.3	3.1	0.60	9.8	4.93	8.2	F.B.D.
First Active	4.80	5.30 31/5	3.25 2/1	143.2	688	0.135	2.8	2.4	0.33	14.5	2.36	12.8	First Active
Fyffes	1.38	1.57 13/5	1.10 11/2	345.3	477	0.047	3.4	2.3	0.109	12.7	0.79	11.8	Fyffes
Galen Holdings	6.45	11.80 28/2	4.30 26/7	185.5	1,196	0.039	0.6	3.0	0.128	50.4	nil	30.0	Galen
Gartmore Irish Growth	4.04	4.04 11/5	4.04 2/1	22.5	91	-	-	-	-	-	4.05	-	Gartmore Irish
Glanbia	1.52	1.58 1/5	1.11 8/2	292.5	445	0.045	3.0	3.0	0.137	11.1	0.56	-	Glanbia
Glencar Mining	0.04	0.05 2/1	0.02 17/5	97.8	4	-	-	-	-	-	-	-	Glencar Mining
Grafton Group	3.95	5.00 20/5	3.32 10/1	176.1	696	0.08	2.0	4.2	0.336	11.8	1.15	11.4	Grafton Group
Greencore	2.75	3.30 17/4	2.60 12/8	187.3	515	0.126	4.6	-	-	-	nil	-	Greencore
Gresham Hotel	0.69	1.01 26/6	0.66 21/8	78.7	54	0.045	6.5	-	-	-	1.72	-	Gresham Hotel
Heiton Holdings	2.60	3.58 16/5	2.65 29/8	49.4	128.4	0.133	5.1	2.0	0.26	10.0	2.05	10.0	Heiton
Horizon Technology	0.20	0.65 8/1	0.18 13/8	67.9	13.6	-	-	-	-	-	0.20	-	Horizon
IAWS Group	8.05	9.30 12/4	7.60 24/7	123.0	990.1	0.068	0.8	6.1	0.42	19.2	0.05	23.0	IAWS
ICON	22.00	37.50 15/3	19.50 30/7	11.4	251.7	-	-	-	1.22	18.0	7.01	18.0	ICON
IFG Group	0.90	3.60 3/1	1.20 23/8	64.9	58.4	0.022	2.4	5.0	0.12	7.5	nil	-	IFG

Continued on page 128

ABN AMRO

www.abnamro.com

CAMPBELL O'CONNOR & CO

CAMPBELL O'CONNOR & CO.

www.camocon.ie

CAPITA CORPORATE REGISTRARS PLC

www.capitacorporateregistrars.ie

COMPUTERSHARE

www.computershare.com

DAVY STOCKBROKERS

www.davy.ie

DOLMEN BUTLER BRISCOE

www.dolmensecurities.com

EUGENE F. COLLINS

www.efc.ie

FINEX

www.nybot.com

GOODBODY STOCKBROKERS

GOODBODY
STOCKBROKERS

www.goodbody.ie

SCOPE INVESTMENTS

www.escope.ie

KPMG

www.kpmg.ie

LEXUS

www.lexus.ie

MASON HAYES & CURRAN

MASON HAYES & CURRAN
SOLICITORS

www.mhc.ie

MERRION STOCKBROKERS

www.merrion-capital.com

NCB STOCKBROKERS

www.ncbdirect.com

OCTAGON

www.octagononline.ie

Investor Information Websites continued..

PRICEWATERHOUSECOOPERS

www.pwcglobal.com/ie

Listed Company Websites

ABBEY

www.abbeyplc.ie

PRIVATE RESEARCH

PRIVATE RESEARCH

www.privateresearch.ie

CRH

www.crh.ie

DCC

www.dcc.ie

GARTMORE

Gartmore

www.gartmore.com

SHARE SPREAD

www.sharespread.com

HORIZON

www.horizon.ie

IRISH CONTINENTAL GROUP

IRISH FERRIES

www.icg.ie

KERRY GROUP

www.kerrygroup.com

TICN

www.ticn.com

TULLOW OIL

TULLOW OIL

www.tullowoil.ie

UNITED DRUG

United drug

UNITED DRUG PLC

www.united-drug.ie

WATERFORD WEDGWOOD

WATERFORD WEDGWOOD

www.waterfordwedgwood.com

COMPANY NAME	Price € Sept 9 2002	High € 2001	Low € 2001	Shares in issue millions	Market Value €'m	Dividend per share €	Dividend yield %	Dividend cover	Earnings per share €	Price/ earnings ratio	Net tangible assets per share €	Rolling* p/e for 2002 €	COMPANY NAME
Continued from page 125													
Independent News & Media	1.44	2.29 21/5	1.55 13/8	572.9	824.9	0.078	5.4	2.1	0.06	24.0	nil	24.0	Independent News & Media
Iona Technologies	2.07	28.67 16/1	1.80 19/8	32.0	66.3	-	-	-	-	-	3.34	-	Iona Tec
Irish Continental Group	5.70	8.85 3/5	6.00 30/8	27.0	153.7	0.171	3.0	2.0	0.34	16.8	7.28	16.8	Irish Continental
Irish Life & Permanent	12.35	16.98 12/6	11.65 2/1	272.3	3,362.3	0.043	0.3	0.4	0.17	72.7	6.15	72.7	Irish Life & Permanent
IWP International	1.35	2.10 16/1	1.24 7/8	75.5	101.9	0.09	6.7	-	-	-	0.03	-	IWP International
Jurys Doyle Hotel Group	8.20	11.15 19/4	8.20 2/1	62.7	513.8	0.219	2.7	3.0	0.66	12.4	9.88	12.4	Jurys Doyle Hotels
Kenmare Resources	0.18	0.33 31/5	0.18 15/8	262.2	47.2	-	-	-	-	-	0.17	-	Kenmare Resources
Kerry Group	14.50	15.98 13/6	13.30 1/8	185.5	2,689.3	0.10	0.7	7.8	0.82	17.7	0.58	22.6	Kerry Group
Kingspan Group	1.95	3.50 15/1	1.88 29/8	167.7	327.1	0.047	2.4	6.9	0.33	5.9	0.41	5.9	Kingspan
McInerney Holdings	2.15	2.55 13/5	1.35 2/1	32.6	70.1	0.045	2.1	9.3	0.44	4.9	1.57	4.9	McInerney
Minmet	0.11	0.22 24/4	0.11 29/7	497.4	54.7	-	-	-	-	-	0.03	-	Minmet
Navan Mining	0.12	0.68 2/1	0.12 30/8	226.0	27.1	-	-	-	-	-	nil	-	Navan Mining
Norish	0.70	0.90 19/4	0.43 9/1	8.5	5.9	0.053	7.6	-	-	-	0.99	-	Norish
Oakhill	0.08	0.14 7/1	0.05 22/5	56.4	4.5	-	-	-	-	-	0.09	-	Oakhill
Oglesby & Butler	0.44	0.60 12/4	0.30 5/2	12.3	5.4	0.017	3.9	1.5	0.03	14.7	0.46	14.7	Oglesby & Butler
Ormonde Mining	0.05	0.08 29/1	0.05 2/1	72.9	3.8	-	-	-	-	-	0.56	-	Ormonde Mining
Ovoca Resources	0.16	0.26 29/4	0.12 2/1	29.1	4.7	-	-	-	-	-	0.09	-	Ovoca Resources
Paddy Power	5.30	6.00 22/5	4.17 4/1	47.1	249.9	0.051	1.0	3.0	0.15	35.3	0.63	34.0	Paddy Power
Premier Oil	0.27	0.27 23/7	0.23 2/1	1.55bn	419.1	-	-	-	0.02	13.5	0.03	13.5	Premier Oil
Providence Resources	0.006	0.01 2/1	0.005 4/6	887.2	5.3	-	-	-	-	-	nil	-	Providence Resources
Qualceram Shires	1.90	2.70 28/3	1.85 4/2	22.0	48.4	0.053	2.4	1.7	0.09	21.1	0.98	-	Qualceram Shires
Rapid Technology	0.28	0.38 11/1	0.25 1/3	23.1	6.5	-	-	-	-	-	nil	-	Rapid Technology
Readymix	1.30	1.85 29/5	1.16 8/2	107.9	140.3	0.061	4.7	3.2	0.2	6.5	0.96	7.2	Readymix
Real Estate Opportunities	1.35	1.35 2/1	1.35 2/1	256.2	345.9	-	-	-	-	-	1.65	-	Real Estate Properties
Riverdeep Group	2.20	4.23 8/3	2.18 2/7	199.5	438.8	-	-	-	0.23	9.6	0.36	9.6	Riverdeep Group
Ryanair Holdings	5.47	7.20 5/3	4.95 24/7	754.3	4,126.1	-	-	-	0.206	26.6	1.33	26.6	Ryanair
Sherry FitzGerald Group	0.85	1.25 27/2	0.85 19/8	13.6	11.6	0.012	1.4	4.6	0.046	18.5	0.49	185	Sherry FitzGerald
SMF Technologies	0.40	0.40 2/1	0.40 1/1	6.8	2.7	-	-	-	-	-	0.04	-	SMF Technologies
Trinity Biotech	1.68	1.90 22/2	1.68 1/5	39.0	65.5	-	-	-	0.04	42.0	0.41	42.0	Trinity Biotech
Tullow Oil	1.50	1.80 20/5	1.20 2/1	356.5	534.7	-	-	-	0.026	37.5	nil	28.3	Tullow Oil
Ulster Television	5.91	6.10 24/5	4.54 2/1	52.5	310.6	0.144	2.4	1.7	0.24	24.6	nil	24.6	Ulster Television
Unidare	1.10	1.35 1/2	0.95 26/6	19.8	21.8	0.03	2.7	-	-	-	1.42	-	Unidare
United Drug	13.55	15.00 8/1	12.70 14/8	29.0	392.6	0.219	1.6	2.9	0.65	20.8	2.07	19.4	United
Viridian Group	7.80	8.83 25/1	6.89 24/6	132.1	1,030.4	0.49	6.3	-	-	-	2.07	-	Viridian
Vislink	0.40	0.55 4/1	0.40 14/6	102.1	40.8	0.002	0.01	-	-	-	0.10	-	V
Waterford Wedgwood	0.52	0.92 03/1	0.50 24/7	758.3	394.3	0.031	6.0	-	-	-	0.15	-	Waterford Wedg

* Rolling price earnings ratio is a combination of the latest interim earnings per added to the earnings per share for the previous six months.